Working With Women Offenders in the Community

Edited by

Rosemary Sheehan, Gill McIvor and Chris Trotter

WILLAN
PUBLISHING

Published by

Willan Publishing
2 Park Square
Milton Park
Abingdon
Oxon
OX14 4RN

Published simultaneously in the USA and Canada by

Willan Publishing
270 Madison Avenue
New York
NY 10016

First published 2011

ISBN   978-1-84392-887-4 paperback
       978-1-84392-888-1 hardback

British Library Cataloguing-in-Publication Data

A catalogue record for this book is available from the British Library

Project managed by Deer Park Productions, Tavistock, Devon
Typeset by GCS, Leighton Buzzard, Bedfordshire
Printed and bound by T.J. International, Padstow, Cornwall

Working With Women Offenders in the Community

Contents

List of figures and tables

Figures

Tables

List of abbreviations

ART	Aggression Replacement Therapy Programme (London, England)
ASBO	Antisocial Behavour Order (UK)
ASRO	Addressing Substance-Misuse-Related Offending Programme (London, England)
CASA	Centre Against Sexual Assault (Victoria, Australia)
CCATS	Childcare and Transport Subsidy (Australia)
CCS	Community Correction Services (Austalia)
CISP	Courts Integrated Services Programme (Australia)
CJA	Community Justice Authority (Scotland)
CJDP	Criminal Justice Diversion Programme (Australia)
CJS	Criminal Justice System
CPO	Community Payback Order (Scotland)
CPS	Child and Protection Services (USA)
CYTS	Community and Youth Training Services (Australia)
DHHS	Department of Health and Human Services (USA)
DipPS	Diploma in Probation Studies (UK)
DOC	Department of Corrections (USA)
DRR	Drug Rehabilitation Requirement (England and Wales)
DSAT	Differential Substance Abuse Treatment (USA)
DTO	Detention and Training Order (England and Wales)
DTTO	Drug Treatment and Testing Order (UK)
EBP	Evidence-based practice
GAO	Government Accounting Office (USA)
GED	Gender Equality Duty (England and Wales)

GIA	Gender Impact Assessment
GIPA	Gender Informed Practice Assessments (USA)
GRP	Gender-responsive principles
LSI-R	Level of Service Inventory-Revised
NCRS	National Crime Recording Standard (England and Wales)
NEW-ADAM	Arrestee drug abuse monitoring programme (England and Wales)
NIC	National Institute of Correction (USA)
NOMS	National Offender Management Service (England and Wales)
OASys	Offender Assessment System (UK)
OGRS	Offender Group Reconviction Scale
PREA	Prison Rape Elimination Act 2003 (USA)
RAC+	Rental Assistance Coupons Plus (USA)
RAP	Resettlement and aftercare provision (England and Wales)
SAO	Supervised Attendance Order (Scotland)
SPIn-W	Service Planning Instrument for Women (USA)
SSA	Social Security Administration (USA)
SSI	Supplemental Security Income (USA)
SSI/SSDI	Supplemental Security Income/Social Security Disability Insurance (USA)
STC	Secure Training Centre (England)
TANF	Temporary assistance for needy families (USA)
TPC	Transition from prison to the community (USA)
TWP	Together Women Programme (England)
UNCRC	United Nations Convention on the Rights of the Child
VACRO	Victorian Association for the Care and Resettlement of Offenders (Australia)
WISP	Women's Integrated Support Programme (Australia)
WOCMM	Women Offender Case Management Model (USA)
WORP	Women's Offending Reduction Programme (England and Wales)
WRC	Womens's Re-entry Centre (USA)
WRNA	Women's Risk/Needs Assessment (USA)
WTP	Women's Turnaround Project (Cardiff, Wales)
WU	Women Unlimited (USA)
YOT	Youth Offending Team (England and Wales)

Notes on contributors

Delores Blackwell is a qualified social worker, mental health programme consultant and staff psychotherapist at the Albert Ellis Institute, New York. She is also Managing Director of the Harlem United NYNY programme for ex-offenders and people living with HIV/AIDS.

Dr Becky Hayes Boober, Program Officer at Maine Health Access Foundation, was previously the Chief Administrative Officer of the Women's Re-entry Centre in Bangor, Maine, USA, and the Executive Director of the Maine Re-entry Network and Director of Women's Services and Community Development for the Maine Department of Corrections.

Maureen Buell is a Correctional Program Specialist at the National Institute of Corrections, Washington, DC. She manages the National Institute of Corrections' women offender initiative.

Professor Janet Davidson is Assistant Professor of Criminology and Criminal Justice at Chaminade University of Honolulu, Hawaii, USA. Her research focuses on community correctional populations as well as on female offenders.

Dr Jo Deakin is a Research Fellow in the Criminal Justice Research Unit (School of Law) at the University of Manchester, England. She teaches in the undergraduate and postgraduate criminology programmes.

Judith B. Fox JD is Director of the Access to Recovery Project, Rhode Island Department of Behavioral Healthcare, Developmental Disabilities and Hospitals Rhode Island, USA. She designed and implemented the Rhode Island Women's Mentoring Programme.

Professor Loraine Gelsthorpe is Professor of Criminology and Criminal Justice and Director of the M.Phil Programmme at the Institute of Criminology, University of Cambridge, England. She is also a practising psychotherapist.

Dr Dot Goulding is Director of the Centre for Social and Community Research, Murdoch University, Western Australia. Her research concentrates on the criminal justice system and she is a board member of the Prison Reform Group of Western Australia and the Institute of Restorative Justice and Penal Reform.

Professor Carol Hedderman of the Department of Criminology, University of Leicester, England, conducts research and evaluative studies into the most effective ways to improve the lives of offenders, including reducing their offending.

Erica Hansen King is a Policy Associate at the Muskie School of Public Service, University of Southern Maine, USA. She evaluates correctional programmes, provides leadership and training for criminal justice agencies related to evidence-based practices, with focus on gender responsive programming, disproportionate minority contact and other areas.

Dr Nancy Loucks is a criminologist and Chief Executive of Families Outside, a national Scottish charity that works on behalf of families affected by imprisonment.

Professor Gill McIvor is Professor of Criminology and Co-Director of the Scottish Centre for Crime and Justice Research at the University of Stirling, Scotland.

Dr Margaret Malloch is Senior Research Fellow at the Scottish Centre for Crime and Justice Research at the University of Stirling, Scotland. Her key research interests include the experiences of women drug users in prison and the community; and 'holistic' community-based responses to crime and social exclusion.

Phyllis Modley is a Senior Manager, Center for Effective Public Policy, Silver Spring, Maryland, USA, specialising in assistance to criminal justice agencies in the areas of gender-informed practice for women offenders and evidence-based decision-making in local criminal justice systems.

Briege Nugent is an independent criminologist in Scotland, and a lecturer at Glasgow Caledonian University, the Open University and Edinburgh University. She is currently researching projects established to assist offenders with reintegration, including an arts programme for women in prison and working with women on probation.

Dr Shoshana Pollack is an Associate Professor in the Faculty of Social Work, Wilfrid Laurier University in Kitchener, Ontario, Canada. She has worked as a psychotherapist in a women's prison and has conducted research in the area of women's criminalisation and imprisonment for about 20 years.

Dr Kristen J. Quinlan is an independent evaluation consultant and an adjunct faculty member in the Women's Studies Department at the University of Rhode Island, USA.

Dawn Salgado is Visiting Professor of Psychology, Lewis and Clark College, Portland, Oregon, USA. She is an Evaluation Coordinator and Specialist for non-profit organisations in the areas of corrections and education.

Professor Rosemary Sarri is Professor Emerita of social work and social research at the University of Michigan, USA. She is currently researching factors associated with intergenerational incarceration and the 'drift' of youth in child welfare to the juvenile and adult criminal justice systems. She serves on the boards of two agencies serving high-risk urban youth in Detroit, Michigan.

Dr Gilly Sharpe is a lecturer in Criminology at the University of Sheffield, England. She is currently engaged in research on desistance from crime, focusing particularly on women (ex-) offenders and their experiences of probation supervision.

Associate Professor Rosemary Sheehan teaches undergraduate and postgraduate students in the Department of Social Work, Monash University, Victoria and holds a Governor-in-Council appointment to the Children's Court of Victoria to conduct alternative dispute resolution conferences.

Jon Spencer is Director of the Criminal Justice Research Unit (School of Law) at the University of Manchester , England and teaches in the undergraduate and postgraduate criminology programmes.

Associate Professor Chris Trotter teaches in the Department of Social Work, Monash University and is the Director of the Monash Criminal Justice Research Consortium, Victoria, Australia.

Dr Patricia Van Voorhis is Professor of Criminal Justice at the University of Cincinnati, USA. She is the principal investigator for the National Institute of Corrections Women's Classification Project and teaches courses in correctional rehabilitation, applied research, and psychological theories of crime.

Preface and Acknowledgements

Cross-national interest in the specific needs of women offenders led to the international conference 'What Works with Women Offenders: Challenging stereotypes and achieving change', hosted by Monash University, Australia at the Monash Centre in Prato, Italy, 10–12 September 2007. Speakers and delegates addressed the differing needs of women offenders, more effectively met by working with women in the community, and concentrating on programmes and interventions that divert women away from custody and improve their quality of life. Conference delegates confirmed that responses to women offenders which addressed their physical and mental health problems, their relationships with their children and families, their work and life skills, were successful in maintaining women's desistance from offending.

The idea for the book arose out of this conference, convened by Rosemary Sheehan. Research presented suggested strategies that might not only reduce women's offending but also prevent women from entering the criminal justice system. Though many more women offenders are supervised in the community than in custody, much less is known about their needs and effective approaches to their supervision, support and treatment. Authors who contributed to this book challenge policy-makers and corrections systems to concentrate more on community provision for women offenders and to resist popular calls for more punitive responses to all offenders, women included. The range of authors from Australia, Canada, UK and USA all argue that the criminogenic lens applied to women's offending must be gender-responsive if systems are to be successful at addressing the disadvantage and risk associated with offending behaviour.

The book is made possible by the generous support of Brian Willan and Willan Publishing, whose interest in criminology encourages the kind of research and debate found in this book. Our thanks go also to those who contributed to the writing of the book, providing a unique cross-national perspective on making a difference for women in the criminal justice system.

Rosemary Sheehan, Gill McIvor and Chris Trotter

Introduction

Rosemary Sheehan, Gill McIvor and Chris Trotter

The recent increase in women's incarceration around the world has generated significant interest in explaining this growth in numbers and identifying female offenders' distinctive circumstances and needs. It has also prompted a re-examination of community-based alternatives to custody and whether and how enhancements to existing community-based services might stem the flow of women to custody (Ward 2003). Key to this is understanding the contribution that gender makes to patterns of offending and the relevance of gender in developing approaches to the supervision and support of women who offend. In Western jurisdictions, many more women offenders are at any time supervised in the community than are in custody. It is argued that women fare better when managed in the community given their patterns of offending, their circumstances and experiences and the importance of their relationships with children and family.

This book argues that correctional intervention is more effective for women offenders when it is gender responsive, and that the needs of women offenders are best met within the community, by programmes and approaches such as those discussed herein. Gender-responsive community-based sanctions are seen as having the potential to reduce the high number of very short custodial sentences that characterise women's incarceration in many jurisdictions. Women commit fewer crimes and, overall, less serious crimes than men; they are more likely to be convicted of crimes involving drugs or property; and their property offences are economically driven, motivated by poverty, gambling and/or the abuse of alcohol and other drugs (Bloom *et al.*

2003; Bloom *et al.* 2004). Women who offend are generally young, have had limited educational opportunities, are unemployed and have few employment skills. Many women in conflict with the law are also mothers, have significant drug problems, poor physical and mental health and lack social supports. Most are victims of past sexual and/or physical abuse, including domestic violence. Their offending is often linked to relationships with family members, significant others or friends (Bloom *et al.* 2003; Leverntz 2006). The need to form and maintain relationships is key to the success of community-based disposals and interventions (Bloom *et al.* 2003), and this is reflected in the range of programme responses presented in this book.

In recent times, UK, Canadian, US and Australian governments have committed to a distinct approach to women offenders. UK policy, set out in the *Women's Offending Reduction Program: 2003–2005* (2003) in England and Wales and *A Better Way* (2002) in Scotland, emphasises the need for the kinds of 'joined-up' or cross-programme, inter-agency, 'one stop shop' approaches to women who offend that are presented in this book. Policy efforts have also aimed to strengthen diversionary services and community-based sanctions for women. In Victoria, Australia, for example, there has been considerable investment in housing for women on bail, as well as in intensive community supervision for women offenders, with strong, community-based support services, including practical supports such as childcare, work-skills programmes and transport to agencies to comply with court-ordered treatment programmes or community work.

The approach that has been developed in Victoria also focuses on the recruitment, training and role definitions of community corrections staff. In the US, UK, Canada and Australia there is now broad recognition of the need for gender-specific training for staff about issues relevant to women offenders. Attention is given to women's different pathways into the criminal justice system, the distinct characteristics of women who offend and their responses to correctional supervision. What is highlighted is that given the importance of relationships in women's lives, corrections staff – if they are to be effective – need to use role modelling and mentoring with women, recognising that the intersection between the stress of family obligations, their parenting and reunification issues, challenging male relationships, family violence, substance abuse and mental health will significantly affect their capacity for desistance. It is suggested that mentoring also recognises that improving women's self-esteem is a critical focus for intervention (Blyth 2001), given that women in the criminal justice system show much more frequent mental health problems than women in general and than male offenders, including higher levels of depression, anxiety and self-injurious behaviour (Blanchette 2001; Dannerbeck *et al.* 2002; Loucks 2004). This issue is a complex one given the arguments presented by Andrews and Bonta (2003) that depression, anxiety and self-esteem are not 'criminogenic needs' for the criminal population as a whole. The differences in the criminogenic needs of men and women are now widely recognised and are highlighted in several contributions to this book.

Contemporary community corrections' policies focus also on the context and environment in which intervention programmes are offered as much as on the interventions themselves and the role of community corrections staff. Bloom *et al.* (2003) identify the need for community corrections to offer a space for women that is safe and distinctive from the often turbulent relationship and living contexts they experience. A number of writers in this book demonstrate, through the programmes they describe, the importance of interventions that concentrate on the empowerment of women, reducing their powerlessness and promoting agency and self-efficacy. In this regard, mutual engagement rather than authoritarian interactions is important when working with women offenders, as is being clear about rules and expectations, using active listening and empathy as working styles (Carlen 2002; Bloom *et al.* 2003).

These approaches were identified by Austin *et al.* (1992) in the first large-scale US review of community-based correctional responses for women. They found, as is identified by contributors to this book, that the best community supervision programmes dealt specifically with women's issues – as identified above – and were most effective when they combined emotional support with practical skill development and support, and in highly structured, safe environments. This emphasis on 'therapeutic' (or supportive) approaches, rather than on the structured models of correctional treatment used with male offenders, was found to be more effective with women. Structured, clinical approaches often draw on confrontational methods – for example in substance abuse, sex offender interventions and domestic violence interventions – that are not effective with women and may even be damaging for women with histories of abuse (Ward 2003).

This book concentrates on the needs of women who offend, the principles that inform the development of policies on which to build expertise in working with women in the community and gender-responsive practices that have been implemented. What emerges from these initiatives is a template for effective community correctional interventions for women who offend. The book offers a practical focus on the work of those professionals engaged with women in the community – including probation officers, community corrections officers and specialist case managers in areas such as drug treatment, housing, mental health or employment programmes – with a view to promoting women's reintegration in the community and encouraging their desistance from crime.

The first six chapters form part one of the book, examining the governance of female criminality. These chapters set out to identify the structural, social and personal issues facing women in the criminal justice system. The authors examine philosophies and practices that seek to maintain women in the community and divert them from imprisonment. In Chapter 1, Briege Nugent and Nancy Loucks (Scotland) argue that despite the welfare tradition of Scottish criminal justice, conflicts in policy and practices for women have seen women sent to prison in increasing numbers, with negligible attention paid to making greater use of diversionary practices and improving community interventions and services for women offenders. The chapter examines two community-based outreach programmes, using holistic and women-centred approaches, whose strengths-based approaches have reduced reoffending and enhanced self-esteem, with consequent benefits of stability in women's relationships and living situations.

Chapter 2 by Carol Hedderman (England) debates what is considered to be a new response to women offenders developed by government in England and Wales. Policy development has specifically aimed to reduce women's involvement in crime and to divert them from prison. However, Hedderman finds that these policies have had little tangible impact to date. Whilst government policy has provided for community-based disposals and an increase in diversion, courts and judicial decision-makers appear to be 'tough on crime' and continue to remand women in custody even when it is unlikely they will receive a prison sentence, and imprison women for comparatively minor offences. Hedderman argues that if the government is genuinely seeking to reduce offending and reoffending, it needs to alter its policy directions to become 'tough on the causes of crime'.

Chapter 3 by Maureen Buell, Phyllis Modley and Patricia Van Voorhis (USA) discusses the changes and challenges arising from shifting US corrections policy away from male-based interventions to approaches that recognise the unique needs of women. They discuss the women-centred risk assessment initiatives developed by the US National Institute of Corrections that concentrate on identifying gender-based risk factors as a way of reducing offending among women. Chapter 4 by Rosemary Sheehan (Australia) outlines policy initiatives in Australia, exemplified by the gender-specific strategy for working with women offenders in Victoria, known as the Better Pathways Strategy. This gives prominence to community-based approaches and emphasises approaches that address the issues leading to women's offending behaviour. When evaluating this approach, women under supervision in the community and in prison indicated that the combination of material supports offered – with housing, child care and finance – and access to relevant programmes, supported their reintegration into the community and reduced their likelihood of reoffending. Community Corrections staff believed that they had better awareness of the needs of women offenders and that community-based interventions were now more suited to women's needs and therefore better able to offer a constructive alternative to imprisonment. The challenge for Community Corrections in the context of resource and staff constraints is to focus specifically on women, given their relatively small numbers in prison and in the community when compared to men.

Chapter 5 by Delores Blackwell (USA) highlights the extent to which female offenders are particularly vulnerable to coercion from both within and outside the legal system. She argues that while coercive treatment is very much a part of the offender landscape, little has been done with regard to practice development to assist social service professionals in acknowledging the practice of coercion and its ethical implications. She contends that with more attention being focused on risk management, mandated clients are more likely to experience coercive practices in the guise of protecting the individual, the treating professionals and the community at large. Chapter 6 by Shoshana Pollack (Canada) extends this discussion of risk narratives by examining the re-entry experiences of Canadian women from prison to the community, finding that corrections policy and programmes do not adequately address the living circumstances for returning women. They may return to contexts of violence and abuse that led to their initial offending, and while these remain unaddressed, women are at increased risk of reincarceration.

Chapter 7 by Loraine Gelsthorpe (England and Wales) commences the five chapters that form part two of the book, which looks at the practical aspects of working with women offenders in the community. Gelsthorpe debates the success and remaining challenges of new approaches implemented in the last few years, drawing on examples of 'ground level' initiatives in England and Wales, and relevant research findings. Gelsthorpe cautions that whilst some things are definitely working better for women who offend, there is anxiety as to whether this will survive in a criminal justice system that is highly sensitive to political and economic priorities. In Chapter 8, Gilly Sharpe (England) examines the distinctive needs of young women who offend. She argues that changes in police and court processing have inflated girls' official crime rates and propelled them into the youth justice system, receiving more intrusive penalties (including custody) than previously. Young women who come into conflict with the law are often reluctant to comply with statutory supervision, and such non-compliance exposes them to increasingly restrictive penalties. Sharpe argues that unless greater attention is paid to their gendered welfare needs, their powerlessness on account of their age and their impoverished backgrounds, young women are at risk of being propelled further into marginalisation, disadvantage and the criminal justice system.

In Chapter 9, Dot Goulding (Australia) discusses a culturally-specific approach developed to assist Aboriginal women, most of whom identified themselves as belonging to the Nyoongar people, who were leaving prison in Perth, Western Australia. The art-based 'Breaking the Cycle' programme implemented culturally-sensitive strategies to foster the women's resocialisation and their economic independence, raised social competencies and helped develop marketable work skills, and provided training opportunities and qualifications. Aboriginal women in Australia experience entrenched general social disadvantage and have a disproportionately high rate of imprisonment. Their vulnerability and disadvantage and their victimisation by family violence place them at increased risk of offending behaviours, out of necessity and despair at the fragmentation of the self and their communities.

Chapter 10 by Margaret Malloch and Gill McIvor (Scotland) examines the relationship between women's offending and drugs and how policy responses to drug-related crime have impacted disproportionately upon women, in particular those from minority ethnic groups. Traditional community-based responses to drug treatment have not been successful at tackling the associated social and personal difficulties that surround the needs of women or addiction, leading to breaches of orders and reoffending. Malloch and McIvor suggest more effective responses by the justice system to women with addiction issues are gained by using community-based resources that provide support and an opportunity for women to address underlying issues. This focus, they suggest, places drug-related offending within the context of other issues in a woman's life, diverts the focus away from mere punishment and is likely to produce more successful outcomes.

Janet Davidson (USA) in Chapter 11 discusses how increases in the numbers of offenders, both male and female, have led to increased calls for evidence as to what constitutes more effective approaches to the management of offenders. These give prominence to actuarial-based risk/need instruments that can manage both risk as well as the programmatic needs of offenders. There is significant concern, however, when these are applied to women offenders as they appear to ignore gender-specific variables and pay little heed to women's more prevalent histories of physical and/or sexual abuse, mental and physical health problems, and relationship and parental difficulties (as well as other gendered factors) that should be key to assessing risk and needs. Davidson argues that women do not get the sort of supervision and help that they need when, through the use of structured assessment tools that have been developed for men, their needs are either misidentified or ignored.

In Chapter 12, Jo Deakin and Jon Spencer (England) illustrate the significance of fostering networks and supportive relationships for women in the reintegration process. This chapter introduces the third section of the book, which focuses on women and resettlement. Deakin and Spencer argue that positive relationships provide a form of social capital and act as a significant form of social control. They describe the transition from prison to the community as fraught with difficulties influenced by demographic characteristics, contextual factors, and cultural experience. They highlight how for many women incarceration is damaging to their familial, social and support networks, reducing ties to family and friends and increasing the risk of recidivism. They suggest that social, practical and emotional supports – most specially the informal support offered by family and close friends – play a vital role in women's rehabilitation and will have a significant impact on their desistance from crime.

Chapter 13 by Chris Trotter (Australia) examines the mentoring relationships between a professional or volunteer worker and an offender, arguing that high levels of contact on an informal basis, along with the provision of some practical assistance, improves the individual offender's well-being and may prevent their drift into reoffending. He discusses the evaluation of four mentoring programmes offered to women and men following their release from prison in Victoria, Australia, and which aspects of the mentoring individuals said they found most helpful. What the women interviewed said they valued most from mentoring was that the volunteers who worked with them addressed their needs as they, the women, saw them, and jointly developed goals and strategies to deal with these, using strengths-based approaches that made them feel more positive about themselves and their ability to desist from offending.

Chapter 14 by Dawn Salgado, Judith B. Fox and Kristen Quinlan (USA) presents findings about the Rhode Island Women's Mentoring Program. They demonstrate the positive outcomes of community mentoring in the United States, and identify factors that appear to promote long-term reintegration and reduce reoffending among women. They argue that mentoring-based strategies are an economical way to provide continuous support to women while they are incarcerated and after release. The women interviewed for the evaluation said their mentors became an important source of social support and guidance, especially for those who had strained relationships with family and friends.

In Chapter 15, Rosemary Sarri (USA) addresses the characteristics and needs of incarcerated mothers and their children with particular reference to the interventions required for successful family reunification. She notes that, in the US, women are associated with increased recidivism as a result of restrictive parole criteria, lack of access to community treatment programmes and lack of community support after release, especially for women with children. She argues that greater use should be made of community-based diversion programmes that maintain family units, reduce dislocation for children, promote social inclusion and reduce women's recidivism and the potential involvement of their children, when older, in the criminal justice system.

Chapter 16 by Becky Hayes Boober and Erica Hansen King (USA) outlines the contribution made by the Women's Re-entry Centre developed by the US State of Maine, to facilitate women's resettlement needs. It is an approach that adopts a strengths-based and relational focus to help women make the transition to, and remain within, the community. They describe how individual case plans are developed to address women's needs for assistance and to support them to become self-sufficient, beyond the correctional system. They found the programme's evidence-based, gender-responsive principles accommodated well the complexity of women's needs and gave them strategies to continue living with their families and desist from further offending.

Women's offending has recently received greater attention, in part because of the exponential increase in women's incarceration (see, for example, Frost *et al.* 2006), stretched resources and government calls for gender-responsive strategies that encourage and support female desistance from offending. Chapter 17 concludes this book by discussing the themes that have been developed and comes to some conclusions about key approaches that are likely to enhance the efficacy of community-based responses to women who offend. As the contributions to this volume demonstrate, women's offending is distinct from male offending and women have distinctive experiences, characteristics and needs. Where gender-responsive principles inform policies and programmes, there are better outcomes for women. It is clear that the social and personal consequences of imprisonment for women are particularly acute. International developments in policy and in practice are turning to community-based strategies that reduce women's incarceration and draw on responses that are holistic in approach and sensitive to the factors that influence women's offending and their pathways into criminal behaviour. We hope that this book, by adding to the growing literature on the significance of working with community-based approaches to the needs of women who offend, contributes to and encourages ongoing discussion and debate.

References

Andrews, D.A. and Bonta, J. (2003) *The Psychology of Criminal Conduct.* Cincinatti, USA: Anderson Publishing.

Austin, J., Bloom, B. and Donohue, T. (1992) *Female Offenders in the Community: An Analysis of Innovative Strategies and Programs.* Washington, DC: National Institute of Corrections.

Blanchette, K. (2001) 'Effective correctional practice with women offenders', in L. Motiuk and R. Serin (eds) *Compendium of Effective Correctional Programming* (Volume 1, Chapter 20). Ottawa, Ontario: Correctional Service of Canada.

Bloom, B., Owen, B. and Covington, S. (2003) *Gender-Responsive Strategies: Research, Practice and Guiding Principles for Women Offenders.* Washington, DC: National Institute of Corrections.

Bloom, B., Owen, B. and Covington, S. (2004) 'Women offenders and the gendered effects of public policy', *Review of Policy Research*, 21 (1): 31–48.

Blyth, A. (2001) *Literature Review Prepared for the OCSC as Part of the Clinical Audit of Bendigo, Fulham and Dame Phyllis Frost Prisons*, August 2001.

Carlen, P. (2002) 'Women's imprisonment: Cross-national lessons', in P. Carlen (ed.) *Women and Punishment: The Struggle for Justice*. Cullompton: Willan Publishing.

Dannerbeck, A., Sundet, P. and Lloyd, K. (2002) 'Drug courts: Gender differences and their implications for treatment strategies', *Corrections Compendium*, 27 (12): 1–5 and 24–26.

Frost, N.A., Greene, J. and Pranis, K. (2006) *Hard Hit: The Growth in the Imprisonment of Women, 1977–2004*. New York, NY: Institute on Women and Criminal Justice.

Home Office (2001) *The Government's Strategy for Women Offenders: Consultation Report*. London: Home Office.

Home Office (2004) *Women's Offending Reduction Programme (WORP) Action Plan*. London: Home Office.

Leverntz, A.M. (2006) 'The love of a good man? Romantic relationships as a source of support or hindrance for female ex-offenders', *Journal of Research in Crime and Delinquency*, 43 (4): 459–88.

Loucks, N. (2004) 'Women in prison', in G. McIvor (ed.) *Women Who Offend*. London: Jessica Kingsley.

Scottish Office (2002) *A Better Way: The Report of the Ministerial Group on Women's Offending*. Edinburgh: Scottish Office.

Ward, L. (2003) *Effective Community Based Programs for Women Offenders: An Evidence Based Review*. Report commissioned by Corrections Victoria and the Department of Justice, Victoria. Melbourne: Lisa Ward Consulting.

Chapter I

Female offenders in the community: The context of female crime

Briege Nugent and Nancy Loucks

This chapter examines the structural, social and personal issues facing women offenders. This includes strategies that assist women offenders in the community and divert them from imprisonment within the welfare tradition of Scottish criminal justice. It also examines the varying philosophies and practices that view women and children as special cases and the consequent conflicts that arise for policy, welfare services and professional social work practice with women offenders.

Structural, social and personal issues facing women

Since the 1990s, much work has been undertaken where previously little research had identified the issues confronted by women offenders. The first inquiry investigating the use of community sentences and custody for women offenders in Scotland was a response to a series of suicides in Cornton Vale, Scotland's prison for women offenders. The resulting Social Work Services and Prisons Inspectorate report (1998: 13) *Women Offenders – A Safer Way* concluded that 'the backgrounds of women in prison are characterised by experiences of abuse, drug misuse, poor educational attainment, poverty, psychological distress and self-harm'.

The complexity of issues for women offenders emphasises the need for services to be holistic. Gelsthorpe (2007: 301) notes that to be holistic is to be 'treated not as a composite offender but as a fully human, socially and culturally differentiated offender', which she believes engenders reciprocal 'respect' and indirectly promotes compliance. Mutual respect between the offender and any caseworker has been shown to be crucial in the process of desisting from offending (McNeil *et al.* 2005). Taking account of and responding to the individual's characteristics, background, age, social class and learning style is vital, as is an acute awareness of the context of the individual's life. For women offenders, the social, structural and personal issues they face often overlap. As a result, many have chaotic lives, making compliance with community punishment difficult (Barry and McIvor 2009).

Prison and the problems for short-term prisoners

The population of women prisoners in Scotland has increased disproportionately in recent years: while the male population has increased by 29 per cent since 1999–2000, the female population has nearly doubled in that time (Scottish Government 2009a). The high level of vulnerability that women offenders present is one reason why so many are being sent to prison at an increasing rate in Scotland – not to be punished, but to be cared for (Barry and McIvor 2009; Tombs and Jagger 2006; Social Work Services and Prisons Inspectorate 1998). Tombs and Jagger (2006) reported that the judges they interviewed accepted that some offenders are so 'grossly deprived that imprisoning them provides a solution however unpalatable to social problems that other institutions and structures fail to address' (2006: 809). In adopting this 'welfare' approach, female offenders are denied agency; using prison in this way can render the most vulnerable even more helpless.

Prison has arguably become a welfare panacea for many women. It suspends them from facing the issues that brought them to prison in the first place and that will inevitably return them to prison unless they are addressed. However, access to support ends for most at the prison gate: 74 per cent of women sent to prison in Scotland are short-term prisoners (sentenced to periods of less than four years), which means they are not subject to statutory supervision and support on release (Scottish Government 2009a). Short-term prisoners have the highest level of social need and the highest rates of reconviction, and a higher proportion of women than men in prison are serving short-term sentences (Maguire and Raynor 2006; Lewis *et al.* 2007; Scottish Government 2008; Social Work Services and Prisons Inspectorate 1998).

Short-term prisoners face a wide range of issues, forming a 'recalcitrant problem for the agencies involved' (Crow 2006: 15). These problems often relate to the fact that very little effective work can be done with them in prison over a short period of time, yet engaging them in support after release can be exceptionally difficult. Using prison as a welfare panacea, particularly for short-term prisoners where little support can be put in place for them on release, is clearly not a rational or viable way forward.

Prison-based intervention is also not ideal. Any intervention in prison will arguably be limited in its efficacy as it takes place in an environment removed from the realities of women's lives on the outside. For example, many women who offend use drugs as a coping mechanism to deal with trauma from victimisation and mental health problems (Malloch 2004; Covington 1999). Getting someone off drugs is not enough unless any underlying issues are addressed; only then can the person be considered to be 'healthy'. Many women say that they have been able to get 'clean' in prison but have struggled when they are in the community. The realities of what women offenders deal with in the community remain outstanding, so prison is not a lasting solution (Nugent and Loucks 2009).

The need for flexible and comprehensive support

To prevent further offending, women's needs have to be identified and taken into account, particularly those that are barriers to the fulfilment of community-based penalties. For example, reliance on welfare benefits is particularly significant for women compared to men (Scottish Parliament 2009). Women may therefore require help with the basic costs required for compliance with community orders such as transport and childcare, or these needs should be accommodated, such as through home visits. The Asha Centre in England, for example, provides the option of an on-site crèche, which offers information and assistance to mothers, or an allowance to enable them to arrange their own childcare (Rumgay 2004b).

Cornton Vale, Scotland's only prison for women, has a Links Centre that provides a central location for services to work in and to connect women to relevant agencies. Women report feeling that a similar 'one-stop shop' would be ideal in the community (Cavanagh et al. 2007). Only two such services for women exist in the community in Scotland. One is the 218 Centre in Glasgow (see below), which offers comprehensive residential and community-based support for

3

women offenders (Malloch and Loucks 2007; Loucks *et al.* 2006). The service offers a range of supports, primarily targeted at women with substance misuse issues, though tailored to the individual needs of the women and focused on addressing the underlying causes for offending. The other is Sacro's (Safeguarding Communities – Reducing Offending) Community Links Centre in Edinburgh, where the Willow Project was recently piloted. This project supports women offenders in addressing their underlying and criminogenic needs. The project places a strong emphasis on practical support and connecting women to services that exist in the community. The evaluation highlighted that this type of support clearly fills a gap in provision (Nugent *et al.* 2010).

The need for women-centred approaches

Extensive research indicates that women who are involved in offending often have a history of physical and sexual abuse in childhood and into adulthood (Loucks 1998; Social Work Services and Prisons Inspectorate 1998; McClellan 2006). Helping women recognise the resilience and strength that has helped them through these experiences can promote their desistance from offending. Other studies of women highlight the importance of support networks in building and maintaining resilience and in particular for coping with social and personal stress (Green and Rodgers 2001; Werner and Smith 1992, cited in Rumgay 2004b).

Women offenders often report feeling they have little control over their lives. Therefore, providing meaningful options that allow them to make responsible choices is essential. These choices must make sense in terms of their past experiences, abilities and skills. Women feel that being heard is important, so any programmes or interventions should be flexible enough to incorporate their views (Nugent *et al.* 2010). Self-sufficiency, responsibility, self-esteem and confidence can be fostered by ensuring women have opportunities to play a role in their own solutions. Arguably these will be more meaningful when placed within the chaos of their lives in the community.

Desistance from crime is a 'process' rather than a 'quick fix', where maturation, strong social bonds and social capital are all important (Bottoms *et al.* 2004; McNeil 2009). For men, part of the process of desistance from offending can mean meeting their partner and settling (Bottoms 2008); for women, in contrast, part of the desistance process can mean separating from their partner (Nugent and Loucks 2009).

Targeting family relationships has yielded the greatest treatment effects for women offenders on an international basis (Dowden and Andrews 1999, 2005). Consequently, effective support should include helping women offenders identify those relationships in their lives that are not positive and empowering in order to move away from these relationships. Equally, women should receive support to regain past and build present pro-social bonds with families or friends that are genuinely supportive. This includes maintaining and strengthening the relationship they have with their children, where possible. A small number of services in Scotland such as Circle, which is an organisation working to support families, has set up reading groups and parent and child craft classes in the community. These classes give women with an offending background the opportunity to meet and bring their children, and provide mutual support in getting their lives back on track.

In 1998, the Social Work Services and Prisons Inspectorate concluded that almost all women offenders could be safely punished in the community without any major risk of harm to the general population. This may sound like a strong claim, but most convictions for women in prison are for relatively minor offences. Prison has not been used as a punishment but rather as a respite facility for the most vulnerable women in Scottish society. This is not a rational, fair or cost-effective way to treat women offenders.

Strategies to maintain women offenders in the community and divert them from imprisonment

Available community penalties

A vast range of community penalties is available in Scotland as a means of punishing offenders. Fines, compensation orders, admonition and absolute discharge are the most straightforward options. Punishments in the community that require supervision include probation, community service, drug treatment and testing, restriction of liberty (electronic tagging) and supervised attendance orders. More recently, Scotland has also used a peer support model to provide support to offenders in the community. Arguably this could be used in future as part of an alternative to custody.

Fines and fine default

Fines are one of the most important strategies to keep people out of prison; these are imposed for the lowest level of crimes such as the non-payment of television licences. This particular offence affects women more than men simply because they are more likely to be at home when the authorities check for a licence (Pantazis and Gordon 1997). If a fine is not paid, eventually the court can impose a period of time in prison instead. As a result, women are more likely to end up in prison for fine default than men. Imprisonment is intended as the last resort and is the harshest and most severe form of punishment available in the UK; the fact that someone can be sent to prison for default of a fine therefore seems extraordinary. Yet, in 2004–2005, 442 women went to prison for fine default (Scottish Executive 2005).

The impact of imprisonment on both the women and those directly affected, such as their children, is clearly disproportionate. Even a short period in custody in such cases is obviously unnecessary, particularly when non-payment is often because the women cannot afford it or have prioritised other needs above the fine. A Home Office study on offenders fined for various offences found that 78 per cent of those who had not paid their fines had defaulted because they needed the money for things such as shoes and clothing, food and housekeeping, rent and rates, unspecified bills, light and heating, and public transport (Softley 1978, cited in Pantazis and Gordon 1997). Despite the age of that research, the finding remains current, with more recent research identifying women's offending and non-payment of fines as based on need rather than greed (Hedderman and Gelsthorpe 1997; Prison Reform Trust 2000). A study by P. Young (1999) of 21 male offenders who went to prison instead of paying their fines found a similar picture. Young (1999: 191) summarised the decision to go to prison rather than pay the fine as 'both the least troublesome and the most profitable thing to do'. A history of negligible self-support and reliance on welfare benefits is particularly significant for women when compared with men (Scottish Parliament 2009), and therefore payment of fines for women can be more difficult.

In 1995, the Scottish Government implemented Supervised Attendance Orders as an alternative to any fine under the value of £500. The rationale for the order was that it avoided resorting to prison as a punishment for non-payment of fines. The order requires the offender to carry out a range of supervised constructive activities. These activities can range from work on basic practical life skills such as debt or money management to unpaid work in the community. As a result, from 2008–2009, 656 women received this order as opposed to a fine, and the number of women going to prison for fine default in 2008–09 fell to 89 (Scottish Government 2009a) – 21 per cent of the figure in 2004–05.

The 218 Centre

Following the Social Work Services and Prisons Inspectorate (1998) *Women Offenders – A Safer Way* report, an inter-agency forum was created to look at the services for women in the criminal justice system (Scottish Executive 2002). The forum recommended that a 'time out' centre be created, and the resulting 218 Centre in Glasgow was established[1]. Loucks *et al.* (2006: 1) summarised that 'The theory was that female offenders should be able to get "time out" of their normal (chaotic) environment without resorting to "time in" custody, where many of them were being placed.' The centre can work with around 40 women at any one time, including 12–14 on a residential basis. As well as reducing reoffending and drug use, it also focuses on improving the women's health and attaining stable accommodation (Loucks *et al.* 2006).

The positive impact of the service highlights that addressing the underlying needs and taking account fully of the context of the women's lives is essential (Malloch and Loucks 2007). The success of the centre is testimony to the point that women have complex needs which require intensive support. In practice this means that caseloads should be kept low with a range of services and partners utilised. The 218 Centre's initial funding was significant in comparison to other services; however, the average cost of an engagement still only equated to the cost of 2.6 months in prison (Loucks *et al.* 2006). Moreover, the benefits to the women in their desistance from offending are significant in the long term. Although the 218 Centre was highlighted as best practice (Scottish Government 2007a), it has not yet been rolled out across Scotland.

Routes out of Prison

One of the largest providers of support in Scotland to prisoners before and after leaving prison is the Routes out of Prison (RooP) Project. The service is made up primarily of ex-offenders who act as peer support workers to help women and men who are not entitled to statutory support to access the support they need in the community (Nugent *et al.* 2008). Clients point out that the strength of the peer support model is that the worker has 'been there' and understands implicitly the difficulties they are likely to face. Pollak (2004) argues that peer support models are the most effective way of moving away from what she sees as an 'expert' model of service delivery which can be both exclusionary and oppressive. Peer support recognises clients' coping and resistance to oppression and uses their past experiences to build strengths; clients are looked at as a whole rather than simply focusing on their weaknesses. At present, RooP is not being used as an alternative to custody, though it could be a viable model for intervention in the future.

Encouraging the use of community-based approaches

The Scottish Government (2007a) report, *Revitalising Justice – Proposals to Modernise and Improve the Criminal Justice System*, and the Scottish Prisons Commission Report (2008) both advocate the end of short-term sentences and more use of effective community sentences. Both reports point to the fact that community sentences result in a lower rate of reconviction and can be effective in 'paying back' to the community. In this era of 'risk-obsessed' policies (Brown and Pratt 2000; Beck 1992; Giddens 1991), the Prisons Commission pointed out that offenders have strengths as well as risks, and potential that should be nurtured. Support for families in particular was highlighted as one of the key ways of helping offenders rebuild their lives.

Following this, the Scottish Government (2009b) proposed the Criminal Justice and Licensing (Scotland) Bill, which moved to create a single type of community sentence – a 'Community Payback Order' – which has a specific focus on 'payback'. The *Reforming and Revitalising: Report on the Review of Community Penalties* (Scottish Government 2007b) states that community penalties should be based on the principles of i) quality; ii) effectiveness; iii) immediacy; iv) visibility; v) flexibility; and vi) relevancy.

In relation to flexibility, the *Reforming and Revitalising* report advises that the penalty should be responsive to the needs of the community, courts, victims, and offenders rather than designed around the needs of the service. In relation to 'relevancy', the report goes on to recommend that the service rehabilitate offenders and address their underlying needs to help them to move away from offending. It is pointed out, for example, that it is wrong to use prison as a period of respite for troubled women and instead highlights the 218 Centre as being an example of a better option existing in the community for female offenders (Scottish Government 2007a: 19). The report also proposes that women offenders should have a mentor or link worker to help them fulfil the conditions of their order in the community

(2007a: 17). Indeed, this approach is currently being piloted for female offenders by Scotland's South West Community Justice Authority, with support provided through Barnardo's Scotland, part of a UK-wide charity that works to support vulnerable children.

The Community Payback Orders (CPOs) established in the Criminal Justice and Licensing (Scotland) Act 2010 brings together elements of restorative justice and rehabilitation as well as more punitive elements. Originally, the Bill proposed to abolish prison sentences of less than six months. However, the Scottish Parliament initially rejected this element of the bill, eventually compromising by reducing this to three months, which highlights that the resistance to change, despite evidence, still exists. Overall, both reports and the Act are important steps moving away from the punitive order and a revival of the welfare ethos.

The Community Justice approach

A significant number of developments have taken place in criminal justice in Scotland. The Management of Offenders etc. (Scotland) Act 2005 provided for the introduction of Scotland's division into eight Community Justice Authorities (CJAs). The description used in the legislation of the Management of Offenders Act arguably indicates a move to a more punitive 'new penology' policy from a traditional welfare approach (Feeley and Simon 1992, 1994). The CJAs, however, mark an important development as they are tasked with facilitating strategic planning between a broad range of partners. These include local authorities, the Scottish Prison Service, the police, health care, court services, victim services and all individuals and organisations that receive funding to provide services or support to offenders or their families. The point of bringing all these groups and individuals together is to address offending and the reasons behind it in a genuinely holistic manner. This includes increasing information-sharing and sharing responsibility and decision-making for the distribution of resources, all with the aim of reducing reoffending.

Women offenders are one of the priority groups identified within the CJAs, which acknowledges that this is a group with distinctive needs. Further, following a report by the Equal Opportunities Committee (Scottish Parliament 2009), the Scottish Government committed £100,000 for each CJA specifically aimed at reducing the number of women in prison (Currie 2010). As yet, how this money will be spent is not known. However, early indications are clear that this will mean more funding – at least in the short term – for community initiatives specific to the needs of women. Although this is a small step in practical terms, it is a brave step in symbolic terms, which highlights a political drive for change. It moves prison away from being the central mode of punishment and gives community options the support they need. The concern is whether this is again a 'knee-jerk' response to the crisis of a rising prison population or whether it signifies a more lasting change of attitude and approach.

Signs of change?

The Corston Report (2007), which looked into the needs of, and options for, female offenders, recommended that community solutions for non-violent women offenders be the norm. It also argued for a strong, consistent message from the highest level of government, with full reasons given, in support of its stated policy that prison is not the right place for women offenders who pose no risk to the public. Gelsthorpe (2006) lamented that things were not changing for women offenders despite countless reports which highlighted that sending women to prison was not the answer. Four years on from this article, and indeed over ten years since Scotland's Social Work Services and Prisons Inspectorate (1998) *Women Offenders – A Safer Way* Report, we now see signs of an agenda for change. In this instance, crisis has bred innovation, but also, community and welfare approaches finally seem to be regarded as a rational way forward.

Variation in philosophies and practice in Scotland

The shift from welfare to punitivism – and back?

Consistent with this apparent shift in approach towards women offenders, Scotland has traditionally taken more of a welfare approach towards offending behaviour compared with other jurisdictions within the UK. This 'welfare ethos' is most embodied in the 1968 Social Work (Scotland) Act. This act disbanded the Scottish Probation Service and made local authority Social Work Departments responsible for the supervision of offenders in the community and the provision of Social Enquiry Reports to the courts.

Equally, the Kilbrandon Report in 1961, largely influenced by the Scandinavian countries, set out the basis of the Children's Hearing System, which replaced juvenile courts. This model was based on the principle that the welfare of the child is paramount and that children in trouble presented needs where care and protection had to be given, rather than punishment. Hetherington *et al.* (1997: 15) describe the Children's Hearing Panel as an example of child welfare activity that is based on a social mandate, 'drawn not in terms of a division but on inclusion' (cited in Sheehan 2001: 213). Both the Social Work (Scotland) Act 1968 and the Children's Hearing System have proudly set Scotland aside because they mark the strength of the welfare agenda in comparison to the influence of a more punitive neo-liberal ideology fostered by the US. Wacquant (1999) argues that many punitive US policies are translated into 'justice' projects, mainly through the conduit of the UK (cited in Drake *et al.* 2010: 38). For example, policies such as zero-tolerance policing, curfews and electronic monitoring have all originated in the US. Although Scotland has adopted these measures to some extent, it has still maintained a welfare agenda by offering schemes that are different from this policy agenda. Specifically, the Children's Hearing System attempts to divert children away from the criminal justice system, and rehabilitation of the offender is the key premise on which the Social Work Scotland (Act) 1968 is built (Whyte and McNeil 2007). Arguably, the welfare agenda in Scotland has shown it to be a 'healthy' society (J. Young 1999), actually 'doing' social inclusion rather than simply talking about it.

Ironically, since Scottish devolution in 1999, the Scottish Criminal Justice System has 'come under an increasingly intensive and political gaze' (McIvor 2007; McNeil 2004). The result has been a convergence towards a more punitive and 'English' way of doing things, particularly in relation to youth justice, which McAra calls a 'detartanisation' (2006: 142). For example, the use of Antisocial Behaviour Orders (ASBOs), which are civil orders to prevent behaviour that causes or would be likely to cause alarm or distress, was extended to 12–15-year-olds by the Antisocial Behaviour etc. (Scotland) Act 2004. Breach of an order is a criminal offence; the order, in contrast to the Kilbrandon philosophy behind the Children's Hearing System, focuses on deeds and less on needs. The number of ASBOs administered doubled between 2004 and 2007 (DTZ and Heriot Watt University 2007).

The police have also been given additional powers to disperse groups in designated areas, and electronic tagging for children is also now an option (McAra 2006). The emphasis on welfare as existing more in Scotland as opposed to England is even argued by some to be 'largely mythical' (Mooney and Poole 2004: 478). However, 'welfare' has almost become a dirty word in many regards, wrongly synonymous with being 'weak' on crime. The belief in the need to be 'tough on crime' in the New Labour era has gained ground since the punitive tsunami following the terrorist attacks in New York in September 2001 and is regarded as a leap backwards in philosophical and ideological notions of how justice and punishment should be carried out (Wacquant 2005). The influence of the United States on criminal justice policy in England is now well-documented (Simon 2007; Jones and Newburn 2007). Similarly, Scottish criminal justice policy and its welfare traditions have not remained immune and, like so many countries in the neo-liberal West, it appears to have embraced 'actuarial justice'. This means that offenders are seen as needing management rather than help and rehabilitation, which ultimately is both dehumanising and iatrogenic (Feeley and Simon 1992, 1994).

The victim's 'voice' is often invoked by the media and politicians as a fail-safe means of promoting an even more punitive line. However, as with children, victims are rarely asked for their views. The small number of studies conducted show that victims of crime are often much less vengeful than their manufactured public voice would suggest (Erez 1999). For example, the SmartJustice and Victim Support survey, *Crime Victims Say Jail Doesn't Work* (2006), shows that almost two-thirds of victims of crime do not believe that prison works to reduce non-violent crime and offences such as shoplifting, stealing cars and vandalism. Victims showed overwhelming support for programmes that focus on prevention and, in particular, more support for parents, more constructive activities for young people and more drug treatment and mental health provision in the community. In 2007, a further poll conducted again by ICM on behalf of SmartJustice involved 1,006 adult participants. The survey found that 73 per cent of victims did not think that mothers of young children who commit non-violent crime should be imprisoned, and 86 per cent supported community alternatives to prison (SmartJustice 2007).

Furthermore, estimates from the Scottish Government (2008) on the costs of various disposals available to the courts for the financial year 2005–06 show that the cost of six months in prison is just under £16,000, while the average cost of a community service order is approximately £2,200. Reoffending rates for people coming out of prison are also consistently higher than for people sentenced to community penalties. This begs the question that if prison is the most costly option in more than monetary terms, and does not work, who actually supports it?

In this global climate of fear and control, punitivism sells. Despite the fact that the public has little information about, or knowledge of, community penalties, the perception of community penalties is that they are 'soft' (Scottish Government 2007b). Finland was in a similar punitive grip to Scotland and even up until the 1970s had one of the highest rates of imprisonment in Western Europe. However, in the late 1960s academics called for the prison population to be cut and insisted that criminal justice policy should be part of an overall social policy related to employment and educational opportunities. Lappi-Seppala (2006), the head of the national research institute of legal policy in Finland, advises that policy-makers, the media and the public need to be convinced that prison overcrowding is a political problem, and that the political will needs to be there to make the change. In Finland, all the organisations and individuals outlined shared knowledge so that what should happen had a realisable effect. Unlike in British countries, in Finland the media were said to have a generally 'reasonable' attitude to criminal justice; in contrast, this could be a stumbling block for British policy. In Finland there has been a mixture of decriminalising some offences (such as public drunkenness), relaxing sentencing on others, and reducing the minimum prison sentence from four months in 1976 to just 14 days in 1989. In the mid-1970s judges were allowed greater scope to impose conditional sentences as opposed to imprisonment, and in the 1990s community service became popular with the result that only repeat offenders and rare cases were sent to prison (Younge 2001). Finland now has one of the lowest rates of imprisonment in Europe; while the prison population rate in Finland is 67 per 100,000 of the national population, in Scotland it is comparably high at 150 per 100,000 (Scottish Government 2009a).

Overall, the Finnish example is able to show that where the political will exists, there is a possibility of change. The Scottish Prisons Commission (2008) pointed out that the public needs to be engaged in rational debate. However, taking on board the evidence from Finland, rational debate must also include policy-makers including government ministers, the legislators, the judiciary, the police and prosecutors and the media.

Falling between the cracks and contradictions in policy?

At present, criminal justice policy in Scotland is at best ambivalent as it struggles between retaining a welfare outlook and taking a punitive line, best exemplified by the ongoing rates of women's imprisonment. Scotland is now imprisoning more women than ever. Whether this is through increased punitiveness or a misplaced 'welfare' agenda, this is not a rational or lasting solution. The proposed Community Payback Order may provide the compromise necessary to satisfy those who advocate for a punitive approach as well as those who see the merits in welfare. For women offenders who are the sole or main carers of children, this type of sentence could be useful in maintaining them in the community and subsequently ensuring the maintenance of the family structure. The question is whether this approach will include the support necessary to address underlying reasons for offending.

Treating women offenders and their children as special cases

The number of children affected by imprisonment in Scotland each year is estimated at 16,500, though precise figures are unknown (Families Outside 2009). Scotland has one female prison and one hall allocated to females in the male prison at Greenock, which is in the west Central Lowlands of Scotland. This means that the majority of women are far away from their families and children. Mothers report that being away from their children is the hardest part of being in prison and, for many, being back with their children is the main motivating factor for desistance (Nugent and Loucks 2009). These women are often the sole or main carer of their children, so unless a family member assumes the caring role, children are sent to be looked after by the local authority.

There is a dearth of knowledge about the specific impact prison has on children. While there may be cases where the imprisonment of the parent may be in the best interests of the child, research highlights the overwhelming evidence of the negative impacts. These effects include post-traumatic stress disorder, anxiety, problems with attention/concentration and sleeping, flashbacks, problems in school and falling deeper into poverty (Bernstein 2005; Loureiro 2009). Siblings are often separated, children experience moving between carers, and planning for their care in many cases is non-existent (Sheehan and Flynn 2007).

Murray et al. (2007) found that young children who have a parent in prison are twice as likely to go to prison themselves in the future. Other impacts are that grandparents often take up the role of sole carer or 'kinship carers' and often feel unsupported practically and financially by social services. Kinship carers are not entitled to the same payments as foster parents and as a result may struggle financially with their new responsibility for children.

Family contact is not easy when someone is in prison, with transport and the financial costs and length of time to get to the prison cited as the main reasons why many visits do not take place. In a seven-day period in one study, 1,460 children in Scotland visited prison. Children sometimes had to be taken out of school to make the visiting times, which also often meant skipping meals and interrupting their normal schedules (Higgenbotham 2007).

Family involvement reduces reoffending (Holt and Miller 1972, and supported in later research such as Hairston 1991; Loucks 2005). Scotland's Commissioner for Children and Young People (Marshall 2008: 34) reports that 'There is ... scope within current policy for a focus on children as members of prisoners' families; however, this is all within a framework aimed at reducing re-offending, with children appearing as potential contributors to satisfaction of this agenda.' The report goes on to propose that the focus should be on children in their own right rather than merely as a tool for resettlement.

Balancing rights

Sentencing women requires a balance of rights, both in terms of the offender and victim but also for those directly affected by the punishment, in this case primarily children. The principle established in Scotland is that the welfare of the child should be paramount and that decisions should be taken to serve their 'best interests'. However, often when a woman offends, the belief is that she has shown herself to be unfit to look after her child. The reality may be very different. No doubt children, in an ideal world, generally want to be with their parents and for their parents to be fit to look after them, even when those parents are not themselves ideal (Bernstein 2005). Women who have children or indeed any parent who is a sole or main carer should be treated as a special case, deserving particular attention. Echoing Sheehan and Flynn (2007), child-centred practices should be introduced into the adult criminal justice system.

Women who are mothers are sometimes judged only on the basis of whether they are 'good' or 'bad' mothers rather than as women who have committed an offence (Carlen 1983). One Sheriff (the title used for Scotland's judicial officers) even said, 'If she is a good mother, we don't want to take her away. If she's not a good mother it doesn't really matter' (Carlen 1983: 67). This is not the type of approach advocated in the research, but rather the research shows the effects of imprisonment on the children should be considered because the consequences are in many regards deeply negative.

Article 3.1 of the United Nations Convention on the Rights of the Child (UNCRC), of which the UK is a signatory nation, states that the best interests of children should be paramount in any decision that affects them. In Scotland, an ambitious overarching policy supports such international developments. Specifically, the policy *Getting it Right for Every Child* (Scottish Government 2006) sets out an ambitious vision with the aim that children in Scotland are safeguarded, protected and heard by the agencies that work with them. The Implementation Plan, which is central to the policy of *Getting it Right for Every Child*, proposes to introduce legislation to ensure that agencies have a duty to be alert to the needs of children and to act to improve a child's situation (Scottish Government 2006). The question of how this might affect decisions in court remains to be seen.

The case of *S v. M* (Centre for Child Law as amicus curiae) (2007) marked the South African Constitutional Court overturning a decision by the High Court to imprison a mother who was the sole carer of her child. The appeal to the Constitutional Court focused on the duties of the court when sentencing a primary caregiver and ultimately it was declared that it was not in the best interests of the child to send the woman in this instance to prison. Since this landmark case, judges are required to take into account the impact of their decision on any dependent children of mothers awaiting sentence. It is also the court's sole responsibility to ensure, in the event that the accused is sent to prison, that arrangements have been made for the child during the incarceration and that the effects of the imprisonment are mitigated as much as possible. As yet this practice does not happen in Scotland, despite attempts to introduce similar legislation (Adams 2010). One argument is that women sacrifice their rights as mothers when they violate the law. However, women are being sent to prison for relatively minor crimes (Barry and McIvor 2009; Carlen and Tombs 2006; Scottish Government 2009a), and the cost of this for both them and their children is incalculable.

'Social capital' for women can often mainly mean the role of being a mother. Losing this role makes it incredibly difficult for them to rebuild their lives. A shift in their friendship and lifestyle choices must be accompanied by a shift in perspective and personal identity (Giordano *et al*. 2006).

Women offenders report engaging most successfully with workers who help them to move beyond their past and to stop feeling guilty. In particular, women who had children said that having a professional view them as a good mother was important in reinforcing this identity, which was far removed from the label of offender (Nugent and Loucks 2009). Arberlour, which is the largest solely Scottish children's charity, which works with children, young people and families, has been working in partnership with Scottish Prison Service staff to develop a parenting programme for women in Cornton Vale, the only dedicated prison for women in Scotland. The evaluation of the project highlights that the women regarded retaining their identity as a mother as being invaluable. It also found that many women quickly lost confidence in their parenting skills when they did not have the full care of their children (Burgess and Malloch 2008).

Looking at women as special cases, or indeed parents as special cases, should not mean that they have licence to do as they please. However, it should make sentencers recognise that sending someone to prison impacts on children and other dependents and also on the competency or confidence of those who are parents. As far as possible, family stability should be supported and maintained; therefore, where appropriate, community penalties should be used. Funding for community disposals must therefore be adequate to make them effective, innovative and flexible to the needs of both offenders and their families.

Challenges for policy, welfare services and social work with women offenders

As noted above, women are often being sent to prison to be cared for, and the complexity of the needs they present means that an effective community disposal must be flexible and responsive. Social workers in Scotland report a lack of training in working with women who offend (National Development Champions Group 2007). Practitioners often report feeling overwhelmed when working with female clients and believe women are more difficult to work with than men (Bloom *et al.* 2003). The indications are that implementing an effective form of community disposal for women offenders requires significant investment and partnership working between agencies from the statutory and voluntary sector. Ongoing training for staff working in this area, which is focused on providing a gender-responsive approach, is equally imperative.

The importance of relationships

The quality of the relationship between the offender and the worker is crucial in helping women to desist from offending (Rumgay 2004a; McNeil *et al.* 2005). An effective professional relationship requires an empathic approach, mutual respect and understanding of the women's problems, through which positive goals can be set and attained. A high proportion of women offenders have been in local authority care as children (Scottish Parliament 2009) and can consequently be distrustful or wary of authority so that building relationships – particularly with professionals – can be difficult. Professionals need to take account of the women's backgrounds, acknowledge the reasons for resistance and know that overcoming this will take substantial effort. Resistance should not be treated as a weakness but rather as a show of resilience which can be harnessed and used in a positive way.

Women offenders feel they work best with workers who listen to them – who are 'straight up' and do not talk down to them (Nugent and Loucks 2009). Building a relationship with this client group takes time and patience: in practice this should mean that professionals such as social workers are not carrying a heavy caseload and are afforded the necessary time and space to do this. The reality of limited resources and pressures to cut funding may make this more difficult in practice.

Group work and individual needs

Group work programmes can be a great way of helping women build confidence and self-esteem, but one-to-one work needs to support this (Burnett and McNeil 2005). McIvor (2004: 305) noted that, as well as structured group work programmes, 'Greater emphasis correspondingly needs to be placed upon social inclusion and upon putting "people" back into the equation by recognising the importance of the supervisory relationship in enhancing the offenders' motivation not to offend.'

Women offenders are not a homogeneous group, so agencies working with them need to be prepared for and responsive to particular needs. For example, a Scottish study of young violent women involved in gangs found that poor family relationships and family violence were significant factors (Batchelor 2005). Based on this, Batchelor (2009) calls for affordable and accessible leisure activities geared to the specific needs of girls and young women. She argues that such activities need to be staffed by specialist workers who are attuned to, and equipped to deal with, girls' bullying and victimisation.

Positive approaches

Although risk is important, it should not become the main driving factor for interventions with women, as women generally present a low risk of harm to others (Barry and McIvor 2010). Helping women identify and build on strengths as well as resilience can be incredibly empowering for them and has proved to be a factor in desistance (Rumgay 2004b).

Both the 218 Centre and the Asha Centre have been successful in helping women offenders because they provide a 'one-stop shop' for women to have their multiple and complex needs addressed. This approach relies on agencies working together in partnership. Each discipline, such as criminal justice and health, has its own set of aims and ethical backgrounds, and as a result there is potential for organisations to work in silos and only with their own agenda in mind. However, the common aim of helping women address their underlying needs potentially unifies agencies, and with joint investment long-term solutions are more likely to be established. Overall the problems that can arise between agencies in working with women offenders are not insurmountable, and they are much less significant than the need to stop women from being sent to prison unnecessarily.

Conclusion

Women offenders present complex needs, but sending them to prison for respite or 'treatment' is not appropriate. Punishing someone or indeed 'caring' for someone in prison removes them from their community context; such an approach is unlikely to prevent further offending, particularly for short-term offenders. Compliance with community penalties can be equally difficult for women offenders but with appropriate support this can be overcome.

Desistance from offending for women demands comprehensive and realistic approaches to complex problems. Community disposals therefore need investment, with sentences that are innovative and flexible enough to support women to connect with services that address the needs that underpin their offending behaviour.

Scotland has thus far been less susceptible than England to the global punitive turn. Nonetheless, community punishments tend to be viewed as a 'soft' option – a view that needs to be challenged. Crimes take place in communities, and the problems that lead to crime exist in communities. Therefore solutions should be reached and carried out in communities. Scotland should reclaim its welfare approach not only as distinct and innovative but also as a rational and cost-effective way of preventing offending. Scotland has the opportunity to implement a meaningful agenda for change that puts community penalties, and more importantly welfare, at the heart of punishment. This includes giving children whose parents are at risk of imprisonment a greater stake in their own futures.

Note

1   The 218 Centre is so called because 218 is the number of the building in the street in which the project is based.

References

Adams, L. (2010) 'Impact of parent's jail term on children "should be factor"', *The Herald*, Glasgow, 2 March.

Barry, M. and McIvor, G. (2009) *Chaotic Lives: A Profile of Women in the Criminal Justice System in Lothian and Borders*. Peebles: Lothian and Borders Community Justice Authority.

Barry, M. and McIvor, G. (2010) 'Professional decision making and women offenders: Containing the chaos?', *Probation Journal*, 57 (1): 27–41.

Batchelor, S. (2005) '"Prove Me the Bam!" Victimization and Agency in the Lives of Young Women who Commit Violent Offences', *Probation Journal*, 52 (4): 358–75.

Batchelor, S. (2009) 'Girls, gangs and violence: Assessing the evidence', *Probation Journal*, 56 (4): 399–414.

Batchelor, S. and Burman, M. (2009) 'Between Two Stools? Responding to Young Women who Offend', *Youth Justice*, 9 (3): 270–85.

Beck, U. (1992) *Risk Society: Towards a New Modernity*. London: SAGE.

Bernstein, N. (2005) *All Alone in the World: Children of the Incarcerated*. New York: The New Press.

Bloom, B., Owen, B. and Covington S. (2003) *Gender-Responsive Strategies for Women Offenders: Research, Practice and Guiding Principles for Women Offenders*. Washington, DC: National Institute of Corrections.

Bottoms, A. (2008) 'Social Bonds and Desistance', in P. Wikström and R. Sampson (eds) *The Explanations of Crime, Context, Mechanism and Development*. Cambridge: Cambridge University Press.

Bottoms, A., Shapland, J., Costello, A., Holmes, D. and Muir, G. (2004) 'Towards desistance: Theoretical underpinnings for an empirical study', *The Howard Journal of Criminal Justice*, 43 (4): 368–89.

Brown, M. and Pratt, J. (eds) (2000) *Dangerous Offenders: Punishment and Social Order*. London: Routledge.

Burgess, C. and Malloch, M. (2008) *An Evaluation of Parenting and Children Together (PACT) in HMP Cornton Vale*. Stirling: Aberlour Child Care Trust and SCCJR.

Burnett, R. and McNeil, F. (2005) 'The place of the officer–offender relationship in assisting offenders to desist from crime', *Probation Journal*, 52 (3): 221–42.

Carlen, P. (1983) *Women's Imprisonment*. London: Routledge and Kegan Paul.

Carlen, P. and Tombs, J. (2006) 'Reconfigurations of penality: The ongoing case of the women's imprisonment and reintegration industries', *Theoretical Criminology*, 10 (3): 337–60.

Cavanagh, B., Daly, M. and Flaherty, A. (2007) *What Life After Prison? Voices of Women in Cornton Vale*. Edinburgh: Circle.

Corston, J. (2007) *The Corston Report: A Report by Baroness Jean Corston of a Review of Women with Particular Vulnerabilities in the Criminal Justice System*. London: Home Office.

Covington, S. (1999) *Helping women recover: A program for treating addiction*. London: Wiley.

Crow, I. (2006) *Resettling Prisoners: A Review*. York: York Publishing Services.

Currie, B. (2010) 'Extra cash to help female offenders', *Herald Scotland* (online), 15 January. Available at http://www.heraldscotland.com/news/crime-courts/extra-cash-to-help-female-offenders-1.999030 (accessed on 15 January 2010).

Dowden C. and Andrews, D.A. (1999) 'What works for female offenders: A meta-analytic review', *Crime and Delinquency*, 45 (4): 438–52.

Dowden, C. and Andrews, D.A. (2005) 'What works for women offenders? A meta-analytic exploration of gender-responsive treatment targets and their role in the delivery of effective correctional intervention'. Paper presented at the 'What works with Women Offenders' Conference, 20–22 June 2005, Monash University Centre, Prato, Italy.

Drake, D., Muncie, J. and Westmarland, L. (2010) *Criminal Justice: Local and Global*. Devon: Willan Publishing, in association with The Open University, Milton Keynes.

DTZ and Heriot Watt University (2007) *Use of Antisocial Behaviour Orders in Scotland*. Edinburgh (web only): Scottish Government. Available at http://www.scotland.gov.uk/Publications/2005/04/07104508/45091

Erez, E. (1999) 'Who's afraid of the big bad victim? Victim Impact Statements as victim empowerment and enhancement of justice', *Criminal Law Review*, 46: 545–56.

Families Outside (2009) *Support and Information for Children Affected by Imprisonment*. Edinburgh: Families Outside.

Feeley, M. and Simon, J. (1992) 'The new penology: Notes on the emerging strategy of corrections and its implications', *Criminology*, 30: 449–74.

Feeley, M. and Simon, J. (1994) 'Actuarial justice: The emerging new criminal law', in D. Nelken (ed.) *The Futures of Criminology*. London: SAGE, pp. 173–201.

Garland, D. (2001) *The Culture of Control: Crime and Social Order in Contemporary Society*. Chicago: University of Chicago Press.

Gelsthorpe, L. (2006) 'Counterblast: Women and criminal justice: Saying it again, again and again', *The Howard Journal*, 45 (4): 421–4.

Gelsthorpe, L. (2007) 'Dealing with Diversity', in G. McIvor and P. Raynor, *Developments in Social Work with Offenders*. London: Jessica Kingsley Publishers, pp. 290–305.

Giddens, A. (1991) *Modernity and Self Identity: Self and Society in the Late Modern Age*. Oxford: Polity Press.

Giordano, P., Cernkovich, S. and Holland, D. (2006) 'Changes in friendships and relations over the life course: Implications for desistance from crime', *Criminology*, 41 (2): 293–328.

Green, B. and Rodgers, A. (2001) 'Determinants of social support among low income mothers: A longitudinal analysis', *American Journal of Community Psychology*, 29 (3): 419–41.

Hairston, C.F. (1991) 'Family ties during imprisonment: Important to whom and for what?', *Journal of Sociology and Social Welfare*, 18 (1): 87–104.

Hedderman, C. and Gelsthorpe, L. (eds) (1997) *Understanding the Sentencing of Women*. London: Home Office Research and Statistics Directorate.

Hetherington, R., Cooper, A., Smith, P. and Wilford, G. (1997) *Protecting Children: Messages from Europe*. Lyme Regis: Russell House Publishing.

Higgenbotham, M. (2007) *Do not Pass Go … Travel Links to Scottish Prisons*. Edinburgh: Families Outside.

Holt, N. and Miller, D. (1972) *Explorations in Inmate–Family Relationships*. Research Report (46), Sacramento, CA: California Department of Corrections.

Jones, T. and Newburn, T. (2007) *Policy Transfer and Criminal Justice: Exploring US Influence over British Crime Control Policy*. Maidenhead: Open University Press.

Lappi-Seppala, T. (2006) 'Reducing the prison population: Long-term experiences from Finland', in Council of Europe, *Crime Policy in Europe*. Strasbourg: Council of Europe Publishing, 139–55.

Lewis, S., Maguire, M., Raynor, P., Vanstone, M. and Vennard, J. (2007) 'What works in resettlement? Findings from seven pathfinders for short-term prisoners in England and Wales', *Criminology and Criminal Justice*, 7 (1): 33–53.

Loucks, N. (1998) *HMPI Cornton Vale: Research into Drugs and Alcohol, Violence and Bullying, Suicides and Self-Injury, and Backgrounds of Abuse*. Occasional Paper 1/98. Edinburgh: Scottish Prison Service.

Loucks, N. (2005) 'Prison without bars': The experiences of families affected by imprisonment, *In Brief* 1. Edinburgh: Families Outside.

Loucks, N., Malloch, M., McIvor, G. and Gelsthorpe, L. (2006) *Evaluation of the 218 Centre*. Edinburgh: Scottish Executive Justice Department.

Loureiro, T. (2009) *Child and Family Impact Assessments in Court: Implications for Policy and Practice*. Edinburgh: Families Outside.

Maguire, M. and Raynor, P. (2006) 'How does the resettlement of prisoners promote desistance from crime: Or does it?', *Criminology and Criminal Justice*, 6 (1): 19–38.

Malloch, M. (2004) 'Not "fragrant" at all: Criminal justice responses to "risky" women', *Critical Social Policy*, 24 (3): 385–405.

Malloch, M. and Loucks, N. (2007) 'Responding to drug and alcohol problems: Innovations and effectiveness in treatment programmes for women', in R. Sheehan, G. McIvor and C. Trotter (eds) *What Works with Women Offenders*. Devon: Willan Publishing, pp. 91–109.

Marshall, K. (2008) *Not Seen. Not Heard. Not Guilty. The Rights and Status of the Children of Prisoners in Scotland*. Edinburgh: Scotland's Commissioner for Children and Young People (SCCYP).

Maruna, S. (2005) *Making Good: How Ex-convicts Reform and Rebuild Their Lives*. Washington, DC: American Psychological Association.

McAra, L. (2006) 'Welfarism in Crisis? Youth Justice in Scotland', in J. Muncie and B. Goldson (eds) *Comparative Youth Justice: Critical Debates*. London: SAGE.

McClellan, A. (2006). *HM Inspectorate of Prisons: Report on HMP and YOI Cornton Vale – Full Inspection Report of HMP and YOI Cornton Vale*. Edinburgh: Scottish Executive.

McIvor, G. (2004) 'Getting personal: Developments in policy and practice in Scotland', in G. Mair (2004) *What Matters in Probation*. Devon: Willan Publishing, pp. 305–27.

McIvor, G. (2007) 'Developments in Probation in Scotland', in G. McIvor and P. Raynor, *Developments in Social Work with Offenders*. London: Jessica Kingsley Publishers, pp. 82–99.

McNeil, F. (2004) 'Desistance, rehabilitation and correctionalism: Developments and prospects in Scotland', The *Howard League of Criminal Justice*, 43 (4): 420–36.

McNeil, F. (2009) *Towards Effective Practice in Offender Supervision*. Glasgow: The Scottish Centre for Crime and Justice Research.

McNeil, F., Batchelor, S., Burnett, R. and Knox, J. (2005) *21st Century Social Work, Reducing Re-offending: Key Practice Skills*. Edinburgh: Scottish Executive.

Mooney, G. and Poole, L. (2004) 'A land of milk and honey? Social policy in Scotland after devolution', *Critical Social Policy*, 24 (4): 458–83.

Murray, J., Janson, C.G. and Farrington, D.P. (2007) 'Crime in adult offspring of prisoners: A cross-national comparison of two longitudinal samples', *Criminal Justice and Behavior*, 34 (1): 133–49.

National Development (Champions) Group Working with Female Offenders (2007) *Service Provision and Intervention Guidance*. Edinburgh: Criminal Justice Social Work Development Centre for Scotland.

Nugent, B. and Loucks, N. (2009) *Circle Scotland: Throughcare for Female Offenders – Review of the First Year*. Glasgow: The Robertson Trust.

Nugent, B., Loureiro, T. and Loucks, N. (2010) *Evaluation of the Willow Pilot Project*. Edinburgh: Families Outside.

Nugent, B., Schinkel, M. and Whyte, B. (2008, unpublished) *Evaluation of Routes out of Prison: Interim Report*. Edinburgh: Criminal Justice Social Work Development Centre for Scotland.

Pantazis, C. and Gordon, D. (1997) 'Television licence evasion and the criminalisation of female poverty', *The Howard Journal of Criminal Justice*, 36 (2): 170–86.

Pollak, S. (2004) 'Anti-oppressive social work practice with women in prison: Discursive reconstructions and alternative practices', *British Journal of Social Work*, 34 (5): 693–707.

Prison Reform Trust (2000) *Justice for Women: The Need for Reform*. Report of the Committee on Women's Imprisonment, chaired by Professor Dorothy Wedderburn. London: Prison Reform Trust.

Prison Reform Trust (2008) *Bromley Briefings: Prison Factfile*. London: Prison Reform Trust.

Rumgay, J. (2004a) *The Asha Centre: Report of an Evaluation*. London: London School of Economics.

Rumgay, J. (2004b) 'Scripts for safer survival: Pathways out of female crime', *Howard Journal*, 43 (4): 405–19.

S v. M (Centre for Child Law as amicus curiae) (2007), South African Constitutional Court. This can be accessed at http://www.saflii.org/za/cases/ZACC/2007/18.html

Scottish Executive (2002) *A Better Way: The Report of the Ministerial Group on Women's Offending*. Edinburgh: Scottish Executive.

Scottish Executive (2005) *Prison Statistics Scotland 2004/5*. Edinburgh: Scottish Executive National Statistics.

Scottish Government (2006) *Getting it Right for Every Child: Implementation Plan*. Edinburgh: Scottish Government.

Scottish Government (2007a) *Revitalising Justice – Proposals to Modernise and Improve the Criminal Justice System*. Edinburgh: Scottish Government.

Scottish Government (2007b) *Reforming and Revitalising: Report of the Review of Community Penalties*. Edinburgh: Scottish Government. Available at http://www.scotland.gov.uk/Publications/2007/11/20142739/0

Scottish Government (2007c) *Community Sentencing: Public Perceptions and Attitudes*. Edinburgh: Scottish Government. Available at http://www.scotland.gov.uk/Publications/2007/11/15102229/0

Scottish Government (2008) *Costs and Equalities and the Scottish Criminal Justice System 2005/06*. Edinburgh: Scottish Government. Available at http://www.scotland.gov.uk/Publications/2008/09/05103117/0

Scottish Government (2009a) *Statistical Bulletin: Crime and Justice Series: Prison Statistics Scotland: 2008–09*. Edinburgh: Scottish Government.

Scottish Government (2009b) *Criminal Justice and Licensing (Scotland) Bill [as introduced] Session 3 (2009)*. SP Bill 24. Edinburgh: Scottish Parliament. Available at http://www.scottish.parliament.uk/s3/bills/24-CrimJustLc/b24s3-introd.pdf

Scottish Parliament (2009*) Equal Opportunities Committee 3rd Report: Female Offenders in the Criminal Justice System*. Edinburgh: Scottish Parliament. Available at http://www.scottish.parliament.uk/s3/committees/equal/reports-09/eor09-03.htm

Scottish Prisons Commission (2008) *Scotland's Choice: Report of the Scottish Prisons Commission*. Edinburgh: Scottish Prisons Commission.

Sheehan, R. (2001) *Magistrates' Decision-Making in Child Protection Cases*. Aldershot: Ashgate Publishing.

Sheehan, R. and Flynn, C. (2007) 'Women prisoners and their children', in R. Sheehan, G. McIvor and C. Trotter (eds) *What Works with Women Offenders*. Devon: Willan Publishing, pp. 214–40.

Simon, J. (2007) *Governing Through Crime: How the War on Crime Transformed American Democracy and Created a Culture of Fear*. New York: Oxford University Press.

SmartJustice (2006) *Crime Victims Say Jail Doesn't Work*. London: Prison Reform Trust.

SmartJustice (2007) *Public say: Stop locking up so many women*. London: Prison Reform Trust.

Social Work Services and Prisons Inspectorate (1998) *Women Offenders – A Safer Way: A Review of Community Disposals and the Use of Custody for Women Offenders in Scotland*. Edinburgh: Scottish Office.

Tombs, J. and Jagger, E. (2006) 'Denying responsibility', *British Journal of Criminology*, 46 (5): 803–21.

Wacquant, L. (2005) 'The great penal leap backward: Incarceration in America from Nixon to Clinton', in J. Pratt, B. Brown, M. Brown, S. Hallsworth and W. Morrison (eds) *The New Punitiveness: Trends, Theories, Perspectives*. Devon: Willan Publishing, pp. 3–27.

Whyte, B. And McNeil, F. (2007) *Reducing Reoffending: Social Work and Community Justice in Scotland*. Devon: Willan Publishing.

Young, J. (1999) *The Exclusive Society*. London: Macmillan.

Young, P. (1999) 'The Fine as the Auto-Punishment', in P. Duff and N. Hutton (eds), *Criminal Justice in Scotland*. Aldershot: Dartmouth Publishing Company, pp. 182–98.

Younge, G. (2001) 'Land of the free', *The Guardian* (online) 2 February 2001. Available at: http://www.guardian.co.uk/theguardian/2001/feb/02/features11.g2 (accessed on 27 April 2010).

Chapter 2

Policy developments in England and Wales

Carol Hedderman

Introduction

Since 2004, the government in England and Wales has sought to develop what is considered to be a new response to women offenders. The stated objectives are to reduce women's involvement in crime, and to divert them from prison. In order to understand what has shaped this policy, and to understand its impact on practice, this chapter begins with a brief discussion of how far women's offending and their involvement in the criminal justice system has changed over the past two decades. It then explores the origins of current government policies on women offenders and considers how far these build on, or diverge from, previous ones. The discussion then moves on to consider what tangible impact these policies have had to date; and what else might be done to secure a proportionate and effective response to women's offending.

Women's offending and criminal justice responses

Prior to the 1980s there was very little interest in the treatment of women in the criminal justice system in England and Wales among policy-makers or researchers. Smart (1976) suggests that this was because of the relatively small number of females involved in the criminal justice process, either as defendants or professionals. During the 1980s to mid-1990s, this situation changed to the extent that a number of studies examined exactly how women's offending differed from men's and particularly how responses to their offending differed (see, for example, Allen 1987, 1988; Carlen 1983, 1990; Eaton 1983, 1986; Edwards 1984; Farrington and Morris 1983; Gelsthorpe 1989; Genders and Player 1987; Heidensohn 1985, 1986, 1996; Hood 1992; Lees 1992; Morris 1987; Pearson 1976; and Worrall 1987, 1990). While the results of any one of these studies may not have been definitive, together they raised enough concerns about women's treatment for a Conservative Government in the early 1990s to include considerations of gender in s. 95 of the Criminal Justice Act 1991. This legislation required the Government to publish information which would enable those involved in the administration of justice to 'avoid discriminating against any persons on the ground of race or sex or any other improper ground'.[1]

The first 's. 95' paper on gender was published by the Home Office in 1992. No further editions emerged until 1999, although s. 95 papers appeared regularly on race, perhaps because the murder of black teenager Stephen Lawrence, and subsequent criticism of the police response, made race harder to ignore (see Macpherson 1999; Home Affairs Committee 2009).

Comparing the s. 95 papers on women over time shows that offending by women consistently accounts for far less crime each year than men's, although the proportion has grown slightly over the past decade (Institute for Criminal Policy Research 2009). For example, in 1998 one in five individuals convicted or cautioned for offences in England and Wales were female whereas by 2007 this figure was one in four (Ministry of Justice 2008a). Women also have shorter criminal careers. Only 9 per cent of women are convicted of a criminal offence before the age of 40 compared with 32 per cent of males (Home Office 2003a). Eighty per cent of females who start offending stop within a year; this is true for only around half of male offenders (Home Office 2003a).

Women's offending has also remained generally less serious than men's, according to both self-report and police recorded crime figures (Institute for Criminal Policy Research 2009). Their involvement in different forms of offending is also quite different. Table 2.1 summarises the statistics relating to offenders who were cautioned or found guilty of 'indictable' (more serious) offences in England and Wales, by sex and type of offence in 2007. It shows that women tend to be involved in property offences: 60 per cent of female offences are theft related, compared to only 35 per cent of male crime. The crime for which women are most commonly convicted is shoplifting. For this reason, shoplifting is sometimes thought of as a female crime

Table 2.1 Sex differences in offences resulting in a caution or conviction, 2007

Indictable offences	% of males	% of females
Violence against the person	19	17
Sexual offences	2	0
Burglary	7	2
Robbery	2	1
Theft and handling stolen goods	30	51
Fraud and forgery	5	9
Criminal damage	4	3
Drug offences	19	9
Other (excluding motoring offences)	11	7
Motoring offences	1	0
Total	416,500	101,900

Source: Ministry of Justice (2008a) Table 3.10

even though men commit substantially more of these offences. For example, in 2007, 47,245 men were convicted of theft from shops compared with 15,320 women (Ministry of Justice 2008a).[2]

The fact that violence has recently become the offence for which females are most frequently arrested has attracted much comment in the media (e.g. McVeigh 2009; Whitehead 2009), who are quick to explain it in terms of binge drinking and girls behaving more like boys. However, men are arrested at a rate of 53 per 1,000 population in England and Wales whereas the rate for women is 10 per 1,000 (Institute for Criminal Policy Research 2009). Also, whilst the percentage of women cautioned or convicted for violence (see Table 2.1) shows that the proportion of women dealt with for violence has grown to be close to that of men, Ministry of Justice statistics (2008a) show that a much higher proportion of the women cautioned or convicted for violence are cautioned. This suggests that their violence remains less serious as well as less common than men's, and that the criminal justice response to women and girls is changing at least as much, of not more, than the underlying behaviour.

Comparing the s. 95 papers on how women are treated once they are convicted shows that many of the issues which were identified as a cause for concern in the very first paper have remained so. These include the escalating use of custody; the increasingly disproportionate presence of ethnic minority women in custody; the impact on women's families of their imprisonment; the extent of mental illness and self-harm in the female prison population; and the continuing under-representation of women in senior positions in all criminal justice agencies. This is disappointing, as is the fact that so many of the gaps in knowledge identified in the first paper remain unaddressed. For example, the first s. 95 paper (Home Office 1992) noted that women who are remanded in custody are much less likely than men to receive a custodial sentence subsequently and suggests that research is needed to explain the difference. Far from being able to point to research results which explain the gap, the s. 95 paper for 2007–8 (Institute for Criminal Policy Research 2009) has to rely on old figures and those from policy documents as this information is no longer provided separately for men and women in the main statistics on criminal proceedings (Ministry of Justice 2008a). The most recent s. 95 paper (Ministry of Justice 2010) drops the discussion entirely. It has also been dropped from the Offender Management Caseload Statistics supplementary tables (Ministry of Justice 2009a). Yet the last time such figures were published in full (RDS NOMS 2006),[3] they showed that this continues to be an important element in the story of how women are treated. As Table 2.2 demonstrates, '[t]wo-thirds of the women who go to prison do so on remand and more than half of them do not go on to receive a custodial sentence, with one in five acquitted' (Corston 2007: 17). This suggests that at least some of those remands were not justified. Also, the figures on remand that are still published show that between 2002 and 2006, the rate at which women were remanded before trial was either higher than that for men, or fell by a smaller amount than that for men (Institute for Criminal Policy Research 2009). It can be argued from these figures that some women are being doubly punished as they effectively serve weeks or months in custody and then receive a community sentence in addition.

Given that women's involvement in crime has become only a little more prevalent, and the seriousness of their offending has either increased marginally or remained static, it is hard to see why the number of females in custody rose by 68 per cent[4] between 1997–2008 to 4,505 (Ministry of Justice 2009a). The scale of the increase is even more surprising given that the male prison population rose by a comparatively modest 35 per cent. Gelsthorpe and Morris (2002) link this disproportionate increase to simultaneous increases in the social and economic marginalisation of women and to legislational changes. A further explanation is the harsher sentencing climate fuelled by media demands for the courts to use custody and not let offenders 'go free from court' by using community sentences (Hedderman 2004a).

Table 2.2 Final court outcome for persons remanded in custody at some stage in magistrates' court proceedings

Final court outcome	MALES						FEMALES					
	2000	2001	2002	2003	2004	2005	2000	2001	2002	2003	2004	2005
Acquitted	23	21	21	22	20	19	22	21	20	19	18	18
Convicted	77	78	79	78	80	81	78	78	80	81	82	82
Discharge	3	3	3	3	3	3	6	5	5	5	5	4
Fine	6	4	4	4	5	4	6	5	5	5	4	4
Community Sentence	15	13	16	16	17	16	23	19	22	23	25	24
Suspended Sentence	–	–	–	–	–	1	1	–	–	–	1	2
Immediate Custody	48	51	50	49	52	53	36	42	41	40	41	43
Total	100	100	100	100	100	100	100	100	100	100	100	100

Source: RDS NOMS (2006) Table 7.11

The impact on women's imprisonment has been greater because the baseline numbers are smaller and because this tougher climate has affected the sentencing of their less serious offending (especially theft and handling) particularly severely.

The consequences of imprisonment for women also seem to be more keenly felt. The small number of female prisons means that women are often held much further from home (Prison Reform Trust 2000). Once in prison, they have greater mental and physical health needs and higher rates of self-harm and suicide than men (Corston 2007). Their resettlement plans on release are also less certain in that they are less likely to have accommodation or training and employment in place (Niven and Olagundoye 2002; Niven and Stewart 2005). As more than two-thirds of women receive sentences of less than one year, they also receive minimal help with these or other problems on release, as such short sentences are not subject to statutory supervision. Despite this, women have consistently lower reconviction rates than men. It is hard to track reconviction figures since the early 1990s as the methodology used by the Ministry of Justice has been revised several times since 2000. However, all of the figures show women reoffending less frequently than men (though the difference varies between 5 and 15 per cent depending on the measurement used). For example, the figures provided in the s. 95 publication for 2008–9 (Ministry of Justice 2010) show that of the 6,463 women and 43,818 men released from custody or commencing a court order in the first quarter of 2007, 34 per cent of women (N=2,074) and 40 per cent of men (N=17,500) were reconvicted within a year.

Recent developments in government policy

The Labour Government came to power in 1997, with a majority of 179 seats. Often governing parties must compromise on legislation, but the scale of this majority meant that the Government was in an unusually strong position to put its ideas into practice. Expectations were high that this would mean that equal weight would be given to both aspects of their Manifesto commitment to be 'tough on crime and tough on the causes of crime' (New Labour 1997). However, Labour showed itself more immediately interested in being seen as 'tough on crime'. Judging from the fact that more than 50 criminal justice bills were put forward between 1997–2008 and more than 3,000 new criminal offences have been created (Travis 2006; Open University 2008–9), this seems to have remained the case. Yet at

31

least three clear differences can be identified between the incoming government's criminal justice policies and those of their predecessors. First, its Manifesto statement made explicit acknowledgement of the fact that crime had social as well as individual causes. Second, it attempted from the outset to establish 'what works' in tackling crime and dealing with offenders (see, for example, Vennard *et al.* (1997) and Underdown (1998)). Third, the new Government sought to ensure that work with offenders took account of such evidence although, at that point, little thought seems to have been given to the fact that the evidence base consisted mainly of studies of young males or that 'what works' for women might be different from 'what works' for men (see, for example, Hedderman 2004b).

Given the new Government's unwillingness to talk down the use of imprisonment, it is unsurprising that the prison population continued to increase during its first term. Hopes that its 'Social Exclusion Unit' report (2002), which showed that those in prison were among the most socially disadvantaged, would be used to argue against the use of custody were also largely unrealised. As the title of the report – *Reducing Re-Offending by Ex-Prisoners* – made clear, this report was not arguing for decarceration and a welfarist response but for prison to be made more effective. The problem, as the then Prime Minister explained in the foreword, was not that too many men and women were in prison but that there had been a failure 'to capitalise on the opportunity prison provides to stop people offending for good' (Social Exclusion Unit 2002: 3). The report was open about the fact that women's needs were often greater than men's, that the female prison population was growing at a faster rate, and that '[b]ecause of the relatively small numbers of women in the prison system overall, their needs are often felt to be overlooked, or dealt with within a system designed primarily for male offenders' (Social Exclusion Unit 2002: 139). However, in trialling the prospect of the Women's Offending Reduction Programme (WORP) as a solution to these problems, the report eschews any mention of avoiding custody. Instead it explains (Social Exclusion Unit 2002: 142):

> The Programme's plan of action, to be formally launched later in 2002, will provide a framework for building on existing good practice to reduce women's offending. It will also enhance the growing recognition across the criminal justice system that there needs to be a distinct response to the particular needs of women.

The WORP Action Plan was not actually published until 2004, although work on the plan had commenced the previous year (Home Office 2004). The wait seemed worthwhile as it began with an uncompromising and clear statement of what so many researchers working in the field understood so well:

> Statistics show that the courts have been using custody more frequently for women over the last few years, even though the nature and seriousness of their offending has not, on the whole, been getting worse. ... The evidence suggests that courts are imposing more severe sentences on women for less serious offences. (Home Office 2004: 3)

Its aims were also generally welcomed:

> Its purpose is to reduce women's offending and the number of women in custody, by providing a better tailored and more appropriate response to the particular factors which have an impact on why women offend. The intention is not to give women offenders preferential treatment but to achieve equality of treatment and access to provision. (Home Office 2004: 5)

Given the acknowledgement that women's offending was not a large or worsening problem, the reference to reducing offending may seem a little unnecessary, but this was an essential nod towards being 'tough on crime', in a document that was otherwise heavily focused on addressing the 'social exclusion'[5] needs of women who had offended in the community. Also, it was reasonable to assume that, given so many of the women who do offend are involved in property crime, tackling issues such as poverty and unemployment would, at least in the longer term, reduce offending.

The approach was described as seeking to embed a consideration of the needs of women in existing systems and approaches. Those who understand 'policy-speak' will appreciate that this is a reference to the fact that no new or specific funding was to be allocated to secure delivery. However, to combat the institutional malaise with which new but unfunded policy initiatives are usually met, the plan's developers had ensured that objectives and time frames had been agreed with the agencies tasked with delivering them, taking account of the resources available.

Disappointingly, only one 'objective' listed under the six delivery plan areas (Bail and Remand; Sentencing; Community Provision;

Prisoner Resettlement; Women Offender Management; Crime Prevention) was actually an outcome. This, listed under the 'Resettlement' heading, was to achieve 'fewer women reoffending', although even here no specific numbers were mentioned. The other objectives took the form of aspirational statements about process and information sharing. For example, the sentencing outcomes were (Home Office 2004: 19):

- better information and understanding of the reasons behind the courts' increasing use of custody for women;

- sentencers influenced to consider credible alternatives to custody;

- perception challenged that prison is the 'safest' place for women with mental health and substance misuse problems, supported by increased opportunities for women to access appropriate community provision;

- the Sentencing Guidelines Council invited to consider guidance and instructions on how the new sentencing powers in the Criminal Justice Act 2003 may impact differently on women.

It is important to recognise and applaud the positive developments, which were undoubtedly the direct result of the WORP (see Women's Policy Team 2006), particularly given the lack of additional funding. These included setting up a cross-departmental liaison group, and encouraging the development of guidance concerning services for women on probation. The WORP also added support and impetus to other initiatives which were already in train, such as arrangements to improve community-based responses to the mental health needs of all women. Given the health needs identified among offending women, it is reasonable to expect them to benefit from such developments.

Building on these achievements, the Home Office Women's Policy Team, tasked with coordinating the WORP, eventually managed to obtain over £9 million to support a demonstration project – 'Together Women' – which sought to provide holistic support for women who were current or former offenders or whose social exclusion needs were considered to put them 'at risk of offending (see Hedderman *et al.* 2008; and Gelsthorpe, Chapter 7 herein). However, many of the criticisms levelled by Carlen (2002) and Tombs (2004) at previous policies to reduce the use of custody for women are equally applicable to the WORP. In particular, the assumption that providing sentencers with more information and better community options would reduce their use of custody runs entirely counter to the evidence. This approach did not work in England and Wales in the 1980s (Women's National Commission 1991) or the 1990s (Prison Reform Trust 2000), nor did it work in Scotland in the 2000s (Tombs 2004).

In the same way that Stephen Lawrence's death focused government thinking on racism, the deaths of six women in one prison drew attention once more to the record number of women entering prison and the negative effects this had on them and their families. The deaths led the Government to commission Baroness Corston (2007) to review 'women with particular vulnerabilities' in the criminal justice system. The phrasing here is revealing: the implication is that the system works for the majority of ordinary women; it was the vulnerable ones who needed special consideration. Fortunately, Corston chose to interpret her brief liberally, not least because:

> There are many women in prison, either on remand or serving sentences for minor, non-violent offences, for whom prison is both disproportionate and inappropriate. Many of them suffer poor physical and mental health or substance abuse, or both. Large numbers have endured violent or sexual abuse or had chaotic childhoods. Many have been in care. (Corston 2007: i)

The Government accepted 25 of Corston's 43 recommendations for change outright and a further 14 in principle or in part (Ministry of Justice 2007). Together with the WORP and the Gender Equality Duty (GED)[6], which took effect in April 2007, Corston's report has raised the profile of women offenders under supervision in the community and in prison. This has led the National Offender Management Service (NOMS) to issue a national service framework for women offenders setting out the sorts of services that were to be provided (NOMS 2008a) and a guide to 'support the implementation of the Government's strategic aims and objectives as set out in the National Service Framework for Women' (NOMS 2008b: 2). The Prison Service (2008) issued related guidance on regimes and standards of care. As these require the preparation of 'detailed, costed service specifications' (NOMS 2008a: 4), it is to be hoped that these will ultimately feed through into more effective assistance for women in the community and better conditions for women in prison.

Unfortunately, Corston's (2007: i) optimism in taking on the review that '[t]here are signs that the government would welcome a radical approach to these issues' was misplaced in four critical respects. First, while agreeing in principle with Corston's conclusion (2007: 8) that '[t]he continued use of prison for women appears to offer no advantages at huge financial and social cost', the Government persisted with the line that sentencing was a matter for the courts. All that could appropriately be done, it insisted, was to re-emphasise to the courts 'how intensive packages of requirement on a community order, together with supportive interventions and services, can be more effective in responding to women's needs and reducing re-offending' (Ministry of Justice 2007: 19). Second, but in contrast, the Government's emphasis on judicial independence seems to have been strangely absent when it designed and implemented breach provisions in the Criminal Justice Act of 2003 which curtailed sentencers' discretion, to make imprisonment for breach of a community sentence much more likely. Third, the Government rejected the idea that women who were unlikely to receive a custodial sentence should not be remanded in custody. And finally, although the 2006 WORP progress report (Women's Policy Team 2006: 21) also acknowledged 'the particular challenges of meeting the resettlement needs of women because of the limited number of women's prisons and their geographical spread', the Government ultimately rejected Corston's recommendation that large prisons for women should be replaced by small custodial units sited closer to women's homes (Ministry of Justice 2008b). This was partly on the grounds that such small units (20–30 women) would not meet all needs efficiently or effectively and partly on the grounds of cost. Instead there was a carefully worded promise to 'utilise any headroom gained from increased community provision to re-configure the prison estate *if* necessary, and *if* resources allow, so that women's establishments are of optimum size and specification for meeting women's needs' (Ministry of Justice 2008b: 15, emphasis added). Of course, those two 'ifs' kill off any real prospect of action or investment, particularly in the current economic climate.

What impact have recent policy changes had?

One year after the Government responded to Corston's recommendations, it reported on progress (Ministry of Justice 2008b). This was discussed under four headings. First, the report noted the publication of a national framework for service provision (NOMS 2008a). Second, under community provision, there is reference to an additional £40 million funding to promote effective community provision 'particularly where offenders are at risk of receiving short custodial sentences' (p. 6). It is important to appreciate that this money was not earmarked specifically for women, it was simply assumed that, as most of the custodial sentences imposed on women are short, they would benefit automatically. The remainder of this section of the progress report refers to guiding, scoping and exploring future improvements, but no concrete achievements are mentioned. In the third section, describing progress on improving custodial provision, 'achievements' are couched in such a way that it is not clear which have actually been achieved and which are still in progress. In the final section on mental health, the list of achievements comprises a list of future intentions. It may seem unreasonable to suggest that more could have been done in the year immediately after Corston reported, but this is four years after the WORP was published, nearly 10 years after the Prison Reform Trust identified the same issues, and 20 years after the Women's National Commission did so.

Extra resources specifically earmarked to divert women from custody are mentioned in a further progress report published two years after Corston (Ministry of Justice 2009b). Although, whether this £15.6 million is additional to the £40 million mentioned in the first progress report, or part of it, is not clear. Also, although this report was optimistically entitled 'Diverting women away from crime', it was only able to report that the reoffending rate for adult women was stable and that, while the rate for girls had fallen, the fall for boys was greater. Strangely, this report neglects to mention that there were also increases in reoffending following release from custody for both women and men or that 'whilst men have shown little change in reoffending following a court order, the rate of reoffending for women has increased' (Ministry of Justice 2010: 67).

Another piece of 'good news' reported in the second progress report also repays close scrutiny: 'There has been a 4.2 per cent reduction in the number of women in prison over the past two years' (Ministry of Justice 2009b: 5). The figures on which this claim is based are not presented in the progress report but Table 2.3 shows the female prison population since 2004. This shows a reduction of 0.7 per cent for the past two years and 0.8 per cent for the whole period. Even this reduction is not caused by a fall in the number of women being sentenced to custody. As the latest s. 95 report reveals (Ministry of Justice 2010: 50): 'In 2008, 8,359 women received an immediate custodial sentence, which represented a seven per cent increase in the numbers of sentences of immediate custody issued in 2007 (7,795).'

Prison populations are affected by the number being sentenced to imprisonment each year, but also by the length of those sentences and the number and length of sentences imposed in previous years. The most recent fall in the prison population is associated with an

Table 2.3 Changes in the female prison population

Year	Female prison population	% change on previous year	% change 2006 to 2008	% change 2004 to 2008
2004	4,448			
2005	4,467	0.4		
2006	4,447	−0.4		
2007	4,374	−1.6		
2008	4,414	0.9	−0.7	−0.8

Source: Ministry of Justice (2010) Table 7.01 (and Ministry of Justice 2009a, Table 7.7)

11 per cent *increase* in the proportion of women being received on very short sentences (under six months). It seems that efforts to persuade the courts not to use short custodial sentences for women have so far, yet again, been ineffective. Further evidence for this lies in the fact that of those sentenced to custody '63 per cent of women compared to 46 per cent of men received sentences up to 6 months' (Ministry of Justice 2010: .52), and the fact that nine per cent of the women sentenced to less than six months had no previous convictions compared to four per cent of men.

The second progress report also noted that there had been 'a corresponding one per cent increase in community orders for women between 2007 and 2008; an increase of 181 (14,906 to 15,087) ...' (Ministry of Justice 2009b: 5). Even this is not unalloyed good news, as all of that increase occurred in orders of one year or less. Taken together with the fact that in 2008 there were over twice as many women as men with no previous convictions (23 per cent compared with 11 per cent) under community supervision, it seems that far from diverting socially excluded women from the criminal justice system, recent policy changes have led to an increasing number of less serious cases being dealt with by means of a community sentence. Thanks to the breach provisions of the Criminal Justice Act 2003, if women breach the terms of these orders, they could easily end up in prison. The unremarked rise in the use of suspended sentence orders from 5,552 in 2007 to 5,959 in 2008 (Ministry of Justice 2010) raises similar concerns, given that breaching such orders, at best, leads to additional conditions (and an increased risk of further breach) and, at worst, leads to the suspended term being converted directly into immediate imprisonment.

Future directions

> Those who cannot remember the past are condemned to repeat it.
>
> (George Santayana 1905)

The overall pattern apparent in the most recent section 95 paper (Ministry of Justice 2010) is depressingly similar to that reported in the first edition (Home Office 1992): women still generally commit low-level offences, their offending is infrequent and their criminal careers are shorter. Despite this, more women are being sent to prison, either as a misguided attempt to get them access to help, which most do not receive, or because they have been swept up in the generally tougher sentencing climate. Most of these women pose no threat and their offences do not seem to justify such treatment: nearly one third of the custodial sentences imposed on women in 2008 were for theft and handling. Once in prison they find it harder to bear and they come out to an even more uncertain future than their male counterparts. While women's reconviction rates are generally lower than men's, there are signs that these have increased as the proportion of women being sentenced to short terms of imprisonment has increased. A study by the New Economics Foundation (2008) found that, when the social, environmental and economic outcomes of sending women to prison are ascribed monetary values, imprisoning women who are mothers for non-violent offences carries a cost of at least £17 million over ten years. This is not only because of the damage imprisonment does to the women's future life chances but because their children are more likely to be unemployed and out of education, more likely to become problem drug users and more likely to offend themselves.

Recent government policy documents specifically focused on women offenders seem to accept at least some aspects of this picture. The fact that specific policy documents exist on women which acknowledge the range of problems they face and the need to divert those who offend away from the criminal justice system, and particularly prison, is indeed a step forward, as is the considerable activity documented in the WORP and Corston progress reports. However, the practical impact to date, particularly on the use of custody, has been negligible at best. As explained above, there are even signs of 'unexpected and retrogressively oppressive consequences of the best-intentioned reforms' (Carlen 2002: 220). There are three main reasons for this. First, recent policy statements on dealing with women offenders, as with those of the previous 20 years, rely on increasing the range of non-custodial options and on informing, encouraging and exhorting sentencers to use them rather more and to resort less frequently to custody for women. This approach did not work in the 1980s, or the 1990s, and it has not worked in the 2000s. Second, and related to this, extending the development of community options specifically for women offenders and, particularly, for those 'at risk', may lead to socially excluded women who have never committed an offence, and are unlikely to do so in the future, being given a community order in a misguided attempt to get them access to help. The fact that all of the increase in community penalties reported in the second progress report on implementing Corston's recommendations shows that only short orders have increased suggests that this is exactly what has happened. This is not to suggest that community resources should revert to being divided into those for offenders and non-offenders, but that how these options are made available to sentencers needs to be reconsidered.

Finally, while government policy on women offenders is now relatively internally consistent, it fails to take account of the way its other activities work to undermine it. Most obviously, at exactly the same time that WORP was being published, a range of provisions of the Criminal Justice Act 2003 were being implemented, which increased magistrates' sentencing powers and decreased their discretion over how to deal with breaches in ways which were clearly going to disproportionately affect women (see Player 2005, for example). The argument that it is for sentencers to decide on individual sentences is valid, but it is the Government that has expanded the range of judicial officers' sentencing powers. Generally curtailing magistrates' powers to imprison women for comparatively trivial offences would have immediate and beneficial effects on the size of the sentenced prison population for women, without interfering with judicial discretion in individual cases. Similarly, taking away the power to remand for offences which are too low level to ultimately result in a custodial sentence would reduce the female remand population. Again, this would not interfere with sentencers' decisions about individual cases. Perhaps the real issue at stake is not judicial independence, but the continuing preference for being seen to be 'tough on crime' rather than genuinely seeking to reduce offending and reoffending by being 'tough on the causes of crime'.

Notes

1 Criminal Justice Act 1991 (Chapter 53).
2 The official statistics showing the numbers cautioned for theft from shops are not broken down by sex of the offender.
3 RDS NOMS was created when one part of the Home Office 'Research, Development and Statistics Directorate' (RDS) became part of the National Offender Management Service (NOMS) in 2002/3. It retained the name 'RDS NOMS' when it moved to the new Ministry of Justice, which was created in 2007. RDS NOMS no longer exists. Its work has been split across a number of different parts of the Ministry.
4 There were 2,675 women in prison in 1997 (Home Office 2003b).
5 I share Carlen's (2002) concern that the term 'social exclusion' is sometimes used to draw attention away from race and class, but it is used here as a collective term to include these as well as poverty and debt, lack of education, unemployment, mental health problems, a history of abuse etc.
6 The GED imposes a legal duty on all public authorities to eliminate unlawful sexual harassment and to promote equal opportunities for men and women.

References

Allen, H. (1987) *Justice Unbalanced*. Milton Keynes: Open University Press.
Allen, H. (1988) 'One law for all reasonable persons?', *International Journal of the Sociology of Law*, 16: 419–32.
Carlen, P. (1983) *Women's Imprisonment: A Study in Social Control*. London: Routledge and Kegan Paul.
Carlen, P. (1990) *Alternatives to Women's Imprisonment*. Milton Keynes: Open University Press.
Carlen P. (2002) 'New discourses of justification and reform for women's imprisonment in England' in P. Carlen (ed.) *Women and Punishment*. Cullompton, Devon: Willan Publishing.
Corston, J. (2007) *The Corston Report: a review of women with particular vulnerabilities in the criminal justice system*. London: Home Office.
Eaton, M. (1983) 'Mitigating circumstances: Familiar rhetoric', *International Journal of the Sociology of Law*, 1: 385–400.
Eaton, M. (1986) *Justice for Women?* London: Open University Press.
Edwards, S. (1984) *Women on Trial: A Study of the Female Suspect, Defendant and Offender in the Criminal Law and Criminal Justice System*. Manchester: Manchester University Press.
Farrington, D. and Morris, A. (1983) 'Sex, sentencing and reconviction', *British Journal of Criminology*, 23: 229–48.

Gelsthorpe, L. (1989) *Sexism and the Female Offender: An Organisational Analysis*. Aldershot: Gower.

Gelsthorpe, L. and Morris, A. (2002) 'Women's imprisonment in England and Wales: A penal paradox', *Criminal Justice*, 2: 277–301.

Genders, E. and Player, E. (1987) 'Women in prison: The treatment, the control and the experience', in P. Carlen and A. Worrall (eds) *Gender, Crime and Justice*. Milton Keynes: Open University Press.

Hedderman, C. (2004a) 'Why are more women being sentenced to custody?', in G. McIvor (ed.) *Women who Offend*. London: Jessica Kingsley.

Hedderman, C. (2004b) 'The "criminogenic" needs of women offenders: What should a programme for women focus on?', in G. McIvor (ed.) *Women who Offend*. London: Jessica Kingsley.

Hedderman, C., Palmer, E. and Hollin, C. (2008) *Implementing services for women offenders and those 'at risk' of offending: Action research with Together Women*, Ministry of Justice Research Series 12/08. London: Ministry of Justice.

Heidensohn, F. (1985) *Women and Crime*. London: Macmillan Press.

Heidensohn, F. (1986) 'Models of justice: Portia or Persephone? Some thoughts on equality, fairness and gender in the field of criminal justice', *International Journal of Sociology of Law*, 14: 287–8.

Heidensohn, F. (1996) *Women and Crime* (2nd edn). Basingstoke: Macmillan.

Home Affairs Committee (2009) *The Macpherson report ten years on*. London: House of Commons.

Home Office (1992) *Gender and the Criminal Justice System*. London: HMSO.

Home Office (1999) *Statistics on Women and the Criminal Justice System: A Home Office publication under Section 95 of the Criminal Justice Act 1991*. London: Home Office.

Home Office (2003a) *Statistics on Women and the Criminal Justice System: A Home Office publication under Section 95 of the Criminal Justice Act 1991, 2003*. London: Home Office.

Home Office (2003b) *Prison Statistics, England and Wales, 2001*. London: HMSO.

Home Office (2004) *Women's Offending Reduction Programme (WORP) Action Plan*. London: Home Offce.

Hood, R. (1992) *Race and Sentencing*. Oxford: Clarendon Press.

Institute for Criminal Policy Research (2009) *Statistics on Women and the Criminal Justice System*. London: Ministry of Justice. http://webarchive.nationalarchives.gov.uk/+/http://www.justice.gov.uk/docs/women-criminal-justice-system-07-08.pdf

Lees, S. (1992) 'Naggers, Whores and Libbers: Provoking Men to Kill', in J. Radford and D. Russell (eds) *Femicide: The Politics of Women Killing*. Buckingham: Open University Press.

Macpherson, Sir W. (1999) *The Stephen Lawrence Inquiry*. London: HMSO.

McVeigh, T. (2009) 'Teenage girls driven to violence by feuds, drink and jealousy', *The Observer*, 22 November 2009, p. 21. http://www.guardian.co.uk/uk/2009/nov/22/teenage-girls-crime-bullying-increase

Ministry of Justice (2007) *The Government's Response to the Report by Baroness Corston of a Review of Women with Particular Vulnerabilities in the Criminal Justice System*, Cmnd 7261. London: TSO.

Ministry of Justice (2008a) *Criminal Statistics 2007 England and Wales*. Statistical Bulletin. London: Ministry of Justice.

Ministry of Justice (2008b) *Delivering the Government Response to the Corston Report: Progress Reports on Meeting the Needs of Women with Particular Vulnerabilities in the Criminal Justice System*. London: Ministry of Justice. http://www.justice.gov.uk/docs/corston-progress-report.pdf

Ministry of Justice (2009a) *Offender Management Caseload Statistics 2008*. London: Ministry of Justice.

Ministry of Justice (2009b) *A Report on the Government's Strategy for Diverting Women Away from Crime*. London: Ministry of Justice.

Ministry of Justice (2010) *Statistics on Women and the Criminal Justice System: A Ministry of Justice publication under Section 95 of the Criminal Justice Act 1991*. London: Ministry of Justice.

Morris, A. (1987) *Women, Crime and Criminal Justice*. Oxford: Blackwell.

New Economics Foundation (2008) *Unlocking Value: How we all Benefit from Investing in Alternatives to Prison for Women Offenders*. London: NEF.

New Labour (1997) Manifesto http://www.labour-party.org.uk/manifestos/1997/1997-labour-manifesto.shtml

Niven, S. and Olagundoye, J. (2002) *Jobs and Homes: A Survey of Prisoners Nearing Release*, Findings 173. London: Home Office.

Niven, S. and Stewart, D. (2005) *Resettlement Outcomes on release from prison*, Findings 248. London: Home Office.

NOMS (2008a) *National Service Framework Improving Services to Women Offenders 2008*. London: Ministry of Justice.

NOMS (2008b) The *Offender Management Guide to Working with Women Offenders*. London: Ministry of Justice.

Open University (2008–9) 'Endless new criminal laws, a massive increase in people jailed, and a rise in fear of crime', *Society Matters*, 11: 4.

Pearson, R. (1976) 'Women defendants in magistrates' courts', *British Journal of Law and Society*, 3: 265–73.

Player, E. (2005) 'The reduction of women's imprisonment in England and Wales: Will the reform of short prison sentences help?', *Punishment and Society*, 7 (4): 419–39.

Prison Reform Trust (2000) *Justice for Women: the Need for Reform. The Report of the Commission on Women's Imprisonment*. London: Prison Reform Trust.

Prison Service (2008) *Prison Service Order 4800: Women Prisoners*. London: Prison Service.

RDS NOMS (2006) *Offender Management Statistics, 2005*. Home Office Statistical Bulletin 18/06. London: Home Office.

Smart, C. (1976) *Women, Crime and Criminology*. London: Routledge and Kegan Paul.

Social Exclusion Unit (2002) *Reducing Re-Offending by Ex-Prisoners*. London: Office of the Deputy Prime Minister.

Tombs, J. (2004) 'From "A Safer to a Better Way": Transformations in Penal Policy', in G. McIvor (ed.) *Women who Offend*. London: Jessica Kingsley.

Travis, A. (2006) 'Fifty bills add 700 offences as jails fill up', *The Guardian*, 26 June: 4.

Underdown, A. (1998) *Strategies for Effective Offender Supervision: Report of the HMIP What Works Project*. London: Home Office.

Vennard, J., Sugg, D. and Hedderman, C. (1997) *Changing Offenders' Attitudes and Behaviour: 'What Works'*, Home Office Research Study 171. London: Home Office.

Whitehead, T. (2009) 'Rise of "ladette" culture as 241 women arrested each day for violence', *Daily Telegraph*, 1 May 2009. http://www.telegraph.co.uk/news/newstopics/politics/lawandorder/5251042/Rise-of-ladette-culture-as-241-women-arrested-each-day-for-violence.html

Women's National Commission (1991) *Women and Prison: Report of an ad hoc Working Group*. London: Cabinet Office.

Women's Policy Team (2006) *Women's Offending Reduction Programme: 2006 Review of Progress*. London: Home Office.

Worrall, A. (1987) 'Sisters in Law? Women Defendants and Women Magistrates', in P. Carlen and A. Worrall (eds) *Gender, Crime and Justice*. Milton Keynes: Open University Press.

Worrall, A. (1990) *Offending Women: Female Lawbreakers and the Criminal Justice System*. London: Routledge.

Chapter 3

Policy developments in the USA

*Maureen Buell, Phyllis Modley and
Patricia Van Voorhis*

Over the past three decades, American correctional practices have
made the transition from prioritising the goals of punishment and
incapacitation to emphasising the importance of rehabilitation.
Progress in the field of corrections through the latter portion of the
20th century paralleled social and political movements affecting all
American society. Over time, offender rights and services slowly
improved. Newer practices were increasingly informed by research
instead of political forces (Cullen and Gendreau 2001). Yet, even
in the context of these transitions, women offenders were, at best,
assumed to have the same needs as men – at worst they were
ignored. Research informing innovative practices was based almost
exclusively on samples of male offenders, and all aspects of the
correctional experience, including rules, treatment programmes and
procedures for identifying offender risk levels and programme needs,
were based on a male model.

Simply put, adequate attention to the needs of women offenders
came much too slowly to the United States. Even with opportunities
provided by the civil rights and the women's movements, advocacy
for women in corrections was limited to the work of a very small
number of practitioners and feminist scholars. It was not until the
late 1980s that agencies within the United States Department of
Justice, and the National Institute of Corrections (NIC) in particular,
called attention to the unique needs of women offenders. For the
most part, progress in community and institutional corrections
occurred in tandem. That is, innovation in one area impacted on the
other.

This chapter traces the historical context of these developments: their origins, results, and future directions. Against this historical background, we move to a focus on recent research on women's risk factors and the development of specific programmatic and service delivery models that promise to substantially change services to women offenders in the community. As will be seen, much of this work began at the federal level, through initiatives funded by the NIC and implemented by universities, public/private partnerships and a number of state and local departments of corrections.

The historical context

The decade of the 1970s stands as a significant time in the US criminal justice system – marking both endings and beginnings. The social revolution of the 1960s was giving rise to an era of increasing political awareness and the women's movement was gaining momentum and raising issues about equality and justice (Rafter 2006). Across the country other factors were at play with regard to civil rights, education, science and technology, during a time of increasing inflation and unemployment. There were larger numbers of women in the workplace, improved birth control and family planning, and a move towards equal rights for women. Women were being elected to political office, they were NASA astronauts, and Title IX of the Education Amendments of 1972, was enacted prohibiting discrimination on the basis of sex for any programme or activity that would receive federal funding. *Ms.* Magazine was founded by Gloria Steinem. Eleanor Maccoby and Carol Jacklin (1974) wrote *The Psychology of Sex Difference*, a meta-analysis of studies investigating gender-based differences; Jean Baker Miller (1976) wrote *Toward a New Psychology of Women* and Carol Gilligan (1982) wrote *In a Different Voice*. The corrections field was changing as well, with a move away from rehabilitation towards an increased emphasis on incapacitation as the dominant goal of sentencing. As part of a research team, Dr Robert Martinson surveyed 231 studies on offender rehabilitation and reported in national publications and forums that 'rehabilitative efforts have no appreciable effect on recidivism' (Martinson 1974). This pronouncement had a significant impact on criminal justice policy for the next 30 years. Although Martinson later refuted his earlier statements (Martinson 1979), before his untimely death, the damage had been done and the US embarked upon decades of emphasising incapacitation goals over rehabilitative efforts in sanctioning and managing offender populations.

Another significant event that would have a resounding impact on criminal justice practices was the September 1971 riots at New York's Attica State Prison. Thirteen hundred inmates took over the prison and held 40 correctional officers hostage. The riots ultimately ended in the deaths of 43 people, including ten hostages, after negotiations failed. Inmates were demanding improvements to living conditions and increased training and educational opportunities.

In response to public concern regarding criminal justice policies and in a search for realistic solutions to the problems in US prisons, President Richard M. Nixon ordered the convening of a national conference on corrections. In December 1971, Attorney General John N. Mitchell convened The National Conference on Corrections in Williamsburg, Virginia. It was attended by 450 participants including researchers, policy-makers, members of the executive, legislative and judicial branches of government and other stakeholders. In a keynote speech, the Attorney General called for existing federal entities to work with states and localities in the 'establishment of a national center for correctional learning, research, executive seminars and development of correctional policy recommendations' (Mitchell 1971).

Among the major addresses at the 1971 National Conference on Corrections was a presentation by Dr Edith Elisabeth Flynn, Associate Director, National Clearinghouse for Criminal Justice Planning and Architecture at the University of Illinois. The talk was entitled 'The Special Problems of Female Offenders' (Flynn 1971). Dr Flynn noted that in the 1967 report from the President's Commission on Law Enforcement and Administration of Justice, *The Challenge of Crime in a Free Society* (1967: 113), not a 'single paragraph or statistic on the female offender could be found in any of the material'. Her presentation focused on two main points: that prevailing theories of criminal conduct were mostly inapplicable to women, and that an improved understanding of the aetiology of women's criminal conduct had important implications for managing and treating female offenders. Among her recommendations were:

- Develop equal opportunity staff training;

- Re-examine the issue of victimless crime and re-evaluate the wisdom of investing extensive resources in the prosecution of prostitution, vagrancy, abortion and disorderly conduct;

- Develop crime prevention and diversion programmes to screen socio-medical problems (i.e. addiction, alcoholism) from criminal prosecution;

- Increase the use of pre-trial diversionary techniques (ROR – release on own recognisance in lieu of bail, conditional release or bail);

- Maximise alternatives to incarceration;

- Develop suitable prison programmes but follow recommended patterns of community-based programmes (i.e. restore community and family ties; use community resources; create educational/ vocational programmes to develop self-sufficiency, self-respect and fully functioning community members; reduce the line of distinction between community and institutions; normalise institutional environments; and pursue regionally located facilities);

- Conduct research to combat the dearth of information on women offenders.

In the subsequent 30 years, NIC and the corrections field were to come to understand the importance of Dr Flynn's early set of recommendations for the improvement of supervision and treatment of women offenders in all correctional settings.

The 1971 criminal justice conference and the riots at Attica set the stage for legislation that created the National Institute of Corrections in 1974. Today, NIC (2008: ii) remains a 'center of learning, innovation and leadership that shapes and advances effective correctional practice and public policy'. The Institute provides training, technical assistance, information services and policy/programme development assistance to federal, state and local corrections agencies. NIC also plays a leadership role in shaping correctional policies and practices nationwide in areas of emerging interest and concern to correctional executives and practitioners as well as public policy-makers (National Institute of Corrections 2008).

Emerging awareness of women in prison

Focusing on the broad needs represented by jails, prisons and community corrections, NIC began its mission of training and technical assistance and soon received its first gender-specific request, to assist a state Department of Corrections in creating programmes for women inmates. Dr Flynn's warning about the appalling lack of research became apparent immediately. While it was evident to some that women presented differently from their male counterparts, there existed little information on the needs of women, the causes of their criminal behaviour, programmes available to them, and the current conditions of their supervision and confinement.

Sorely needed research on women offenders initially took the form of surveys and qualitative studies. In the late 1970s the US Government published two documents: *A National Study of Women's Corrections Programs* (Glick and Neto, US Department of Justice 1977) and *Female Offenders: Who are They and What are the Problems Confronting Them?* (US Government Accounting Office 1979). Both documents attempted to assess the needs of women across the criminal justice continuum in order to better design gender-responsive programmes and practices. During the 1980s, NIC sponsored additional national surveys of women offenders and conducted focus groups to increase the level of understanding about this population. Studies addressed institutional programmes, the needs of inmate mothers, legal issues and facility design. Well-known qualitative studies followed and continued to be published over subsequent decades (e.g., see Arnold 1990; Browne *et al.* 1999; Chesney-Lind 1997; Chesney-Lind and Rodriguez 1983; Chesney-Lind and Shelden 1992; Daly 1992; Gilfus 1992; Holsinger, 2000; Owen 1998; Richie 1996).

At the same time, state and local jurisdictions as well as public/ private entities were launching their own initiatives to begin to meet the needs of imprisoned women. The Family in Corrections Network www.fcnetwork.org was established as a national clearing house focused on families and incarceration. A handful of states, sensing the challenges they faced with managing women offenders, created positions within corrections departments for oversight of this population.

In 1985, the First National Adult and Juvenile Female Offender Conference was held. It was described as a 'grassroots movement begun to provide a forum for women and men in the corrections profession to come together and share information and concerns regarding the needs, management and treatment of the female offender' (http://mdoc.state.ms.us/ajfo/history.html). The event attracted participants from across the US and Canada, representing prisons, community corrections and jails.

In 1993, NIC published *A Guide to Programming for Women in Prison* (Education Development Center, Inc. 1993). Included in the recommendations for programme development with relevance to community transition were:

- Building skills and developing responsibilities to assist women in becoming productive and contributing members of their communities;

- Promoting support for community reintegration by encouraging participation of community agencies and volunteers;

- Coordinating linkages between prison and community-based services.

Notwithstanding these initial contributions, the entire field of corrections in the late 1980s and 1990s was consumed with managing the massive increase in offender populations in all settings – not just prisons. Largely the result of several policy shifts, especially mandatory prison sentences for drug use and sales and the closing of state mental health hospitals, rather than increases in serious crimes *per se*, the impact on the growth of women in the criminal justice system was especially acute (Austin *et al.* 2001). In fact, between 1990 and 1998 the number of women with criminal justice involvement grew 48 per cent compared with the growth rate of men at 27 per cent (Bureau of Justice Statistics 1999).

A number of state and federal laws also had severe consequences for criminal-justice-involved women and their families, both in prison and the community. The Adoption and Safe Families Act of 1993 was enacted to free children for adoption who were languishing in foster care. One of the law's provisions was the requirement that states initiate termination of parental rights if there was not sufficient contact between parents and children for 15 out of 22 consecutive months. Although this impacted on both men and women, women were hit particularly hard given the high percentage who had been primary caregivers of their children prior to going to prison. External systems responsible for protecting children were reluctant to facilitate contact between incarcerated parents and their children, and correctional systems for their part did little to foster the necessary contacts to avoid termination proceedings. Many women lost parental rights although they had not been found to present a danger to their children.

In the early 1990s a major lawsuit challenged a state department of corrections for inappropriate staff sexual misconduct with female inmates (*Cason v. Seckinger*, Civil Action File No. 84-313-IMAC). A number of correctional staff were indicted. The event not only changed the field of corrections with regard to the issue of sexual safety in institutions but began to draw the attention of some correctional policy-makers to the challenges of effectively managing women offenders. The issue of women's safety in prison became a national and international issue drawing the attention of Amnesty International, the US Government Accounting Office (GAO) and Human Rights Watch.

This, and similar litigation, did much to prompt US Congressional passage of the Prison Rape Elimination Act (PREA) in 2003. The bill was designed to 'prevent and detect incidents of sexual violence' (Prison Rape Elimination Act of 2003, Public Law 108–79, 108th Congress). A provision of the Act designated NIC as the national information clearing house and technical assistance provider for criminal justice entities responsible for the detection, prevention, investigation and sanctioning of sexual misconduct. In addition to a focus on male adult offenders, PREA specifically mentions concern for the impact of sexual misconduct on women, youth, and gay, lesbian and transgender justice-involved populations. With this broad charge, NIC developed a broad range of materials: briefing packets, issues' analyses, training curricula (face to face and online) and strategies to respond to the PREA mandates. NIC remains a key resource to the field on this topic. The materials and learning have been incorporated into the development of products specifically for women in prisons, jails and the community. To date, all 50 states have enacted legislation criminalising staff sexual misconduct.

Other initiatives impacting on women included the creation of an NIC-sponsored curriculum, developed with the National Association of Women Judges, entitled 'Sentencing Women Offenders: A Training Curriculum for Judges' (Cicero and DeCostanzo, 2000). In 2001, Congress awarded four million dollars for three years to NIC to establish a Federal Resource Center for Children of Prisoners, and create planning and implementation sites to address the issue of the impact of parental incarceration on children.

Broadening the focus on women offenders from prisons to the community

Concern for women offenders supervised in community settings was also becoming a priority within the NIC. In 1989, NIC held a special topic session, 'Women Offenders Under Community Supervision', designed to help NIC sharpen its understanding of specific needs of women offenders supervised in the community. Researchers and practitioners from across the country identified service gaps in areas critical to women offenders, particularly concerning treatment needs and the lack of valid community classification tools for women. Attention was devoted to identifying the differences between women's and men's experiences under community supervision and the ways in which these differences could contribute to revocation of probation or parole status and reoffending. It became increasingly evident that identical sanctions and supervision strategies could have dramatically different impacts on men and women.

NIC sought to improve the community supervision of women in a number of ways. First, the field needed to understand what comprised women-specific programming and where those programmes were located. NIC published surveys and analyses of programmes for women offenders in the community, first in 1992 (Austin *et al.* 1992) and again in 2000 (NIC Information Center 2000). The most recent effort to identify and describe women-specific programmes was an online National Directory of Programs for Women with Criminal Justice Involvement, launched in 2009. NIC also utilised its established 'networks' of corrections agency directors to build awareness concerning the latest research, and unique needs and challenges of women under community supervision. This was a deliberate process of putting critical information about women offenders on the radar screens of top management, not just the practitioners already interested in women's programmes. One such meeting assembled the directors of state probation and parole, state community corrections oversight agencies, and large urban probation departments.

By 1991 NIC began direct, two-year partnerships with criminal justice policy teams to promote improvements in the range and effectiveness of community sentencing options for women offenders. The Intermediate Sanctions for Women Offenders project (later called Improving Community Responses to Women Offenders) assisted 16 jurisdictions over five funding periods. The project had three important components:

- The *full participation of a diverse group of criminal justice policy-makers, human service decision-makers and community leaders*, working collaboratively as a policy team, to address the unique issues and problems of women defendants and offenders;

- The *establishment of a problem-solving and strategic planning approach* that involved careful information gathering and analysis prior to the identification of change targets and implementation plans; and

- The *development of community partnerships* to enhance the achievement of intended outcomes.

Improving Community Responses to Women Offenders resulted in creative and effective models of criminal justice practice, many of which continue to meet the needs of women offenders in local jurisdictions. The results in two jurisdictions, Cook County (Chicago), Illinois and Hamilton County (Cincinnati), Ohio, are especially noteworthy.

In Hamilton County, Ohio, for example, the Pretrial Services Agency screens all accused persons for pretrial risk and refers female and male, *medium risk, high need* defendants (pretrial status), offenders (detained on a probation violation or arrested for a new crime) and *homeless* defendants to a Pretrial Early Intervention and Transition Project. There, a team of intervention specialists designs release supervision plans based on an Inventory of Need. When necessary, additional in-depth assessments of mental illness, treatment engagement, and stages of change are conducted by the court's psychiatric clinic. The Inventory of Need was developed as a gender-informed pretrial risk and needs screen for women by the University of Cincinnati; it explores many gender-specific factors. Its effectiveness is currently being studied with both female and male defendants. A critical aspect of the project is the network of partnerships with public and private human services, a comprehensive array of women's services, and trained mentors. The extraordinary collaborations across diverse agencies in Hamilton County are, in large measure, the result of the efforts of the high-level policy team of decision-makers from judicial, executive and legislative branches.

Another exemplary programme is seen in Cook County, Illinois (Chicago) where the Sheriff's Department of Women's Justice Services (DWJS) has created a comprehensive array of gender-informed sanctions and services for women in pretrial and sentenced (local jail) status to prepare them for release and successful re-entry from jail to the community. DWJS begins discharge planning at jail intake with a comprehensive screening process that employs a Women's Risk/Needs Assessment. A team of case managers, counsellors and mental health externs work with each defendant/offender to identify immediate needs and begin developing a service and discharge plan. DWJS operates three programmes itself: an intensive inpatient substance abuse and mental health treatment programme; an outpatient day reporting programme where women report for case management and treatment services while returning to their homes at night; and a MOM's Program, an off-site treatment programme for dually diagnosed pregnant and parenting women that promotes mother–child bonding. Like Hamilton County, DWJS has developed a powerful set of partners in the mental and physical health and criminal justice areas. Two of its recent initiatives include a project providing comprehensive mental health treatment, case management and peer support for women serving a probation sentence under supervision of a mental heath court; and a Domestic Human Trafficking Project that provides direct outreach at the point of arrest for street prostitutes and 'Craig's List' victims of sexual solicitation. (Craig's List is a worldwide online directory of classifieds and forums, including sources for prostitution under headings of massage, escort services etc.).

One of the most influential policy initiatives affecting community corrections during the 1990s and beyond was a model of service delivery developed by Canadian correctional psychologists Donald Andrews, James Bonta, Paul Gendreau, Robert Hoge and others (see Andrews and Bonta, 2009). Based on a series of meta-analyses, the authors formulated a strong, empirically supported set of principles guiding correctional practice, referred to as the Principles of Effective Intervention. Their work was widely adopted and provided invaluable evidence for moving American correctional practices away from the punitive model to one that focused on psychologically informed programming for needs that were likely to predispose offenders to future criminal activity. In fact, one of the principles embodied in the Canadian Model, *the needs principle*, maintained that the most effective correctional treatment programmes, those most likely to reduce offender recidivism, were those that targeted *criminogenic needs* (needs correlated with future offending) rather than needs found to be unrelated to future offending, e.g. wilderness skills (see Andrews and Bonta 2009; Andrews *et al.* 1990; Gendreau 1996).

The gender-neutral Principles of Effective Intervention required the use of risk/needs assessments to aid the process of identifying and targeting needs for programming. A series of validation studies and later meta-analyses found the new assessments to be valid for women (see Andrews *et al.* 2001; Smith *et al.* 2009). Other meta-analyses also noted that some risk factors were more predictive that others. Researchers observed the most predictive factors consisted of the 'Big 4': criminal history, criminal personality (impulsivity, grandiosity and egocentricity), criminal thinking, and criminal associates (Andrews *et al.* 1990; Andrews and Bonta, 2009; Gendreau *et al.* 1996). It followed from this that criminal personality, antisocial thinking and antisocial associates should be the major foci of most correctional treatment enterprises. A primary concern regarding the gender-neutral risk/needs assessments, notions of the 'Big 4', and the research, however, was the absence of assessment scales many believed to be more relevant to women offenders, such as dysfunctional relationships, depression, parental issues, self-esteem, self-efficacy, trauma and victimisation (Blanchette 2004; Blanchette and Brown 2006; Bloom *et al.* 2003; Brennan 1998; Brennan and Austin 1997; Farr 2000; Hardyman and Van Voorhis 2004; Reisig *et al.* 2006; Van Voorhis and Presser 2001). Added to this concern was the realisation that the *needs principle* was acting as a policy directive, of sorts, encouraging correctional agencies to prioritise the treatment of antisocial attitudes and antisocial associates while ignoring the gender-responsive needs listed above. Thus, the fact that the gender-responsive needs were not noted on the current generation of risk/needs assessments risked inattention to essential programming for women (Hannah-Moffat 2009).

In rather stark contrast to the gender-neutral models embodied in the Principles of Effective Intervention, thoughtful practitioners who understood the unique circumstances of women involved in the criminal justice system worked to establish and operate interventions specifically designed for women offenders. Dr Barbara Bloom and Dr James Austin identified some of these promising programmes in their 1992 publication on innovative strategies. They included day reporting programmes, halfway houses and residential programmes designed specifically for women and some for women and their children. Subsequent efforts sought to describe supervision strategies (implemented by probation and parole agencies) as well as stand-alone treatment programmes. Efforts by Kay Harris, Temple University, NIC and the Women's Prison Association (2009) sought to tease out and describe the key aspects of gender-informed programmes: the theoretical grounding, goals and objectives, change targets and strategies, staff training and eligibility requirements that practitioners felt made them particularly efficacious for women offenders. These interventions acknowledged and addressed the histories of abuse, co-occurring substance abuse and mental health issues, dysfunctional relationships with partners, parenting responsibilities, needs for childcare and transportation and so forth.

To bring gender-responsive treatment priorities into greater relevance to women offenders, NIC published *Gender-Responsive Strategies: Research, Practice and Guiding Principles for Women Offenders* (Bloom *et al.* 2003). This document was the result of two years of research that included focus groups with researchers, practitioners and women offenders. The work identified the following six general principles of gender-responsive strategies:

- Gender: acknowledge that gender makes a difference;

- Environment: create an environment based on safety, respect and dignity;

- Relationships: develop policies, practices and programmes that are relational and promote healthy connections to children, family, significant others and the community;

- Services and supervision: address substance abuse, trauma, and mental health issues through comprehensive, integrated and culturally relevant services and appropriate supervision;

- Socio-economic status: provide women with opportunities to improve their socio-economic conditions;

- Community: establish a system of community supervision and re-entry with comprehensive, collaborative services.

This publication was the foundation of a series of NIC bulletins specific to women offenders, which to date include a summary of the original publication, two publications addressing jail and community corrections applications of the gender-responsive principles, the use of jail exit surveys to identify the specific needs of locally detained women, and case studies of two programmes successfully providing services to women offenders. Finally, in response to intense national interest in prisoner re-entry, NIC supported the development of a practitioner-focused summary of research and practice on gender-responsive approaches to women offender re-entry (Berman, 2005), which employed NIC's own system change model for Transition from Prison to the Community (TPC) as its framework.

Concern for the ongoing lack of attention to gender-responsive needs, and the continued growth in the size of women's correctional populations prompted NIC to shift focus to the development of specific assessments, programmes and other tools for applied use with women offenders. The female prison population had grown by 832 per cent from 1977 to 2007 compared with 416 per cent for males during the same time period (Bureau of Justice Statistics 2008a). At year end 2007, there were nearly a million women on probation, and women represented 12 per cent of the overall parole population (Bureau of Justice Statistics 2008b).

These initiatives funded both the development of the tools and the training of jurisdictions in their use. The first was an initiative to develop a gender-responsive risk/needs assessment for women.

The second was a gender-responsive approach to case management and counselling of women offenders. And the third was a facility assessment tool to provide feedback to correctional facilities on a number of measures of organisational and programmatic factors.

Development of assessments, programmes, and other tools

The development of these three tools marked a shift in NIC's approach to women offenders. Where earlier work sought to encourage jurisdictions to change and to point them in meaningful directions, these larger initiatives designed the change itself. End products were intended to be in the public domain, available to be handed to interested jurisdictions to use as long as appropriate assurances were made regarding staff training and other methods of quality assurance.

Risk/needs assessments

In early 2002, NIC sponsored the Gender-Responsive Assessment meeting in Washington, DC to develop a research agenda on assessment strategies for women offenders. Participants included prominent researchers in correctional assessment and practitioners known for their innovative work with women offenders. Recommendations from that meeting included the development of research standards, establishment of multidisciplinary research teams to explore issues related to women's criminal behaviour, the funding of demonstration projects emphasising research design and replicability and the provision of technical assistance to test models and processes as they were developed.

In response to concerns that current risk/needs assessments were identifying risk/need factors that were not relevant to women offenders (e.g. the 'Big 4'), NIC partnered with the University of Cincinnati in 2004 to construct a gender-responsive risk/needs assessment for women that would contain scales pertaining to gender-responsive needs. The intent was to develop two types of assessments. The first, the Women's Risk/Needs Supplement (WRNA Supplement) was designed to supplement existing dynamic risk/needs assessments such as the Level of Service Inventory-Revised (Andrews and Bonta 1995) and the Northpointe Compas (Brennan et al. 2006). It was assumed that jurisdictions currently invested in the popular, gender-neutral instruments would find it more cost-effective to supplement them with a gender-responsive 'trailer' (as it is often called) rather than change to an entirely different assessment. The second assessment was designed to be used on its own, as a 'stand-alone' Women's Risk/Needs Assessment (WRNA). The WRNA provided gender-neutral as well as gender-responsive scales.

Extensive literature searches and focus groups with correctional administrators, treatment practitioners, line staff and women offenders informed both of the assessments. Studies that examined female pathways to crime and recidivism, discussed earlier, were extremely helpful. As a result, the UC research team developed scales measuring: a) self-esteem; b) self-efficacy; c) victimisation as an adult; d) child abuse; e) parental stress; and f) relationship dysfunction.

The NIC/UC project involved four jurisdictions (Colorado, Maui, Missouri and Minnesota) in the development and validation of the WRNAs. In addition, UC worked with the Missouri Women's Issues Committee to reframe a number of traditional, gender-neutral, risk/ needs scales in more gender-responsive terms. For instance, housing problems tapped safety and violence within the home and were not limited to issues of homelessness and antisocial influences. Indicators of mental illness were disaggregated to account for current symptoms of depression, anxiety and psychosis. A family domain was expanded to differentiate between intimate relationships, family of origin matters, and parental concerns. Finally, in contrast to many gender-neutral assessments, items were added to identify strengths, or protective factors, such as support from others and educational assets. Accounting for strengths better mapped the assessment process on to strategies emerging in the areas of positive psychology (Seligman 2002; Sorbello et al. 2002; Van Wormer 2001) which was finding many advocates among gender-responsive scholars (Blanchette and Brown 2006; Bloom et al. 2003; Morash et al. 1998; Prendergast et al. 1995; Schram and Morash 2002; Van Wormer 2001).

Results of the research are presented in greater detail in other publications (see Salisbury et al. 2009; Van Voorhis et al. 2008; Van Voorhis et al. 2010; Wright et al. 2007, all provided at www. uc.edu/womenoffenders). At the conclusion of the project, separate instruments were constructed for probation, pre-release and prison settings. The scales included in each instrument are shown in Table 3.1.

Once these assessments were developed, the NIC/UC cooperative agreement disseminated the results through publications, conferences and various internet venues. Online orientations were made available

Table 3.1 Structure of gender-responsive instruments*

Probation	Institutional	Parole
Section I: Items for risk scale		
Criminal history	**Criminal history**	**Criminal history**
Antisocial attitudes	**Antisocial attitudes**	**Antisocial attitudes**
Antisocial friends	**Family conflict**	**Antisocial friends**
Educational challenges	**History of mental illness**	**Educational challenges**
Employment/financial	*Substance abuse*	**Employment/financial**
Family conflict	*Dynamic substance abuse*	**History of mental illness**
Substance abuse history	Depression/anxiety symptoms	Depression/anxiety symptoms
Dynamic substance abuse	Psychotic symptoms	Psychotic symptoms
Relationship dysfunction	Child abuse	**Substance abuse history**
Anger	Anger	Dynamic substance abuse
Housing safety	Relationship dysfunction	Adult victimisation
Depression/anxiety symptoms		Anger
Psychotic symptoms		
Parental stress		
Strengths:	Strengths:	Strengths:
Educational assets	Family support	Educational strengths
Family support		Family support
Self-efficacy		
Section II: Other items		
Other:	Other (re-entry).	Other:
Mental health history	**Mental health history**	*Self-efficacy*
Child abuse	**Antisocial friends**	Family conflict
Adult victimisation	**Educational challenges**	Child abuse
	Employment financial	*Housing safety*
	Adult victimisation	*Parental stress*
	Parental stress	
	Self-efficacy	
	Housing safety	

*Items in bold are gender-neutral items; others are gender-responsive.
Items in italics were inconclusive in the construction validation research and are undergoing additional research at present.

to interested jurisdictions, and a number of training curricula were developed. At the time of going to press, these public domain assessments had been or were in the process of being implemented in eight state and three local agencies. These adoptions are affording an opportunity to validate and perhaps further refine the WRNAs on large samples.

Moving beyond patterns for the gender neutral risk/needs factors to the tests of gender-responsive factors, the NIC/UC research supports more serious consideration of most of the gender-responsive variables tested. We note some degree of sample variation for both the gender-neutral and gender-responsive scale. Even so, these studies suggest the importance of programmes targeted to depression and other mental health issues, parental stress, healthy relationships, abuse, self-efficacy, anger and safety. Some will fault recommendations for a new set of treatment priorities for women, asserting that we do not have the benefit of years of controlled studies to show that targeting these factors reduces recidivism. However, this may be changing as well, albeit at a very slow pace.

Women Offender Case Management Model (WOCMM)

In 2005, NIC, in collaboration with Dr Marilyn VanDieten of Orbis Partners, Inc. of Ottawa, Canada, developed and began to test a Women Offender Case Management Model (WOCMM) (Van Dieten 2008). WOCMM was designed to be a seamless case management model that would accompany a woman throughout her sentence – from prison to community release and supervision. Similar to the development of new risk and needs assessment instruments for women, the WOCMM model sought to merge evidence-based and gender-responsive principles and research.

The goals of the case management model were not only to reduce future criminal behaviour but also to increase the health and well-being of women, their families and communities. The model was guided by an extensive review of the criminal justice, mental health and child welfare literature, and involved a working group of practitioners and researchers. WOCMM is intended for use with women sentenced directly to probation or prison and throughout the re-entry process, including in-prison assessment and programming, pre-release planning, and community supervision.

Among the most critical aspects of the model is the use of a gender-informed dynamic risk instrument for women and a 'team approach' to delivery of case management services. The team consists of the woman herself, a correctional case manager, human and health service providers and other supports. The team works intentionally to engage the woman in the change process while respecting the woman's right to choose what needs and challenges to address and in what order. The process also involves identifying and mobilising the woman's strengths. The WOCMM team (and the administrators of its representative agencies) works to build essential partnerships with service providers to ensure that critical resources are available and readily accessible. Also, service is intended to be 'limitless', that is, available to the woman and her family long after the termination of criminal justice supervision. The model employs 12 guiding practices that are fully described in the WOCMM model document, available at http://www.nicic.org/Library/021814. WOCMM is currently being piloted in three jurisdictions, one with probation cases and two others with women making the transition from prison to the community. Research is under way to test its effectiveness.

Gender-Informed Practice Assessment (GIPA)

The latest tool was begun in 2008, when NIC, through a cooperative agreement with the Center for Effective Public Policy, produced a tool designed to assess environments and practices within correctional facilities for women. GIPA was designed to assess facilities on the following criteria: a) leadership and philosophy; b) external support; c) facility operations, including physical plant; d) management and operations; e) staffing and training; f) facility culture; g) offender management (incorporating sanctions and discipline); h) assessment and classification; i) case management and transitional planning; j) programming; and k) services (e.g. medical, mental health, transportation, food services, legal and victim services). Like other NIC tools, GIPA was built upon a foundation of gender-responsive and evidence-based practices. Jurisdictions undergoing a GIPA analysis could find the tool valuable in a number of ways. For example, the tool could serve as a gap analysis of current institutional practices specific to women. Jurisdictions could then use the results to provide empirical support for funding requests. In addition the GIPA could also support quality assurance processes and provide the feedback needed to improve current programmes and other aspects of the facility (e.g. staffing, culture, services and physical plant). At present, the tool is being piloted in several locations and is in the process of revision based on the pilot study results. Overall, the feedback has been quite positive reflecting the field's desire to develop or enhance current practices to improve outcomes with women.

Emerging research on the effectiveness of gender-informed interventions

Sadly, many of the earlier gender-responsive programmes begun during the 1990s and early 2000s were not sustained; they too easily fell victim to lagging interest, poor support and budget cuts. Clearly, the dearth of evaluative research on these promising and gender-responsive programmes hampered their sustainability and progressive improvement. Understandably, policy officials and funders in the 1990s were sharply focused on public safety; that is, effective strategies for controlling offenders and reducing recidivism. Policy-makers were calling for 'evidence-based programs' (MacKenzie 2000), and that meant that any new programme models would have to show supporting evidence from controlled studies that found significant reductions in recidivism. There were many such studies, but nearly all had been conducted on male offenders. Practitioners simply did not have the research grounding to support their arguments that programmes focused on the gender-specific risk and needs factors of women would result in improved public safety outcomes. Fortunately, this situation is changing as a small but steady stream of new evaluations of gender-informed programmes is appearing. More recent research is lending support to broader counselling and case management approaches (Lipsey 2009) and programmes targeted to self-efficacy (Gehring *et al.* 2010); childcare (Olds *et al.* 2004); parenting (Piquero *et al.* 2009; Showers 1993); substance abuse (Hall *et al.* 2004; Hein *et al.* 2004); and trauma (Najavits *et al.* 1998, 2006). Discussed below are some of the better-known gender-responsive programmes in the United States. This list draws from *Gender Responsive Programming: Promising Approaches* by Krista Gehring and Ashley Bauman, University of Cincinnati (see www.uc.edu/womenoffenders):

- *Moving On*, a 26-session, curriculum-based programme, developed by Dr Marilyn Van Dieten (Van Dieten and MacKenna 2001). Its goals are to provide women with opportunities to mobilise and enhance existing strengths and access personal and community resources. The programme incorporates cognitive-behavioural techniques with motivational interviewing and relational theory. A recent (2009) evaluation of its use with women on probation in Iowa confirmed its effectiveness in reducing recidivism (Gehring *et al.* 2010).

- *Beyond Trauma: A Healing Journey for Women* and *Helping Women Recover: A Program for Treating Addiction* by Dr Stephanie Covington. The first programme uses psycho-educational and cognitive skills approaches to help women develop coping skills and emotional wellness to counter the effects of physical, emotional, and sexual abuse. The second programme integrates four theories of women's offending and treatment: pathways, addiction, trauma and relational theories. Evaluation results are favourable (Grella 2005).

- *Seeking Safety* by Dr Lisa Najavits, a present-focused therapy to address the co-occurring disorders of trauma/PTSD and substance abuse (see Najavits 2002). It draws from research on cognitive-behavioural treatment of substance abuse disorders, post-traumatic stress treatment and educational research. While not designed specifically for women, most clients of the programme tend to be women (since women suffer from these disorders at higher rates than men). It is the most studied treatment programme for dually diagnosed individuals. 'Improvements were [in the areas of] social adjustment, general psychiatric symptoms, suicidal plans and thoughts, problem-solving, sense of meaning, depression and quality of life' (see Najavits *et al.* 1998, 2006).

- *Forever Free*, a programme of the California Institution for Women, is a modified therapeutic community, designed specifically for incarcerated women. Its goals are to reduce in-prison disciplinary actions as well as substance use and recidivism; it provides substance abuse treatment and relapse prevention services. One programme evaluation demonstrated that participants had fewer arrests or convictions during parole than participants in a comparison group (Hall *et al.* 2004).

- *The Center for Substance Abuse Treatment* (CSAT) guide to substance abuse treatment of women offenders identifies 17 areas that are critical to the model. It has been implemented in a number of state women's facilities; the Forever Free programme described above is one of those implementation efforts (Kassebaum 1999).

- *Female Offender Treatment and Employment Programs* (FOTEP) is a residential programme that aims to assist in the successful reintegration of women parolees into the community, with particular attention to employment, substance use, criminal involvement and parenting. It employs intensive case management, vocational and family services, and facilitates reunification with dependent children if appropriate. Preliminary results of an ongoing evaluation are promising (Grella 2005).

- *The Nurses Program* is a rather well-known visiting nurses programme for at-risk mothers providing support in the areas of child health and child management skills. It has had favourable results for both mothers (who had lower post-programme recidivism rates) and children (Olds *et al.* 2004; Piquero *et al.* 2009).

It is also noteworthy that women-only caseloads are beginning to be used by community-based agencies. While not as structured as the WOCMM model, discussed above, women-only caseloads generally utilise a gender-responsive approach to achieve reductions in recidivism and improve the well-being of women and children. Officers have received specialised training on women's unique criminal pathways and needs and have developed various techniques to address those needs. While the content of these case management models may vary dramatically across programmes, a key component seeks to expand women's ongoing access to community services. In 2002, for example, the Missouri Department of Corrections, Division of Probation and Parole, began to implement the Gender Specific Caseload Project, piloting these caseloads in six districts across the state. A preliminary study comparing the women-only caseloads to other specialised programmes in the Department (drug court, intensive supervision, electronic monitoring, and community treatment) revealed very promising outcomes with less than 10 per cent (9.11) returned to prison one year post-programme entry (compared to 10.06 per cent for drug court, 21.56 per cent for intensive supervision, 28.16 per cent for electronic monitoring, and 28.73 per cent for community treatment) (Missouri Department of Corrections 2005).

Future directions

Many of the initiatives outlined above are continuing to develop. For example, the Women's Risk/Needs Assessments are currently undergoing large-scale revalidation and refinement. The NIC/ University of Cincinnati cooperative agreement is continuing to work with interested states and localities on careful, rigorous implementation and testing of the instruments. It will be equally important to foster the process and outcome evaluations of the WOCMM model and other gender-specific interventions and to make emerging research findings available to the corrections field. Authors of the prison assessment tool (GIPA) intend to develop an assessment tool for community supervision settings as well.

Interest in gender-informed practice at the front end of the criminal justice system is growing. This will involve policy-makers, practitioners and judicial authorities focusing on the decisions and supervision practices regarding pretrial release, detention and transition to the community. There is a strong and growing need to address the seemingly endless flow of repeat offences among women for such high-volume offences as misdemeanour property, simple assault, illegal substance use, resisting arrest, prostitution, and shoplifting. As discussed above, exemplary programmes, such as the Cook County and Hamilton County project exist but they have not been widely replicated.

In sum, women offenders have received renewed attention over the past two decades in the United States. Research has substantiated the importance of gender-responsive risk factors. Contrary to earlier correctional treatment guidelines, poverty, parental stress, substance abuse, mental health, relationship dysfunction, trauma and self-efficacy are key to women's offending and reoffending and must be addressed by correctional agencies. Over time, a number of innovative practices addressing these needs have sustained empirical research and been found to be effective. On the horizon is the hope that courts and community social service agencies will recognise the importance of pre-entry programmes and form partnerships to reverse the ever growing numbers of women entering prisons and other correctional agencies with mental health and substance abuse-related offences.

References

Andrews, D.A. and Bonta, J. (1995) *Level of Service Inventory-Revised*. North Tonawanda, NY: Multi-Health Systems.

Andrews, D.A. and Bonta, J. (2009) *The psychology of criminal conduct* (5th edn). Cincinnati, OH: Anderson.

Andrews, D.A., Bonta, J. and Hoge, R.D. (1990) 'Classification for effective rehabilitation: Rediscovering psychology', *Criminal Justice and Behavior*, 17: 19–52.

Andrews, D., Bonta, J., Wormith, S., Guzzo, L. and Brews, A. (2008) *The relative and incremental predictive validity of gender-neutral and gender-informed risk/need.* Unpublished manuscript, Carleton University, Ottawa, Ontario, Canada.

Andrews, D.A., Dowden, C. and Rettinger, J. (2001) 'Special populations within corrections', in J.A. Winterdyck (ed.) *Corrections in Canada: Social reactions to crime.* Toronto, Ontario, Canada: Prentice Hall, pp. 179–212.

Arnold, R. (1990) 'Processes of victimization and criminalization of Black women', *Social Justice,* 17: 153–66.

Austin, J., Bloom, B. and Donahue, T. (1992) *Female Offenders in the Community: An Analysis of Innovative Strategies and Programs.* San Francisco, CA: National Council on Crime and Delinquency.

Austin, J., Bruce, M.A., Carroll, L., McCall, P.L. and Richards, S.C. (2001). The use of incarceration in the United States: American Society of Criminology National Policy Committee. *Critical Criminology: An International Journal,* 10: 17–41.

Belknap, J. and Holsinger, K. (2006) 'The gendered nature of risk factors for delinquency', *Feminist Criminology,* 1: 48–71.

Berman, J. (2005) *Women Offender Transition and Reentry: Gender Responsive Approaches to Transitioning Women Offenders from Prison to the Community.* Washington, DC: National Institute of Corrections.

Blanchette, K. (2004) 'Revisiting effective classification strategies for women offenders in Canada', *Feminism and Psychology,* 14: 231–36.

Blanchette, K. and Brown, S.L. (2006) *The Assessment and Treatment of Women Offenders: An Integrative Perspective.* Chichester: Wiley.

Bloom, B., Owen, B. and Covington, S. (2003) *Gender-Responsive Strategies: Research Practice and Guiding Principles for Women Offenders.* Washington, DC: USDOJ, National Institute of Corrections.

Brennan, T. (1998) 'Institutional classification of females: Problems and some proposals for reform', in R.T. Zaplin (ed.) *Female Offenders: Critical Perspectives and Effective Interventions* (pp. 179–204). Gaithersburg, MD: Aspen Publishers.

Brennan, T. and Austin, J. (1997) *Women in Jail: Classification Issues.* Washington, DC: USDOJ, National Institute of Corrections.

Brennan, T., Dieterich, W. and Oliver, W. (2006) *COMPAS: Technical manual and psychometric report Version 5.0.* Traverse City, MI: Northpointe Institute.

Brennan, T., Dieterich, W., Ehret, B., Breitenback, M., Arredondo Mattson, S. and Mattson, B. (2008) *California Department of Corrections and Rehabilitation (CDCR) pilot study report.* Golden, CO: Northpointe Institute for Public Management, Inc.

Browne, A., Miller, B. and Maguin, E. (1999) 'Prevalence and severity of lifetime physical and sexual victimization among incarcerated women', *International Journal of Law and Psychiatry,* 22: 301–22.

Bureau of Justice Statistics (1999) *Special report: Women Offenders.* Washington, DC: US Department of Justice.

Bureau of Justice Statistics (2008a) *Prisoners in 2007*. Washington, DC: US Department of Justice.

Bureau of Justice Statistics (2008b) *Probation and Parole in the United States, 2007*. Washington, DC: US Department of Justice.

Chesney-Lind, M. (1997) *The Female Offender: Girls, Women, and Crime.* Thousand Oaks, CA: Sage.

Chesney-Lind, M. and Rodriguez, N. (1983) 'Women under lock and key', *Prison Journal*, 63: 47–65.

Chesney-Lind, M. and Shelden, R. G. (1992) *Girls, Delinquency, and Juvenile Justice*. Belmont, CA: Thompson Wadsworth.

Cicero, J.H. and DeCostanzo, E.T. (2000) *Sentencing Women Offenders: A Training Curriculum for Judges*. Washington, DC: National Institute of Corrections and National Association of Women Judges.

Cullen, F.T. and P. Gendreau. (2001) 'From nothing works to what works: Changing professional ideology in the 21st century', *Crime and Delinquency*, 81: 313–38.

Daly, K. (1992) 'Women's pathways to felony court: Feminist theories of lawbreaking and problems of representation', *Southern California Review of Law and Women's Studies*, 2: 11–52.

Education Development Center, Inc., Center for Equity and Cultural Diversity (1993) *A Guide to Programming for Women in Prison*. Washington, DC: National Institute of Corrections.

Farr, K.A. (2000) 'Classification for female inmates: Moving forward', *Crime and Delinquency*, 46: 3–17.

Farrington, D. and Painter, K. (2004) *Gender differences in risk factors for offending* (Home Office RDS Online Report OLR09/04).

Flynn, E. (1971) *The Special Problems of Female Offenders*. Paper presented at the National Conference on Corrections, Williamsburg, VA, 6 December 1971.

Gehring, K., Van Voorhis, P. and Bell, V. (2010) '"What Works" for female probationers? An evaluation of the Moving On Program', *Women, Girls, and Criminal Justice*, 11 (1): 1, 6–10.

Gendreau, P. (1996) 'The principles of effective intervention with offenders', in A.T. Harland (ed.) *Choosing Correctional Options that Work: Defining the Demand and Evaluating the Supply*. Thousand Oaks, CA: Sage, pp. 117–30.

Gendreau, P., Little, T. and Goggin, C. (1996) 'A meta-analysis of the predictors of adult offender recidivism: What works!', *Criminology*, 34: 575–607.

Gilfus, M.E. (1992) 'From victims to survivors to offenders. Women's routes of entry and immersion into street crime', *Women and Criminal Justice*, 4: 63–90.

Gilligan, C. (1982) *In a Different Voice*. Cambridge, MA: Harvard Press.

Glick, R.M. and Neto, V.V. (1977) *A National Study of Women's Correctional Programs*. US Government Printing Office, Washington, DC #027-000-00524-I.

Grella, C. (2005) *Female Offender Treatment and Employment Project* (FOTEP): *Summary of Evaluation Findings 1999–2004*. UCLA Integrated Substance Abuse Programs.

Hall, E., Prendergast, M., Wellisch, J., Patten, M. and Cao, Y. (2004) 'Treating drug-using women prisoners: An outcome evaluation of the Forever Free program', *The Prison Journal*, 84: 81–105.

Hannah-Moffat, K. (2009) 'Gridlock or mutability: Reconsidering gender and risk assessment', *Criminology and Public Policy*, 8: 209–19.

Hardyman, P.L. and Van Voorhis, P. (2004) *Developing Gender-specific Classification Systems for Women Offenders*. Washington, DC: USDOJ, National Institute of Corrections.

Hein, D., Cohen, L., Litt, L., Miele, G. and Capstick, C. (2004) 'Promising empirically supported treatments for women with comorbid PTSD and substance use disorders', *American Journal of Psychiatry*, 161: 1426–32.

Holsinger, A.M., Lowenkamp, C.T. and Latessa, E.J. (2003) 'Ethnicity, gender, and the Level of Service Inventory – Revised', *Journal of Criminal Justice*, 31: 309–20.

Holsinger, K. (2000) 'Feminist perspectives on female offending: Examining real girls' lives', *Women and Criminal Justice*, 12: 23–51.

Holtfreter, K., Reisig, M.D. and Morash, M. (2004) 'Poverty, state capital, and recidivism among women offenders', *Criminology and Public Policy*, 3: 185–208.

Kassebaum, P. (1999) *Substance abuse treatment for women offenders: Guide to promising practices*. Rockville, MD: US Department of Health and Human Services, Substance Abuse and Mental Health Services Administration, Center for Substance Abuse Treatment.

Lipsey, M. (2009) 'The primary factors that characterize effective interventions with juvenile offenders: A meta analytic overview', *Victims and Offenders*, 4: 124–147.

Maccoby, E.E. and Jacklin, C.N. (1974) *The Psychology of Sex Difference*. Palo Alto, CA: Stanford University Press.

MacKenzie, D. (2000) 'Evidence-based corrections: Identifying what works', *Crime and Delinquency*, 46: 457–71.

Martinson, R. (1974) 'What Works? Questions and answers about prison reform', *The Public Interest*, 35: 22–54.

Martinson, R. (1979) 'New findings, new reviews: A note of caution regarding sentencing reform', *Hofstra Law Review*, 7: 243–58.

Messina, N. and Grella, C. (in press) *Gender-responsive Treatment for Women in Prison* (Grant 1R21DA 18699-01A1). Bethesda, MD: National Institute of Drug Abuse.

Miller, J.B. (1976) *Toward a New Psychology of Women*. Boston: Beacon Press.

Miller, J.G. (1989) *The Debate on Rehabilitating Criminals: Is it True that Nothing Works? Washington Post*, March.

Missouri Department of Corrections (2005) 'Internal memorandum: Summary report on gender specific program', 7 February.

Mitchell, J. (1971) *New Doors, Not Old Walls.* Keynote address at the National Conference on Corrections, Williamsburg, VA, 6 December 1971.

Morash, M. (2009) 'A great debate over using the Level of Service Inventory – Revised (LSI-R) with women offenders', *Criminology and Public Policy*, 8: 173–81.

Morash, M., Bynum, T.S. and Koons, B.A. (1998). *Women Offenders: Programming Needs and Promising Approaches.* Washington, DC: USDOJ, National Institute of Justice.

Najavits, L. (2002) *Seeking Safety: A Treatment Manual for PTSD and Substance Abuse.* New York: Guilford Press.

Najavits, L., Gallop, R. and Weiss, R. (2006) 'Seeking safety therapy for adolescent girls with PTSD and substance abuse: A randomized controlled trial', *Journal of Behavioral Health Services and Research*, 33: 453–63.

Najavits, L., Weiss, R., Shaw, S. and Muenz, L. (1998) 'Seeking Safety: Outcomes of a new cognitive-behavioral psychotherapy for women with posttraumatic stress disorder and substance dependence', *Journal of Traumatic Stress*, 11: 437–56.

National Institute of Corrections (2008) *Technical Assistance, Information and Training for Adult Corrections.* Washington, DC: US Department of Justice.

National Institute of Corrections, Information Center (2000) *Directory of Community Based Programs for Women Offenders.* Longmont, CO: National Institute of Corrections.

National Institute of Corrections and Women's Prison Association (2009) *National Directory of Programs for Women with Criminal Justice Involvement*, an online searchable database, www.nicic.gov/WODP

Olds, D., Robinson, J., Pettitt, L., Luckey, D., Holmberg, J., Ng, R., Isacks, K., Sheff, K. and Henderson, C. (2004) 'Effects of home visits by paraprofessionals and by nurses: Age 4 follow-up results of a randomized trial', *Pediatrics*, 114: 1560–68.

Owen, B. (1998) *In the Mix: Struggle and Survival in a Women's Prison.* Albany, NY: State University of New York Press.

Piquero, A.R., Farrington, D.P., Welsh, B.C., Tremblay, R. and Jennings, W.G. (2009) 'Effects of early family/parent training programs on antisocial behavior and delinquency', *Journal of Experimental Criminology*, 5: 83–120.

Prendergast, M., Wellisch, J. and Falkin, G. (1995) 'Assessment of services for substance-abusing women offenders and correctional settings', *The Prison Journal*, 75: 240–56.

President's Commission on Law Enforcement and the Administration of Justice (1967) *The Challenge of Crime in a Free Society.* Washington, DC: US Government Printing Office.

Prison Rape Elimination Act of 2003, Public Law 108–79, 108th Congress, USA.

Rafter, N.H. (2006) 'Women's prison reform: Past, present and future', in Russ Immarigeon (ed.) *Women and Girls in the Criminal Justice System:*

Policy Issues and Practice Strategies. New York, NY: Civic Research Institute, pp. 1–3.

Reisig, M.D., Holtfreter, K. and Morash, M. (2006) 'Assessing recidivism risk across female pathways to crime', *Justice Quarterly*, 23: 384–405.

Rettinger, L.J. and Andrews, D.A. (2010) 'General risk and need, gender specificity, and the recidivism of female offenders', *Criminal Justice and Behavior*, 37: 29–46.

Richie, B. (1996) *Compelled to Crime: The Gendered Entrapment of Battered Black Women.* New York: Routledge.

Salisbury, E.J. and Van Voorhis, P. (2009) 'Gendered pathways: An empirical investigation of women probationers' paths to incarceration', *Criminal Justice and Behavior*, 36: 541–66.

Salisbury, E., Van Voorhis, P. and Spiropoulis, G. (2009) 'The predictive validity of a gender-responsive risk/needs assessment', *Crime and Delinquency*, 55: 550–85.

Schram, P.J. and Morash, M. (2002) 'Evaluation of a life skills program for women inmates in Michigan', *Journal of Offender Rehabilitation*, 34: 47–70.

Seligman, M. (2002) *Authentic Happiness: Using the New Positive Psychology to Realize your Potential for Lasting Fulfillment.* New York: The Free Press.

Showers, J. (1993) 'Assessing and remedying parenting knowledge among women inmates', *Journal of Offender Rehabilitation*, 20: 35–46.

Smith, P., Cullen, F. and Latessa, E. (2009) 'Can 14,737 women be wrong? A meta analysis of the LSI-R and recidivism for female offenders', *Criminology and Public Policy*, 8: 183–208.

Sorbello, L., Eccleston, L., Ward, T. and Jones, R. (2002) 'Treatment needs of female offenders: A review', *Australian Psychologist*, 37: 198–205.

Taylor, K. and Blanchette, K. (2009) 'The women are not wrong: It is the approach that is debatable', *Criminology and Public Policy*, 8: 221–29.

US Government Accounting Office (1979) *Female Offenders – Who are They and What are the Problems Confronting Them?* NCJ 060496.

Van Dieten, M. (2008) *Women Offender Case Management Model.* Funded by the National Institute of Corrections, 07WOI02GJQ3.

Van Dieten, M. and MacKenna, P. (2001) *Moving On Facilitator's Guide.* Toronto, Ontario, Canada: Orbis Partners.

Van Voorhis, P., Pealer, J., Spiropoulis, G. and Sutherland, J. (2000) *Validation of Offender Custody Classification and Needs Assessment Systems in the Colorado Department of Corrections.* Cincinnati, OH: University of Cincinnati Criminal Justice Research Center.

Van Voorhis, P. and Presser, L. (2001) *Classification of Women Offenders: A National Assessment of Current Practices.* Washington, DC: USDOJ, National Institute of Corrections.

Van Voorhis, P., Salisbury, E., Wright, E. and Bauman, A. (2008) *Achieving Accurate Pictures of Risk and Identifying Gender-responsive Needs: Two*

New Assessments for Women Offenders. Washington, DC: United States Department of Justice: National Institute of Corrections.

Van Voorhis, P., Wright, E., Salisbury, S., and Bauman, A. (2010) 'Women's risk factors and their contributions to existing risk/needs assessment: The current status of gender responsive assessment', *Criminal Justice and Behavior*, 34: 261–88.

Van Wormer, K. (2001) *Counseling Female Offenders and Victims: A Strengths-restorative Approach*. New York: Springer.

Wright, E., Salisbury, E. and Van Voorhis, P. (2007) 'Predicting the prison misconducts of women offenders: The importance of gender-responsive needs', *Journal of Contemporary Criminal Justice*, 23 (4): 310–40.

Chapter 4

Policy developments in Australia

Rosemary Sheehan

Introduction

This chapter examines policy initiatives in Australia as exemplified by the *Better Pathways* Strategy implemented by the Department of Justice, in Victoria, Australia. This gender-specific strategy for working with women offenders places great emphasis on community-based approaches, incorporating therapeutic approaches to the treatment of issues that lead to women's offending behaviour, with the aim to not only reduce offending but also achieve more effective outcomes for women.

Women offenders in Victoria

The significant increase in the number of women in prison in Victoria was the impetus for Corrections Victoria, the statutory authority responsible for prison and offender management in Victoria, Australia, to develop a specific policy response to the needs of women offenders. Since 1995, the number of women sentenced or remanded in prison custody in Victoria (with a 2010 population of some five million people) between 1998 and 2003 increased by 84 per cent, from 8.4 to 14.3 per 100,000 of the Victorian adult female population; moving from 5.4 to 7.5 per cent of all individuals in prison custody in Victoria (Corrections Victoria 2006: 6), almost triple the growth in the male prisoner population over the same five-year period. In March 2009, there were 268 women in prison in Victoria, a 14 per cent increase (from 235) in the previous 12-month period, compared with just over 100 in mid-1995. The majority of women in prison in Victoria are aged 25 to 29 years; eight per cent are between 18 and 24 years, eight per cent are indigenous women (E*Justice@ 1 June 2008).

This increase is in line with international trends: that the female prisoner population is on a sustained growth curve that shows no indication of slowing without intervention (Corrections Victoria 2006: 6). The significant growth in the number of women entering prison custody in Victoria placed the state's women's prison system under unprecedented pressure. This increase in women's imprisonment not only incurred economic costs but also had social implications, not only for the women themselves but also for their families – especially their children. An increasing number of children were, as a consequence of their mother's imprisonment, experiencing dislocated and disadvantaged lives and increasing the likelihood of their own contact with the criminal justice system later in life.

The increase in women in the corrections system

When Corrections Victoria looked for factors that might explain the increase in female imprisonment they found distinctive risk factors relating to health, addiction, trauma, victimisation, debt, family issues and homelessness, but also changed community and legal responses to women offenders (Corrections Victoria 2006: 7). Whilst there was an increase in the number of women entering prison custody for serious violent offences (i.e. robbery offences and offences against the person) and drug-related offending, leading to more women prisoners serving longer sentences, there was an increased use of remand (see Figure 4.1), particularly for women with inadequate accommodation and complex treatment and support needs. In the 12-month period 2008–09, there was a 41 per cent increase (from 56 to 79) in the number of unsentenced women prisoners remanded in the women's prison.

There was an increase also in the number of women sentenced to a short term of imprisonment (i.e. less than one month) (see Figure 4.2). Of 255 women sentenced between July 2008 and May 2009, 35 (14 per cent) were serving less than one month and 25 (10 per cent) were serving between one and three months. The increase was also explained by a decline in the use of prison as a 'last resort' sentencing option, with women sent to prison for the first time bypassing the

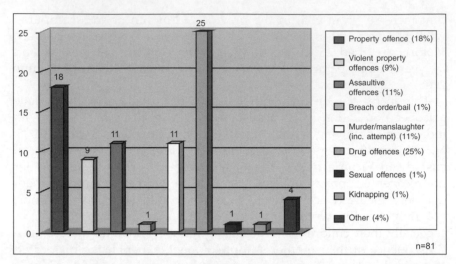

Figure 4.1 Increased use of remand for women in Victoria, as at June 2009
Source: Department of Justice, Victoria, November 2009

use of community-based orders. More women were being imprisoned for breaching non-custodial orders, particularly suspended sentences, affecting about one-tenth of all women going into prison custody annually.

Women were also more likely to reoffend; approximately one-third of all women released from prison at the end of their sentence returned to prison custody within two years. In May 2009, of the 81 women on remand, 62 per cent had prior contact with the Corrections system. Of 49 women on remand with previous Community Corrections Services contact, 39 (80 per cent) had previously breached an order.

The profile of women prisoners had also changed, to include a significant increase in the number of women prisoners from culturally and linguistically diverse communities, particularly Vietnamese-born women; 25 Vietnamese-born women were in prison custody in Victoria in June 2005 (9.7 per cent of women in prison) compared with just five (3.3 per cent) in June 1998. In May 2009, 14 of 81 women in remand were born in Vietnam (see Figure 4.3). This particular increase was driven by serious drug offences, anecdotally believed to be linked to settling debts incurred as a result of problem gambling (Corrections Victoria 2006: 8).

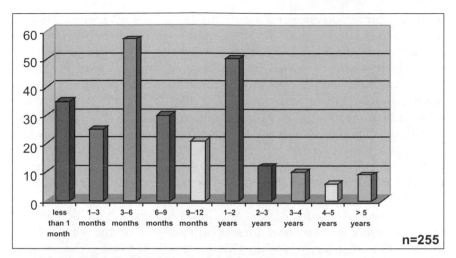

Figure 4.2 Sentence lengths for women in Victoria, 2008–09
Source: Department of Justice, Victoria, November 2009

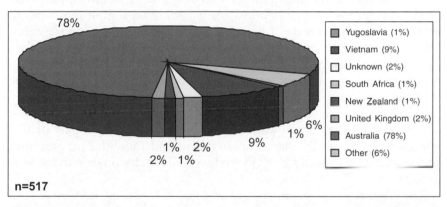

Figure 4.3 Country of origin of women entering prison in Victoria, 2008–09
Source: Department of Justice, Victoria, November 2009

Better Pathways: An integrated response to women's offending

What emerged was that women entering prison custody in Victoria had a complex range of unmet treatment and support needs that were linked to their offending, reoffending and subsequent imprisonment. They are, as found by the Equal Opportunity Commission, Victoria (2006: 21) a high-needs group compared with women in the general community. Bloom *et al.* (2005) report that substance abuse, male partners, family violence and their struggle to support themselves and their children are the main factors that drive women into crime. This is mirrored in the Victorian figures (see Figure 4.1) where women are more likely to be convicted of crimes involving property or drugs, which are motivated by poverty, gambling and/or substance abuse. Mental illness, abuse and trauma are also important factors: more women than men experience sexual, physical and psychological abuse and these experiences appear to contribute to women's criminality and shape their patterns of offending (Rumgay 2005; McIvor 2004; Carlen 2002). Their needs for support are linked not only to such victimisation but also to their child rearing responsibilities and self-esteem (Gelsthorpe *et al.* 2007).

Recognising the contribution the legal system might be making to the increase in women's imprisonment, one of the aims of the *Better Pathways* strategy is to provide information to the judiciary and defence lawyers about trends in women's offending and sentencing options. Community Correctional Services (CCS) Court Services Unit staff, who make recommendations to the courts about appropriate order conditions and suitability for specialist programmes, are to ensure the specific needs of female defendants are taken into account when preparing assessment reports and court advice. Key issues they need to alert the court to in, for example, the making of community-based orders, are around a woman's capacity to comply with the conditions of such an order – attending programmes etc., when they may have primary carer responsibilities. The development of a risk assessment tool specifically for women offenders is also part of this approach, to assess the risk of reoffending and therefore programmes and services that should be delivered to best meet women's individual needs.

The Victorian Government had in 2001 introduced its Corrections Long Term Management Strategy to invest in programmes and facilities that could curb the growth in prison populations. There was a renewed focus on rehabilitation and diversion, and on introducing evidence-based offending, behavioural and cognitive skills programmes, to reduce reoffending. Whilst separate standards for women prisoners had been introduced in 1995, they were broadly similar to those for men. International experience and research was demonstrating however that prison systems do not respond effectively to women's needs in environments, which are designed primarily to manage males. Further, Bloom *et al.* (2005) argued that the obstacles faced by women offenders are specifically related to their status as women. Thus, the *Better Pathways* strategy was developed, to be implemented over a four-year period (2005–09) to target factors that contribute to women's risk of offending, and to explore options to divert women from prison custody, and reduce the risk of reoffending by women involved in the correctional system. It provided for a range of initiatives that were gender responsive, recognising that women's needs, characteristics and life experiences differed from those of men who offend. Approaches that recognised that women respond best to relationship-focused and holistic responses were sought out, services and programmes that could address many of the women's needs simultaneously (Gelsthorpe *et al.* 2007). Attention was given also to adolescent girls' antisocial and offending behaviour, to determine how existing interventions might be tailored to better meet the specific needs of 'at-risk' adolescent girls and young women.

The women's correctional services framework, an initiative of *Better Pathways*, introduced in August 2007, provides a structure with which to sustain these developments in the longer term. It describes a model for the delivery of correctional services that takes into account the distinct needs, characteristics, life experiences and family circumstances of women offenders. Its focus is as much on the needs of women in prison as those on community-based orders, supervised by Community Correctional Services and women under the supervision of the Home Detention Program. It acknowledges women respond to correctional intervention differently from men. They tend to have shorter periods of supervision, meaning less opportunity for intervention; are more likely to expose their vulnerability, talk about problems and ask for help; may display violent or aggressive behaviour differently from men, often with an emotional basis; and seek greater access to health services, including prescription drugs (Corrections Victoria 2006). A further challenge for the corrections system is the relatively small number of women under its supervision. As noted, women comprise less than seven per cent of the total Victorian prison population; approximately 1,550 women (19 per cent of offenders) are on community-based orders (E*Justice @ 1 June 2008), spread across approximately 50 office locations around Victoria. The majority of the women are in the 20–29 years age group; six per cent are indigenous women. They share many of the same characteristics of women in prison: poor education and few employment skills, many are mothers with few social supports, have drug abuse problems and are victims of abuse and maltreatment.

Gender responsiveness: principles and policy

Bloom *et al.* (2005) argue that women offenders respond best to interventions that understand the realities and relationships that shape their lives. Women develop a sense of self and self-worth when their actions arise out of, or lead back to, connections with others. This is a strong motivation for women; this relational context is critical in order to successfully address the reasons why women commit crime, the motivation behind their behaviours, how they change their behaviours, and their reintegration into the community. Given the centrality of relationships in women's lives, and their particular needs, the services that underpin those needs are more effective if they are holistic and strengths-based in their approach. Women need significant practical support to balance their correctional obligations and carer responsibilities. Whilst all offenders confront the problems of re-entry into the community, Bloom *et al.* (2005: 4) comment that women offenders face particular obstacles. Many women are mothers and a major consideration is reunification with their children. Their requirements for safe housing, economic support, medical services and other needs must include the ability to take care of their children. They may also need, in ways men will not, gender-specific services such as protection from abusive partners, childcare, access to reliable transport and realistic employment opportunities that allow for self-support.

Baldry (2007) argues that what is key to effective responses to women offenders is continuous, coordinated and integrated management; the principles of *throughcare* provide this, commencing with assistance and support to offenders while in custody or on community supervision. Clay (2002: 41) suggests that such case management, with consistent interventions across community and custody, is better at reducing recidivism and assisting community integration. This case management approach, in which planning and services are implemented at the women's first point of contact with corrections services, is the approach of mental health services (Borzycki 2005). It is an approach that can be used with women on remand or short sentences, who are disadvantaged by approaches that commence only with sentenced women. It is an approach that mirrors what Bloom *et al.* (2005) confirm, that coordinated case management with wraparound services, which are collaborative and multidisciplinary, are more effective. No one agency can realistically be expected to meet the diverse needs women will have, dealing with issues of alienation, unemployment, low self-esteem, finances, housing and carer responsibilities. It is what the NSW Department of Corrective Services (2002) refers to as seamless services, offering women better chances for successful reintegration into the community and avoiding duplication and isolated work practices that see women bounce from service to service to comply with conditions (Stevens 2002). However, these wraparound services need proper funding.

What Bloom *et al.* (2005) argue is essential in this approach is that case planning and management must negotiate the relationships between the women, the programmes they are to participate in, and the broader community if they are to be successful. If case plans fail to meet women's needs for, for example, housing, their physical and psychological safety, for education, job training and opportunities, for community-based substance abuse treatment and economic support, then their re-entry to – and maintenance in – the community is compromised. It is an approach that sees corrections and service staff as providing positive role models for women as they deal with managing compliance with orders and any prescribed interventions. For this to work, however, relations and communication between custodial and community corrections staff need to be transparent and open; they need to share also the same aims and philosophy about responding to women if case management is to be effective and women reintegrated into the community.

Better Pathways: Gender principles in practice

Recognising this, the *Better Pathways* strategy developed gender-specific principles to underpin its programmes and other initiatives. These principles recognised women's different pathways into the criminal justice system (Bloom *et al.* 2005) and their responses to correctional interventions; the importance of relationships in women's lives, issues associated with separation and reunification; and, as already noted, the link between substance abuse, mental health issues and past victimisation and offending behaviour and the need to address these within the context of these issues. Importantly, disability awareness is included, with strategies to appropriately manage women offenders with a disability. The principles aimed to improve organisational culture in correctional services; they promote strong representation of female staff at all levels of correctional services, the importance of positive role models of both genders, and the provision of mandatory training in gender-responsive principles for all staff recruited to work in prisons and community corrections settings. The principles emphasise that education and training and other types of skill development are pivotal to reducing women's risk of reoffending. These initiatives exemplify what Andrews and Bonta (1998) describe as responses to dynamic risk factors, which are more amenable to change: such as education, employment and substance abuse; compared with static risk factors, such as criminal history, which cannot be changed. They found that programmes that dealt with social and behavioural problems reduced the probability of reoffending.

What *Better Pathways* set out to do was challenge the system-level lack of programmes and services designed and targeted for women, to provide better community support and more holistic responses to women. This would reduce their need for involvement with multiple human service agencies as they struggle to support themselves and their children when released from prison. *Better Pathways* specifically focused on working with women offenders in the community, recognising that community-based correctional services are delivered at various points in the criminal justice system, for those individuals involved with diversionary programmes, on bail or community-based orders, including parole, as well as those leaving prison. *Better Pathways* established partnerships between the government and non-government sectors to cater for women after their release from prison or on community orders.

The emphasis is on rehabilitation and addressing the victimisation common to the experience of women offenders. A material example of this is the appointment of a Vietnamese liaison officer (Multicultural Liaison Officer) at the women's prison. The large number of Vietnamese women, now representing approximately one-tenth of all women in prison, have distinct needs not readily met in established programmes. The liaison officer also communicates with community-based agencies to assist women post-release, most particularly around problems they experience with debt. In 2007, a Problem Gambling Program for Vietnamese women was developed and implemented to acknowledge the relationship between problem gambling and Vietnamese women's offending.

It is accepted that the issues women offenders have are neither simple nor uniform, most particularly when matters relating to their involvement in the criminal justice system may be unresolved and still capable of interfering in their life (Gelsthorpe *et al.* 2007). Furthermore, the very fact of their involvement in the criminal justice system may give rise to new problems, compounding the difficulties the women are experiencing – such as the debt problems experienced by Vietnamese women, noted above. It is the Community Correctional Services that provide a range of non-custodial programmes for women post-release who may still have reporting conditions, and for women on community-based orders. These orders will vary in the extent and nature of supervision required by conditions on the order, and any restrictions on the woman living in the community. Figure 4.4 shows the number of remanded women – slightly more than 50 per cent – who have returned to the community; many on orders that will be supervised by Community Corrections.

Hamlyn and Lewis (2000: 79) in their UK study established how central accommodation is to reintegration; they found one-fifth of women leaving prison have no address to go to, and no means of paying a housing bond and rent. Where accommodation does not include children, women may feel compelled to return to violent partners on release (Cook and Davies 1999). Housing for women and their children is crucial for women who are seeking to regain access to their children who may have been placed in 'care' of one type or another. The key initiatives of *Better Pathways* focused on practical support: additional transitional housing for women on bail, including indigenous women; women, particularly those with inadequate accommodation and complex treatment and support needs, who were being more readily remanded after their arrest and initial court appearance. The extent of this problem for women is demonstrated by the community outcomes for remanded women in Figure 4.4.

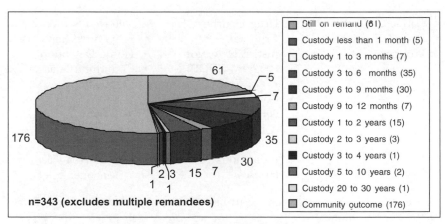

Figure 4.4 Outcomes for remanded women, 2008–09
Source: Department of Justice, Victoria, November 2009

Diversion and community-based responses

The Better Pathways practical supports are also embedded in the range of diversion options available to the courts for women appearing before them (see Figure 4.5). The community-based programmes address the key factors identified as integral to women's re-integration: accommodation, family responsibilities, and access to holistic services. Baroness Corston in her Report on *Women with Particular Vulnerabilities in the Criminal Justice System* in England and Wales (2007) also emphasised multi-agency and holistic approaches to work with women, which could serve to encourage courts to make greater use of community disposals for women and custody is only used as a last resort (National Offender Management Service, 2005: 3).

The CREDIT/Bail Support Program was implemented to offer access to supported transitional houses, to divert women from prison custody. Corrections Victoria, the Magistrates' Court of Victoria, the Victorian Government's Office of Housing, Women's Housing Ltd and HomeGround (the latter are both non-government agencies, funded by government for this project) work in partnership to improve the chances of eligible female defendants being granted bail and

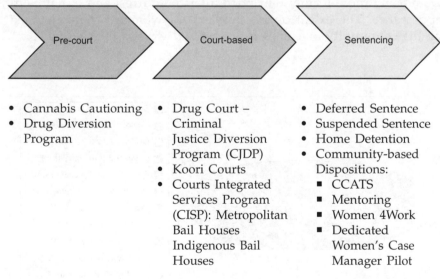

Pre-court	Court-based	Sentencing

• Cannabis Cautioning
• Drug Diversion Program
	• Drug Court – Criminal Justice Diversion Program (CJDP)
	• Koori Courts
	• Courts Integrated Services Program (CISP): Metropolitan Bail Houses Indigenous Bail Houses
		• Deferred Sentence
		• Suspended Sentence
		• Home Detention
		• Community-based Dispositions:
		  ▪ CCATS
		  ▪ Mentoring
		  ▪ Women 4Work
		  ▪ Dedicated Women's Case Manager Pilot

Figure 4.5 Interface between court-based diversion outcome and *Better Pathways* programmes
Source: 'Strengthening Diversion Options', Department of Justice, Victoria, February 2010

successfully completing their bail periods. *Better Pathways* provided funding for ten dedicated transitional bail properties in metropolitan Melbourne for women participating in the programme who are unable to find stable, secure housing. Two additional transitional properties have been established in Mildura and Shepparton, two regional cities in Victoria, specifically for indigenous women offenders who are released on bail, or are being supervised by Corrections Victoria and who are at risk of reoffending due to unsatisfactory housing. Between 2008–2009, indigenous women represented 52.4 per cent of the indigenous female remand population. They were less likely to receive bail: of the 33 indigenous women who were remanded, only 12 received bail. Accommodation difficulties feature largely for indigenous women on remand, a combination of no housing and unsatisfactory housing, and the need to not return to violent partners. Their offences were, by and large, property offences (51 per cent), followed by offences against the person (18 per cent) and breaches of Parole and Drug Treatment Orders (11 per cent).

Other key programmes that exemplify *Better Pathways* initiatives are WISP, Women4Work and CCATS. The Women's Integrated Support Program (WISP) is a Corrections Victoria and community agency partnership that provides intensive pre- and post-release case management and support for up to 12 months to at least 90 women prisoners each year. It exemplifies the kind of wraparound services Bloom *et al.* (2005) suggest are most effective for women exiting prison. WISP provides support to women around long-term, affordable, secure housing; the management of legal and court issues; family reunification; parenting skills; financial management; independent living skills; access to education, training and employment programmes; drug and alcohol support; assistance with general and mental health issues; pathways for reintegration into the community; and referral to specialist support programmes. Since October 2006, WISP has provided assistance and support to more than 190 women exiting prison:

> WISP has always been there for me, when I had no place to go, when I needed food, a tram ticket, even if it was somebody to talk to. I'd not be where I am today without the support, perhaps not even alive. (WISP client)

The Women4Work Program commenced in July 2006 to help women exiting prison find secure employment. The programme is run by Melbourne Citymission, a non-government agency, and funded through *Better Pathways* grants. It provides women with individualised job searching and planning, information about work opportunities, as well as access to vocational training and support, to help women maintain meaningful employment. A key element of the programme has been 'Employment Expos', offered in each of the two women's prisons, which bring employers into the prison to meet the women, to speak to them about employer/employee expectations and participate in 'mock' job interviews. Since July 2006, the Program has placed 80 women in employment, 46 of whom have been employed for a minimum period of 16 weeks:

> If it wasn't for the experience of the 'Employment Expo' while I was in prison, who knows where I'd be today. Before going to the expo, I had no immediate intention of changing my lifestyle. I didn't feel there was any reason to. I'm now drug free and on my way to working in a job that I had always wanted to do. (Woman prisoner following her participation in an Employment Expo)

The Childcare and Transport Subsidy (CCATS) Program offers practical support to women offenders on supervised community-based orders. Corrections Victoria, when examining factors around increases in women's offending rates, found women offenders are more likely to breach supervised community-based orders by failing to comply with order conditions rather than by reoffending. What they found was that many women experience difficulty complying with the conditions of their orders due to competing primary carer responsibilities and transport difficulties. Since July 2006, Corrections Victoria, in partnership with VACRO (Victorian Association for the Care and Resettlement of Offenders), has provided more than 2,000 childcare and transport subsidies to women offenders.

> Money-wise, it would have been hard with five kids. I get paid on Thursday so by Monday, there's not much spare change for tickets to get into the city for appointments that I need to go to. (Participant who receives public transport tickets)

Women's needs from supervision

Bloom *et al.* (2005) emphasise the need for role models offering mentoring to women trying to turn away from offending behaviour.

The VACRO Women's Mentoring Program was initially established as a post-release programme to assist women exiting prison to reintegrate successfully into the community. The programme now supports women on Community Correctional Orders by matching them with a volunteer mentor to support them in the community. Recognising the difficulties faced by indigenous women, the Aboriginal Women's Mentoring Program was established in 2002 under the Victorian Aboriginal Justice Agreement (2000) to offer indigenous women undertaking supervised community-based orders a flexible model of supervision, and mentoring and support provided by female indigenous elders/respected persons. The programme's dual aims are to improve order completion rates and reduce reoffending, the former directly related to the latter. Mentoring also addresses the isolation, low self-esteem and social exclusion experienced by women offenders (Bloom *et al.* 2005). The importance of mentoring is evident in what women say about the Women's Mentoring Program offered by the Wellington Centre, Collingwood. This is a community-based agency supported by the local Roman Catholic parish of an inner city Melbourne area, situated next to a large public housing estate, which is home to many families with complex needs, refugees, and people with marginal income. A programme participant said her mentor helped her address many of her problems:

'She will come to court with me and will help me keep appointments,' she said. 'It is a new thing for me to have someone who listens to me.' (*Melbourne Leader*, 1 March 2010: 7)

Local police refer women who have been charged to the Wellington Centre, who match women caught up in the criminal justice system with trained volunteer mentors to offer practical assistance and, importantly, friendship. The social work coordinator reported that the approach of applying prison sentences to break the cycles of substance abuse and crime simply does not work. 'Frequent prison terms of less than six months render women ineligible for educational or rehabilitation programs ... Sometimes these are very disadvantaged women and often find themselves locked into a cycle of self-harm and crime ... and a life of prison cells, community-based orders, drug addiction and theft' (*Melbourne Leader*, 1 March 2010: 7). Her comments echo what researchers say about the distinct needs of women offenders: 'Many women caught up with the law have poor life skills and have many demands on them from children and family ... They are often ill-equipped to deal with life. They don't have enough money, they may have mental health and drug and alcohol issues. Many are friendless' (*ibid*.). The police confirmed the utility of such an approach: 'It's an opportunity for us to have a really positive impact on crime by reducing recidivist offending but, more importantly, to have a positive impact on that person's situation' (*ibid*.).

A key initiative of *Better Pathways* is strengthening the community work programme for women offenders. Many women will be placed on orders directing them to work in community settings. Community Corrections is seeking to increase both work options and places for women on community-based orders, so that settings in which they are placed are meaningful and offer skill development that can be transferred to paid employment. Examples of community placements are: canteen work, cleaning, graffiti removal, gardening, sorting goods, opportunity shop work and other retail settings (Women's Community Work Options Information Kit, Department of Justice 2009). This Information Kit provides an overview of community work sites offering gender-specific services in each region in Victoria and an outline of gendered considerations that are important for identifying suitable community work options.

Women undertaking unpaid community work hours are also, where possible, to work with a female supervisor and co-worker (Corrections Victoria 2005). An important planned policy change is the recognition of participation in rehabilitation programmes as part of the unpaid community work requirements of these orders. The debate is whether programme attendance hours, including hours undertaken to complete programmes such as life skills or financial planning courses, should be credited towards the community work component of a supervised community-based order. This is particularly significant given the competing demands women with dependent children have on their time, their difficulties with transport, as well as their need to improve their life skills and opportunities through education and training.

Community Correctional Services are employing specialist advisors to both build the expertise of community corrections staff in managing women offenders and strengthen relationships with community-based agencies that provide treatment programmes and support services. Dedicated women's case managers are to be based in areas where there are a number of high-risk women, or women with complex needs, and the case managers will be provided with specialised training, recognising the need for such targeted training (Bloom *et al*. 2005). *Better Pathways* also provides ongoing education for staff about the needs and characteristics of women offenders and best practice responses to these, to incorporate a gendered approach in everyday practice. Emphasis is on staff as female role models, offering mentoring, as noted above, encouraging women to learn from and support each other in working towards their rehabilitation, and maximising their participation in, and control over, the development of their case plans. Emphasis is also on giving women clear, accurate, accessible and timely information about rules, regulations and other correctional processes, as well as sanctions, making sure that should the latter be necessary they match the particular woman's behaviour, needs and circumstances. The Women's Case-Management Guide has recently been developed by VACRO, funded by Corrections Victoria (in 2010), to provide all Community Corrections staff with information about how best to respond to women who are offending; information about local agencies and service pathways who can assist women and support their community reintegration; and, importantly, information about the range of factors that influence women's lives and offending behaviour.

The majority of women who come into contact with the criminal justice system come from a background of profound socio-economic disadvantage and marginalisation (Gelsthorpe *et al.* 2007). *Better Pathways* (2006: 33) principles and initiatives offer women the resources, skills or opportunities to move beyond entrenched disadvantage and offending behaviours. The challenges for Community Corrections staff in managing women include resistance and challenging behaviours, multiple and complex needs versus their compliance with orders, balancing their history of victimisation with their offender/perpetrator role, managing the women's criminal peers/partners, keeping the women on track, and staff maintaining professional boundaries – and knowing when to refer on (Corrections Victoria 2009: 4).

Providing for women in the community: More effective responses to complex problems

The gender-responsive strategy of *Better Pathways* recognises that women offenders' needs, characteristics and life experiences differ from those of men who offend. Ogilvie (2001: 1) comments that, for women offenders, attempting to reintegrate into the community has much in common with post-traumatic stress disorder (PTSD). Their return from prison to the wider community involves dealing with the negative experiences of imprisonment in contexts all too often characterised by isolation, accommodation difficulties, financial and material constraints and a lack of significant material support. Women especially vulnerable to a lack of post-release support are those with mental illness and indigenous groups. Bloom *et al.* (2005: 6) underline the need to offer gender responses in a therapeutic context, recognising that the often complex needs of the women, their likely past trauma, issues with substance abuse and mental illness, will influence their capacity for understanding and taking responsibility for offending behaviour. They emphasise the importance of all-women group settings and individual counselling as appropriate, and being flexible around women and their needs, to facilitate their participation and better outcomes.

Tye and Mullen (2006) found that approximately two-thirds of women assessed over a 12-month period at the women's prison in Victoria in 2000 met the criteria for a mental disorder, with depression, PTSD and drug use disorders featuring the most. This mirrors Baroness Corston's findings (2007) in England where 78 per cent of women coming into custody displayed some form of psychological disorder, compared with 15 per cent of the general population. The significant increase in the number of women entering prisons and the high rate of mental illnesses among them has major implications for Corrections Services. Ogloff and Tye (2008) argue that unless prison services identify and treat such mental illness, women with major mental illnesses will continue to cycle between the community and prison. They note also that greater focus on the mental health needs of women in the community could reduce the number of women with mental illnesses entering into custody. Community treatment and diversion offer more therapeutic responses to women who, Ogloff and Tye (2008) remind, are at the margins of custody (i.e. women who are not violent or are drug dependent offenders), but are featuring more in prison. As a response to this, Corrections Victoria built a 20-bed mental health unit at the major women's prison (Marrmak Mental Health Unit) to offer specialist treatment to women coming into the prison who have a mental illness. It has an inpatient unit, as well as outpatient, outreach and consultancy services.

Ogilvie (2001: 3) refers to the financial difficulties women experience when they return from prison to the wider community. These material difficulties are often embedded in broader issues around relationships and the reasons why they went into prison in the first place. Corrections Victoria introduced a pilot project to assist women prisoners to manage and minimise debt, in collaboration with community welfare agencies, electricity and gas retailers, and water companies. The WISP programme, referred to earlier, has incorporated assistance with these practical supports, as part of the holistic approach it takes to supporting women exiting prison or on community orders. Offering a range of services within the one setting creates better linkages for this vulnerable group of women. Recognising the post-release period as high risk, when women are dealing with readjustment and any unresolved problems that flow from their incarceration, Corrections Victoria extended post-release support from six to 12 months for women with significant needs, whose vulnerability puts them at risk of reoffending.

Bloom *et al.* (2005: 7) remind that drug abuse features strongly in women's offending and this is borne out in the figures which feature elsewhere in this chapter. They argue the strong connection between trauma and addiction and the vulnerability that accompanies this. Experiences of abuse, both in childhood and in adulthood, are extremely common among women prisoners. Corrections Victoria funds specialist sexual assault counselling offered by Victoria's Centres Against Sexual Assault (CASA) to deliver sexual assault counselling, advocacy and support services to women prisoners, recognising the link between past victimisation and offending behaviour. Since October 2006, more than 60 women prisoners have accessed CASA's services. This therapeutic context offers women the opportunity to explore past trauma and move to recovery. A further key programme that addresses victimisation is the Family Violence Program, a pilot programme introduced at the women's prison in 2009. Melbourne CityMission (non-government agency funded to work with offenders) evaluated the initial programme and reported that whilst the women found it emotionally challenging, it was helpful in providing information and supportive in building self-esteem and confidence. A second pilot programme commenced in February 2010.

The importance of relationships to women has already been flagged. Brimley (2009) found, in his English study of continuity, compliance and women offenders, as had Bloom *et al.* (2005) in the US, that relationship problems were more likely to underpin female offending than male offending, and that relationship issues also affect women more in the supervision process. This was twofold: women were affected by relationship matters as they tried to fulfil community requirements, and also placed more emphasis on relationships with supervisors in the community work settings. The implications of this in the design of services for women are evidenced in the holistic packages of services that address multiple needs, such as those offered by WISP. What also characterises such interventions is that they are strengths-based and promote skill-building with the women.

How effective is *Better Pathways?*

Better Pathways evaluated its range of community and transitional support programmes (Corrections Victoria 2009b) to establish the extent to which these initiatives have kept women out of prison. The women offenders and prisoners they interviewed identified accommodation and family reunification as their highest priorities, with health, education and employment as subsequent needs. The programmes that provided them with support in these areas or facilitated contact with family had the greatest impact. The evaluation found that although the availability of longer-term recidivism data and the short duration of the direct impact of programmes made it difficult to assess the direct impact of *Better Pathways*, there was strong evidence that programmes such as WISP, CREDIT/Bail Housing and Women4Work were meeting women's needs. Given that these programmes are targeted at women with complex and multiple needs, their positive impact was encouraging.

Since the introduction of the CREDIT/Bail transitional housing programme in 2006–07, the 10 available properties have housed 16 women, with an average tenancy of eight months, with only one of the 16 women returning to prison. Two dedicated supported transitional housing properties have been established in regional Victoria, in indigenous communities, so that indigenous women could be eligible for bail. They have housed five women, one of whom returned to custody. These houses are now available to indigenous women placed on Community Correctional Orders.

Women using the services of CCATS (the Childcare and Transport Support) said it helped them comply with community correctional orders. The demand for this programme in Community Corrections Services continues to increase. During July to September, 2009, 17 women received 241 instances of childcare and 121 women were assisted on 715 occasions with transport. The high uptake of childcare and transport assistance confirms how essential these material supports are if women are to reintegrate into the community. The wraparound services provided by WISP have seen only nine per cent of the women in the programme return to prison during the support period, which is much lower than the state average recidivism rate. The Women4Work programme provides employment support and advice for women exiting prison and on Community Correctional Orders to improve their chances of finding employment in the community. Between July 2006 and July 2009, 104 women were placed in employment through Women4Work; 59 of these were placed in employment of a minimum of 30 hours per week, for a period of 13 weeks or longer, a significant achievement for this highly complex cohort. The VACRO Women's Mentoring Program, initially established as a post-release programme to assist women exiting prison reintegrate into the community, has been extended to support women on Community Correctional Orders and matches them with a volunteer mentor to support them in the community. From July to September 2009, 40 women were working with the Mentoring Program, with referrals from both the prison and Community Corrections. Corrections Victoria is currently focusing on unsentenced women and those with sentences of less than three months to reduce the number of women entering the system and to reduce the impact of this on women and their families, most particularly the impact on housing and children.

The evaluation found that the combination of these programmes, with efforts made by Community Corrections Women's Portfolio Holders to educate their staff, had raised their awareness of the needs of women offenders, especially their non-criminogenic needs. Members of staff were more likely to view non-custodial sentencing options as more successful, with programmes such as those just noted helping women to stay out of prison and meet the requirements of their parole or orders. However, it remains a challenge for Community Corrections to focus specifically on women, given the relatively small number, when compared to men, exiting prison and on orders, and the difficulties of resource and staff constraints.

Whilst the Women4Work programme has successfully helped women find and maintain work, women with a conviction will have diminished opportunities. Criminal history checks made by employers make it impossible for them to work in traditional areas of employment and volunteering for women: teaching, nursing, childcare and home-based care of older people. Women's Health Victoria (2009: 3) presented a submission on the proposed Spent Convictions Bill, currently before the Victorian Parliament, which brings attention to the impact of criminal history checks on individuals involved in the criminal justice system. The proposed bill recommends that certain criminal convictions (excluding sexual offences) be discarded for a sentenced adult who has spent less than 12 months in prison or less than 24 months in juvenile detention. Women's Health Victoria (*ibid.*) argues that this offers women offenders the opportunity 'to break the cycle of disadvantage and improve their health and well-being and that of their dependent children'. They submit that this proposal would benefit 40 per cent of women prisoners in Victoria who serve less than 12 months, are in the 29 to 49 years age bracket, and with potentially significant numbers of years in the paid and unpaid workforce (*ibid.*: 3–4).

A direct challenge to therapeutic and community-based responses to women offenders comes from the increasing dominance of the risk paradigm being applied within the criminal justice system (Hannah-Moffat 2005; Stenson and Sullivan 2001). Women are particularly affected when this occurs as the social problems that bring them into contact with criminal justice – intellectual disability, mental health, dual diagnosis, drug- and alcohol-related behaviour problems and homelessness – are classified as high risk. Hudson (2001: 144) suggests risk undermines rehabilitation, imposing a surveillance framework on people and services, requiring community corrections staff to have an increasing policing role, and drawing resources away from therapeutic and rehabilitative programmes. Yet it is such programmes – as offered by *Better Pathways* – that are emphasised by contemporary corrections policy as key to diversion and reducing reoffending (Gelsthorpe *et al.* 2007).

Gelsthorpe *et al.* (2007) found the flexibility afforded by community approaches worked better at unravelling the complex and interrelated problems presented by women offenders. They offered the time needed to build relationships to promote change in a way that the time-limited and risk-focused cognitive skills programmes cannot. Worrall (2002: 144) notes also that women are less driven to commit offences because of cognitive deficits but more from the needs and demands that surround them. Dowden and Andrews (1999), McIvor (1999) and Hannah-Moffat and Shaw (2000) confirm that such approaches are less likely to address women's criminogenic needs, and Covington (1998) suggests they do not recognise that women learn best in collaborative settings, in which their needs for health care, childcare and mental health are better addressed.

The *Better Pathways* initiatives recognise the need to address the personal and social problems that can lead women to offend. They exemplify what Gelsthorpe *et al.* (2007: 51) recommend about policy provision for women offenders in the community in England, 'joined-up policy across probation, health and housing sectors'. It will be important to continue to evaluate these approaches and provide the evidence that confirms their efficacy, and the greater value of diversion and community reintegration over increasing calls for more punitive responses to women and their offending. Gelsthorpe *et al.* (2007: 13) argue that unless community provision is given prominence then courts may think the only place where women's needs will be met is prison, suggesting there is a 'danger in seeing prisons as the new social services'. The *Better Pathways* strategy of liaising with judges and legal practitioners to give information about women's pathways into offending and the impact of incarceration on women, aims to give legitimacy to diversion and community-based approaches. Community-based approaches such as those articulated in *Better Pathways* address factors that are unique to or more relevant for women who offend (Hedderman 2004: 241), thus more effectively working to reduce both vulnerability and reoffending.

References

Andrews, D.A. and Bonta, J. (1998) *The Psychology of Criminal Conduct* (2nd edn). Cincinnati, USA: Anderson Publishing Co.

Baldry, E. (2007) 'Throughcare: making the policy a reality', keynote address, *The Reintegration Puzzle Conference*. Sydney, NSW, Australia, 7–8 May 2007.

Bloom, B., Owen, B. and Covington, S. (2005) 'Gender-responsive strategies for women offenders: A summary of research, practice, and guiding principles for women offenders'. National Institute of Corrections, Washington DC: US Department of Justice, May 2005.

Borzycki, M. (2005) 'Interventions for prisoners returning to the community'. A report prepared by the Australian Institute of Criminology for the Community, Safety and Justice Branch of the Australian Attorney-General's Department, Canberra, ACT: Australian Attorney-General's Department.

Brimley, J. (2009) 'Effective offender management: Continuity, compliance and women offenders', *Issues of Community and Criminal Justice*. Monograph No. 8, published by SAGE for the British Society of Criminology.

Carlen, P. (ed.) (2002) *Women and Punishment: The Struggle for Justice*. Cullompton: Willan Publishing.

Clay, C. (2002) 'Case management and throughcare – can it work?' Available at www.corrections.sa.gov.au

Cook, S. and Davies, S. (1999) 'Neglect or punishment? Failing to meet the needs of women post-release', in S. Cook and S. Davies (eds) *Harsh punishment: international experiences of women's imprisonment*. Boston, USA: Northeastern University Press.

Corrections Victoria (2000) 'Women's Community Work Options Information Kit', September, 2009. Melbourne, Victoria, Australia: Department of Justice, Victoria.

Corrections Victoria (2005) *Principles and Standards for the Management of Women Prisoners in Victoria, 2005.* Melbourne, Victoria: Department of Justice, Victoria.

Corrections Victoria (2006) *Better Pathways: An Integrated Response to Women's Offending and Re-offending.* Melbourne, Victoria, Australia: Department of Justice, Victoria.

Corrections Victoria (2008) *Better Pathways Report Card,* April 2008. Melbourne, Victoria, Australia: Victorian Department of Justice.

Corrections Victoria (2009a) *Correctional Management Standards for Women Serving Community Correctional Orders,* released 10 February 2009. Melbourne, Victoria: Department of Justice, Victoria.

Corrections Victoria (2009b) *Evaluation of the Better Pathways Strategy,* prepared for by PriceWaterhouse Coopers for Corrections Victoria, April 2009. Melbourne, Victoria: Victorian Department of Justice.

Corston, J. (Baroness) (2007) *The Corston Report: A Report by Baroness Jean Corston of a Review of Women with Particular Vulnerabilities in the Criminal Justice System.* London: Home Office.

Covington, S. (1998) 'The relational theory of women's psychological development: implications for the criminal justice system', in R. Zaplin (ed.) *Female Offenders: Critical Perspectives and Effective Interventions.* Gaithersburg, Maryland: Aspen Publishers, Inc.

Department of Justice, Victoria, Women's Policy Unit (2009) 'Explanation for change in female prisoner profile 2008–09'. Presentation to the Women's Correctional Services Advisory Committee, November 2009.

Department of Justice, Victoria, Women's Policy Unit (2010) 'Strengthening diversion options'. Presentation to the Women's Correctional Services Advisory Committee, February 2010.

Dowden, C. and Andrews, D.A. (1999) 'What works for female offenders: A meta-analytic review', *Crime and Delinquency,* 45 (4): 438–52.

E*Justice @ 1 June 2008, Victorian State Government Resources website.

Equal Opportunity Commission Victoria (2006) *Women Prisoners in Victoria.* Report to Victorian Attorney-General concerning a formal investigation into systemic discrimination against women in Victorian prisons. Released 19 December 2006, available at www.eoc.vic.gov.au

Gelsthorpe, L., Sharpe, G. and Roberts, J. (2007) 'Provision for women offenders in the community'. Report for the Fawcett Society. London: Fawcett Society.

Hamlyn, B. and Lewis, D. (2000) *Women Prisoners: A Survey of their Work and Training Experiences in Custody and on Release.* Home Office Research Study 208. London: Home Office.

Hannah-Moffat, K. (2005) 'Criminogenic needs and the transformative risk subject', *Punishment and Society,* 7 (1): 29–51.

Hannah-Moffat, K. and Shaw, M. (eds) (2000) *An Ideal Prison? Critical Essays on Women's Imprisonment in Canada.* Halifax: Fernwood Publishing.

Hedderman, C. (2004) 'The Criminogenic Needs of Women Offenders', in G. Mclvor (ed.) *Women Who Offend.* London: Jessica Kingsley.

Hudson, B. (2001) 'Punishment, rights and difference: defending justice in the risk society', in K. Stenson and R.R. Sullivan (eds) *Crime, Risk and Justice*. Cullompton, Devon: Willan Publishing, pp. 144–72.

McIvor, G. (1999) 'Women, crime and criminal justice in Scotland', *Scottish Journal of Criminal Justice Studies*, 5 (1): 67–74.

McIvor, G. (ed.) (2004) *Women Who Offend*. London: Jessica Kingsley Publishers.

Melbourne Leader (2010) Report by Hamish Heard, 1 March: 7.

National Offender Management Service (2005) *Women's Offending Reduction Programme: Annual Review 2004–05*. London: Home Office.

New South Wales Department of Corrective Services (2002) *Throughcare Strategic Framework 2002–2005*. New South Wales Department of Corrective Services, Throughcare and E-Case Management Unit, Sydney, NSW.

Ogilvie, E. (2001) 'Post release: the current predicament and the potential strategies', Australian Institute of Criminology, http://www.aic.gov.crc/reports/ogilivie.html

Ogloff, J. and Tye, C. (2008), 'Responding to the mental health needs of women offenders', in R. Sheehan, G. McIvor and C. Trotter (eds) *What Works with Women Offenders: International Perspectives*. Cullompton, Devon: Willan Publishing, pp. 142–81.

Rumgay, J. (2005) *When Victims Become Offenders: In Search of Coherence in Policy and Practice*. Occasional Paper. London: Fawcett Society.

Stenson, K. and Sullivan, R.R (2001) *Crime, Risk and Justice*. Cullompton: Willan Publishing.

Stevens, L. (2002) 'The challenges of implementing throughcare'. Paper presented at *Probation and Community Corrections: Making the Community Safer* conference, 23–24 September, Perth, W.A.

Tye, C.S. and Mullen, P.E. (2006) 'Mental disorders in female prisoners', *Australian and New Zealand Journal of Psychiatry*, 40 (3): 266–71.

Victorian Aboriginal Justice Agreement (2000) A joint initiative of the Victorian State Government (the Departments of Justice and Human Services), the Victorian Aboriginal Justice Advisory Committee (VAJAC), the Aboriginal and Torres Strait Islander Commission (ATSIC) and the Aboriginal community (through the Aboriginal Regional Councils of Tumbukka and Binjurru), released 1 January 2000, available at http://www.atns.net.au/agreement.asp?EntityID=1059

Women's Health Victoria (2009) 'Draft Model Spent Convictions Bill: Response to Consultation Paper', January. Melbourne: Women's Health Victoria.

Worrall, A. (2002) 'Rendering them punishable' in P. Carlen (ed.) *Women and Punishment: The Struggle for Justice*. Cullompton, Devon : Willan Publishing.

Chapter 5

Coercion and women offenders

Delores Blackwell

Introduction

As the frontline staff in many traditional and non-traditional service environments, social workers are placed in situations where they are being asked to coerce clients into treatment. Coercion is of major concern when working with women offenders, because of the presence of numerous biopsychosocial issues such as addiction, mental illness and poverty to name a few. Because of their multiple stressors female offenders are particularly vulnerable to coercion from both within and outside of the legal system. While coercive treatment is very much a part of the offender landscape, little has been done with regard to practice development to assist social workers and other social service professionals in acknowledging the practice of coercion and its ethical implications. This chapter will focus on the identification and definition of coercion, the practice of coercion and the ethical considerations as it relates to the treatment of and practice with women offenders.

Over the past decade, criminal justice trends suggest that more and more women are offending and entering the various levels of the criminal justice system. While women offenders are still much lower in numbers than their male counterparts, their presence in criminal justice systems around the world is increasing at a dramatic rate. Women offenders traditionally commit less violent offences than their male counterparts and therefore serve fewer long-term sentences. However, women who do commit violent crimes are punished more harshly as their commission of violent offences is deemed more of a violation of the natural image of women in our society. Women are committing crimes such as larceny, property crimes and violent offences such as assault and murder. An analysis of criminal justice trends suggests that women's offending is because of, or directly related to, their abuse of illicit substances. Further profile analysis of female offenders indicates that when incarcerated, women are more intensively entrenched in their substance use and/or abuse. Women 'have more extensive histories of disability, disadvantage and misfortune' (Kruttschnitt and Gartner 2003: 2) than male offenders.

While rates for women who are being incarcerated are rising drastically across the world, it should be acknowledged that many of these women are from oppressed groups. Female offenders from these oppressed groups such as African Americans and Latinos have a higher rate of overall incarceration and tend to garner longer sentences particularly for violent crimes (Kruttschnitt and Gartner 2003). Another distinction for female offenders is that they are more likely than their male counterparts to be the primary caregiver in their families, with many being single parents. They have a higher prevalence of mental health issues both before and after their involvement with the criminal justice system with diagnoses ranging from depression to trauma (Kruttschnitt and Gartner 2003). Female offenders have a higher rate of abuse histories including verbal and physical abuse and have higher levels of vulnerability to physical maladies such as HIV and AIDS, particularly among Latino and African American populations (Kruttschnitt and Gartner 2003).

Because of their status as primary caregivers, women offenders are more likely than not to have their children used as an external motivator for them to engage in treatment. Women who are seeking to re-establish relationships with their children or to regain custody are subjected to increased pressure from both the penal system and community agencies once released to engage in treatment. They are coerced into treatment to prove their viability as a parent and/ or to prove that they truly are reformed. This reformation is seen as a testament to not only their willingness to conform to societal standards, but also their motivation to remain as parents to their children.

All these issues make women offenders more susceptible to coerced treatment to either avoid incarceration, regain custody of children or to care for their families. As caregivers, women offenders are exposed to multiple avenues by which they can be coerced into treatment. It can begin at the initiation of their involvement in the criminal justice system and can continue well into their reintegration into the community. These sanctions can move along a continuum from threats of incarceration to the sanctions of necessary cash benefits needed to care for their families.

Because of their multiple vulnerabilities, women offenders can be coerced by any number of social control bodies that may or may not have complete information as to their history. They may be coerced into various programmes just because of their offender status. Female offenders who are either involved in criminal justice agencies or other social control bodies may find themselves in front of these entities when they are at their most vulnerable and fearful. They are forced to make decisions that can have lifelong consequences, under duress, leaving female offenders powerless in the face of interactions with those deemed more powerful. It is hoped that with this chapter, practitioners will begin to look at their beliefs about coercion. It is hoped also they will begin to critically look at their practice with women offenders and how coercion impacts on their daily practice and the implications of those practices on both the offender and the practitioner who utilises them.

Defining coercion

The use of coercion is not a new concept. While one may be tempted to view coercion within a single lens it is in fact a complex combination of ideas. To define coercion, all of these variables must be examined objectively by both the practitioner and offender to appropriately plan for and participate in the treatment and services provided in the community. Coerced treatment, which is used interchangeably with a number of terms, most notably mandated treatment, requires the presence of distinct pressures with clear consequences to get individuals to attend treatment (Goldsmith and Latessa 2001: 657).

A comprehensive definition of coercion includes not just the implications of the referral source but also the subjective interpretation of the offender as to whether they feel that they are being coerced. Female offenders who have issues may not believe that they in fact have a choice when they are in front of social control bodies such as judges, parole officers and/or other social service practitioners. When faced with coercion they may not be able to identify the coercion itself, but rather the way that it makes them feel. These feelings, which may be initially identified as resistance, may in fact be the manifestation of their feelings of powerlessness in dealing with a system that seeks to control them and define who they are as individuals. These feelings, which increase and decrease in intensity over time, may be directed at the personification of their oppressor, the worker assigned to their case. This may play a significant role in their ability to accept treatment and to comply with treatment goals.

Polcin (2001) suggests that individuals who are mandated to treatment have different interpretations of that coercion depending upon their status as a legally or non-legally mandated client. In practical terms there is a clear difference between offenders who are legally and non- legally coerced. The most apparent difference between the two defining types of coercion is that legally coerced offenders may be coerced into treatment or other sanctions prior to or after incarceration. They can also be mandated after incarceration as a condition of their parole or their release on probation. Offenders who are struggling with mental health issues can be civilly committed and coerced into treatment or controlled behaviours by hospital or treatment facility workers. Civilly committed offenders, once released to intensive community treatment programmes, may also be coerced by workers attempting to justify their practices as a way of assisting the offender to remain in the community. However, in all of these instances, the prevailing theme of legal coercion is that an offender faces some sort of incarceration or detainment as a consequence of not meeting defined mandates.

The consequences for non-legally coerced offenders in the community may not be as clearly defined as with legally coerced clients. Offenders who have a multitude of biopsychosocial stressors may be coerced into certain behaviours or treatment in a variety of ways. For example, female offenders who have children who have been placed in the foster care system during their incarceration may have to submit to certain mandates in order to gain visitation or to regain custody. Women may be coerced into parenting classes, substance abuse and/or mental health treatment based upon the recommendations of child welfare workers. Whilst coercing women into these mandates, in many instances workers are untrained to provide appropriate assessments of offenders' true treatment needs; they may mandate certain programme sanctions based upon prior or secondary reports of behaviours deemed maladaptive such as substance abuse or criminal involvement. Offenders may also be coerced into programmes or other activities solely on their past history of incarceration and must prove to practitioners that they are in fact viable as parents despite their offending behavior (Rittner and Dozier 2000).

Non-legally mandated offenders can be coerced into controlled behaviours by public assistance programmes in order to receive cash and other benefits. They can be coerced into drug, alcohol and other forms of treatment as a condition of the continued status as an entitlement recipient. While the concept of coercion and the definition of the coercion may be the same, the external motivators, the level and choice of sanctioning by social control bodies may be very different. While at first glance it may appear that offenders who are not legally bound to sanctions and mandates have more choices, this is in fact an illusion. Although they may not face incarceration, they face other forms of sanctions, which for some may be far worse than incarceration.

Implications of coercion for women offenders

Any critical look at coercion must include the implications of the coercion for the person or persons who are experiencing it. Coercive practices can be justified by those who practise them as a way to reach clients who traditionally have been seen as hard to reach, resistant and difficult to engage in treatment. It is thought that these individuals, who are clearly in need of assistance to deal with a multitude of issues – whether they be criminal behaviour, substance abuse or mental health treatment – will not voluntarily engage in treatment due to their inability to recognise either the presence or extent of their problem. These problems are maladaptive and negatively impact not only on the offenders but also on the lives of those around them and – more globally – the community.

It is believed that while offenders are not thought to be initially motivated to seek out treatment, at some point during the treatment process the external motivator of sanctions will eventually give way to a recognition of the extent of their problem and lead to a willingness to change it through treatment and other means (Burke and Gregoire 2007). While the theories are ever present as to the effectiveness of mandated treatment there is in fact conflictual evidence in the literature as to its actual effect on treatment outcomes and retention.

Although there is some dispute in the literature as to the viability of coerced treatment and its impact on treatment outcomes and retention, there is very little attention given to the actual effects of coercion on offenders (Polcin 2001). Coercive practices are thought by many to be an opportunity to improve the quality of life for offenders and those with whom they interact. Society is thought to benefit from offenders who have been through treatment and/or are involved in activities that address such issues as mental illness, substance abuse and poverty.

While these are lofty and amiable expectations there is one concept lost – little thought is given as to how coercive practices may impact on the psychological health of offenders who are coerced both through legal and non-legal mandates. Practitioners who work with coerced offenders must be prepared to deal with the powerlessness that an offender may feel to be coerced into treatment. There is a natural power imbalance built into the therapeutic or helping relationship as the offender is coming in need of assistance, whether defined by the offender or another entity such as the courts.

Bacharach and Baratz (1963) suggest that there are three relational characteristics with this social power. First, there must be a conflict of interest between two or more persons or groups; second, power emerges only if the person actually bows to the source's wishes; and, third, power only exists if the source threatens to use sanctions. This paradigm of power is at the core of coercive practices with women offenders.

During the process of referral, an offender is defined according to their problem by a third party whether it be in the community or within the penal system. They are labelled and treated in line with this label as they navigate throughout the system and that label follows them into the community. They are pressured to commit to treatment to avoid consequences which can include incarceration, the loss of custody or loss of benefits that they need to survive. It stands to reason that female offenders are labelled as they move throughout the penal system and the same labels such as offender, and drug user, follow them into the community. In the community this label plays a role in how the now ex-offender is perceived by social control agencies such as child protection, social service agencies, families and society as a whole. Given their ex-offender status, the women now have even more difficulties in securing employment. Women offenders, who are statistically less educated, are more vulnerable to involvement with social control agencies such as welfare, making them even more vulnerable to coercion in the form of sanctions against their benefits if they fail to comply. Women offenders, who also have higher levels of trauma, may also be more vulnerable because of their mental health status to returning to inpatient hospitals and other treatment facilities due to the stress of re-entry (Davis 2002).

All these factors come to bear with female offenders when they re-enter the community. The pressure of legal or non-legal consequences can define their treatment both therapeutically and behaviourally, combined with feelings of powerlessness. These feelings define the working relationship with practitioners who 'attempt to achieve a therapeutic alliance with their clients, workers who come in contact with these feelings may feel stymied by their client's resistance and feel the urge to evoke coercive power' (Anderson and Levine 1993: 336), based on this emotional response.

This willingness by some practitioners to evoke this coercive power leads to a further divide in the offender–worker relationship. This coercive power may be as small as the withholding of privileges or as intense as the threat of incarceration, if the person does not comply with the practitioner's wishes. The evoking of coercive power negatively affects the offender's self-esteem. It is in this space within the relationship that both the offender and the practitioner are operating from an emotional place versus a place of collaboration. It can also become a missed opportunity for the offender and the practitioner to negotiate ways in which the offender can gain some power within the practitioner and offender relationship.

Further compounding this issue is the fact that the offender's problem is defined not by the offender, but by an outside entity such as a judge, probation officer or child welfare worker. While the offender may be aware that there needs to be some change in their life, to acknowledge this thought to a practitioner is also to acknowledge that perhaps the system is correct about them. The offender may not be ready to acknowledge this issue even if the manifestation of the problem led to their incarceration. Coercion can be seen by some workers as a useful tool to engage resistant individuals into the therapeutic process. While it may be helpful in areas such as retention, it may not be as helpful in others such as overall treatment goal compliance.

Another more concrete perception of client coercion is that the client may feel that no matter how helpful the practitioner may appear to be, they are a part of the oppressing system – the same system that they are either fighting or have seen others have negative experiences of fighting. This is of particular interest to offenders from oppressed populations and speaks to a need for practitioners who work with these offenders to also be versed in culturally competent techniques (NASW 2005). These factors have major implications for clients who are coerced into treatment and can impact not only on the engagement into treatment, but also on active participation in the treatment process.

Practitioners who come into contact with offenders who have been mandated to treatment can have a number of reactions to their resistance. These reactions can include the personalisation of such resistance as something that they have done or that the client is in denial and does not truly want help. Less experienced practitioners may also feel that their ability to help the client is impaired because of the so-called wall of resistance that interferes with the formation of a therapeutic bond with the offender, and may feel ill-equipped to deal with it in the treatment process. Ultimately, in order to appropriately address coercion in treatment, the practitioner must be ready to actively engage the client around their perceptions of the coercion. They will need to identify possible stigmas around the offender's defined problem, the offence committed and their thoughts about their role as both practitioner and an agent of social control.

The offender must decide if the practitioner is in fact an advocate for them and working collaboratively or is part of the system that seeks to further oppress her. It is this decision that impacts on the early efforts to engage women offenders into the treatment process. It must be revisited throughout the course of treatment as both the practitioner and the offender perceptions of each other change as the relationship changes. Practitioners should recognise the feelings of powerlessness that a coerced offender may feel and discuss these openly and honestly to assist clients in processing coercion and developing alternatives to their feelings of powerlessness.

The day-to-day practice of coercion with women offenders

As the numbers of women who become involved with criminal justice systems increase so too does their vulnerability to the coercive power. In looking at the day-to-day practices of coercion, one need look no further than the criminal justice system. A prime example of coercion in day-to-day practice is during the pretrial phase when women who offend are placed in situations in which they have to make choices under duress (Goldsmith and Latessa 2001). Any of these choices are based upon multiple issues such as substance abuse and/or use, prior criminal history, the presence of mental health issues or on their roles as primary caregivers. If the offender decides to enter into custody, she may be compelled to either formally or informally enter treatment while in jail in order to shorten her sentence or to improve her chances with the parole board. She may also be compelled to enter treatment to improve her chances of regaining custody of her children when she is released, if she is a primary caregiver.

If at pretrial the offender decides to enter treatment in lieu of incarceration, she may be compelled to observe certain sanctions as a condition of her release. She may be coerced into entering treatment in lieu of incarceration, which may include drug and alcohol treatment, mental health treatment and other programmes deemed necessary by the courts. In the case of substance abuse treatment, the offender may be compelled to submit to regular urinalysis testing and the disclosure of information to the courts on a regular basis to remain in compliance with her sentence. Many of the programmes that the offender may be compelled to enter are abstinence based with no room for relapse even though by all accounts relapse is a part of the recovery process. The abstinence-based programmes that many jurisdictions rely on may leave some women offenders who are legally mandated to treatment vulnerable to increased supervision or to additional sanctions if they relapse during treatment. The offender who is not legally mandated may be faced with additional sanctions such as being required to work with child protection and social service agencies like public assistance (Flavin 2001).

In the area of mental health the offender may be compelled to enter an intensive treatment programme where she may be coerced into entering psychiatric treatment, and taking psychotropic medication as a part of her sanctioned treatment. In day-to-day interaction with staff she may be coerced into following through with programme recommendations, may have her monies managed and may even have her contact with her family monitored – all in the guise of assisting her to improve her quality of life. Women may have to comply with visits to their homes, disclosure of their records to law enforcement bodies and exposure to increased supervision or hospitalisation for failure to comply. Offenders who are mandated to mental health treatment are more vulnerable to coercion because of the emotional stress they may experience on re-entry into the community. It is during this stressful time that while they may want to reach out for help they are afraid to do so because of mandatory reporting (Anderson and Levine 1993). If the offender is in emotional distress she may be afraid of reporting symptoms of her illness and other psychosocial stressors for fear they will be reported to social control agents, resulting in her being returned to hospital for detainment or, if legally mandated, to prison.

When thinking about the regular use of coercion, no review would be complete without a discussion of the child welfare system.

Women offenders who are primary caregivers are particularly at risk of coercion from the child welfare system because of the statistical correlation between offending and substance abuse (Rittner and Dozier 2000). As previously stated, women are more likely to be the primary caregivers of their family. As the primary caregiver, their behaviour is subjected to more scrutiny by systems outside the home if a child welfare issue arises. Rittner and Dozier (2000) suggest that there is a high correlation between substance abuse, criminal behaviour and child maltreatment. Practitioners who are influenced by the belief that substance abuse, criminal behaviour and child maltreatment go hand in hand may believe that a female offender will at some point place her child at risk. In response, they may feel compelled to evoke coercive practices. While it is not suggested that offenders should not be monitored if they are in a high-risk category, the belief that all offenders who use substances will eventually mistreat their children should not be used as a guidepost for these cases. Each case should be assessed on the facts of the case and not on a belief that may in fact not be applicable to an individual case.

The dual stigma of being an offender and a substance abuser may put workers in these systems in a mindset that the parent needs to be monitored more closely to prevent harm before it happens. Offenders who have a history of substance abuse are routinely coerced into a variety of mandated services, which can include treatment and supervised visitation. The threat of having a child removed from their home is a strong external motivator for an offender to comply with sanctions, whether they agree with the recommendations or not. Once a child is removed, an offender may be even more vulnerable to coercion as the need to do anything that the child welfare officials require in order to have their child returned is an even stronger inducement to participate in mandated services.

Ethical and legal implications of coercive practices

Overall, coercive practices have a major implication with regard to social work ethics. One of the basic tenets of the social work profession is its focus on the concept of self-determination. 'Social Workers respect and promote the rights of clients' self determination and assist clients in their efforts to identify and clarify their goals' (NASW 1996: 5). This is a major barrier for clients who are mandated to treatment in lieu of incarceration. Workers who engage in practice with mandated clients face an ethical dilemma with regard to assisting clients to identify their issues and clarify their goals. Clients may want to work on very specific issues that impact on their lives, but their involvement in the criminal justice system removes many of their treatment choices. Offenders who are mandated to treatment are mandated by legal entities because of an already identified core issue. Substance abuse, for example, may be a core issue, but other core issues may be present as well. While it is understood that a legal entity or social control agent may identify a specific issue for clinical focus, other issues such as lack of education and poverty, which are prevalent among female offenders, may be of less importance in the treatment than the issue that leads to the mandated sanction.

Workers in forensic practice, in particular, may see substance use and criminal behaviour as part of a larger issue. However, as with the offenders, their treatment choices are in large part driven by the recommendations of the mandating body. Practitioners in practice face an ethical dilemma in working with a client whose issues have been identified for them prior to actual engagement in the service planning process. It is a direct contradiction of a worker's ethical responsibility to assist clients to determine and clarify their own goals. In the formation of a truly helpful working alliance, practitioners must have the tools to resolve ethical dilemmas and utilise their knowledge and skills to assist clients in making treatment choices that comply with treatment mandates. However, there is little in their training to assist workers to make these ethical decisions with regard to offender treatment. Rather than a strict focus on the actual mandate for treatment, practitioners working with coerced offenders can work with the offender from a strengths perspective to identify options that they can exercise with regard to the development of treatment tasks and goals.

A related ethical issue may also arise from the dual role of practitioners as a treatment provider and as an agent of social control with mandated clients. 'Despite its important and necessary responsibilities, a question that resurfaces periodically focuses on the potential conflicts and ethical dilemmas: can social workers simultaneously satisfy dual roles of fostering improved functioning and maximum self determination of clients, while promoting the general welfare of society according to ethical principles' (Burman 2004: 197). While social workers have an ethical responsibility with regard to social justice, their work with mandated clients creates a dilemma in respect of the social control aspect of mandates to treatment. The dilemma arises in that the majority of individuals involved in the criminal justice system are from oppressed and vulnerable populations (Burman 2004). Social workers may have difficulty managing the dual roles of being promoters of social justice and carrying out the social control aspect of work with mandated clients. Work with mandated clients in itself shifts the focus from the rights of the individual to the safety of the larger society. The ethical question then becomes: are social workers who practise with coerced clients from oppressed populations acting as agents of continued oppression or as providers of assistance in dealing with oppression – in the form of social control? This duality of roles may be difficult for workers to handle as it has larger implications concerning their professional mission versus their role as members of law enforcement, child welfare workers or entitlements specialists. While this a relevant issue with any population it has a stronger relevancy to those from oppressed groups and their work with practitioners who represent both the helping professions and agents of social control.

Lastly, there are also legal considerations in practice with mandated clients. More and more attention is being focused on risk management (Wild *et al.* 1998). The practitioner working with mandated clients faces an increased possibility of professional liability. This can come in the form of a mandated client engaging in activities that place others at risk, thus increasing the possibility of legal action against the practitioner providing care. This is of particular importance to offenders who are struggling with severe mental health issues and residing in the community. While they are vulnerable to the use of coercion in their care, there is also an increased risk of a female offender putting others at risk at a time of emotional duress. This risk can put practitioners who work with them in line for legal action if the offender does in fact hurt someone. This possible risk may lead some practitioners who work with offenders who are also mentally ill to utilise a higher level of coercive practice to protect themselves from litigation in the guise of protecting the community at large.

Conclusion

The use of coercive practices with women offenders is not a new paradigm. Coercive practices have been utilised for offenders since the early 1800s and appear to have no end in sight (Wild *et al.* 1998). A review of coercion literature suggests that coercion is more prevalent for use in addiction and mental health treatment. However, because of their status as offenders and/or ex-offenders, women are also extremely susceptible to the use of coercion by members of law enforcement agencies, officials of the courts and other systemic practitioners such as child welfare workers. Given the numerous biopsychosocial stressors that females face both during incarceration and after, they are at an increased risk of being coerced into actions that seek to control their behaviour under the guise of improving their quality of life.

While it is hoped that practitioners who work with offenders are mindful of the effects of coercion in their day-to-day practice, ultimately it is societal control that sanctions the use of coercion. Practitioners must make the decision to practise coercion, if necessary, in a way that maintains the offender's sense of self while assisting them to meet mandates that ultimately will lead to a better quality of life after coercion.

References

Anderson, E. and Levine, M. (1993) 'Coercive uses of mandatory reporting in therapeutic relationships', *Behavioral Sciences and the Law*, 11: 335–45.

Bacharach, P. and Baratz, M. (1963) 'Decisions and non decisions: An analytical framework', *American Political Science Review*, 57: 632–43.

Bishop, D. and Frazier, C. (1992) 'Gender bias in juvenile processing: Implications of the JJDP Act', *The Journal of Criminal Law and Criminology*, 82 (4): 1162–86.

Burke, A. and Gregoire, T. (2007) 'Substance abuse treatment outcomes for coerced and non coerced clients', *Health and Social Work*, 32 (1): 7–16.

Burman, S. (2004) 'Revisiting the agent of social control role: Implications for substance abuse treatment', *Journal of Social Work Practice*, 18 (2): 197–210.

Davis, S. (2002) 'Autonomy versus coercion reconciling competing perspectives in community mental health', *Community Mental Health Journal*, 38 (3): 239–50.

Flavin, J. (2001) 'Of punishment and parenthood: Family based social control and the sentencing of black offenders', *Gender and Society*, 15 (4): 611–33.

Goldsmith, J. and Latessa E. (2001) 'Coerced treatment of addictions in the criminal justice system', *Psychiatric Annals*, 31 (11): 657–63.

Kruttschnitt, C. and Gartner, R. (2003) 'Women's imprisonment', *Crime and Justice*, 30: 1–81.

National Association of Social Workers (1996) *NASW Code of Ethics*. Washington, DC: National Association of Social Workers.

National Association of Social Workers (2005) *NASW Standards for Social Work Practice with Clients with Substance Use Disorders*. Washington, DC: National Association of Social Workers.

Polcin, D. (2001) 'Drug and alcohol offenders coerced into treatment: A review of modalities and suggestions for research on social model programs', *Substance Use and Misuse*, 36 (5): 589–608.

Rittner, B. and Dozier, C. (2000) 'Effects of court-ordered substance abuse treatment in child protective service cases', *Social Work*, 45 (2): 131–40.

Roberts, D. (1973) 'The meaning of gender equality in criminal law', *The Journal of Criminal Law and Criminology*, 85 (1): 1–14.

Tedeschi, J.T., Bonoma, T. and Brown, R. (1971) 'A paradigm for the study of coercive power', *Journal of Conflict Resolution*, 15 (2): 187–223.

Wild, C., Newton-Taylor, B. and Alletto, R. (1998) 'Perceived coercion among clients entering substance abuse treatment: Structural and psychological determinants', *Addictive Behaviors*, 23 (1): 81–95.

Chapter 6

Victimisation and governance: Gender-responsive discourses and correctional practice

Shoshana Pollack

Introduction

Canada has become known internationally for having gender-responsive correctional policies for women in federal prisons (Moloney and Moller 2009). However, since the development of the 1990 policy document, *Creating Choices* (Task Force on Federally Sentenced Women 1990), which recommended federal prisons become more sensitive to the ways in which women prisoners are different from male prisoners, it has become quite clear that gender-responsive policy rhetoric does not necessarily lead to substantial changes in how incarcerated women are treated. In fact, many have illustrated that the language of gender sensitivity when deployed by institutions designed to punish and control is simply a new discursive strategy for governing women (Pollack 2000; Pollack and Kendall 2005; McCorkel 2003; McKim 2008; Shaylor 2009; Hannah Moffat 2004).

One of the vehicles by which dominant (masculinised, racialised and classed) correctional norms are transmitted, even when couched within gender-responsive rhetoric, is through risk narratives. Assumptions about risk form the bedrock of correctional practice and thus provide the institutional narratives for both prison and community practice with criminalised[1] people. Institutional narratives of organisations – the ideologies and discourses that shape practice mandates, intervention methods, and perspectives about clients – provide the frameworks for working with people on parole/probation.[2] Work within correctional systems (whether institutional or community) is organised around assessing and managing people's 'riskiness'. Although researchers, activists and scholars have illustrated the racialised, classed and gendered biases inherent in assumptions about riskiness, the taken-for-grantedness of risk narratives in correctional practice remains. Further, proponents of gender responsiveness have not interrogated the risk framework, thereby merely absorbing correctional assumptions about criminal behaviour and 'criminals', into liberal feminist language about gender equality and empowerment.

Drawing upon data from a national qualitative study about women's post-prison experiences in Canada, this chapter illustrates how parole policies construct women who have been abused by men as dangerous or 'at risk' of behaving dangerously. These notions are embedded in parole practices and policies that define who the women are, what they need, and how to 'manage' their 'risk'. While participants in this study spoke of myriad socio-economic obstacles to reintegrating/resettling into their communities, a central story emerged emphasising the role that parole practice plays in compounding their difficulties and perpetuating the gendered arm of social control. Thus these findings offer an important contribution to the literature on women's post-prison experiences since, as Turnbull and Hannah-Moffat (2009: 532) observe, researchers have 'largely ignored how penal techniques are used to govern women and extend the carceral gaze upon release'.

This chapter begins with an examination of the racial and gender biases inherent in assumptions of riskiness and proposes that such critical reflection on practice is an ethical imperative for human service professionals. Findings from a study with women on parole in Canada are then presented, which illustrate the consequences of unreflective adoption of feminist-inspired language without a parallel interrogation of dominant constructions of riskiness. Participants in this study raised epistemic issues in relation to how they are '(un)known' through the institutional narrative of riskiness. Further, data from this study indicate that gendered rhetoric about victimisation and empowerment has led to gender-specific correctional strategies for regulating the 'dangerous victim'.

'The orthodoxy of effective practice': Gendered and racialised implications

Debates about probation training in the UK suggest that in addition to offering skills-based correctional education, programmes also attempt to train probation workers in critical reflection skills (Nellis 2003; Treadwell 2006; Goldhill 2010). The tension in this literature, perhaps best symbolised by the UK's move to separate probation worker training from professional social worker training, seems to be whether people working in probation should be 'skilled technicians' of correctional practice or whether they should be taught theories and critical analysis reflective of the wider field of social service work. In professional social work, the development of critical reflective skills is generally seen as an ethical imperative. These skills include understanding one's 'self'; the beliefs, feelings, experiences, values and identities that we bring to our work. A further component of critical reflection is analytical engagement with social inequalities that shape people's experiences and the ways in which professional practice may reproduce these inequalities through structural, institutional and/or practice approaches (Mandell 2007). Although the field of corrections is not generally a bastion of critical reflexivity, the Diploma in Probation Studies (DipPS) in the UK has attempted to train students in Schön's classic approach to 'the reflective practitioner' in which he outlines two types of reflective thinking: reflection *in* action and reflection *on* action (Schön 1991). According to Goldhill's (2010) evaluation of the DipPS, however, there are structural impediments to operationalising a reflective stance in probation work. In addition to the discomfort of some students with examining their own feelings and values, Goldhill (2010) found that institutional factors posed significant barriers to the student's ability to apply reflective skills to their actual practice. These impediments, resulting from neo-liberal policy and management approaches, included high caseloads, discourses of efficiency and resources, and a focus upon enforcement rather than relationship (Goldhill 2010: 67). In his earlier examination of the UK DipPS, Nellis (2003: 944) similarly points to the barriers that an over focus on managerialism, technical skills and 'the orthodoxy of effective practice' pose to critical thinking skills and reflection on practice.

'The orthodoxy of effective practice' (Nellis 2003: 944), also known as 'what works', relies upon social learning theories of crime and cognitive behaviour models of intervention, both of which underpin risk narratives. The power of this discourse lies, in part, in its claims to be evidence-based and empirically validated (Bonta and Wormith 2007). The desire for a standardised global approach to risk assessment – regardless of national context, culture, gender, race, immigrant or refugee status – also fuels the momentum of risk narratives. Yet, the risk/need assessments utilised in correctional practice have been critiqued for their claims to universality and gender neutrality, the exclusive focus on predictive validity, and for the problematic assumptions about why people come into conflict with the law embedded within them. For example, an energetic debate has recently emerged in regard to using male-based actuarial instruments to assess and manage the risk of criminalised women and racialised groups. For the most part, this literature is quantitative and focuses on the Level of Service Inventory (LSI-R) as well as similar actuarial risk assessment measures, used across many English-speaking jurisdictions to classify and manage criminalised people both in and out of prison. Not surprisingly, the architects of these tools claim predictive validity across gender and race (Bonta and Wormith 2007; Rettinger and Andrews 2010), while others provide evidence of the gender, class and racial biases of these types of instruments (Taylor and Blanchette 2009; Davidson and Chesney-Lind 2009; Brown and Bloom 2008; Turnbull and Hannah-Moffat 2009). The emerging qualitative research in the area illuminates the specific ways in which gender and racial biases are embedded in actuarial instruments that declare they are gender and race neutral. Bramhall and Hudson's (2007) research from the UK, for example, investigated how 201 pre-sentence reports and risk assessment tools constructed the riskiness of Caucasian and Asian men in racialised ways. Although utilising ostensibly objective and race-neutral risk assessment measurements, their research found that in situations where white and Pakistani (predominately Muslim) men were assessed as 'medium risk', probation officers were more likely to recommend community sanctions to white men and prison sanctions for Pakistani men. Their analysis found that racialised stereotypes related to Islam and South Asians led to Pakistani men being scored as more 'risky' and therefore given custodial rather than community sanctions.

In the US, Davidson and Chesney-Lind (2009) conducted a multi-method study examining the gender biases inherent in the LSI-R and concluded that hetero-normative assumptions about men upon which this assessment tool is based decontextualised the meaning of risk for criminalised women. Moreover, their findings suggest that women are penalised (given higher risk ratings) on factors that actually may reflect help-seeking behaviours, such as receiving mental health or addiction treatment. In addition, women may be given lower risk ratings if they are in a relationship, since in many correctional risk assessments involvement in a heterosexual relationship is considered evidence of 'stability'. Given that criminalised women have high rates of being abused by men in intimate relationships, it is concerning that being in a heterosexual relationship lowers assessments of women's risk to reoffend. In fact, risk narratives as embodied within parole decisions 'are based on "idealized lifestyles" that reflect whiteness, heterosexuality, able-bodiedness and middle-class norms' (Turnbull and Hannah-Mofffat 2009: 548). Although standard risk assessments such as the LSI-R do not adequately account for the effects of abuse in women's lives (Davidson and Chesney-Lind 2009), gender-responsive discourses have raised the issue of both childhood and adult abuse as contextual factors in the criminalisation of women. However, risk narratives can transform abuse into risk factors. Hannah-Moffat (2004) analysed parole decision-making processes in regard to women with non-violent criminal convictions. Her findings illustrate that decisions about women's recidivism are often based on how a woman responded to male violence (e.g. whether she used violence against her abuser). She concludes that the omission of an analysis of gender and power in risk narratives not only distorts the dynamics of violence against women but 'formulates a spurious link between resistance in the context of a violent relationship and the potential for violent recidivism' (Hannah-Moffat 2004: 376). This current study on the post-prison experiences of criminalised women contributes to the literature on the racialised, classed and gendered effects of discourses and policies spawned by correctional risk narratives. Findings from this study suggest the need for increased critical reflection upon 'the orthodoxy of effective practice' of risk assessments as well as how feminist-inspired language is co-opted and made complicit in the gendered regulation of criminalised women.

Reintegration of women after prison: the Canadian experience

The purpose of this qualitative study was to examine the experiences of women released from federal prisons in Canada by exploring reintegration from their point of view.[3] Sixty-eight women who had served federal prison[4] sentences were interviewed for this study between 2004 and 2006. The interview questions were open-ended and semi-structured. Women were asked about prison programming and services (including release planning), and about their experiences of being released back into the community. Interviews were between one and one and a half hours long and were tape-recorded with the permission of the participants (two women did not wish to be tape-recorded, and so the interviewer took handwritten notes). The interviews were conducted by the principal investigator (Pollack), a community research partner, and graduate students involved with the project; they took place in halfway houses, individual homes, shelters, treatment centres, and community organisations in eight provinces and 19 cities and towns across Canada. Participants were recruited through individuals and organisations that work with women who have spent time in prison, as well as through some of the participants themselves who, following their own interviews, referred their friends. Participants were paid an honorarium of $40 (Canadian) for their time and expertise. Every effort was made to ensure that women who saw the flyer within the context of service delivery agencies were aware that participation (or not) in the study would in no way affect the services they were receiving. This point, as well as assurances of confidentiality and anonymity, was clearly articulated in an information letter and consent form.

Participants came from a variety of backgrounds and had different types of experiences with the correctional system. In recruiting participants, efforts were made to obtain diversity in living arrangements (e.g. halfway houses, treatment centres, living on one's own), racial and cultural backgrounds, age, lengths of prison sentences (two years to life), time out of prison, and types of parole (e.g. day, full, completed parole).

Forty-one participants were identified as Caucasian (60.3 per cent); 22 (32.3 per cent) as Aboriginal, Métis, or Inuit; and four (5.9 per cent) as black. The racial/ethnic background of one participant was unknown. Fifty participants (73.5 per cent) were sentenced to two to five years in prison; four (5.9 per cent) were sentenced to six to nine years; four (5.9 per cent) were sentenced to 10 to 18 years, and nine (13.2 per cent) had life sentences. The sentence length for one participant was unknown. The age range of participants was 20 to 63 years with a mean age of 38 years. Participants were interviewed in British Columbia (10), Alberta (11), Manitoba (1), Saskatchewan (3), Ontario (18), Quebec (10), Nova Scotia (10) and New Brunswick (5).

The findings discussed here are those pertaining to how women experienced constructions of their riskiness while on parole in the community and the concrete impact of these narratives on their post-prison relationships, opportunities and subjectivities. (For further discussion of this research please see Pollack 2009a, 2009b, 2010). In this chapter I first focus upon the epistemic issue of being '(un)known' through risk narratives that decontextualise women's gendered, racialised and classed realities. This is followed by an examination of the shackling effects of the consequent construction of abused women as 'dangerous victims'.

Being '(un) known': Institutional risk narratives

Data from interviews with criminalised women illustrate the ways in which their subjectivities – assumptions and discourses about who they are (not) and who they should be – pervaded their engagement with correctional professionals (parole officers, halfway house staff, psychologists). Specifically, many participants spoke of how professional narratives about riskiness discounted their own understandings and usurped alternative constructions of their past experiences and present needs. As Julie 1[5] observed, even when prison and/or parole personnel 'come face-to-face with somebody, really face-to-face – they can't even see you.' In many ways, 'not being seen' on an individual level is built directly into the structure of risk assessments. As Garland (1997) points out, risk assessment tools are not individually tailored, but are based upon assumptions about what constitutes riskiness. 'The individual is viewed not as a distinct, unique person, to be studied in depth and known by his or her peculiarities, but rather as a point plotted on an actuarial table' (Garland 1997: 182).

The configuration and implementation of risk assessment practice reflect the ideologies of the institutional setting in which it emerges. The ideological narratives of corrections supersede women's 'primary narratives' (Smith 1990) about their own experiences and needs. Smith (1990) refers to *primary narratives* as one's subjective account of events: how we make sense of our own experience. *Ideological narratives* transform personal accounts into forms that are intelligible to institutional goals and norms. Being 'known' through the ideological narratives of corrections is not only an epistemological erasure but also promotes individualistic and pathologising approaches, which disqualify the effects of structural factors such as racism, poverty and gendered violence. In fact, risk assessment approaches are theoretically grounded upon (derogatory) masculinist assumptions about learned behaviour and antisocial personality characteristics, such as impulsiveness, thrill-seeking, egocentrism, poor self-control and callousness (Bonta and Wormith 2007: 141).

Participants in this study offered various articulations of how risk goes way beyond personality issues and reflects the impact of gendered, racialised and classed inequalities. In discussing the complexities of negotiating her release with very little money and only perfunctory addictions counselling while in prison, Steph explains:

I know that today a woman gets out [of prison] and she doesn't want to use [drugs] but she doesn't have no money either, so she thinks I'll just go turn a trick [work in the sex trade] and make 100 bucks. But as soon as you do, that puts you at higher risk to use because then you feel shitty about yourself and you wanna numb that pain or that ugliness. So you use and then starts the whole cycle. So I mean even having no money, I mean as crazy as it sounds, puts you at risk.

Steph qualifies her statement about the connection between poverty and risk with 'as crazy as it sounds'. Within the correctional context, references to factors that are not individual are heard as a denial of responsibility or as rationalisations for criminal behaviour (Fox 2001). Thus, Steph is in fact offering a 'crazy' alternative that lies beyond the bounds of what can be said within correctional risk discourses.

Policy and programme discourse can influence how those who are subject to its regulation constitute their subjectivity, struggles and goals. In outlining the various tensions within feminist criminology's construction of the female criminalised subject, Snider (2003: 361) questions whether the subjectivity of criminalised women created by feminist 'expert knowers' has 'percolated down the social order to (re)constitute the female offender herself'. She is particularly interested in victimisation discourses, as they have been mobilised by feminists to advocate for improved prison programming and to challenge the demonisation of imprisoned women. Victimisation discourses have indeed percolated down to correctional policy and practice, and criminalised women employ them in various ways to constitute their subjectivity as well as to negotiate and challenge the correctional system. Women are rewarded for reproducing correctional renditions of risk in order to provide evidence of a reformed self; no longer incapable of managing the risk she poses. Self-regulation is often encouraged through the language of self-esteem and empowerment (familiar liberal feminist notions) common to gender-responsive correctional approaches. Within this framework, an empowered criminalised woman is one who takes responsibility for her own risk. The next section discusses how risk narratives merge with feminist-informed empowerment/self-esteem discourses to govern abused women in the community context though the subjectivity of the 'dangerous victim'.

The 'dangerous victim'

Canadian correctional researchers have drawn upon a branch of feminist psychology called relational psychology (now called 'relational-cultural' psychology) to substantiate the assertion that women's psychology should be the foundation upon which gender-specific programming is built (Fortin 2004). Relational-cultural psychology was developed by feminist psychologists at the Stone Center at Wellesley College in Massachusetts, USA, as a way of understanding how women's psychological development differs from that of men. Traditionally, developmental psychological theories have posited that the journey towards mature development is one that culminates in autonomy, independence and separation (Jordan 1997). However, relational-cultural theory argues that women's development differs from the traditional male model of psychological development and asserts that women's sense of self is cultivated through connection rather than separation and is in fact damaged by disconnections. Relational disconnections and violations, such as child abuse, rape and male violence, are thought to render some women susceptible to drug abuse, street life and criminalisation. Using the work of Bloom *et al.* (2003), correctional researchers implicitly connect relational disconnections to women's lawbreaking and thereby construct relationships as risk factors.

Once something becomes equated (either empirically or discursively) with criminal behaviour, it typically becomes, in correctional lexicon, a 'criminogenic factor'. Criminogenic factors are those aspects of an individual that are thought to be linked with criminal behaviour. The recent emergence of relational theory as an organising framework for conceptualising gender-specific programming for women prisoners has become enmeshed with risk discourses that aim to predict and manage women's potential for 'pro-criminal behaviour' (Fortin 2004: 39). Thus, *risk* and *relationships* become entwined.

When asked about their experiences of returning to the community, participants in this study who had been abused by men in intimate relationships stated that they were required to report to their parole officer any new relationships in which they became involved (this appeared to be the case for both heterosexual and lesbian relationships). Quinn, whose criminal charges were *not* in the context of violence against women but who had disclosed to prison correctional officers that she had a history of being abused, stated, 'I have to report all intimate relationships … they think that I have issues around … *intimacy.*' Even if Quinn agreed (which she did not) with the pop psychological notion that she had 'intimacy issues', it is difficult to follow the logistical thread of how the risk apparatus transforms these 'issues' into risk factors for her own criminal activity. Constructing victimisation as intimacy issues not only dramatically undermines the realities of violence against women but also translates into increased regulation. Intimate relationships therefore become a gendered site of surveillance and regulation of the criminal justice system. Tania, for example, states that because she was abused by her ex-husband:

> They want to know about any changes in my relationship with my [current] husband. If we're having problems, they want to know. If we break up, they want to know. Because of my *ex*-husband ... *I'm* being punished for what *he* did to me.

Some of the criteria used to evaluate the impact of a relationship on women's level of risk are whether their partners have been incarcerated and how 'stable' the relationships are deemed to be. Women need to balance their own safety and well-being with the requirements of the risk apparatus in which they are entangled. Dawn, for example, was in a relationship that was abusive, yet felt that her risk level would be elevated should she disclose this information to her parole officer (as this might result in more intensive controls over her life). She decided to stay within an abusive relationship until she was eligible for full parole, at which time she would no longer be required to have her risk (and relationships) intensively monitored:

> [Corrections] says that you have to be stable before you get full parole, and if you don't maintain this relationship and look like you're having a stable type of deal, then guess what's happening? ... and there was a lot of abuse going on. So I'm thinking to myself, 'You know what? Full parole is coming, full parole is coming ... it's going to be OK. As soon as full parole hits, dissolve the relationship.'

Correctional approaches that draw on relational psychology sub-stantiate Dawn's concern. Correctional research asserts that 'the loss of valued relationships play[s] a greater role in female offending' (Bloom *et al.* 2003, as quoted in Fortin 2004: 38). Losing a relationship, perhaps due to experiencing abuse, could then be read by correctional and/or parole staff as increasing a woman's risk of reoffending. Barb's comments reflect the perspective that the loss of a valued relationship puts her at risk of extreme emotions and getting in trouble:

I have to have my relationships monitored … when I get into a relationship, it usually turns abusive and then, I get in trouble. You know, in the long run, I get in trouble, because breaking up is an emotional time for me … I get really angry … I'd get beat up, you know, so I'd turn around, go to the pub and have a few drinks and then jump in my truck and go back home, and bang … I know now, the parts where, you know, everything had to be my way in the relationship and stuff like that. And, it was hard and I would get mad.

Barb's description of herself as angry and as needing everything her way echoes correctional programme and policy documents that stress women's inability to regulate their emotions and control their anger (Pollack and Kendall 2005). That Barb's relationships usually turn abusive and that she would get beaten up is only relevant insofar as it relates to ideas about her risk or getting into trouble. Women's prior behaviour is disconnected from the context of abuse and is taken to mean that *relationships in general* are sites in which they may behave violently.

Women who have defended themselves against male violence are encouraged to see themselves as lacking self-esteem and as violent. As Selma stated:

I'd have to report what kind of relationships I have, because they kind of don't want you to go into a relationship intimately, because they know what's going to happen, you know … like me, for example, once I got into a relationship, that's all I focused on. I didn't focus on getting well, I didn't focus on taking care of me, I didn't focus on, you know, loving me and whatever.

The psychologised risk thinking that permeates correctional practice with criminalised women has concrete policy implications as well as a direct impact on women's articulations of their subjectivity. Dorothy reproduces correctional discourses that link abused women's victimisation with a propensity for violence: 'If we have self-esteem, we're powerful; if we don't love ourselves, we're dangerous.'

Whereas some women reproduced 'dangerous victim' discourses, others offered nuanced attempts to grapple with the complexities of resisting male violence. Sam, for example, was abused in several of her relationships with men, but her criminal charges were unrelated to being abused. Yet she was required to have her relationships monitored because, as she said, 'relationships are bad for me'. She also stated, however, that she 'won't let nobody hurt me ever again', and that she will defend herself physically against 'the next [violent partner] who screws with me'. Sam's comments reflect the importance of contextualising women's responses to violence against women and the problems with correctional invocations of risk discourses. To some degree, Sam sees the logic of monitoring her relationships in that she knows she will defend herself should someone attempt to abuse her. However, it is she who experiences punitive responses to her attempts to protect herself from male violence.

'Gender-responsive' correctional agendas and techno-rational correctional practice

Gender-responsive approaches to working with criminalised women emerged from a recognition that male-based correctional programming was being imported into women's prisons without consideration of women's different experiences of criminalisation and imprisonment. Gains have been made through the scholarship and activism of feminist criminologists who have exposed the gendered and racialised faces of criminalised women's trajectories to and within prison. As outlined above, however, analyses of women's victimisation by men are often transformed into regulatory risk strategies that position past experiences of abuse as risk factors for women's recidivism. Certainly, this is unlikely to be the outcome that feminist activists and scholars envisioned in their analyses of how violence against women and structural marginalisation such as institutional racism and poverty contribute to the criminalisation and imprisonment of women.

Data from this study revealed that criminalised women are shackled to a risk subjectivity devoid of social context or of their own experiential knowledge. This raises an epistemological issue germane to the problematics of risk discourses; that it is not possible to be 'known' as a gendered, classed and racialised subject within the risk frame. Turnbull and Hannah-Moffat (2009) also uncovered the gendered ramification of decontextualised risk narratives in their textual analyses of parole decisions for criminalised women in Canada. They state that:

> Through the decision narratives, the paroled subject is variously positioned as a victim, a follower, a recovering addict, someone who lacks sufficient impulse control and makes poor choices,

and/or someone who suffers from low self-esteem. Her law-breaking is understood not in relation to larger social and material conditions, but as a consequence of her personal failures, which are considered to be her gendered 'risk factors'. (Turnbull and Hannah-Moffat 2009: 5)

As strategies for the regulation of social marginality, risk practices in general are heavily intertwined with therapeutic and quasi-therapeutic discourses and practices. Adaptations of feminist relational psychology have fostered a story about relationships as sites of criminal risk for women rather than viewing violent men as a risk to women (to her safety, opportunities, social connections, etc.). An arsenal of therapeutic programmes may be mobilised to act on the selves of those who have failed to appropriately manage their own risk, in order to 'empower' them to be self-regulating (Cruikshank 1996; Kemshall 2002; Rose 2000). Thus, the concept of *self-regulation* is central to processes of risk management (Kemshall 2002). Correctional discourse and policy – ostensibly gender-specific or women-centred – encourages imprisoned women to think about themselves as relationally deficient; as being unable to 'do' relationships properly, appropriately take care of themselves, even love themselves enough. The reproduction of this discourse fosters self-regulation and compliance with the norms of correctional practice. Thus, as Foucault (1977) has illustrated, the embodied self is rendered a site of self-surveillance.

Increasingly, both within the context of probation and parole work as well as in other areas of human services, a privileging of a managerial technocratic approach to professional practice with a focus on risk and accountability has occurred. Kemshall (2010: 9) argues that 'proceduralism' has 'resulted in a focus on monitoring and information exchange at the expense of understanding, problem solving and client engagement'. These contexts contribute to a 'text box' mentality that takes precedence over critical engagement with ideas, discourse and people (Kemshall 2010: 8). Critical engagement and critical reflection are central components of ethical practice. Working from a 'text box' proceduralist framework is antithetical to client-centred and anti-oppressive human service work. As Butler, Ford and Tregaskis (2007: 292) state, in reference to social work practice in general, workers should:

... allow theoretical and procedural frameworks to act as a resource for reflection and understanding, rather than to restrict the way in which we listen (Schön 1991). In this way there is potential for service users to discover and strengthen their own voices rather than to fit into the available narratives.

Conclusion

This chapter has argued that when the only 'available narrative' for articulating one's experiences is risk-based, criminalised women are bound to correctional stories and policies that perpetuate misinformation about violence against women and sanction women for resisting. Not only should critically reflective correctional practice include anti-oppressive approaches (Nellis 2003) but practitioners should also examine their own perspectives, values and discourses and how probation/parole work may reproduce the very inequalities that inform the criminalisation of women.

Notes

1 I use the term 'criminalised' rather than the commonly used 'offender' to signal state processes and practices rather than a reified identity. As Laberge (1991) pointed out almost two decades ago in reference to women, the term 'criminalised' foregrounds the fact that what and who is considered criminal is socially constructed and based upon socio-historical relationships between the state and particular people and behaviours.
2 Within the Canadian context, 'parole' refers to those on conditional release from *federal* prisons while 'probation' refers to those under *provincial* correctional community supervision. For most of the chapter I use the term 'parole' as I am referring to women who are completing their *federal* sentences in the community.
3 I gratefully acknowledge the Social Sciences and Humanities Research Council of Canada for funding this research.
4 In Canada there are two correctional systems. The federal system is operated by the Correctional Service of Canada, which incarcerates those who receive a prison sentence of two years plus a day. There are 13 provinces and territories in Canada, all of which operate their own correctional facilities that incarcerate people who receive a sentence of less than two years.
5 Women chose pseudonyms for themselves to protect their identity. Two women chose the name 'Julie' and thus I have called them 'Julie 1' and 'Julie 2'.

References

Bloom, B., Owen, B. and Covington, S. (2003) *Research, Practice, and Guiding Principles for Women Offenders: Gender Responsive Strategies*. Washington, DC: US Department of Justice, National Institute of Corrections.

Bonta, J. and Wormith, S. (2007) 'Risk and need assessment', in G. McIvor and P. Raynor (eds) *Developments in Social Work with Offenders*. London: Jessica Kingsley Publishers, pp. 131–52.

Bramhall, G. and Hudson, B. (2007) 'Criminal justice and "risky" masculinities', in K. Hannah-Moffat and P. O'Malley (eds) *Gendered Risks*. New York: Routledge-Cavendish, pp. 127–44.

Brown, M. and Bloom, B. (2008) 'Colonialism and carceral motherhood: Native Hawaiian families under corrections and child welfare control', *Feminist Criminology*, 4 (2): 151–69.

Butler, A., Ford, D. and Tregaskis, C. (2007) 'Who do we think we are?: Self and reflexivity in social work practice', *Qualitative Social Work*, 6 (3): 281–99.

Cruickshank, B. (1996) 'Revolutions within: Self-government and self-esteem', in A. Barry, T. Osborne and N. Rose (eds) *Foucault and Political Reason: Liberalism, Neo-Liberalism and Rationalities of Government*. Chicago: University of Chicago Press.

Davidson, J. and Chesney-Lind, M. (2009) 'Discounting women: Context matters in risk and need assessment', *Critical Criminology*, 12: 221–45.

Fortin, D. (2004) 'A correctional programming strategy for women', *Forum on Corrections Research*, 16 (1): 38–9.

Foucault, M. (1977) *Discipline and Punish: The Birth of the Prison*. New York: Vintage Books.

Fox, K. (2001) 'Self-change and resistance in prison', in J.F. Gubrium and J.A. Holstein (eds) *Institutional Selves: Troubled Identities in a Postmodern World*. Oxford, UK: Oxford University Press, pp. 176–92.

Garland, D. (1997) '"Governmentality" and the problem of crime: Foucault, criminology, sociology', *Theoretical Criminology*, 1 (2): 173–214.

Goldhill, R. (2010) 'Reflective practice and distance learning: problems and potentials for probation training', *Reflective Practice*, 11 (1): 57–70.

Hannah-Moffat, K. (2004) 'Losing ground: Gendered knowledges, parole risk, and responsibility', *Social Politics*, 11 (3): 363–85.

Jordan, J. (1997) 'A relational perspective for understanding women's development', in J. Jordan (ed.) *Women's Growth in Diversity: More Writings from the Stone Center*. New York: Guilford, pp. 9–24.

Kemshall, H. (2002) 'Effective practice in probation: An example of "advanced liberal" responsibilisation', *The Howard Journal*, 41 (1): 41–58.

Kemshall, H. (2010) 'Risk rationalities in contemporary social work policy and practice', *British Journal of Social Work*, 40: 1247–62.

Laberge, D. (1991) 'Women criminality, criminal women, criminalized women? Questions in and for a feminist perspective', *The Journal of Human Justice*, 2 (2): 37–56.

McCorkel, J. (2003) 'Embodied surveillance and the gendering of punishment', *Journal of Contemporary Ethnography*, 32 (1): 41–76.

McKim, A. (2008) '"Getting gut-level": Punishment, gender, and therapeutic governance', *Gender and Society*, 22 (3): 303–23.

Mandell, D. (ed) (2007) *Revisiting the Use of Self: Questioning Professional Identities*. Toronto: Canadian Scholars' Press Inc.

Moloney, K.P. and Moller, L.F. (2009) 'Good practice for mental health programming for women in prison: Reframing the parameters', *Public Health*, 123: 431–3.

Nellis, M. (2003) 'Probation training and the community justice curriculum', *British Journal of Social Work*, 33 (7): 943–59.

Pollack, S. (2000) 'Dependency discourse as social control', in K. Hannah-Moffat and M. Shaw (eds) *An Ideal Prison? Critical Essays on Canadian Women's Imprisonment*. Halifax: Fernwood, pp. 72–81.

Pollack, S. (2009a) '"Circuits of exclusion": Criminalized women's negotiation of community', *Canadian Journal of Community Mental Health*, 18 (1): 83–95.

Pollack, S. (2009b) 'You can't have it both ways: Punishment and treatment of imprisoned women', *Journal of Progressive Human Services*, 20 (2): 112–28.

Pollack, S. (2010) 'Labelling clients "risky": Social work and the neo-liberal welfare state', *British Journal of Social Work*, 40: 1263–78.

Pollack, S. and Kendall, K. (2005) '"Taming the shrew": Regulating prisoners through women-centred mental health programming', *Critical Criminology: An International Journal*, 13 (1): 71–87.

Rettinger, L.J. and Andrews, D.A. (2010) 'General risk and need, gender specificity, and the recidivism of female offenders', *Criminal Justice and Behaviour*, 37 (1): 29–46.

Rose, N. (2000) 'Government and control', *British Journal of Criminology*, 40 (2): 321–39.

Schön, D.A. (1991) *The Reflective Practitioner: How Professionals Think in Action*. Aldershot: Ashgate.

Shaylor, C. (2009) 'Neither kind nor gentle: The perils of "gender responsive justice"', in P. Scraton and J. McCulloch (eds) *The Violence of Incarceration*. London: Routledge, pp. 145–63.

Smith, D. (1990) *The Conceptual Practices of Power: A Feminist Sociology of Knowledge*. Toronto: University of Toronto Press.

Snider, L. (2003) 'Constituting the punishable woman: Atavistic man incarcerates postmodern woman', *British Journal of Criminology*, 43 (2): 354–78.

Task Force on Federally Sentenced Women (1990) *Report of the Task Force on Federally Sentenced Women – Creating Choices*. Ottawa: Ministry of the Solicitor General.

Taylor, K. and Blanchette, K. (2009) 'The women are not wrong: It is the approach that is debatable', *Criminology and Public Policy*, 8 (1): 221–9.

Treadwell, J. (2006) 'Some personal reflections on probation training', *The Howard Journal*, 45 (1): 1–13.

Turnbull, S. and Hannah-Moffat, K. (2009) 'Under these conditions: Gender, parole and the governance of reintegration', *British Journal of Criminology*, 49: 532–51.

Chapter 7

Working with women offenders in the community: A view from England and Wales

Loraine Gelsthorpe

Introduction

As outlined in Chapter 2, responses to women offenders in England and Wales have been reshaped in the past few years to focus more directly on what we know about women's needs, and to divert them from both crime in general and prison specifically. Five particular prompts have led to innovative community-based initiatives: First, an unprecedented rise in the number of women sentenced to imprisonment between the early 1990s and early 2000s (Home Office 2007) with concerns about both the high level of their personal and social needs, and the general failure to address them; second, the establishment of the Women's Offending Reduction Programme (WORP) in 2004 (itself a reflection of the increasing concerns about women and the failure to address their distinctive needs); third, the Equality Act 2006;[1] fourth, a report from Baroness Jean Corston on vulnerable women within the criminal justice system (Corston 2007); and fifth, the setting up of the National Offender Management Service (NOMS) in 2008. The dramatic increases in women's imprisonment, the Women's Offending Reduction Programme, and the Corston Report have all been described in some detail in Chapter 2 of this book, thus I dwell only on the creation of NOMS here. I do so because it has facilitated some of the innovations in the delivery of services that we have seen.

The NOMS emerged from a Correctional Services Review (Carter 2003) to create a single correctional organisation with a primary purpose of reducing reoffending and placing particular emphasis on increased cooperation and coordination between prisons and probation. Informed by ideas from 'New Public Management' (Clarke *et al.* 2000), Lord Carter's vision of correctional services included a probation system underpinned by market competition through a process of what has come to be known as 'contestability' (a synonym for competition). According to the principle of 'contestability', the Probation Trusts[2] would become both part-purchasers and part-providers of services (with NOMS 'Commissioners' being appointed to take on the role of choosing service deliverers). The pros and cons of this restructuring and contestability have been widely debated (Hough *et al.* 2006) but what is of interest here is how this move has facilitated greater links with third sector (voluntary sector) providers, many of whom have a good deal of experience of working with women in the community. Indeed, as will be shown later, the development has led to some imaginative partnerships between women's centres in the community and criminal justice agencies.

Certainly there are exciting developments in England and Wales which deserve a place in this book on the community. In the first section of the chapter I briefly summarise what we know about women and their needs and I address issues relating to the need for gender-specific provision. In the second section I refer to the Fawcett Society's survey of available provision for women offenders in the community and to the challenges for the newly established commissioners of services within NOMS. In the third section I give some examples of important 'ground level' initiatives in England and Wales, and discuss evaluation findings thus far. In the fourth and final section of the chapter I draw out some of the lessons to be learned from various community-based initiatives, and discuss some of the remaining challenges.

What do we know about women offenders in the community from the research literature and from service providers?

Consistent messages from the research literature on women offenders include the fact that women offenders tend to have a history of unmet needs in relation to sexual and violent victimisation, physical and mental health, housing and income, and training and employment. Substance misuse and childcare responsibilities often compound these problems. (See Hedderman 2004 and Gelsthorpe *et al.* 2007 for overviews of the research literature relating to women's 'criminogenic' needs.) Desistance studies serve to highlight the complexity of factors relating to women's pathways into crime and point to the need for broadly based provision that can be individually tailored. (See, for instance, Rumgay 2004a; Carlen 2002; MacRae *et al*. 2006; Malin 2004; Hamlyn and Lewis 2000; Gelsthorpe and Sharpe 2007.) Moreover, service providers highlight a lack of or unsuitable accommodation for women offenders (the application process itself, a shortage of accessible accommodation, and rent arrears all feature here; see Gelsthorpe and Sharpe 2010). Service providers and researchers also support claims that there may well be indirect relationships between abuse and mental health, labour market participation, and substance abuse, all of which are associated with risk of reoffending (Hollin and Palmer 2006a). In other words, 'victimisation' creates psychological sequelae, which can lead to offending behaviour. Consequently, the provision of 'helping' services within a criminal justice framework can be fully justified.

Translating these broad needs into deliverable provision for offenders of course is quite another matter. It has been suggested that it may be important to consider two levels of criminogenic need: first, criminogenic needs experienced by both women and men; and, second, women-specific criminogenic needs (Blanchette 2002) each of which might inform programme interventions and other provisions for women offenders in the community. Even when women and men appear to have similar criminogenic needs, however, the ways in which these intersect may still differ. Moreover, even where there is overlap in needs this still does not mean that they can be or should be addressed in the same way for men and women in the light of evidence to suggest that there are differential ways of learning and differential responses. Let me consider these points further in relation to offending-related programmes.

In England and Wales, there has been no specific evaluation of women's performance on community programmes that are part of Community Orders, to which offenders may be sentenced by the courts. This represents a significant gap in our understanding of effective interventions for women. Indeed, whilst interventions have increasingly been driven by a concern with 'evidence-based practice' these practices are not necessarily responsive to women and their needs (Kaschak 1992; Hollin and Palmer 2006a). The problem is encapsulated very well in the reference to women as 'correctional afterthoughts' (Ross and Fabiano 1986). There are also claims that what works for men will work for women too.

What works for men may work for women too ...

In 2006, Jenny Cann examined the impact of Enhanced Thinking Skills programmes on women, as compared with men, and found that there were no statistically significant differences in the one- and two-year reconviction rates between female offenders who participated in prison-based cognitive skills programmes delivered between 1996 and 2000 and a matched comparison group of men. But leaving the fact that this was a prison-based programme rather than a community-based programme and methodological limitations aside here (targeting the 'purity' of the matched comparison group and so on), Cann acknowledges that there may be an issue around the responsivity of female offenders to cognitive skills programmes. As Anne Worrall (2002) has argued, women who offend are often driven to do so not by 'cognitive behavioural deficits' but by the complexity of the demands placed upon them. Worrall goes on to suggest that '... [women] not only believe that they have few legitimate options, but in reality, they have few positive options. Important as enhanced thinking skills are, they can only be, at best, a prerequisite to empowering women to make better choices, if the choices genuinely exist' (2002: 144). More recent research by Veronica Hollis (2007) has argued that there may be no clear differences between men and women in the impact of General Offending Behaviour Programmes on reconviction rates, although the limitations of the findings on women have to be recognised because of the very small sample sizes and the fact that the findings are not statistically significant. Indeed, the overall effectiveness of the mixed-gender General Offending Behaviour Programme has remained virtually unexamined. Further disappointment comes in relation to the rapid evidence assessment of interventions produced by the Ministry of Justice, which has produced relatively little beyond suggesting that targeting women's antisocial attitudes and general educational needs through interventions might be useful, especially if combined with residential treatment after prison. Yet even these results are limited by the fact that they emerge from just 16 North American and Canadian studies (in the main) and three meta-analyses (Lart *et al.* 2008). Thus without addressing the question of women's performance it is difficult to say whether current programmes meet the Government's expectations that they would reduce women's offending and their moral obligation to do so. It is arguable that there should be a legal obligation too.[3] One recent study has tried to take things forward by exploring women's lower rate of completion on the community-based General Offending

Programme (Martin *et al.* 2009). Compliance is an important step on the way to (but not interchangeable with) non-offending (Lewis *et al.* 2007), making clear that its promotion is important for researchers, policy-makers and providers. The study indicates that despite some similarities, the predictors of programme completion (OASys)[4] not only vary for men and women, but also operate differently between them. The findings support the 'gender-responsiveness' position that men and women should be approached differently, and suggest, moreover, that men are more likely to engage in instrumental compliance and women more likely to achieve normative compliance (Martin *et al.* 2009).

Notwithstanding the fact that we have been somewhat hampered in the task of facilitating gender-responsiveness in programmes and interventions because the state of research and programme development for women generally lags behind that for men, we do in fact know quite a bit about what is likely to work with women.

Different ways of learning and the need for gender-informed responses

Looking more at gender-specific developments, among foundational work on gender and learning is Belenky *et al.*'s *Women's Ways of Knowing* (1986), which argues that women's learning differs from men's learning, both in terms of its developmental sequence and in terms of underlying theory (see also Covington 1998). The researchers suggest that most women prefer to learn in collaborative, rather than competitive, settings. If we put this alongside evidence that suggests that women-only environments facilitate growth and development (Zaplin 1998) we can see that the evidence adds up to a need to work with women in non-authoritarian cooperative settings, where women are empowered to engage in social and personal change. A sound analysis of the 'responsivity' principle conducted by Blanchette and Brown (2006), concerning *how* treatment should be delivered in different criminal justice settings,[5] emphasises not only the importance of matching treatment style to learning styles, but also that alongside structured behavioural interventions case-specific factors should also be addressed. These include 'women-specific' factors such as health care, childcare and mental health together with factors relating to race and gender combined. Certainly, substance abuse treatment effects are thought to be more robust when such factors are conceptualised as responsivity factors (Ashley *et al.* 2003).

On the basis of analysis of work in Canada, Blanchette and Taylor (2009) take us further in advocating the integration of a number of gender-informed theories and methodologies in responses to women. Specifically, they recommend gendered pathways (Salisbury and Van Voorhis 2009), the use of relational theory (Miller 1986), strengths-based approaches (Van Wormer 2001; Worell and Remer 2003), the use of positive psychology (Gillham and Seligman 1999) and use of the 'good lives model' (Ward and Brown 2004), all of which are critical frameworks for intervention with women. We might add to this the need for such interventions to be sensitive to 'trauma' (Messina *et al.* 2007).

With some clear messages from research and service providers on women's needs, and from gender-informed theoretical work, we turn to look at practice on the ground.

Viewing the possibilities

In 2007, the Fawcett Society commissioned a review of community-based provision for women. From a national survey of provision, 120 projects or services for women in the community were identified (Gelsthorpe *et al.* 2007). There was geographical unevenness and many of the projects or services were specific to particular needs such as housing, mental health, drug treatment and advice. Moreover, not all the services identified in the survey specifically worked with women offenders. At the same time, a good deal of the work was clearly innovative, it had evolved intuitively in a way that reflects what research has established as being most likely to work with women, and a good number of those with whom we spoke expressed a willingness to engage with criminal justice partners (funding arrangements permitting) so as to work with women offenders in the future.

Four case studies were looked at in the attempt to weigh up the merits of different kinds of provision and to assess 'what works'. Centre 218 (sponsored by the Scottish Executive and now known simply as '218') has its origins in reviews and consultation processes following a series of suicides in Scotland's only prison for women at Her Majesty's Prison and Young Offender Institution, Cornton Vale. The centre provides residential and non-residential support services for women offenders in Glasgow. It is based on the idea that female offenders should be able to get 'time out' of their normal (and perhaps chaotic and stressful) environments without resorting to 'time in' custody. 218 thus serves as a diversion from prosecution and as an alternative to custody, and more generally it offers particular support (residential or daily – for detoxification and support and outreach to health, social work or housing services). Up to 12 women can be accommodated in the residential unit at any one time (Loucks *et al.* 2006). The ethos is therapeutic in intention and there is much emphasis on providing a safe environment for the women. There are no childcare facilities so as to facilitate a focus on the women themselves. When the centre was set up, there were three main programmes: 'Safe', 'Connections' and 'Loss' (implicitly, if not explicitly, drawing on attachment theory in psychoanalytic thinking) although there have obviously been some adaptations. The work of the centre has been evaluated and continues to find support, although the work has changed shape (Malloch *et al.* 2008). The initial challenges for the centre lay in the area of establishing links with outside agencies so as to facilitate reintegration into the community. Subsequent challenges have revolved around competing objectives, especially between the criminal justice agencies and the more general aims of the centre, to work through the 'Safe', 'Connections' and 'Loss' programmes. Greater criminal justice involvement appears to have come at a cost of losing some of the original ethos, with more focused work on offending behaviour rather than on the general social and personal problems that make women vulnerable, and more probation-led groupwork and less centre staff involvement in the design of programmes. Moreover, the drop-in function has been replaced by more restricted follow-up of just 12 weeks. This is worrying because it may not reflect women's real needs. More worrying still is the fact that the centre has had no real impact on the use of imprisonment; the number of women in prison in Scotland has continued to rise (Malloch *et al.* 2008).

The Asha Women's Centre (West Mercia) is one of three such centres in Worcestershire, England at present; it owes its existence to women-centred work by the local probation service, developed over nine years between 1992–2001. A thematic report by Her Majesty's Inspectorate of Probation in 1991 had criticised probation services for failing to make appropriate provision for women offenders. The local service then developed a non-residential group programme (in effect an empowerment programme) based centrally in women-only premises (Roberts 2002). Controversially, the programme did not achieve 'accredited' status from the Home Office Accreditation Panel in 1996 (arguably because the panel was operating on narrow 'criminogenic' criteria rather than broader criteria, which would have encompassed the women's particular pathways into crime).[6] As a consequence, it was subsequently realised that it might be more appropriately delivered and developed from an independent, voluntary sector setting. The Asha Women's Centre thus opened in 2002 with a grant from the regional crime prevention directorate and is a registered charity that now derives its funding from charitable and statutory sources, including the probation service and the Ministry of Justice. Asha serves around 110 women at any time, including some who are supported by a specific worker for ex-offenders.

The distinctive ethos of the Asha Centre is its generic intake (women only) and its aim to link women isolated by disadvantage to resources that will help them improve their social and economic potential. Probationers involved in the Asha Centre have indicated that it has provided them with considerable support, especially since it facilitates multifaceted, multi-agency provision (Roberts 2002; Rumgay 2004b). The Asha Centre was identified by the Department of Health in 2003 as a model of good practice for women with mental health problems, and in 2005 was one of two initiatives identified by the Home Secretary (the other being Centre 218) as a basis for the development of the Together Women Programme demonstration projects for women offenders and women at risk of offending (see below). Moreover, an early evaluation showed positive effects in terms of reoffending (compared with a custodial sample) (Roberts 2002). However, the Asha Centre experiences the advantages and disadvantages of being a voluntary sector provider. It has the freedom to innovate and pursue promising features of practice. At the same time, funding constraints severely limit how far things can be pursued. Assured levels of funding from health, probation and the local authority (especially children's services) would assist the centre to maintain stability and further develop its activities.

Another case study was the Camden Probation Women's Centre in London, where at the time of the research there was specialist provision for women offenders via a stand-alone offending-related programme (the Women's Programme based on an earlier 'acquisitive crime' programme for women).[7] The programme is based on a Canadian women-specific offending behaviour programme developed by T3 Associates. About four programmes are run each year, including an Aggression Replacement Therapy programme (ART) and an Addressing Substance-Misuse-Related Offending Programme (ASRO) – both programmes designed for men, but adapted for women. The Women's Programme consists of three phases (delivered in 31 two-hour sessions). Phase One is designed to motivate women offenders to think about change by considering the long- and short-term costs and benefits of their behaviour. Phase Two is designed to help offenders prepare for and begin the change process. Phase Three focuses on ways of maintaining change and preventing relapse. Women have to be on a Community Order and to have an Offender Group Reconviction Scale (OGRS) score of 30[8] and above in order to be eligible for the programme. The centre is housed in the basement of a London building in Camden (with separate access) and funded by the London Probation Service. Off-site childcare is paid for by the Probation Service. The programme was evaluated (Lovbakke and Homes 2004) during a pilot period (when it was called the Real Women Programme) but it is not clear whether it has subsequently been evaluated in terms of its effectiveness. At the time of the Fawcett Society Survey in 2007, the key issues appeared to revolve around intermittent referrals, the excessive amount of material used in each session and the guidelines for delivering the material within two-hour sessions. In addition, it has been recognised that there is need to make the language and contents of the materials better suited to a British group of women, the need to inform women about the nature of the programme prior to commencement, the need for tutors to be given better training and practice in running sessions, and the need to inform others involved in the management of the offenders what the programme entails so that they can better support the women following the programme.

The fourth case study was the Cambridge Women's Resources Centre in East Anglia, set up by a group of local women in 1982, with a mission to empower women by providing information, support and training. Again, it has a generic intake (women only) and can provide up to 200 places on the different courses at any one time. The centre comprises a detached two-storey building (and an outside children's play area). It attracts a wide range of women, including those who are unemployed and those who have additional needs (mental health or education) as well as the partners of visiting academics to the two city universities. At the time of the survey, the centre did not know whether any service users were offenders. However, participation in the Fawcett Society Survey later prompted interest in engaging with criminal justice agencies and the Dawn Project was created as a result. The Dawn Project is still in the early phases of implementation and delivery, but involves the two local women's centres in Cambridge and Peterborough working more closely with Probation and Prisons in particular, accepting referrals from these sources and working with women at risk of offending or reoffending,

135

supporting women upon release from prison, and making provision for women offenders on its various courses. An evaluation of the work is under way.

Models of provision: general observations

All four case studies, reflecting very different models of provision and funding, had something to commend them. Indeed, the survey and case studies prompted deep thinking about the pros and cons of different kinds of statutory and voluntary provision and about what would be 'ideal'. Our impressions were that whilst statutory provision can offer more stable funding than voluntary sector provision, the voluntary sector appears to enjoy a greater degree of flexibility and freedom to meet women's real needs. Voluntary organisations also tend to be relatively flexible in their approach, and are able to provide personalised and tailored services as they are developed from the bottom up to respond to their service users. Certainly, narrow eligibility criteria and narrow agency boundaries do not fit well with the complexity of women offenders' lives. Some statutory providers experience a dearth of referrals, which threatens the sustainability of women-offender-specific provision. Voluntary sector provision can be chameleon-like, changing the focus of work to catch funding streams. Too much involvement with statutory agencies can mean a risk of these voluntary agencies losing their distinctive identity and skills base. This may also undermine voluntary agencies' ability to deliver appropriate provision for women because they are anxious not to lose out on contracts and funding. A further challenge to increasing the voluntary and community sector's contribution to the provision of services is the fact that commissioners may not fully understand how the third sector operates. Equally, voluntary sector providers may not understand or be equipped to deal with monitoring and evaluation. Prescriptive contracts may undermine the value that third sector providers can bring through their involvement; a focus on processes and systems rather than outcomes may limit innovation and flexibility in delivery.

Developing provision for women in the community: towards good practice

The main conclusion of the Fawcett Society survey (Gelsthorpe *et al*. 2007) was that ideally, community provision for women that is designed to meet their needs and be flexible enough to address changing needs might be funded by statutory bodies but delivered by voluntary agencies. There was evident capacity within the voluntary sector already working with women to suggest that NOMS might be able to utilise and build on the available provision. As a result of all the findings from the survey and an analysis of previous research we highlighted nine lessons for NOMS commissioners of services charged with the task of deciding upon provision for women offenders in regional and local criminal justice systems.

Nine Lessons

Such provision should:

1 be women-only to foster safety and a sense of community and to enable staff to develop expertise in work with women;

2 integrate offenders with non-offenders so as to normalise women offenders' experiences and facilitate a supportive environment for learning;

3 foster women's empowerment so they gain sufficient self-esteem to directly engage in problem-solving themselves, and feel motivated to seek appropriate employment;

4 utilise what is known about the effective learning styles with women;

5 take a holistic and practical stance to helping women to address social problems that may be linked to their offending;

6 facilitate links with mainstream agencies, especially health, debt advice and counselling;

7 have capacity and flexibility to allow women to return for 'top ups' or continued support and development where required;

8 ensure that women have a supportive milieu or mentor to whom they can turn when they have completed any offender-related programmes, since personal care is likely to be as important as any direct input addressing offending behaviour;

9 provide women with practical help with transport and childcare so that they can maintain their involvement in the centre or programme.

We also identified nine challenges for NOMS commissioners of services in the hope that this would encourage them to think creatively about the possibilities of community provision for women, using third sector organisations where appropriate.

Nine questions for commissioners of services

1 What is available within the NOMS region specifically for women (including young women, ethnic minority women, older women and other disadvantaged women)?

2 To what extent could existing provision for women be utilised for women offenders? Are there useful partnerships that could be forged between agencies to help address women offenders' needs (including both intra and inter voluntary and statutory provision)?

3 In what ways could any barriers to working with women who offend, within existing service provision, be addressed and overcome?

4 Do any of the potential service providers have a stable setting or building which might be used as a base for women's services?

5 Would other users in the same setting enhance or militate against effective work with women? (For example, Women's Aid or counselling might enhance work with women; a motorcycle maintenance class for men might militate against effective work since women might be afraid to enter the building.)

6 Is there appropriate childcare provision? If not, could childcare provision be created?

7 Is the building or setting easily accessible and otherwise conducive to women's needs? Could transport be provided?

8 Does the project initiate styles of working with service users which are conducive to women's learning needs?

9 Does it provide opportunities for women to be integrated within non-offending groups?

An overview of new initiatives

As will be clear, there has been considerable momentum to create appropriate provision for women offenders in the community over the past few years. Centre 218, The Asha Centre, the Women's Offending Reduction Programme, the Fawcett Society survey of provision and challenges for NOMS, combined with the creation of NOMS itself, and of course the Corston Report of 2007, have all featured in the developments. One might say that there have been both 'top down' and 'bottom up' imperatives for change.

As indicated in Chapter 2, in March 2005 the Home Secretary announced that there would be provision of £9.15 million for the Together Women Programme (TWP) for two demonstration projects for women offenders and those at risk of offending. Ministry of Justice policy frameworks and good practice guides have followed (Ministry of Justice 2008a, 2008b). During 2009 alone, the Ministry of Justice committed over £25 million to voluntary organisations to take the lead in working with statutory agencies to provide extra and enhanced community support for women at risk of offending. To maintain the momentum, between September 2009 and January 2010 the Government Equalities Office organised ten 'Women in Focus' events in the regions, each of them bringing together statutory and third sector (voluntary) agencies to consider how best to work together to divert women away from crime (Ministry of Justice 2010a).

In working towards a conclusion, I now turn to observations on how matters have been working out in practice in relation to the TWP and other new initiatives on the ground.

Together Women[9]

Together Women, as the Government's demonstration programme, and funded for three years on this basis, began operating between late 2006 and early 2007 at five centres in two areas in England: the North-West, and Yorkshire and Humberside National Offender Management Service (NOMS). Whilst the approaches in the two areas have been different, they have shared the stated objectives of Together Women to offer a one-stop-shop centre that would provide holistic and individual support packages for women to reduce reoffending and to divert 'women at risk' of offending from becoming offenders. Secondary aims are to divert women offenders from prosecution and custody. Although the exact range of support varies slightly between the five centres according to local demand and partnership arrangements, provision for women includes training on such issues as parenting, managing mental health, life skills, thinking skills, and addressing offending behaviour. Each (women-only) centre holds surgeries covering a range of issues (relating to benefits, housing and so on) but also functions as a drop-in centre where women can access activities such as reading groups and complementary therapies. Together Women aims to identify gaps in provision and fill them; it also seeks to link up and extend local services without duplicating them. The Yorkshire and Humberside approach was delivered by one supplier, a consortium of five voluntary organisations with various strengths, and one of the one-stop shops was developed from an existing women's centre; in the North-West two separate providers run the centres – each with different strengths and local links. An overall summary of Together Women (Jackson 2009) drew on the nine lessons identified in the Fawcett Society Report (Gelsthorpe *et al.* 2007) and on an early evaluation of the implementation of TWP (Hedderman *et al.* 2008) with the following observations and conclusions:

- *Women only space* This has received very positive feedback (especially among women who have experienced domestic violence). There has been local adaptation so as to facilitate access for suppliers and contract managers (e.g. by either restricting the 'women only space' to certain hours or by managing the issue sensitively by making women aware and asking for their consent whenever there are male visitors).

- *Drop-in and peer support* Another principle relates to women being allowed 'top ups' of support. From the outset, the centres involved in Together Women have functioned as drop-in centres to reinforce the structured services available. This facilitates both problem sharing and problem resolution via peer support. Some of the services that centres have been able to offer include internet access, breakfast clubs, and promotional material. Service user meetings and focus groups also serve to reinforce the philosophy and practice of the centres.

- *One-stop shop* In practice, as well as delivering a number of services in this way, (which obviously makes it easier for women with complex needs, children, and little money) it seems that Together Women has proved to be as much about encouraging women to attend and engage with the most appropriate services – even if outside the centres – and key worker and mentor/volunteer support has been crucial to this. Work based in the centres would arguably benefit from greater statutory health provision, especially in relation to mental health and substance misuse. Needless to say, services that are delivered from a variety of providers and sectors, in different locations, with different specialisms and with different funding arrangements, is an exceedingly complex undertaking. One centre was able to attract a general practitioner and nurse to work at the centre for two days a week, with positive effects in terms of increasing women's confidence in using other local services.

- *Other outside services* When services such as Debt Advice, Legal Advice and Domestic Violence Support are provided, women are seemingly more inclined to use them when they are readily accessible. As Jackson (2009: 11) describes, 'What is proving particularly effective is not just the signposting and "hand holding" into other services but those services having a "face" or a presence within Together Women which increases women's confidence in that service and encourages them to attend the service on another site.'

- *Holistic support* The 'wraparound' service for each woman involved in Together Women starts with a robust needs assessment covering: accommodation, substance misuse, poverty and debt, children and families, employment and education, mental and physical health, domestic abuse, and prostitution. The assessment is converted into a support plan, which is reviewed every six weeks to measure progress and track changes. The 'wraparound' service has proved to be particularly successful with Probation clients who have attended the centres for standard appointments connected with their Community Order, but then have chosen to engage with other aspects of the centres' provision as well.

- *Empowering and enabling culture* The centres have been established and marketed with a positive culture, so that those using or visiting the centres can see that the environment and service are enabling and empowering. Working in this kind of culture and spirit also makes for good teamwork (among key workers, crèche workers, mentors, volunteers, managers, external providers and reception staff) and service users have reported that they feel attached to the centre rather than just to individuals. The approach also avoids the difficulties that may occur where there is strong attachment to a particular staff member who then leaves.

- *Mentors and volunteers* Volunteers and mentors appear to play a key role in supporting the work of the centres and in supporting women (accompanying them on outside appointments for instance).

They also encourage women to maintain the changes they have made and act as a link between the women and the centre; this role supports confidence-building and skills development when the woman has begun to complete some tasks on her support plan. Some service users have gone on to train as mentors and volunteers.

- *Practical and emotional support* Counselling has proved to be in high demand, but the type of support and advice offered can range from budgeting and cooking to personal hygiene. There are structured group work programmes that promote self-esteem and self-worth, but in practice these aims are woven into the culture and philosophy of the centres and not confined to the group work.

- *Multi-agency provision* Probation partnerships – with probation staff using the centres for appointments with offenders – have reduced the rate of breaches for non-attendance. In one area there is a prison partnership where a Together Women Programme worker is based full-time in a women's prison. The worker delivers services to women in custody and thus increases the chances of engagement with the centre upon release.

- *Voluntary sector involvement* The evidence thus far is that Together Women benefits from being led by third sector (voluntary sector) organisations. Women feel less stigmatised than they do when being involved directly with the criminal justice system.

- *Mix of women eligible* The focus on women offenders alongside other vulnerable women has served to promote the idea of the Together Women work being for women, and not just a reducing reoffending project. It is thought that the mix of clients has allowed the women to challenge their perceptions of themselves and each other; and, indeed agency perceptions of the women have been challenged too.

- *Peer support* Some of the centres have been able to create service user meetings and focus groups alongside welcoming breakfast clubs and internet access, all of which serve to reinforce the philosophy and practice of the centres.

- *Children and families* The initial plans were to offer crèche facilities to increase women's access to the centres and their services (mirroring the practice at Centre 218 in Glasgow). However, work relating to children and parenting has become a major focus of the work in the centres (direct positive play with children under eight years, parenting skills, healthy eating, teenage pregnancy and other health information). Staff in the centres have also worked in partnership with a range of agencies to deliver services to women and their children, including Surestart, Children's Services, and Education and Health providers. In some cases staff have been able to work with the mothers and agencies to facilitate mothers and children being 'reunited' after the mother has been imprisoned.

• *Education* Women have also had access to education through taster sessions within the centres, and through group work on parenting, self-esteem and confidence-building, motivation and thinking skills, managing money and coping with loss (a significant feature of vulnerable women's lives).

Concluding reflections: What works with women offenders in the community?

The emerging evidence on Together Women is thus very positive in relation to 'what works'. Certainly TW has received very positive feedback from both service users and local stakeholders. However, as the evaluators (Hedderman *et al.* 2008) have argued, there is arguably further to go in making explicit exactly how TW has impacted, particularly in relation to outcome measures, whether this be contact that involves outside agencies, or indeed in relation to 'models of change'; in essence the work with women is under-theorised. Work with women that addresses criminogenic needs (in both narrow and broad senses) obviously has to demonstrate how the 'broad' work relating to social and personal needs impacts on women's pathways into crime. For the most part, the changes recorded on the Together Women database reflect key worker assessments of change.[10] Moreover, there are no comparison or control groups being followed up (e.g. non-starters following referral to the Together Women centres or non-completion). The difficulty of measuring change is perhaps compounded by the fact that it is invariably difficult to measure change within 'individually tailored' support plans, especially when aims and targets may change (Hedderman *et al.* 2008). The involvement of the evaluators after Together Women became operational also meant that the database was limited in relation to research purposes (although fine for management purposes), and the variation in data collection mechanisms across the centres has also constrained research on the impact of Together Women (Hedderman *et al.* 2008). The evaluation team has also reported that interviews with magistrates and court legal advisors suggest that Together Women's aim of diverting women from custody is not yet being achieved, despite programme staff believing that they were achieving this. Certainly the project has been welcomed by service users and one year into the project, service users felt very positive about the assistance being provided (Hedderman *et al.* 2008).

There have been many other initiatives beyond Together Women. For instance, the Women's Turnaround Project (WTP), set up in Cardiff in 2007 for NOMS CYMRU (Wales) and evaluated 18 months into its existence, showed clear evidence of high demand for the services offered and a general welcome for the resource (Holloway and Brookman 2008). Having functioned for many years as a generic Women's Centre, in May 2007 Calderdale Women's Centre (again in Yorkshire) was funded by a charitable organisation (The Tudor Trust) to develop and demonstrate its approach to work with women offenders. The Evolve project (Calderdale) was set up as a result and funded to run for two years. The project aimed to provide integrated individualised packages of support and intervention for women offenders and women at risk of offending in the area. In adopting Baroness Corston's notion of a one-stop shop Evolve aimed, in the long term, to reduce the likelihood of reoffending and to achieve positive outcomes for women. Evolve has involved providing intensive individual support to women offenders (only), some of whom have been in prison. From an evaluation report by Nacro (2009), the key findings were that the women accessing Evolve had all significantly improved in their personal, domestic and socio-economic circumstances; many had achieved change in relation to skills development, strengthened relationships with children, and improved self-esteem, and had reduced the likelihood of reoffending through holistic support.

Looking around at the various developments in the regions,[11] we are reminded of the need for effective communication between agencies involved (health and housing included); the need to recognise women's children in provisions, and the fact that what women pick up on, what really counts, is genuineness of efforts and concerns. We also need to avoid confusions between *women-centred* and *women-only* provision. If there is dedicated space or if there are dedicated days for women in a centre, that may be perfectly acceptable, depending on what the other activities are, of course. In one initiative, the providers were so intent on a new one-stop shop for women being in a single-use building, women only, that it sat unused for some months, because whilst the funding paid for one project worker, health and safety rules required two workers in the building at all times. One-stop shops were always meant to be creative networks too, and thus there is scope to think about dispersed provision and outreach, and not just activities within a single building. The initiatives have also prompted learning anew that newly forged partnerships need some working out; it is important to recognise different working cultures, and sort out different working practices from the outset; it takes time to develop trust (more frequent meetings in the beginning stages of partnerships are thus helpful). Some voluntary organisations are also so used to functioning on a crisis intervention basis and 'hand to mouth' existence that the notion of business plans and planned provision has come as a shock. We also know that monitoring and evaluation are important for quality assurance purposes and to help secure continued funding. Following up women in this regard is challenging and requires particular effort; one has to work at the relationships. More than this we know that supporting women in the development of new scripts for survival, and new identity, means establishing the right ethos across the piece – including the courts if a woman reoffends – so that they know what efforts the woman has been making and what the team aims are across the agencies involved. With these further lessons in mind there is a good deal of optimism about achieving changes in practice.

A Government website – *Link Up Link In*[12] – provides examples of best practice case studies and useful guidance on collaboration and working with vulnerable client groups. It is also thought that Problem-Solving Courts might be an effective means of addressing the needs of women offenders, following the development of specialist Drug Courts and Mental Health Courts. Moreover, it is anticipated that the use of the Conditional Caution to refer low-level, low-risk women offenders to a women's centre such as those described above will be an effective way of ensuring commitment from the criminal justice system, and an effective way of addressing women's needs. In this context the condition attached to the caution (which is a pre-court disposal) commits a woman offender to attend a women's centre for a full needs assessment. A full evaluation report is shortly to be published, but the pilots indicate that the initial findings are promising in terms of linking women in to the centres, with many of them continuing to engage with the centres on a voluntary basis after the completion of their assessment, which thus provides them with an opportunity to address the causes of their offending.

Finally, notwithstanding the fact that the Government has baulked at the suggestion that women's prisons should be used as a very last resort, it is also important to mention that the Ministry of Justice has committed £300,000 per year (for three years) to develop a demonstration project in Bristol, Eden House,[13] piloting an integrated approach to women offenders and providing access to a range of community-based *and* residential services (not unlike Centre 218 in Glasgow). The possibility of *residential* units for women in the community then may be nearer in sight than first imagined.

In reviewing policy developments in England and Wales, Carol Hedderman (see Chapter 2 of this book) rightly draws attention to the positive steps forward and rightly observes that there is need to take account of other activities that may undermine these activities, notably the expansion of sentencing powers. In reviewing practical initiatives on the ground in this chapter, there is much cause for optimism that some things are definitely working for women offenders, but there are also some cautionary lessons. Women offenders were in focus for the latter part of the Labour Government's tenure, but there is anxiety as to whether this will hold in a criminal justice system so readily shaped by political and economic priorities of the day.

Notes

1 Public sector equality duties (regarding religion, race, disability and so on) are developing apace in the United Kingdom. A key part of the Equality Act 2006 was the 'gender duty', which brought equality issues concerning women in line with other public sector equality duties. In particular, the legislation promoted the introduction of Gender Impact Assessments (GIA). This is a move that highlighted the need to give further attention to what works for women in sentencing because equality of treatment need not be equated with the same treatment. The Equality Act 2010 harmonises previous equality legislation; public sector duties will come into place in April 2011.

2 Following the Management of Offenders Act 2007, Probation *Services* have became Probation *Trusts*.

3 It is arguable that there should be under the Equality Act 2010 of course, but forays into other areas of law which could be used to support the idea of a legal obligation on the part of Government to sentence offenders only to interventions that 'work' have been all too rare.

4 OASys is a comprehensive assessment tool used by probation staff and others to determine levels of risk and need for each offender.

5 Blanchette and Brown (2006) refer to 'treatment', but it is perhaps questionable as to whether or not the language of service provision

should in fact be a language of 'treatment'. Comment and observations from those working with women on the ground suggest that terms such as enabling, training and facilitating may be more helpful and have fewer (pathological) connotations.

6 The Correctional Services Accreditation Panel (as it is now known, having had previous titles) was set up by the Home Office and the Prison Service in 1999 as part of the Government's Crime Reduction Programme. It is a non-departmental public body. Essentially, its role is to accredit offender treatment programmes against a set of 'what works' principles for prison and probation services to use in reducing reoffending. The principal aim of the accreditation process is to produce a core curriculum of demonstrably effective programmes.

7 This is the only accredited programme for women. Whilst the nationally recognised accreditation programme has meant some benefits and standardisation, the criteria upon which accreditation is based have come under criticism for not addressing women's distinctive needs in an appropriate manner (Hollin and Palmer 2006b).

8 A high-risk score is 72 plus; a score of 20–37 means low risk.

9 The Together Women Programme is more commonly referred to as 'Together Women' by those actively involved in its delivery. This reflects the fact that it has little in common with other programmes for offenders in that it does not involve a manual, and it does not involve predetermined levels of risk or need.

10 In West Yorkshire, there is an attempt to examine TW assessments with OASys and probation officer assessments on a small subsample of women offenders in order to check the validity of TW assessments.

11 See the Ministry of Justice (2010b) *A Guide to the Women's Community Projects*.

12 http://www.hmg.gov.uk/linkuplinkin.aspx.

13 The Eden House Project provides both a day support service and a residential service for women offenders, including, but not exclusive to, ex-prisoners. Service delivery commenced in August 2009, with the first residential service users moving there in October 2009. Personal communication with Eden House's project manager in November 2009 indicated that the project can cater for 12 women *and their children* living in single or shared rooms in a single residential site with 24-hour staff cover. The residential aspect of the project provides a high level of support for women (ex-) offenders at medium or high risk of reoffending and with complex needs, including those with dependent children. No children had been involved in the project at the time of the communication (by which time five women were resident at the project), although there were pregnant women service users whose babies were expected to reside in Eden House. The project intends gradually to accept women with babies, and then women with dependent children up to the age of 12 years. See http://www.edenhouseproject.org/

References

Ashley, O., Marsden, M. and Brady, T. (2003) 'Effectiveness of substance abuse treatment programming for women: A Review', *American Journal of Drug and Alcohol Abuse*, 29: 19–53.

Belenky, M., Clinchy, B., Goldberger, N. and Tarule, J. (1986) *Women's Ways of Knowing*. New York: Basic Books.

Blanchette, K. (2002) 'Classifying female offenders for effective intervention: Application of the case-based principles of risk and need', *Forum on Corrections Research*, 14: 31–5.

Blanchette, K. and Brown, S. (2006) *The Assessment and Treatment of Women Offenders*. Chichester: John Wiley and Sons.

Blanchette, K. and Taylor, K. (2009) 'Reintegration of female offenders: Perspectives on "what works"', *Corrections Today*, 71 (6).

Cann, J. (2006) *Cognitive Skills Programmes: Impact on Reducing Reconviction Among a Sample of Female Prisoners*. Home Office Research Findings 276. London: Home Office Research Study 277.

Carlen, P. (2002) *Women and Punishment. The Struggle for Justice*. Cullompton: Willan Publishing.

Carter, P. (2003) *Managing Offenders, Reducing Crime: A New Approach*. London: Prime Minister's Strategy Unit.

Clarke, J., Gewirtz, S. and McLaughlin, E. (2000) *New Managerialism. New Welfare?* London: SAGE in association with the Open University.

Corston, J. (2007) *The Corston Report: A Report by Baroness Jean Corston of a Review of Women with Particular Vulnerabilities in the Criminal Justice System*. London: Home Office.

Covington, S. (1998) 'The relational theory of women's psychological development: Implications for the criminal justice system', in R. Zaplin (ed.) *Female Offenders: Critical Perspectives and Effective Interventions*. Gaithersburg, Maryland: Aspen Publishers, Inc.

Fawcett Society (2004) *Women and the Criminal Justice System. A Report of the Fawcett Society's Commission on Women and the Criminal Justice System*. London: Fawcett Society.

Gelsthorpe, L. and Sharpe, G. (2007) 'Women and Resettlement', in A. Hucklesby and L. Hagley-Dickinson (eds) *Prisoner Resettlement. Policy and Practice*. Cullompton: Willan Publishing.

Gelsthorpe, L. and Sharpe, G. (2010) *The Re-Unite Project. Early Development Phase Evaluation Report*. London: Commonwealth Housing.

Gelsthorpe, L., Sharpe, G. and Roberts, J. (2007). *Provision for Women Offenders in the Community*. London: The Fawcett Society. (See www.fawcettsociety.org.uk)

Gillham, J. and Seligman, M. (1999) 'Footsteps on the road to a positive psychology', *Behaviour Research and Therapy*, 37 (Supplement 1): S163–S173.

Hamlyn, B. and Lewis, D. (2000) *Women Prisoners: A Survey of their Work and Training Experiences in Custody and on Release*. Home Office Research Study 208. London: Home Office.

Hedderman, C. (2004) 'Why are more women being sentenced to custody?', in G. McIvor (ed.) *Women Who Offend*. London: Jessica Kingsley.

Hedderman, C., Palmer, E. and Hollin, C. with the assistance of Gunby, C., Shelton, N. and Askari, M. (2008) *Implementing services for women offenders and those 'at risk' of offending: Action research with Together Women*. Ministry of Justice Research Series 12/08.

Hollin, C. and Palmer, E. (2006a) 'Criminogenic need and women offenders: A critique of the literature', *Legal and Criminological Psychology*, 11: 179–95.

Hollin, C. and Palmer, E. (eds) (2006b) *Offending Behaviour Programmes. Development, application, and controversies*. Chichester: Wiley.

Hollis, V. (2007) *Reconviction Analysis IAPS*. London: RDS/NOMS (December 2007).

Holloway, K. and Brookman, F. (2008) *An Evaluation of the Women's Turnaround Project*. Report prepared for NOMS CYMRU. University of Glamorgan, Pontypridd: Centre for Criminology.

Home Office (2007) *Sentencing Statistics 2005 England and Wales*. Home Office Statistical Bulletin 03/07. London: Home Office.

Hough, M., Allen, R. and Padel, U. (2006) *Reshaping Probation and Prisons. The New Offender Management Framework*. University of Bristol: The Policy Press.

Jackson, M. (2009) *Together Women Project. Key Lessons Learned to Date*. Report. London: Ministry of Justice.

Kaschak, E. (1992) *Engendered Lives: A New Psychology of Women's Experience*. New York: Basic Books.

Lart, R., Pantazis, C., Pemberton, S., Turner, W. and Almeida, C. (2008) *Interventions Aimed at Reducing Re-offending in Female Offenders: A Rapid Evidence Assessment (REA)*, Ministry of Justice Research Series 8/08. London: Ministry of Justice, NOMS.

Lewis, S., Maguire, M., Raynor, P., Vanstone, M. and Vennard, J. (2007) 'What Works in Resettlement? Findings from seven pathfinders for short-term prisoners in England and Wales', *Criminology and Criminal Justice: An International Journal*, 7: 33–53.

Loucks, N., Malloch, M., McIvor, G. and Gelsthorpe, L. (2006). *Evaluation of the 218 Centre*. Edinburgh: Scottish Executive Social Research.

Lovbakke, J. and Homes, A. (2004) *Focus on Female Offenders: The Real Women Programme – Probation Service Pilot*. Home Office Development and Practice Report 18. London: Home Office.

MacRae, R., McIvor, G., Malloch, M., Barry, M. and Murray, L. (2006) *Evaluation of the Scottish Prison Service Transitional Care Initiative*. Edinburgh: Scottish Executive Social Research.

Malin, S. (2004) *Supporting People: Good News for Women Ex-Prisoners?* Research Paper 2004/1. London: The Griffins Society.

Malloch, M., McIvor, G. and Loucks, N. (2008) '"Time Out" for women: Innovation in Scotland in a context of change', *Howard Journal of Criminal Justice*, 47 (4): 383–99.

Martin, J., Kautt, P. and Gelsthorpe, L. (2009) 'What works for women?: A comparison of community-based general offending programme completion', *British Journal of Criminology*, 49 (6): 879–99.

Messina, N., Grella, C., Burdon, W. and Prendergast, M. (2007) 'Childhood adverse events and current traumatic distress: A comparison of men and women drug-dependent prisoners', *Criminal Justice and Behavior*, 34 (11): 1385–1401.

Miller, J. (1986) 'What do we mean by relationships?' *Work in Progress No. 33*. Wellesley, Mass.: Stone Center, Working Paper Series.

Ministry of Justice/NOMS (2008a) *National Service Framework. Improving Services to Women Offenders*. London: Ministry of Justice.

Ministry of Justice (2008b) *Offender Management Guide to Working with Women*. London: Ministry of Justice, NOMS.

Ministry of Justice (2010a) *Women in Focus: Promoting equality and positive practice*. London: Ministry of Justice, Government Equalities Office.

Ministry of Justice (2010b) *Government's Strategy to Divert Women Away from Crime: A Guide to the Women's Community Projects*. London: Ministry of Justice.

Nacro (2009) *Evaluation of the Evolve Project*. London: Nacro (Prisons and Resettlement Research).

Roberts, J. (2002) 'Women-centred: The West Mercia community-based programme for women offenders', in P. Carlen (ed.) *Women and Punishment: The Struggle for Justice*. Cullompton: Willan Publishing.

Ross, R. and Fabiano, E. (1986) *Female Offenders: Correctional Afterthoughts*. Jefferson, NC: McFarland.

Rumgay, J. (2004a) 'Scripts for safer survival: Pathways out of female crime', *Howard Journal of Criminal Justice*, 43: 405–19.

Rumgay, J. (2004b) *The Asha Centre: Report of an Evaluation*. Worcester: Asha Centre.

Salisbury, E. and Van Voorhis, P. (2009) 'Gendered pathways: A quantitative investigation of women probationers' paths to incarceration', *Criminal Justice and Behavior*, 36 (6): 541–66.

Van Wormer, K. (2001) *Counseling Female Offenders and Victims: A Strengths-based Approach*. New York: Springer.

Ward, T. and Brown, M. (2004) 'The good lives model and conceptual issues in offender rehabilitation', *Psychology, Crime and Law*, 10 (3): 243–57.

Worell, J. and Remer, P. (2003) *Feminist Perspectives in Therapy: Empowering Diverse Women* (2nd edn). Hoboken, NJ: John Wiley and Sons.

Worrall, A. (2002) 'Rendering women punishable: The making of a penal crisis', in P. Carlen (ed.) *Women and Punishment: The Struggle for Justice*. Cullompton: Willan Publishing.

Zaplin, R. (ed.) (1998) *Female Offenders. Critical Perspectives and Effective Interventions*. Gaithersburg, Maryland: Aspen Publishers.

Chapter 8

Beyond youth justice: Working with girls and young women who offend

Gilly Sharpe

Introduction

In recent years frequent reports that young women's offending, and especially their violence, is escalating have led to calls that more must be done to tackle the growing 'problem' of girls' offending behaviour. However, neither youth justice policy nor academic study of youth justice practice has paid any serious attention to young women. This chapter begins by analysing recent trends in the criminalisation and punishment of young women and argues that it is principally changes in police and court processing that have inflated girls' official crime rates and propelled them into the youth justice system. For those girls who appear in court, the penalties they receive are more intrusive and more often custodial than previously, and the rate at which they are punished for non-compliance has also increased. The second part of the chapter, which draws on data collected for a larger study of girls and youth justice, illustrates that young women themselves may experience statutory supervision as stigmatising, irrelevant to their needs and apt to terminate abruptly, leaving them without support and effecting no real change in the material circumstances of their lives. I argue that more does indeed need to be done with girls, not because of the risk they pose to public safety, which is minimal, but on account of their gendered welfare needs, their powerlessness on account of their age and their impoverished backgrounds. I conclude by proposing that more attention ought to be paid to the needs of *all* young women – many of whom share similar experiences with girls who have offended – and that working with young female offenders outside the youth justice system has the potential to normalise offending girls' needs and experiences, rather than single them out as 'bad' girls. Moreover, such a normalising strategy may pay dividends by encouraging solidarity and mutual support among girls.

Recent trends in female youth crime and criminalisation

Young women offend significantly less than young men, and those who do break the law commit less serious offences, less frequently, and 'grow out of crime' (Rutherford 1986) sooner than their male counterparts (Burman 2004; Gelsthorpe and Sharpe 2006). Young women are responsible for only around one-fifth of recorded youth crime in England and Wales. However, the number of them entering the youth justice system has increased dramatically in recent years. Offences committed by girls resulting in a formal disposal increased by 38 per cent in the five years between 2002/03 and 2007/08, compared with a three per cent decrease among their male counterparts (Youth Justice Board 2004, 2009). Violent crimes have shown the biggest increase for both sexes, official data indicating a 78 per cent rise in girls' violent offences compared with a 49 per cent rise in those committed by boys in just three years between 2002/03 and 2005/06 (Youth Justice Board 2004, 2007), subsequent rates remaining relatively stable. Similar patterns are in evidence in Australia (Carrington with Pereira 2009), Scotland (Burman and Batchelor 2009) and the United States (Steffensmeier and Schwartz 2009).

There is much debate as to whether girls' increased share of violent arrests is indicative of changes in their behaviour, or rather an artefact of 'tougher' policing and court practices, which have resulted in penal responses to misdemeanours that might previously have been dealt with informally or via welfare mechanisms (Steffensmeier *et al.* 2005). Popular commentators have been quick to attribute the officially recorded upward trend in female youth violence to so-called 'ladette culture' (Worrall 2004), the assumption of the headlines being that there is a 'new breed' of violent girls who apparently represent the 'dark side' of feminism (Carrington 2006). The very frequency of such headlines can perhaps be interpreted as a warning to young women of the unpleasant consequences of seeking equality with men at work and in social life (Chesney-Lind and Irwin 2008).

In contrast to the media hype, the conclusions of more critical analysis of both official statistics and self-reported lawbreaking by girls converge in broad support of a 'criminalisation' hypothesis.

Briefly put, the argument is that changes in police and court processing – notably pre-emptive intervention in the name of crime prevention at the 'front end' of the system, and stricter enforcement and less tolerance towards those more deeply entrenched in it – are primarily to blame for the burgeoning population of girls in the youth justice system (Nacro 2008; Steffensmeier *et al.* 2005). Minor assaults by young women have risen steeply around the world (e.g. Burman and Batchelor 2009; Carrington 2006; Chesney-Lind and Irwin 2008), and such 'crimes' are particularly vulnerable to changes in policing. In England and Wales, for example, the National Crime Recording Standard (NCRS), introduced in 2002 in order to improve the integrity and geographical consistency of police recording practices, requires the police to record *any* notifiable offence that comes to their attention, even in the absence of any supporting evidence.[1] This has led to more petty offences (including minor assaults, which constitute the majority of girls' violent crimes) resulting in arrest. Moreover, general increases in child criminalisation of 26 per cent between 2002 and 2006 alone in England and Wales have, as Morgan (2007) has argued, been largely a product of the police pursuing 'low-hanging fruit' in the shape of teenagers causing mischief, including drinking, smoking cannabis, and fighting in public (see also Bateman 2008).

Chesney-Lind and Shelden (2004), writing from the North American context, have drawn attention to two further practices that have served to reconstruct vulnerable and defiant girls as violent offenders. Firstly, the practice of relabelling status offences, such as running away and being a 'person in need of supervision' – categories in which girls have traditionally been significantly over-represented – as violent crimes, and secondly, the proactive policing of domestic assaults, where parents may press charges against their daughters in the aftermath of family disputes or situations of mutual combat.

Until the latter part of the twentieth century, girls were more likely to be drawn into the criminal justice system as a result of gender-inappropriate behaviours relating to sexual activity and running away from home, than for straightforward criminal activity (Cox 2003; Shacklady Smith 1978). More recently, as the foregoing discussion indicates, it seems that violence has overtaken sexuality as the central site of anxiety about young womanhood and girlhood delinquency (Chesney-Lind and Irwin 2008; Sharpe 2008). In practice, however, the picture may be rather more complex than one set of concerns displacing the other; indeed, there is some evidence that patriarchal-protective discourses about girls' (sexual) vulnerabilities persist. In England and Wales, the jurisdiction from which I write, a retrenchment of the welfare state and, in particular, a reduction in services for young people in difficulty, has coincided with the industrial-scale expansion of the youth justice system following the establishment of multidisciplinary Youth Offending Teams (YOTs) by the Crime and Disorder Act 1998 (Goldson and Muncie 2006). YOT employees now include health, education and social welfare professionals, as well as those from a probation or policing background. Consequently, and partly by virtue of workers' professional and ideological inclinations to 'help' young people (as offenders) who have previously been ignored or short-changed by the state (as children in need), youth justice professionals may 'plug the gaps' (Phoenix 2009) by offering welfare services to compensate for the state's abrogation of its responsibilities towards needy and/or vulnerable young people, thereby paradoxically drawing girls who are needy or 'at risk', but who pose no danger to the public, into the criminal justice system (Sharpe 2009). Whilst such an approach may be motivated by benevolent intentions, the penal/ punitive framework in which youth justice workers operate, and the risk discourse that dominates contemporary criminal justice practice, ironically serve to render vulnerable children *more* punishable, by way of recommendations that they require more intensive criminal justice intervention/control, resulting in what Phoenix (2009: 128) has referred to as 'repressive welfarism twenty-first century style'.

Punishing girls

At the 'deep' end of the system, the expansion of the female youth custodial population has given particular cause for concern. In England and Wales, the introduction of more permissive youth sentencing powers by the Crime and Disorder Act 1998 (Bottoms and Dignan 2004), as well as the requirement that half of a detention and training (custodial) order – the latter 'training' half – be served under supervision in the community, have undoubtedly had a negative impact on girls, whose welfare needs have traditionally meant that they have been considered both in need of 'protective' incarceration (Cox 2003) and suitable subjects for supervision (Harris and Webb 1987). The effect of the 1998 act was an upsurge in the proportion of female juvenile prisoners from 3.9 per cent to 7 per cent of all young people in penal custody within just two years of its implementation in 2000 (Bottoms and Dignan 2004: 107). In subsequent years, as shown in Table 8.1, it is principally an increase in *short* detention and training orders (DTOs) of just four months' duration that has further

Table 8.1 Girls and young women sentenced to penal custody, England and Wales, 2002–2008

	2002/03	2003/04	2004/05	2005/06	2006/07	2007/08
DTO 4 months	165	184	244	263	272	295
DTO 4 months to						
2 years	297	260	284	330	324	290
Custodial sentence						
> 2 years[2]	36	32	26	30	25	27
Total sentenced to						
custody	498	476	554	623	621	612

Source: Youth Justice Board Annual Workload Data 2002/03–2007/08

swelled the female youth custodial population. This trend – which can scarcely be justified in terms of public protection, given that just two months are spent in custody – is not discernible among boys.

Table 8.2 shows the proportionate use of different youth sentences in England and Wales during the period 1998–2008. The use of discharges and fines decreased significantly over the decade, while the rate at which girls were sentenced to supervision in the community increased exponentially: community sentences constituted three-quarters of sentences imposed by the courts in 2008, up from just 30 per cent ten years earlier. In numerical terms, this represents an increase of 215 per cent, from 3,301 to 10,390, compared with a (less dramatic but nonetheless considerable) rise of 92 per cent among boys (Ministry of Justice 2010). The fact that custody *rates* remained fairly stable, despite a rise in the *number* of custodial sentences imposed on girls, is due to an overall increase in the number of girls entering the youth justice system and, importantly, sentenced by the courts. Interestingly, comparable data incorporating young people of both sexes (most of whom are young men) indicate a decline in the proportionate use of custody over a similar time period (Morgan 2009: 66), notwithstanding a steady increase in the number of imprisoned young people.

Concern has also been expressed about the increased number of conditions that are attached to community penalties (Morgan 2009), making compliance more difficult. The rate at which girls are breached for non-compliance with a statutory order – most often involving a failure to attend appointments – has increased by 134 per cent in just five years in England and Wales,[4] and breach is now the third largest

Table 8.2 Proportionate (%) use of sentences for girls aged 10–17 years, England and Wales, 1998–2008

Sentence	1998	1999	2000	2001	2002	2003	2004	2005	2006	2007	2008
Discharge	42	43	34	24	16	15	14	13	13	13	13
Fine	22	17	16	15	9	8	7	7	5	6	6
Community sentence[3]	31	33	42	50	66	70	72	74	76	75	76
Custody	3	4	4	4	5	4	3	4	3	3	3
Other	2	4	4	6	4	4	4	3	3	3	2

Source: Ministry of Justice 2010

primary offence group for which young people (the gender breakdown of whom is not recorded) are sent to custody (Youth Justice Board 2009: 39). Similarly, in the US, almost one-third of detained girls have been charged with 'technical violations' (Snyder and Sickmund 2006). The dearth of programmes tailored specifically towards girls' needs may result in them receiving 'standard' interventions designed to meet the needs of, and control the risks presented by, young male offenders, which are inappropriate to their circumstances, fail to actively engage them, and which may thus reduce their likelihood of compliance.

What works with girls who offend?

This apparently straightforward question is notoriously difficult to answer. Gender-specific programmes with girls are in very short supply and evaluations of the few that do exist, mostly in the US, provide little evidence as to their effectiveness (Chesney-Lind *et al*. 2008). Studies of the needs of girls and young women who offend offer some insights into promising targets for programmes. Whilst much of this research has been conducted in custodial establishments, there is evidence that the needs of girls in custody and those subject to community supervision are strikingly similar in nature, if not in degree (Sharpe 2008; Williams 2008).

Young women offenders are an acutely damaged and deprived population in whose backgrounds violent victimisation, damaged family relationships, trauma and loss, substitute care and poor educational attainment frequently feature (Batchelor 2005; Chesney-Lind and Pasko 2004; Her Majesty's Inspectorate of Prisons 2004;

Howard League 1997; Sharpe 2008; Tye 2009). Many have been 'failed' by their families and by the 'care' system, and a high proportion have experienced toxic relationships with family members characterised by violation, rejection and conflict. Some are parents themselves. A higher proportion of female than male young offenders have experienced homelessness (Arnull *et al.* 2007), and many more have experienced disrupted or unstable living arrangements (Sharpe 2008). A recent international review of the health needs of female prisoners concluded that young women's very high levels of psychiatric disturbance, self-harm and substance misuse render them more vulnerable than both young men and adult women in penal detention (Douglas and Plugge 2006).

Reviews of the needs of girls who offend have offered several pointers for promising interventions. Firstly, programmes should be gender-specific: they should acknowledge the victimisation and other gender- (and age-) specific histories of their young female participants, rather than simply deliver programmes designed for boys, or indeed for adult women (Batchelor and Burman 2004; Greene *et al.* 1998). Secondly, relationships play a central role in girls' psychosocial development (e.g. Gilligan 1982) and also feature in their offending (Batchelor 2005). Consequently, interventions should aim to harness the positive aspects of girls' relationships and also, perhaps, work with their families, with whom girls' relationships are often a root cause of their distress (Chesney-Lind *et al.* 2008). Thirdly, group work in non-authoritarian settings is likely to respond better to girls' collaborative learning styles. Fourthly, programmes should be facilitated by committed and well-trained staff, and women-only environments may be necessary in order for many girls to feel safe, and to avoid young men dominating the 'air space'. Fifth, interventions should foster girls' strengths and aim to empower them to make positive decisions, but without blaming individuals if they fail to engage with programmes or if they are unable to effect change in their lives in the face of overwhelming structural obstacles (cf. Hannah-Moffat 2001). Additionally, and acknowledging the multifaceted nature of girls' needs, provision should be holistic and have capacity for follow-up where required (Patton and Morgan 2002).

An important paradox should be noted here. The intensity of the needs of girls in the youth justice system and the high levels of disadvantage that characterise their backgrounds are not generally matched by the seriousness or the persistence of their offending. Moreover, despite substantial increases in the punishment and criminalisation of young women, as the preceding analysis indicates, the majority have limited contact with the formal youth justice system and those who are supervised in the community typically receive services for relatively short periods of time. There may thus be insufficient time to address girls' considerable needs within the confines of a short community order. Conversely, there are dangers that practitioners will redefine girls' welfare needs as risks, or 'criminogenic needs' (Maurutto and Hannah-Moffat 2006), which may result in the recommendation of excessively intrusive penalties that are out of proportion to the seriousness of their offending. Finally, girls themselves may experience criminal justice involvement as controlling, rather than supportive.

Little attention has been paid to listening to the views of the growing population of young women who are subject to youth justice governance as to what works (and what does not) in facilitating their pathways out of crime and achieving a successful, non-criminal transition into adulthood. The remainder of this chapter attempts to address this gap by focusing on what girls and young women have to say about their experiences of youth justice supervision.

What works and what matters: A view from the girls

The findings reported here derive from a larger study of young women and youth justice (Sharpe, forthcoming). The aims of that study were to examine and analyse understandings of girls' pathways into crime, offending girls' needs, and the effectiveness of the 'new' youth justice system *vis-à-vis* young women, from the perspectives of both criminalised young women and youth justice professionals. The research centred on three case studies: two youth offending teams (YOTs) in shire counties in central England and one secure training centre (STC).[5] Semi-structured interviews were conducted with 52 young women aged between 13 and 19 years. The majority (43) of the sample was, or had recently been, subject to youth justice supervision in the community and the remainder of the young women were interviewed in custody. Mirroring national trends, theft and handling, violence, criminal damage and public order offences respectively appeared most frequently on the girls' criminal records.

'When you leave you forget all about it'

In discussing what had led them into offending and into the youth justice system, the girls' accounts of their pathways into crime and into the youth justice system involved both social and psychological explanations. Social attributions included getting into trouble with friends and associates – scenarios that took place in public spaces, on the streets of their local neighbourhoods and estates. Here, groups of young people with no money to spend on organised entertainment (and, for those in rural areas, very limited access to public transport) would (usually) drink, (sometimes) use drugs and engage in disorderly or 'antisocial' behaviour, such as fighting and causing criminal damage. Simultaneously, many girls attributed their offending, albeit rather less directly, to psychological, personal and family troubles: to generalised feelings of anger, having no one to care about them, and to conflicts or 'clashes' with their mothers. Such altercations were frequently perceived to result in heightened emotionality which, in turn, could 'explode' in expressive offending, particularly acts of violence (Sharpe 2008).

In relating these explanatory schema to their needs in relation to desistance from further offending, a common view was that their welfare and developmental needs had been ignored or neglected and that, as a consequence, they had turned to alcohol, drugs and alternative (anti)social means of relieving boredom and achieving a degree of social recognition (cf. Barry 2006) from their peers. They defined their needs in terms of participation in social life, which meant having access to affordable leisure activities, and not being excluded from them, or 'harassed' while there on account of their youth and criminal records. In addition, many girls wanted practical support with finding accommodation as well as someone they could talk to about their experiences of victimisation at home, in school and in public spaces – an adult who would listen to their experiences as young women living in dangerous and violent circumstances, and not relate to them solely as 'young offenders'.

Few of the young women had access to any source of personal or practical support outside the YOT, and their own families, if the women were still living with them, were often unable or unwilling to provide much in the way of emotional or material assistance. 'Helping' agencies, in particular social services, had let them down in the past, they felt, even when they themselves had *requested* help. Several girls described previous child welfare social workers who, they felt, had given up on or abandoned them, 'dropping' their 'case' without warning or explanation because they 'didn't want nothing to do with us no more' (Rowan, 13 years old). Others, such as Kate

(19 years old), had received support while at school – in Kate's case from a mentor – but on subsequently being excluded from school, either officially or by 'voting with their feet', these relationships with helping adults had also come to an abrupt end. In a handful of cases, a lack of prior support due to the state's abrogation of its duty to protect them and promote their welfare ironically resulted in relief at having been prosecuted, since this led to involvement with the YOT and thus to much-needed practical and emotional support. As April (16 years old) put it, 'until I became a youth offender I didn't know who to ask for help.' However, many girls felt angry and resentful that their social and developmental needs had only been taken seriously when (and sometimes not even when) the focus of attention had shifted to their lawbreaking.

The young women had been involved with their local YOT for anything from two weeks to several years. However, the majority were subject to a relatively short period of community supervision (or post-release supervision in the case of those who had served custodial sentences); for half of the sample (n=26), this would last for no longer than six months. As discussed above, many had received little or no formal support prior to their involvement in the youth justice system, and for the majority, the end of the YOT's statutory involvement would signal the abrupt termination of any professional help.[6] The girls felt – unsurprisingly, in view of the short duration of youth justice services many of them were receiving – that youth justice supervision was unlikely to effect change in their everyday circumstances:

> They don't want you to get into trouble, but as soon as your referral order ends, you've still got nothing to do, and you're in the same situation. So you're still gonna keep on getting in trouble. (Holly, 16 years old)

> When you come off your licence you don't get anything. (Rhiannon, 17 years old)

> You only see them [YOT worker], like, once a week for half an hour, but when you leave you forget all about it. (Zoë, 18 years old)

Some young women acknowledged that they had rejected the support – or regulation, as many understood it – that social workers and others had offered them in the past, because of their own 'bad attitude' when they were younger. More commonly, though, girls said that they had *wanted* help (although not from social workers, perhaps due to fears that they would remove them from their homes and force them to enter state 'care') but that no help was forthcoming or, as highlighted above, that help had ended suddenly and without explanation.

Relationships with workers

It was above all their responses to individual workers that determined girls' evaluations of the quality of YOT interventions. In line with findings from other studies (e.g. Batchelor and McNeill 2005; Covington 1998; McNeill 2009; Trotter 2007), relationships with workers were deemed particularly important. Highly valued worker attributes included trustworthiness, 'being there' to talk to, and the ability to understand their own lives and experiences, 'knowing where we come from', as Letitia (15 years old) put it. Workers' personal qualities in these respects were more important to most of the young women than their agency role or professional background.

Worker gender was important for half of the girls I asked, and almost all of these expressed a preference for a female worker, on the grounds of finding women easier to talk to, believing that 'girls don't talk to blokes', or that women 'understand where you're coming from'. Chloë (15 years old), who was glad that she had not been allocated a male YOT worker, elucidated:

> I definitely couldn't talk to a man. I prefer talking to a lady. I feel more confident talking to [her female YOT worker]. I don't think the girls would really let their feelings out to a man.

Previous experience of being abused by men, as well as a generalised fear and distrust of males, were also important considerations for some girls. Jessica (16 years old), for example, did not want a male worker, since 'if you're on your own in a room, you don't know what they're gonna do'. Recent research by Williams (2008) similarly found that girls reported feeling more comfortable with female workers and more able to talk openly with them. Some girls in the current study gave specific examples of 'good' male workers, however, and there was not universal support for a blanket policy of female-only case allocation. Some female workers will have little in common, in terms of ethnic and class background, or even sexual orientation, with their supervisees, and these latter characteristics may feature more prominently in girls' self-identities. Nonetheless, it was clear that female workers were 'better' for a significant proportion of individuals, indicating that female-only caseworker allocation merits serious consideration, at the very least in order to ensure that girls feel safe.

Importantly, some girls who resented what they perceived to be the officialdom of YOT officers were more positive about lay mentors or befrienders with whom they had become involved at school or via a YOT referral. This seemed especially beneficial for girls who were reluctant to trust or engage with professionals. Melissa (16 years old), whom I interviewed in the STC, was very positive about her resettlement and aftercare provision[7] worker, and believed that he 'understood' her because he too had spent time in prison. She contrasted this with her experience of some YOT workers, who 'are just, like, posh, and they don't know what it's like ... [and] stereotype people'.

Although generally negative about the impact YOT interventions had had on her life (she characterised YOT supervision as 'interference' and feared that workers would disclose information to the police if she discussed her offending with them), Laura (19 years old) talked at length, and extremely positively, about her long-standing involvement with a female boxing coach who ran a Girls' Group in one of the study YOTs. The coach had initially been Laura's mentor – organised by her YOT worker – when Laura was on conditional bail several years earlier. Interestingly, Laura did not associate the boxing coach with the YOT, despite the fact that she had effectively supervised Laura throughout several court orders. The coach continued to be heavily involved in Laura's life, even though Laura had not been subject to YOT supervision for some time.

Growing enthusiasm for youth mentoring (even Michelle Obama recently launched a mentoring scheme for high school girls at the White House) has unfortunately not been equalled by evidence of its effectiveness. A recent evaluation of a range of mentoring projects in England was somewhat equivocal in its conclusions: whilst mentoring programmes enjoyed some success in terms of increasing mentees' involvement in education, training and employment, they had no measurable impact on reoffending rates (Newburn and Shiner with Young 2005). Nonetheless there are indications that, if youth justice professionals link young women offenders into informal community support mechanisms that outlast periods of statutory supervision, such referrals will be appreciated, not least since so many girls have been excluded from school where they might otherwise have been offered support and advice.

Reparation

Reparation has been given significant emphasis within the contemporary youth justice system in England and Wales, and is now explicitly named as one of the purposes of youth sentencing,[8] and a 'fundamental part of any community sentence for a young offender' (Her Majesty's Government 2008: 51). In practice, the majority of reparative activities are indirect, the recipient being the 'community at large'. In such cases the underlying principle is perhaps more accurately described as 'coerced restitution' (Bottoms and Dignan 2004: 162), than restoration or offence resolution.

Indirect reparation, or 'community payback', was a supervision requirement for the majority of the young women who were subject to community supervision, and it was almost universally disliked; indeed, several girls had refused to complete the reparation element of their court orders despite otherwise being compliant, and considered the reparation tasks they were required to do to be demeaning, 'slave labour', or treating them 'like little kids'. Several girls were required to do manicuring in an elderly people's home as reparation. YOT professionals, notwithstanding jokingly acknowledging that the project reinforced gender stereotypes as well as having questionable benefits for its recipients, highlighted the relational benefits of the work, as well as the fact that the girls were learning a potentially useful vocational skill in the process. However, Ellen (17 years old) said that the prospect of manicuring elderly women's nails made her 'feel sick', while Tegan (13 years old) seemed to be rather unsuited to the task, given her somewhat aggressive and unpredictable behaviour.

Few girls considered reparation to be relevant either to their offending or to the victims of their crimes, and few understood its relevance even as a punishment.[9] April (16 years old), for example, who had been required to undertake conservation work in some woods, which involved a 35-mile round trip from her home, reflected that 'I don't think digging holes is going to stop me getting into trouble!' Their experiences contrasted starkly with the intended benefits of reparation, as set out in recent good practice guidance for Youth Offending Teams, wherein the most effective reparation is said, *inter alia*, to be 'restorative … contribute to repairing harm … fully "owned" by the young person, and builds the young person's skills and learning' (Youth Justice Board 2008: 4).

Community involvement

The handful of girls who had become engaged in leisure and activity projects via a referral from the YOT or another agency spoke extremely positively about them. Several young women were involved, variously, in a youth project led by the fire service, army cadets, and a girls' boxing and fitness group. The young women's accounts of these activities revealed a positive impact on their feelings of self-worth, most notably when their efforts had been recognised by certificates and positive feedback from staff – forms of recognition that many had not previously received via the education system. Laura (19 years old), for example, proudly showed me a file full of certificates that she had obtained after completing numerous boxing and fitness courses.

Participation in projects not specifically targeted at offenders has several potential benefits. The normalising effect of integrating offenders with non-offenders – for example, through voluntary sector provision – seems to have particular benefits for female offenders (Gelsthorpe *et al.* 2007; Roberts 2002) by reducing the stigma associated with projects for offenders only and thus bolstering offenders' non-criminal identities. Mainstream services have the further benefit of avoiding some of the difficulties associated with including very small numbers of females in male-orientated and male-dominated group programmes for offenders – including a reluctance to attend on the part of girls and women, due to previous experiences of victimisation by men (Gelsthorpe *et al.* 2007), and issues of sustainability. Perhaps of greatest importance is the voluntary, non-coercive nature of involvement and the fact that, in contrast to statutory youth justice programmes, participation is generally not contingent either on prior offending or assessed risk of future offending and may, where appropriate, extend beyond the rigid time limits of court-ordered supervision. Third sector involvement may also lead to opportunities to adopt a prosocial 'identity script' (Rumgay 2004) by becoming a volunteer oneself.

Youth (in)justice: Unwelcome interference

The young women in the *Girls in the Youth Justice System* study were frequently the victims of exclusionary educational and social practices which, exacerbated by their youth and financial hardship, limited their capacity for active citizenship. Their alternative strategies for social inclusion and resisting boredom, which often included attempts to have fun amongst, and gain recognition from, their peers, led them periodically to engage in lawbreaking. Many felt a sense of injustice at having been criminalised for these delinquent inclusionary strategies, given that they had no access to affordable and accessible alternative pursuits. Many had received little or no professional support prior to their involvement in the criminal justice system, in spite of their histories of school exclusion, family distress and violent or sexual victimisation, and their experiences of youth justice services were, as often as not, fragmentary and transient. The end of the YOT's statutory involvement usually signalled the termination of any support, mirroring disruption experienced in other areas of their lives and replicating the manner in which they had been dropped – or symbolically *abandoned* – by other professionals, and often by their own families, in the past.

A common view among the girls was that the legitimacy of YOT intervention (or interference, as they frequently understood it) was undermined by the absence of prior support, echoing Pat Carlen's contention that ignoring or neglecting young people's welfare needs, but at the same time subjecting them to the full weight of the criminal justice system, represents an 'asymmetry of citizenship':

> Instead of a moral reciprocity of citizen rights, there is an asymmetry of citizenship, with young people being punished for not fulfilling their citizenship obligations even though the state fails to fulfil its duties of nurturance and protection towards them. (Carlen 1996: 2)

Conclusion: beyond the youth justice system

Responses to young people who offend in Britain have become increasingly articulated within a formal youth justice system (Rutherford 2002). Girls and young women have consistently been overlooked within this system, despite entering it in increasing numbers and receiving more restrictive penalties. Official claims that the contemporary youth justice system in England and Wales is highly 'effective' contrast starkly with the subjective assessments of the girls I interviewed, who felt that youth justice services did not improve the social and material conditions of their lives, to which they attributed much of the 'trouble' they had got into. Rather, their experiences of the youth justice system mirrored disruption and disconnection in other areas of their lives. Many experienced youth justice supervision as stigmatising.

It is imperative (and much overdue) that policy-makers start taking troublesome young women seriously (Burman and Batchelor 2009). However, a vital and rarely asked question relates to where and how offending girls' needs are best met. Young women do not, in general, pose much risk to the public and they are relatively unlikely to embark upon lengthy criminal careers. Whilst robust evidence regarding the ideal components of programmes for girls remains elusive, the principle of non-maleficence is an important one, not least since so many young women in the justice system have suffered significant harm in the past. Moreover, we must heed the warnings of recent research that *any* form of exposure to the formal youth justice system has the potential to stigmatise and to impede desistance (McAra and McVie 2007).

While writing this chapter, I contacted Rhiannon (not her real name), whom I met five years ago when she was aged 17 years and on supervision after serving a custodial sentence for an offence of grievous bodily harm. In 2005, Rhiannon was depressed, unable to access counselling, and bemoaned the lack of support she was receiving from her local YOT. She reflected back then that, if *she* were to miss an appointment with her YOT worker, she would be recalled to prison, whereas there were no such consequences if her YOT worker did not find the time to see her. In the intervening period, Rhiannon has trained to become a peer mentor, and subsequently found employment with a large young people's organisation, where she is now a team leader. Research on women's pathways out of crime has emphasised not only structural barriers to desistance such as housing and poverty, but also the importance of cognitive shifts in self-identity (Giordano *et al.* 2002) and the acquisition of prosocial 'identity scripts' (Rumgay 2004). The importance of relationships, reciprocity and generativity – a concern for, or 'giving back' to the next generation – also seem to play a role in young women's ability to leave crime behind (Barry 2007; McIvor *et al.* 2004). Rhiannon's transformation from prisoner to professional helper is testimony to this, as well as a reminder that, if they are offered meaningful opportunities to make good, girls are usually keen to take them.

A key question is to what extent are services able to assist young women to desist from crime when they are situated within an increasingly risk- and punishment-oriented youth justice system in which young people, and especially young women, in need of support are subjected to intensified net-widening supervision and surveillance (Piacentini and Waters 2006)? And what happens when statutory supervision comes to an end? Perhaps one answer might be to transfer (and ring-fence) resources from youth justice into developing gender-specific provision for girls within mainstream children and youth services, or within the voluntary sector, to which youth justice professionals can refer (and divert) young women, but which are accessible to *all* girls in difficulty, many of whom have similar needs to girls in the youth justice system. Such projects might also be well positioned to develop opportunities for girls to undertake reparation in ways that are meaningful to them, and which benefit the wider population of young women in difficulty. Perhaps most importantly, and as Annie Hudson (1989) pointed out some time ago, defining girls' problems and needs in collective (but not criminogenic) terms would both acknowledge the experiences they have in common as well as empower them to actively provide meaningful and lasting support and friendship to one another, rather than consigning them to becoming the passive recipients of what they may experience as unreliable and stigmatising youth justice services.

Notes

1 See Maguire (2007) for a detailed discussion of the impact of the NCRS.
2 Includes detention under Sections 90–92 of the Powers of Criminal Courts (Sentencing) Act 2000 (murder and other grave crimes punishable by 14 or more years' imprisonment in the case of adults over 21 years), and Sections 226 (detention for public protection) and 228 (extended sentence for serious violent or sexual offences) of the Criminal Justice Act 2003.
3 Includes referral orders and reparation orders, both known as 'first-tier' penalties. Referral orders were introduced in 2002 and now make up over half of youth community disposals, having displaced the fine and the discharge to a large extent. Referral orders are given to defendants aged 10 to 17 appearing in court for the first time and who plead guilty, unless the offence is considered so serious as to warrant a custodial sentence.

The young person is required to attend a youth offender panel, which is made up of two volunteers from the local community and a member of the youth offending team. Panel attendees must draw up a 'contract' that the young person agrees to abide by, which must include reparation either directly to the victim or indirectly to the wider community, as well as activities aimed at preventing further offending (see Morgan 2009: 61–2). The length of the order, which is decided by the court, is between three and 12 months, and the conviction is 'spent' once the contract has been successfully completed. Reparation orders comprise a maximum of 24 hours' reparation – again, either direct or indirect – which must be completed within three months of the imposition of the order.

4 The number of girls sentenced for breach of a statutory order increased from 1,171 in 2002/03 to 2,741 in 2007/08. Comparable numbers for boys were 7,085 and 14,101, representing a 98 per cent rise (Youth Justice Board 2009).

5 There are four secure training centres (STCs) in England (and none in Wales), each run by a private company. They are custodial establishments housing young prisoners aged 12 to 17 years. The location of the study STC is not given, in order to preserve its anonymity. The majority of the girls incarcerated there at the time of this research were 16 or 17 years old.

6 The professionals interviewed as part of the broader study (Sharpe, forthcoming) frequently complained that mainstream welfare, and sometimes education, services 'drop' young people as soon as they become involved with youth offending services, which strongly suggests that any support that preceded the girls' offending may well have ended when YOT involvement began.

7 Resettlement and aftercare provision (RAP) is attached to YOTs and provides support to young people with substance misuse problems during the community part of a detention and training order.

8 Criminal Justice and Immigration Act, section 9(3)(d).

9 There was no evidence that any of the girls interviewed had undertaken direct reparation to the victims of their crimes. Had they done so, their views might perhaps have been different from those expressed here.

References

Arnull, E., Eagle, S., Gammampila, A., Patel, S., Sadler, J., Thomas, S. and Bateman, T. (2007) *Accommodation Needs and Experiences of Young People who Offend*. London: Youth Justice Board.

Barry, M. (2006) *Youth Offending in Transition: The Search for Social Recognition*. Abingdon: Routledge.

Barry, M. (2007) 'The transitional pathways of young female offenders: Towards a non-offending lifestyle', in R. Sheehan, G. McIvor and C. Trotter (eds) *What Works with Women Offenders*. Cullompton: Willan Publishing.

Batchelor, S. (2005) '"Prove me the bam!" Victimisation and agency in the lives of young women who commit violent offences', *Probation Journal*, 52 (4): 358–75.

Batchelor, S. and Burman, M. (2004) 'Working with girls and young women', in G. McIvor (ed.) *Women Who Offend*. London: Jessica Kingsley.

Batchelor, S. and McNeill, F. (2005) 'The young person-worker relationship', in T. Bateman and J. Pitts (eds) *The RHP Companion to Youth Justice*. Lyme Regis: Russell House Publishing.

Bateman, T. (2008) '"Target practice": Sanction detection and the criminalization of children', *Criminal Justice Matters*, 72: 2–5.

Bottoms, A. and Dignan J. (2004) 'Youth justice in Great Britain', in M. Tonry and A. Doob (eds) *Youth Crime and Youth Justice: Comparative and Cross-National Perspectives*. Crime and Justice: A Review of Research, Vol. 31. Chicago: University of Chicago Press.

Burman, M. (2004) 'Turbulent talk: Girls making sense of violence', in C. Alder and A. Worrall (eds) *Girls' Violence: Myths and Realities*. Albany: State University of New York Press.

Burman, M. and Batchelor, S. (2009) 'Between two stools? Responding to young women who offend', *Youth Justice*, 9 (3): 270–85.

Carlen, P. (1996) *Jigsaw: A Political Criminology of Youth Homelessness*. Buckingham: Open University Press.

Carrington, K. (2006) 'Does feminism spoil girls? Explanations for official rises in female delinquency', *Australian and New Zealand Journal of Criminology*, 39 (1): 34–53.

Carrington, K. with Pereira, M. (2009) *Offending Youth: Sex, Crime and Justice*. Leichhardt, Australia: The Federation Press.

Chesney-Lind, M. and Irwin, K. (2008) *Beyond Bad Girls: Gender, Violence and Hype*. New York: Routledge.

Chesney-Lind, M., Morash, M. and Stevens, T. (2008) 'Girls' troubles, girls' delinquency, and gender responsive programming: A review', *Australian and New Zealand Journal of Criminology*, 41 (1): 162 89.

Chesney-Lind, M. and Pasko, L. (2004) *The Female Offender: Girls, Women, and Crime* (2nd edn). Thousand Oaks, CA: Sage.

Chesney-Lind. M. and Shelden, R.G. (2004) *Girls, Delinquency and Juvenile Justice* (3rd edn). Belmont, CA: Wadsworth.

Covington, S. (1998) 'The relational theory of women's psychological development: Implications for the criminal justice system', in R. Zaplin (ed.) *Female Offenders: Critical Perspectives and Effective Interventions*. Gaithersburg, MD: Aspen Publishers.

Cox, P. (2003) *Gender, Justice and Welfare: Bad Girls in Britain, 1900–1950*. Basingstoke: Palgrave Macmillan.

Douglas, N. and Plugge, E. (2006) *Female Health Needs in Young Offender Institutions*. London: Youth Justice Board.

Gelsthorpe, L. and Sharpe, G. (2006) 'Gender, youth crime and justice', in B. Goldson and J. Muncie (eds) *Youth Crime and Justice*. London: SAGE.

Gelsthorpe, L., Sharpe, G. and Roberts, J. (2007) *Provision for Women Offenders in the Community*. London: Fawcett Society.

Gilligan, C. (1982) *In a Different Voice*. Cambridge, MA: Harvard University Press.

Giordano, P., Cernkovich, S. and Rudolph, J. (2002) 'Gender, crime and desistance: Toward a theory of cognitive transformation', *American Journal of Sociology*, 107 (4): 990–1064.

Goldson, B. and Muncie, J. (2006) 'Critical anatomy: Towards a principled youth justice', in B. Goldson and J. Muncie (eds) *Youth Crime and Justice*. London: SAGE.

Greene, Peters and Associates (1998) *Guiding Principles for Promising Female Programming: An Inventory of Best Practices*. Washington, DC: Office of Juvenile Justice and Delinquency Prevention, US Department of Justice.

Hannah-Moffat, K. (2001) *Punishment in Disguise: Penal Governance and Federal Imprisonment of Women in Canada*. Toronto: University of Toronto Press.

Harris, R. and Webb, D. (1987) *Welfare, Power and Juvenile Justice: The Social Control of Delinquent Youth*. London: Tavistock.

Her Majesty's Inspectorate of Prisons (2004) *Girls in Prison: The education and training of under-18s serving Detention and Training Orders. A thematic report by the Office of Standards in Education in consultation with HM Chief Inspector of Prisons*. London: Her Majesty's Inspectorate of Prisons.

Her Majesty's Government (2008) *Youth Crime Action Plan 2008*. London: Home Office.

Howard League (1997) *Lost Inside: The Imprisonment of Teenage Girls*. London: The Howard League.

Hudson, A. (1989) '"Troublesome girls": Towards alternative definitions and policies', in M. Cain (ed.) *Growing Up Good: Policing the Behaviour of Girls in Europe*. London: SAGE.

McAra, L. and McVie, S. (2007) 'Youth justice? The impact of system contact on patterns of desistance from offending', *European Journal of Criminology*, 4 (3): 315–45.

McIvor, G., Murray, C. and Jamieson, J. (2004) 'Desistance from crime: Is it different for women and girls?', in S. Maruna and R. Immarigeon (eds) *After Crime and Punishment: Pathways to Offender Reintegration*. Cullompton: Willan Publishing.

McNeill, F. (2009) 'Supervising young offenders: What works and what's right?', in M. Barry and F. McNeill (eds) *Youth Offending and Youth Justice*. London: Jessica Kingsley.

Maguire, M. (2007) 'Crime data and statistics', in M. Maguire, R. Morgan and R. Reiner (eds.) *The Oxford Handbook of Criminology* (4th edn). Oxford: Oxford University Press.

Maurutto, P. and Hannah-Moffat, K. (2006) 'Assembling risk and the restructuring of penal control', *British Journal of Criminology*, 46 (3): 438–54.

Ministry of Justice (2010) *Sentencing Statistics: England and Wales 2008*. Statistics Bulletin. London: Ministry of Justice.

Morgan, R. (2007) 'A temporary respite', *The Guardian*, 19 February.

Morgan, R. (2009) 'Children and young people: Criminalisation and punishment', in M. Barry and F. McNeill (eds) *Youth Offending and Youth Justice*. London: Jessica Kingsley.

Nacro (2008) *Responding to girls in the youth justice system*. Youth crime briefing. London: Nacro.

Newburn, T. and Shiner, M. with Young, T. (2005) *Dealing with Disaffection: Young People, Mentoring and Social Inclusion*. Cullompton: Willan Publishing.

Patton, P. and Morgan, M. (2002) *How to Implement Oregon's Guidelines for Effective Gender-responsive Programming for Girls. Oregon Commission on Children and Families*. Available at: http://www.oregon.gov/OCCF/Documents/JCP/GenderSpecific.pdf

Phoenix, J. (2009) 'Beyond risk assessment: The return of repressive welfarism', in M. Barry and F. McNeill (eds) *Youth Offending and Youth Justice*. London: Jessica Kingsley.

Piacentini, L. and Waters, R. (2006) 'The politicisation of youth crime in Scotland and the rise of the "Burberry Court"', *Youth Justice*, 6 (1): 43–59.

Roberts, J. (2002) 'Women-centred: The West Mercia community-based programme for women offenders', in P. Carlen (ed.) *Women and Punishment: The Struggle for Justice*. Cullompton: Willan Publishing.

Rumgay, J. (2004) 'Scripts for safer survival: Pathways out of female crime', *The Howard Journal of Criminal Justice*, 43: 405–19.

Rutherford, A. (1986) *Growing Out of Crime: Society and Young People in Trouble*. Harmondsworth: Penguin.

Rutherford, A. (2002) 'Youth justice and social inclusion', *Youth justice*, 2 (2): 100–107.

Shacklady Smith, L. (1978) 'Sexist assumptions and female delinquency: An empirical investigation', in C. Smart and B. Smart (eds) *Women, Sexuality and Social Control*. London: Routledge and Kegan Paul.

Sharpe, G. (2008) *Girls in the Youth Justice System*. Unpublished PhD thesis, University of Cambridge.

Sharpe, G. (2009) 'The trouble with girls today: Professional perspectives on young women's offending', *Youth Justice*, 9 (3): 254–69.

Sharpe, G. (forthcoming) *Offending Girls: Young Women and Youth Justice*. Cullompton: Willan Publishing.

Snyder, H. and Sickmund, M. (2006) *Juvenile Offenders and Victims: 2006 National Report*. Washington, DC: US Department of Justice, Office of Juvenile Justice and Delinquency Prevention.

Steffensmeier, D. and Schwartz, J. (2009) 'Trends in girls' delinquency and the gender gap: Statistical assessment of diverse sources', in M. Zahn (ed.) *The Delinquent Girl*, pp. 50–83. Philadelphia: Temple University Press.

Steffensmeier, D., Schwartz, J., Zhong, H. and Ackerman, J. (2005) 'An assessment of recent trends in girls' violence using diverse longitudinal sources: Is the gender gap closing?', *Criminology*, 43 (2): 355–406.

Trotter, C. (2007) 'Parole and probation', in R. Sheehan, G. McIvor and C. Trotter (eds) *What Works with Women Offenders*. Cullompton: Willan Publishing.

Tye, D. (2009) *Children and Young People in Custody 2008–2009: An analysis of the experiences of 15–18-year-olds in prison*. London: Her Majesty's Inspectorate of Prisons/Youth Justice Board.

Williams, J. (2008) *Real Bad Girls: The origins and nature of offending by girls and young women involved with a county youth offending team and systemic responses to them*. Unpublished PhD thesis, University of Bedfordshire.

Worrall (2004) 'Twisted sisters, ladettes, and the new penology: The social construction of "violent girls"', in C. Alder and A. Worrall (eds) *Girls' Violence: Myths and Realities*. Albany: State University of New York Press.

Youth Justice Board (2004) *Youth Justice Annual Statistics 2002/03*. London: Youth Justice Board.

Youth Justice Board (2007) *Youth Justice Annual Statistics 2005/06*. London: Youth Justice Board.

Youth Justice Board (2008) *To Develop and Improve Reparation, as part of the Youth Crime Action Plan: Good practice guidance for youth offending teams (YOTs)*. London: Youth Justice Board.

Youth Justice Board (2009) *Youth Justice Annual Workload Data 2007/08*. London: Youth Justice Board.

Chapter 9

Breaking the cycle: Addressing cultural difference in rehabilitation programmes

Dot Goulding

Women in prison are not a homogeneous group. Like all women everywhere, their life experiences and life chances are influenced by factors such as socio-economic status, local cultural norms, religion, ethnicity and race. Although most women who have experienced prison will have some issues in common, in terms of the impact of imprisonment on their lives, there are also issues that are specific to particular sociocultural groups. This chapter focuses on the ways in which one service provider developed a culturally specific approach to assist a particular sociocultural group of women exiting prison in the Perth metropolitan area of Western Australia. The women in question were Aboriginal women, most of whom identified themselves as belonging to the Nyoongar people, Aboriginal Australians from in and around the Perth and south-west areas of Western Australia.

The chapter argues that the 'one size fits all' approach to programme and service delivery for women exiting prison is unlikely to achieve positive outcomes (Goulding 2004). It deviates slightly from the focus of assisting women offenders out in the community. It engages firstly with a particular 'in prison' programme designed for Australian Aboriginal women that, in essence, has its theoretical foundation rooted in the notion that community-based programmes for women exiting prison work most effectively when cultural issues are a primary consideration and relationships of trust are already established. Given this, much of the text is devoted to the 'in prison' programme and its central relationship to the enlistment and retention of Aboriginal women within Community and Youth Training Services (CYTS) community-based programmes, post release.

In particular, this chapter looks at aspects of cultural difference in relation to successful reintegration to community for women exiting prison. The programme, in this instance, initially involved a specific education and training programme delivered to Aboriginal women exiting prison in Western Australia. The chapter looks at an innovative approach used by CYTS to assist indigenous Western Australian women successfully reintegrate into the community upon release from prison. The approach involved the development and delivery of a culturally appropriate art-based training programme for indigenous Australian women exiting prison in Perth, the capital city of Western Australia. A major focus within this programme was relationship building between programme presenters, the training organisation and the women themselves. The chapter illustrates how this innovative approach was central to retaining the women throughout the 'in prison' programme and in their subsequent re-engagement with the organisation (CYTS) upon release.

Most research highlights the importance of establishing relationships with people in prison prior to release as a major contributing factor to successful re-engagement post release (Goulding 2004: 53; Salomone 2002c: 2). Van Wormer's research (1999: 51) supports this, noting that:

> In the criminal justice system, clients often find their very selfhood defined by their crimes. For such persons, whose views of therapy and of all authority figures are apt to be decidedly negative, a positive approach is essential to establish the one crucial ingredient of effective treatment – *trust* [author's emphasis]. Sometimes one encounter or one supportive relationship – whether with a teacher, social worker, or priest – can offer a turning point in a life of crime.

In the Breaking the Cycle programme the relationships of trust were established while the women were still incarcerated. Also, and central to the programme's ethos of cultural appropriateness, the programme content was both *developed* and *run* by Aboriginal women.

The Breaking the Cycle initiative was seen by CYTS as an opportunity to formally acknowledge the primary importance of developing relationships of trust with the women prior to release, as part of a throughcare strategy to present a user-friendly organisational face to encourage, in particular, Aboriginal women to re-engage with CYTS training programmes out in the community. The initiative presented an opportunity for CYTS to develop and deliver culturally appropriate training to indigenous Australian women in prison who traditionally did not access formal training within the prison. This was viewed as a chance to create pathways into further education and/or practical training in order to enhance employment readiness and re-engagement with the organisation out in the community.

The initiative for the development of the Breaking the Cycle programme was borne out of a report which investigated the impact of imprisonment on women's familial and social connectedness: *Severed Connections* (Goulding 2004). The report clearly identified six distinct socio-economic and cultural groupings of women in prison in Western Australia. Although these groupings were not seen to be mutually exclusive, they had, in terms of the impact of imprisonment, issues in common with each other as well as issues specific to each group. For the purpose of the 'Breaking the Cycle' initiative, however, CYTS elected to focus on the sociocultural group identified as 'urban' Aboriginal women. These were, in the main, Nyoongar women from in and around metropolitan Perth and south-west areas of Western Australia. The majority of Aboriginal women in prison in Western Australia are held in the metropolitan area. Bandyup Maximum Security Prison for Women houses 50 per cent of female Aboriginal prisoners with Boronia Pre-release Centre for Women housing 9 per cent. The remaining 41 per cent are held in regional prisons (Department of Corrective Services 2008).

The lives of the women in this group are typified by social and economic marginalisation from mainstream Australian culture. However, they generally have strong kinship ties and remain connected to their families and communities with little if any stigma attached to having experienced imprisonment. Nonetheless, their life chances are significantly diminished in Western terms. This disadvantage is clearly illustrated in the following statistics. Within the West Australian context, Aboriginal women, who make up approximately 3.2 per cent of the general female population, constitute almost 60 per cent of the female West Australian prison population. In short, Aboriginal women in Western Australia are over 40 times more likely to be in prison than their non-Aboriginal counterparts (Salomone 2002b). Notably, Aboriginal women within the criminal justice system are more likely than non-Aboriginal women to be repeat offenders, with around 70 per cent experiencing imprisonment on more than one occasion. This high recidivism rate among Aboriginal women ensures their continuing over-representation in Western Australian prisons.

Socio-economic position of Aboriginal women in Western Australia

Colonisation and its consequences, dispossession from land and culture, and forcible removal of generations of Aboriginal children from their families and communities have had a disastrous impact on Aboriginal people's general well-being and life chances (Salomone 2002b: 1). It is well documented that Aboriginal people suffer entrenched disadvantage in all aspects of life. Aboriginal women in particular are among the most socially and economically disadvantaged members of Western Australian society. They endure deep-rooted poverty, ongoing systemic racism, high rates of unemployment, entrenched high levels of family violence and sexual abuse, high rates of teenage pregnancy, as well as bearing the burden of high levels of mental health problems, alcoholism and increasing substance abuse.

Aboriginal women also often bear sole responsibility for keeping their families and communities together under circumstances negatively impacted on by past and present socio-economic and cultural dispossession (Salomone 2002b: 2). Some of these women experience imprisonment as a real dislocation in their lives. For many though, being imprisoned only exacerbates the many negative socio-economic factors that continually impact on their lives. As Eaton (1993: 80) argues: 'the denial of the right to act as agents on their own behalf is not new to them. They are accustomed to acting in response to the expectations of others.'

Some other social indicators of Aboriginal women's disadvantage include: a life expectancy almost 20 years shorter than that of non-Aboriginal women; infant mortality rates that are twice those of other Australian infants; and Aboriginal women are twice as likely to be sole parents. Disturbingly, they are 45 times more likely to be victims of domestic violence and eight times more likely to be victims of homicide than their non-Aboriginal counterparts (HREOC *Face the Facts* 2005). In addition to such entrenched general social disadvantage, Aboriginal women are also disadvantaged by their disproportionately high rate of imprisonment.

Although they are disproportionately represented in the Western Australian prison system, Aboriginal women seem to be invisible to policy-makers within the criminal justice system. Historically, there has been a distinct lack of culturally and gender-specific service provision and programme design and delivery for Aboriginal women impacted upon by the criminal justice system. Indeed, where gender is considered in criminal justice policy, 'the needs of Indigenous women are generally treated as being met through mainstream services for women (which are not culturally specific)' (ATSIC Social Justice Commissioner 2004: 8). It was within this backdrop of disadvantage, even within the prison system itself, that CYTS developed the Breaking the Cycle initiative.

Developing Breaking the Cycle

Acknowledgement of the value, diversity and richness of their culture should be a priority in any programmes and/or service delivery for this group of urban Aboriginal women. All such programmes should be formulated by appropriately qualified Aboriginal people with a particular familiarity with Nyoongar traditions and the general lifestyle of urban Aboriginal women (Goulding 2004).

In 2005, when the programme was originally developed, there were no culturally specific programmes designed *by* and *for* Aboriginal women held in Western Australian prisons. Neither was there any culturally specific service provision for Aboriginal women newly released from prison. 'Breaking the Cycle', initially an 'in prison' programme, was groundbreaking indeed in that it was designed *by* and *for* Aboriginal women and the trainers who *delivered* the programme were also Aboriginal women. This initiative was in line with one of the recommendations from the *Severed Connections* Report (Goulding 2004: 45–53). In sum, the Breaking the Cycle programme was developed specifically to address some of the needs of imprisoned Aboriginal women from in or around the Perth metropolitan area as they prepared for release back into the community. A primary objective of the programme was to present a user-friendly, non-threatening and welcoming organisational face that would in effect encourage the women to re-engage with CYTS in the community upon release.

The Breaking the Cycle programme specifically targeted 'urban' Aboriginal women for practical reasons. These were because: (a) it was neither economically nor logistically viable for CYTS (a Perth-based organisation with limited and unsecured funding) to offer post-release training to Aboriginal women from regional and remote areas because of the vast distances and costs involved; and, (b) urban Aboriginal women were identified in the *Severed Connections* Report (Goulding 2004: 8) as a group that was socio-economically and culturally distinct in many ways from Aboriginal women from regional towns and remote communities who tended to adhere to more traditional cultural protocols.

Programme design

The Breaking the Cycle programme was designed to enlist those women who did not historically connect with education and/or training programmes either within the prison environs or post release. In line with a recommendation from the *Severed Connections* Report (Goulding 2004: 43), the programme was designed and delivered in a culturally appropriate manner by Aboriginal women trainers in order to address the previously unaddressed needs of imprisoned Aboriginal women. Within the Western Australian prison system it has been the case that, in the main, Aboriginal women tend not to access mainstream post-release support services and/or education. 'Breaking the Cycle' was developed with the primary goal of addressing some of the gaps in this area.

The in-prison training programme was presented as an art-based project designed to culminate in a prison-based art exhibition. The exhibition was to be organised and facilitated by all the women enrolled in the programme. The women were expected to engage in several major art projects both as individuals and in groups. The art projects included painting, jewellery-making and mask-making. The women also had to nominate spokespersons to negotiate with prison authorities and they were also expected to participate in the planning, promoting and presentation of the final exhibition. In this way, the programme was designed to draw out the women's creative talents, enhance their traditional cultural knowledge and draw on more formal skills such as effective communication, negotiation, numeracy and literacy.

The painting component included the completion of at least two individual art works per person and two major group projects. In completing these modules, the CYTS trainers led the women through a variety of skills-based activities that require the employment of and/or development of a variety of proficiencies. The development of these proficiencies was largely hidden within the more enjoyable 'art' projects. However, at the end of each day the trainers identified the range of skills utilised to progress to the next point of the programme. The skills development utilised throughout each module included:

- the enhancement of *cultural knowledge* and connection through storytelling in pictures and words, learning about traditional Nyoongar culture, and using cultural knowledge to promote positive identity and heighten self-esteem;

- the development of *communication skills* in order to deal with everyday conflict through negotiation and compromise, also consideration and respect for the opinions and feelings of others and the acknowledgement that there are consequences of actions;

- the use of *planning skills* to set and complete achievable goals; also, noting the importance of working together in teams to achieve mutually beneficial outcomes and learning to cope with negative outcomes through risk management and alternative strategies;

- *teamwork*: learning the importance of networking, using consensus and encouragement and losing judgemental attitudes towards others;

- *literacy*: developing promotional brochures and posters for the art exhibition; identifying rules for the group; telling their stories and creating stories for their children;

- *numeracy*: developing numeracy skills through use of fractions and ratios in colour-making for paintings; counting beads in jewellery design; designing and planning various art works; costing materials; working out hourly rates and profit margins on sales of art works.

Programme delivery

After discussions between CYTS and senior management at Bandyup Maximum Security Prison for Women it was decided that the Breaking the Cycle programme would be run during 'summer school' time when competition for limited space at the education centre was at a minimum ('summer school' time is the period during December and January when more traditional education courses are in recess, because it is the middle of summer in Australia and school holidays). Also, the timing for the delivery of the programme over the Christmas holiday period was seen to be beneficial for the women as prison activities are at a minimum then and feelings of sadness and disconnection from family and community run high around Christmas. In addition, general feelings of frustration and boredom prevail at this time of year and it was felt that the programme would help alleviate the boredom. The programme was run twice weekly for five weeks during the traditional down time in the education centre, during December 2005 and January and February 2006.

Initial yarning sessions

Notice of the proposed programme was posted around the prison and it was clearly identified as a programme designed specifically for Aboriginal women. In November 2005, prior to the programme's commencement, the programme team visited the prison on two occasions to talk to the women about the programme content. The team consisted of two Aboriginal trainers (a Nyoongar artist and a Nijina woman trainer from the north-west of Western Australia) and two non-Aboriginal women (the Chief Executive Officer (CEO) of CYTS and the author, who was to conduct a formative programme evaluation and who would be present at training sessions to observe programme delivery and to interview the women).

During the two yarning sessions the women had the opportunity to get to know the trainers and the author and ask any questions about the programme. In turn, the trainers were able to gain some sense of the restricted, rule-governed nature of the prison environment, learn about the women's interests and determine any special considerations regarding learning activities. The trainers were made aware that the women would not necessarily be permitted to keep their completed art works in their cells. They were also told what could and could not be brought into the prison by the trainers and the manner in which things must be brought in and taken out.

The yarning sessions proved to be a most valuable ice-breaking tool. The presence of the two Aboriginal trainers was obviously the key to high levels of interest in the programme. Initially, during both yarning sessions, the women engaged solely with the Aboriginal trainers, asking about family names and discovering extended family members in common. Although the women afforded the non-Aboriginal members of the project respect when they spoke of their own particular roles, it was apparent that the familial and cultural links to the Aboriginal trainers were central to the women's strong interest in participating. From a non-Aboriginal observer's perspective, it was clear that a very significant connection between the women and the Aboriginal trainers had taken place. When conversation moved on to the programme and its content the women displayed enthusiasm and offered suggestions regarding art and craft projects in which they might like to participate. Several women said that they were pleased that the programme was designed and taught by Aboriginal women and was only available to Aboriginal women in the prison. Subsequent conversations with the women who participated in the training programme determined that these were *the* most important factors in ensuring its extraordinarily high levels of attendance and enthusiasm.

A credible marker of the programme's success was the extraordinarily high attendance rate. Traditionally, the pattern of programme attendance at Bandyup prison had a starting point of 14 or 15 participants, the numbers usually diminishing significantly over the weeks. The Breaking the Cycle programme started with 15 participants and numbers grew to 30 after two sessions. Numbers should have been capped at 20 participants but because of the nature of imprisonment, women would be called out of class for legal, official or social visits; to receive medication; for attendance at court; called back to their units; called to their workstations. Consequently there was a great deal of coming and going within the classroom, but each session was well attended and a total of 30 women regularly participated in activities and contributed their completed art works to the exhibition. Importantly, all the women who participated said that they were initially interested in enrolling in the Breaking the Cycle programme because it was advertised as being specifically for Aboriginal women. Further interest was initiated when the women realised that the trainers were Aboriginal women. The importance of these two factors to the programme's unprecedented success in terms of participant attendance and enthusiasm ought to be emphasised.

The women's assessment of Breaking the Cycle

Thirty women participated in the programme. Their ages ranged from 18 to 49 years. Six of the women declined to be interviewed on a one-to-one basis. Three of these women agreed to speak about the programme while participating in their art activities. The remaining three had imminent parole issues and all were understandably stressed. All the 24 women interviewed individually had previously served time in prison and/or juvenile detention prior to their current sentence. Sixteen of the women had served three or more prison terms.

The women cited the following expectations as being met by the programme: enhanced cultural knowledge; spiritual healing through the gaining of cultural knowledge; ability to use art to deal with negative emotions such as anger and despair; alleviation of boredom during a particularly monotonous period within the prison's calendar. In addition, each of the 24 women interviewed said that the programme either met or exceeded their expectations and made them feel increased pride in their cultural heritage. All the women said that prior to the programme they had minimal knowledge of traditional Nyoongar culture. They liked the fun-based activities and having something to show for their efforts (jewellery, masks and paintings). They also said that being able to move around the classroom, interact with the trainers and their peers and discuss their projects was a major factor in holding their interest.

In terms of what worked least well, the general consensus was that sometimes the formal skills sessions involving components such as organisational and negotiating skills and voting for various things took up too much 'art' time. The younger women tended to become bored during these sessions, saying that the older women would generally be the decision-makers in any case. Also there were concerns when the women were not permitted to take their finished work back to their cells. Several women were instructed to place their art works in their property boxes, which were unavailable to them during their time in prison. These items could only be collected upon release. Given the differing interpretations of relevant prison rules by various prison officers, this issue was exacerbated. This pertains to the rule-governed nature of prisons and was clarified prior to subsequent programme delivery.

The women generally felt that it would be beneficial for Aboriginal women in the prison if the programme could be run several times throughout the year rather than just during the education centre down time at the Christmas holiday period. They mentioned that this was the only programme specifically for Aboriginal women and that this was an important factor in sustained participation. Several women indicated that, while many of the non-Aboriginal service providers and programme trainers were good people who offered genuine help, they did not know what it was to be Aboriginal and experience many of the negative socio-economic aspects of being an Aboriginal woman. One of the programme participants, a 23-year-old Nyoongar woman, emphasised the importance of this factor in this way:

No disrespect to you; but wadjelas [Nyoongar term for non-Aboriginal Australians] don't know what our issues are. Not really. You might read about them and be sympathetic to us but you can't know what it is to live with violence and racism and put-downs every day of your life in your own country. These women – the Aboriginal trainers – they've lived it too so they know who we are and what we go through. And they've survived it all and made something of themselves. That's inspiration to us. It means that maybe we have some hope of making things better too.

Obstacles to smooth running of programme

In spite of the programme's obvious success in terms of attendance rates and participant satisfaction with content and delivery, there were many obstacles that had to be overcome in terms of delivering the programme within the prison context. These difficulties are arguably generic to all education, service provision and programme delivery provided by 'outside' agencies. Identified problems included (in no particular order of importance):

- competition for time and space within prison education centres; being aware that programmes may be cancelled at short notice due to various other prison-related considerations;

- security issues: police clearance certification for trainers; identifying which items may be or may not be taken into prisons; keeping reasonable relational boundaries;

- being aware of and keeping to local prison rules that may well be interpreted differently by various members of staff;

- individual trainers need some form of induction to the prison environment prior to any programme commencement, including information on prevailing prison culture and the strict rule-governed nature of prisons;

- continuing difficulty specific to the ongoing success of the Breaking the Cycle programme – the availability or otherwise of suitably qualified Aboriginal trainers, being mindful that the single most important factor in the successful participation rates was the holistic involvement of Aboriginal women trainers.

Programme impact

The programme content is relevant to Aboriginal and Nyoongar culture in particular. It was designed to enhance cultural knowledge, draw on and further develop various social competencies, enhance notions of positive cultural identity and individual self-esteem, and promote economic independence through the development of marketable employment skills.

Apart from the programme's emphasis on enhancement of cultural and spiritual well-being, it also focused on some of the most pressing issues facing Aboriginal women both pre- and post-release. In addition to the specifically targeted cultural content, the attendance rate at programme sessions clearly indicated the programme's popularity and perceived importance among the women. In the context of this chapter, the impact of Breaking the Cycle can also be gauged by looking at re-engagement rates with community-based CYTS training programmes, overall participation by Aboriginal women affected by the criminal justice system because of court orders and/or community-based service orders.

Initially, the Breaking the Cycle programme was non-accredited which, in effect, rendered its claim to ongoing space within an already cramped education centre less than a priority. However, the initial programme, having established CYTS as a training organisation with a culturally appropriate and user-friendly face has, in essence, flowed on to the organisation's other accredited training programmes. From the original humble beginnings of a non-accredited art-based training programme specifically designed for Nyoongar women which could only elicit space in the education centre at Bandyup prison during the traditional 'down time', CYTS now runs accredited training programmes at both metropolitan facilities for women (Bandyup Maximum Security Prison for Women and Boronia Pre-Release Centre for Women). It is important to recognise that in Western Australia custodial facilities accredited training is given preference by the prison authorities over non-accredited training. Attendance at accredited training programmes contributes to the positive and increased reporting statistics of each custodial institution while also providing points for consideration at the women's parole hearings.

It is also important to note that the indigenous women who engage with CYTS are those who would most likely be at a disadvantage with more traditional training courses where higher levels of self-direction and motivation are required for successful outcomes. The culturally appropriate trainers conduct classes as well as one-to-one tutoring.

The same trainers service both custodial facilities so that the women, who may move between prisons, have continuity in their training. It is interesting to note that, although accredited training programmes are available to women of all ethnic and racial backgrounds at these facilities, many of the students are Aboriginal women. For many it is the first time that they have connected with any form of vocational educational training. Given this, CYTS offers several lower certificate courses as well as Certificate III, IV and Diploma levels (nationally recognised, standardised training levels approved by the Training Accreditation Council, Australia). This was because it was recognised that for many women, particularly Aboriginal women in prison, commencement at Certificate III level was too great an undertaking in the absence of certain basic educational prerequisites. Put simply, CYTS offers students with limited educational history accredited courses at lower, more manageable levels, with a view to confidence building and the capacity to graduate to Certificate III training or to enter the workforce.

Post release re-engagement with CYTS in the community

In recognition of the particular needs of Aboriginal women and to encourage timely re-engagement with education and training in the community, CYTS has established several user-friendly strategies. These are (in no particular order of importance):

- The women can access the same certificate courses as they did while in prison;

- The women can work with the same trainer/tutor as in prison, either in classes or on a one-to-one basis;

- 'Rolling intakes' allow the women to join at any point in the course that is convenient to them, encouraging a continuity that effectively diminishes drop-out rates;

- Subsidised student packs are available at minimal cost;

- Any fees or purchases of resource texts and/or student packs can be paid for via direct deductions from their welfare payments on a fortnightly basis;

- The women can request extra help with literacy and/or numeracy skills and receive additional tuition to help reduce gaps in comprehension.

In addition to the above, CYTS employs caseworkers who can provide advocacy, referral to other service providers and assistance to women who may have other issues in their lives that might impact on their ability to attend, undertake or continue their education/training.

Many of the women, in particular those who have recently exited prison, live in situations of continuous poverty. Indeed, several of the women who enlisted in the initial Breaking the Cycle programme had lost their homes, furniture and personal belongings while they were in prison and so returned to the community even more disadvantaged than before. In addition, some women indicated that they would be returning to situations of family and domestic violence (Goulding 2004). For these women, education and other forms of training are simply not a priority. Programmes and other forms of service delivery, particularly for Aboriginal women, need to reflect this overarching socio-economic disadvantage. With this in mind, CYTS has established some practical strategies that are designed to encourage regular attendance at training sessions. CYTS routinely provides snacks and refreshments during the day because many of the women attend without having had breakfast, usually due to a lack of forward planning and/or lack of funds. The provision of sustenance also encourages regular attendance as well as punctuality, thus minimising any disruption to classes. Sustenance also helps brain function and increases levels of concentration, rather than focusing on hunger. Also, gathering around food/meals promotes positive socialisation and helps to break down barriers as well as promoting subliminal messages which encourage good eating habits and food choices thus becoming part of the hidden 'improving life skills' experience. Importantly, if the women need to take a break from training, they can advise CYTS of their requirement to either cease or suspend their training until circumstances support their continuance. These very practical strategies have contributed to the success of CYTS in attracting and retaining Aboriginal women in training courses.

The first Breaking the Cycle programme was a successful project in terms of retaining high 'in-prison' attendance rates and enthusiasm among a disadvantaged socio-economic and cultural group that traditionally does not seek out educational training within the prison environment. The programme complied with identified best practice in programmes for Aboriginal women prisoners in that it was designed in a culturally appropriate manner by Aboriginal women, was delivered by Aboriginal women trainers, promoted Aboriginal women's involvement, facilitated their resocialisation and fostered their economic independence and long-term general well-being (Salomone 2002c). Also in accordance with best practice, Breaking the Cycle was designed to enhance notions of self-determination and foster empowerment rather than dependency. It also emphasised strengths rather than deficiencies, fostered family and community involvement, raised social competencies, developed marketable work skills, provided training opportunities and qualifications, established relationships with mentors and emphasised the significance of Aboriginal culture. Finally, and most importantly, Breaking the Cycle at all times included meaningful, rather than tokenistic, involvement of Aboriginal people. This practical application of culturally sensitive strategies has now been implemented in all CYTS accredited training and educational programmes, making them more accessible for Aboriginal women who live in and around the Perth metropolitan area.

From the initial art-based Breaking the Cycle programme, three women reconnected with other CYTS accredited training programmes in the community. Several of the original programme participants were from the regions and returned to their homelands outside the metropolitan area. Some of the women remained in prison for extended periods and two of these are currently studying with CYTS at Certificate III level in Bandyup prison. Several of the original number were released, reoffended and returned to prison. Two of these women who were returned to prison are currently enrolled in a CYTS accredited programme in Bandyup prison.

CYTS reports that approximately 50 per cent of their community-based students are Aboriginal Australians. Also, 50 per cent of their community-based female students are Aboriginal. Indeed, Aboriginal Australians constitute 60 per cent of CYTS in-prison students. In terms of retention rate, which is defined by CYTS as either 'in prison' or community based, the 'in-prison' retention rate for successful programme completion is around 80 per cent. Whereas the retention rate for those women enrolled in community-based programmes is more difficult to quantify. The Chief Executive Officer of Community and Youth Training Services explained it this way:

It's hard to say what the actual retention rate for newly released women is within the community-based programmes. Women coming out of prison have so many things happening in their lives and 'training' is generally the last thing on their minds when they come out. Sometimes they will be reconnected to us through other service providers once they have settled. As an organisation, CYTS understands the basic life challenges they face, particularly the Aboriginal women, and so we are very flexible in terms of deferring and returning to study. Also, we provide sustenance on a daily basis and both of these strategies help us retain students over the longer term. Currently, the overall retention rate, taking into consideration the stopping and starting issue, is around 80 per cent. (Interview: March 2010).

Conclusion

In conclusion, the original Breaking the Cycle art-based programme was a one-off, funded initially as an action research project with a built-in formative evaluative component (McNiff *et al*. 2003). The programme was groundbreaking in that it was designed and delivered *by* Aboriginal women *for* Aboriginal women. Indeed, the programme surpassed all expectations in its popularity and attendance rates and was central in identifying Community and Youth Training Services as an organisation with a user-friendly image. This image has been maintained and CYTS has been asked to run another art-based programme at Bandyup Maximum Security Prison for Women. This programme will be run in collaboration with another local service provider and will also culminate in an art exhibition where the women may present their art works for sale. A percentage of the profits will be returned to the programme to perpetuate the provision of the programme on an ongoing basis.

References

Aboriginal and Torres Strait Islander Social Justice Commissioner (2004) 'Walking with Women – Addressing the needs of Indigenous women exiting prison', Chapter 2 in *Social Justice Report*. Sydney, Australia: Australian Human Rights and Equal Opportunity Commission. http://www.hreoc.gov.au/social_justice/sjreport04/2WalkingWithTheWomen.html

Borzycki, M. and Baldry, E. (2003) 'Promoting integration: The provision of prisoner post-release services', in *Trends and Issues in Crime and Criminal Justice,* September 2003. Canberra, ACT: Australian Institute of Criminology.

Department of Corrective Services, Western Australia (2008) *Profile of Women in Prison*. Report, Planning and Review Branch of Strategic and Executive Services. Perth, Western Australia: Government of Western Australia.

Eaton, M. (1993) *Women After Prison*. Buckingham, UK: Open University Press.

Goulding, D. (2004) *Severed Connections: An Exploration of the Impact of Imprisonment on Women's Familial and Social Connectedness*. Perth, Western Australia: Murdoch University Print.

Goulding, D. (2007) *Recapturing Freedom*. Sydney, Australia: Hawkins Press, Australia.

Harding, R. (2002) *Report of an Announced Inspection of Bandyup Women's Prison*. Office of the Inspector of Custodial Services, Western Australia, June.

HREOC (2005) *Face the facts: Countering Myths about Refugees, Migrants and Indigenous People*. Australian Human Rights Commission, http://www.humanrights.gov.au/racial_discrimination/face_facts

McNiff, J., Whitehead, J. and Lomax, P. (2003) *You and Your Action Research Project*. Routledge: London.

Owen, B., (2003) 'Understanding women in prison', in J. Ross and S. Richards (eds) *Convict Criminology*. Thompson Wadsworth, USA, pp. 231–46.

Salomone, J. (2002a) 'Issues Paper 2: Mothers and Children/Babies', Department of Justice Report, Low Security Women's Prison Project Paper. Perth, Western Australia: Government of Western Australia.

Salomone, J. (2002b) 'Issues Paper 3: Aboriginal Women', Perth, Western Australia: Government of Western Australia.

Salomone, J. (2002c) 'Issues Paper 4: Women's Program Needs', Department of Justice Report, Low Security Women's Prison Project Paper. Perth, Western Australia: Government of Western Australia.

Social Exclusion Unit (2002) *Reducing Re-offending by Ex-prisoners*. Report by the Social Exclusion Unit. London: Home Office.

Van Wormer, K. (1999) 'The strengths perspective: A paradigm for correctional counseling', in *Federal Probation*, Vol. 63. The Administrative Office of the United States Courts, Washington, DC, USA, pp. 51–8.

Chapter 10

Women, drugs and community interventions

Margaret Malloch and Gill McIvor

Introduction

In this chapter we address the relationship between women, drug use and community interventions. The chapter begins by examining the relationship between women's offending and drugs and by considering how policy responses to drug-related crime have impacted disproportionately upon women, in particular those from minority ethnic groups. Although the introduction of programmes in prisons was viewed as a potential way of tackling drug problems among offenders, including women, this has not proved to be particularly successful since associated social and personal difficulties typically remain unresolved. It is argued that traditional community-based responses to women's offending have also failed to take account of the needs of women or addiction, with the result that statutory orders are more likely to be breached and are often associated with high rates of reoffending. Innovative criminal justice approaches to dealing with drug-related crime – such as arrest referral, Drug Treatment and Testing Orders and Drug Courts – attempt to explicitly address the relationship between drug use and crime but have often failed adequately to resolve difficulties women encounter in their contact with the criminal justice system. The chapter concludes by arguing that contemporary evidence suggests that the justice system can respond more effectively to women with addiction issues by using community-based resources that provide support and an opportunity to address underlying issues. This focus, which places drug-related offending within the context of other issues in a woman's life, and attempts to address these issues rather than merely punish, is likely to produce more successful outcomes.

Women, drug use and crime

While drug use has traditionally been depicted as a predominantly male issue, there is evidence that problematic drug use among women is increasing, that it often has different meaning and form for women (Ettorre 2007; Anderson 2008), and that it is having a significant impact on routing women into criminal justice systems internationally.

In the UK, data from the most recent British Crime Survey suggest that among the general population, drug use is more common among men than among women, with 26.3 per cent of the former and 16.4 per cent of the latter reporting drug use in the past year (Hoare and Flatley 2008), though other estimates suggest that around one-third of drug users in the UK are women (Simpson and McNulty 2008). In Scotland, men also report higher levels of illicit drug use than women, with more men than women reporting having used all types of illicit drugs and men more likely to report using more than one type of drug (MacLeod et al. 2009).

However, male and female drug use prevalence rates were similar for arrestees tested in 2001–02 in the NEW-ADAM (arrestee drug abuse monitoring) programme in England and Wales, and women were more likely than men to produce a positive test for opiates, methadone, cocaine, amphetamines and benzodiazepines (Bennet and Holloway 2004). A Scottish study found that women who were drug tested following arrest were almost twice as likely as men (51 per cent compared with 26 per cent) to test positive for opiate use, though men were more likely than women to have been arrested in the previous five years (McKeganey et al. 2002).

The most recent statistics on drug offenders in England and Wales indicate that the majority (88 per cent) were male. Although women represented only 12 per cent of drug offenders overall, higher proportions of women were convicted of the more serious offences of drug dealing (15 per cent) and the production, importation or export of drugs (17 per cent) (Mwenda 2005). Between 1992 and 2002 there was a 414 per cent increase in the number of women imprisoned for drug offences in England and Wales (Councell 2003) and it has been estimated that almost two-thirds of women in prison in England and Wales have a drug problem (Social Exclusion Unit 2002; Borrill et al.

2003). In Scotland, 71 per cent of all prisoners tested on admission to prison in 2007–08 under the Addictions Prevalence Testing scheme produced a positive test for an illicit substance, with a higher percentage of prisoners admitted to HMP and YOI Cornton Vale, Scotland's prison for women, testing positive for drugs (Information Services Division 2008).

Schwartz and Steffensmeier (2007) report that in the USA there has been an increase in female arrests for substance-related offences since 1960 and that rising levels of illicit drug use among women have had an important impact on trends in female crime. The increase in the female prison population in the USA was driven primarily by sentences imposed for non-violent drug offences (Shaffer *et al.* 2009). In the USA, drug offences accounted for around one-third of female state prison sentences in 2002 (Hartman *et al.* 2007) while in 2007, 29 per cent of female state prisoners had been sentenced for a drug offence (West and Sabol 2008). A higher proportion of female than male prisoners report having been under the influence of drugs or alcohol when they committed their offence (Schwartz and Steffensmeier 2007). Overall, 43 per cent of women in federal prisons and 60 per cent in state prisons were assessed as being drug dependent in 2004 (Mumola and Karberg 2006).

In the USA, with the exception of tranquillisers, more women use methamphetamine than any other drug and methamphetamine use has become a national problem (Hartman *et al.* 2007). In 2004, women in both federal and state prisons in the USA were more likely than men to report methamphetamine use, with reported use in the month before imprisonment among female prisoners increasing from 37 per cent to 48 per cent between 1997 and 2004. Female drug court participants in the US state of Ohio were more likely than men to identify crack cocaine as their drug of choice while men were more likely than women to report use of alcohol (Johnson *et al.* 2000). Women entering drug court programmes in Missouri were more likely to use cocaine, stimulants and prescription painkillers and, compared with men, tended to have started using drugs when they were slightly older (Dannerbeck *et al.* 2002).

Analysis of Australian data indicated that in 2002, arrested women were more likely than men to test positive for amphetamines, benzodiazepines and opiates while the number of women incarcerated for drug offences almost doubled between 1992 and 2002 (Willis and Rushforth 2003). More recent data suggest higher levels of amphetamine, heroin, benzodiazepine, street methadone and morphine use among arrested women than among arrested men (Loxley and Adams 2009).

Loxley and Adams (2009) concluded that women are more likely than men to attribute their involvement in criminal behaviour to drug use, with female police detainees being more likely than male detainees to have been using drugs before their most recent arrest. Among female detainees in Australia, the most serious offences for which women are arrested tend to be property offences (though there is also an association between alcohol use and violent crime, especially among indigenous women) (Loxley and Adams 2009). As in other jurisdictions, there is evidence of high levels of drug use among female prisoners in Australia. For instance, Willis and Rushforth (2003) cite an Australian study conducted in New South Wales in which almost three-quarters of women in prison reported a relationship between drug use and their current offence (typically through the commission of property offences for money to buy drugs).

Women's pathways into drug use and crime

The contexts of women's lives are often different from their male counterparts and, unsurprisingly, pathways into both drug use and criminal activity vary across gender groups. Explanations for the underlying basis for these distinctions are diverse, but include the constraining effect of processes of feminisation; differing responsibilities for childcare; and different motivations and coping mechanisms. These factors are presented by way of explanation for women's significantly lower involvement in criminal activity of any kind, and suggest that when they do commit crime, it is more often due to broader social, economic and/or emotional problems than would appear to be the case for men.

Research by Peters *et al.* (1997) indicated that, compared with male prisoners, drug-involved female prisoners in the USA were more likely to have experienced employment problems, earned less, were more likely to use cocaine and were more likely to report previous suicide attempts and physical or sexual abuse. In a more recent analysis, Mumola and Karberg (2006) reported that drug-dependent prisoners were more likely than those who were assessed as not being drug dependent to report experiences of physical or sexual abuse, homelessness, unemployment, parental substance abuse and parental incarceration. In Scotland, 62 per cent of women in drug treatment reported having been physically abused while, as in the study by Peters *et al.* (1997), 36 per cent reported experiences of sexual abuse (McKeganey *et al.* 2002).

Women in the criminal justice system are also more likely than men to report family conflicts and are less likely to report having family support (Dannerbeck *et al.* 2002; Webster *et al.* 2006). Female drug users report higher levels of mental health problems than male drug users, including higher levels of anxiety and depression (Dannerbeck *et al.* 2002) and lower levels of self-esteem (Webster *et al.* 2006). Women involved in substance use are less likely to obtain and maintain employment than similarly involved men because they may face more barriers to employment (such as family responsibilities or lack of vocational skills) and women who do find employment tend to be paid less than men (Staton-Tindall *et al.* 2008).

Female drug users are often socially isolated (Dannerbeck *et al.* 2002). Staton-Tindall *et al.* (2008) found that female drug court participants reported having fewer casual and close friends than did men and suggest that women's relative social isolation may be as a result of their having exhausted the social supports provided by friends. Alternatively, of course, women who are more isolated in the first instance may be more likely to turn to drug use as a source of emotional support. There is, however, evidence that female drug users are more likely than men to recognise their drug use as a problem (Webster *et al.* 2006). As a result, although they are less likely to access treatment of their own volition, they are more likely than men to request drug treatment if arrested for a drug-related offence (Webster *et al.* 2006) and to access resources in prison, when these resources are available (Borrill *et al.* 2003)

International data suggest that there may be important gender differences in the relationship between drug use and crime. For instance, in a study of young people and offending in Scotland, Jamieson *et al.* (1999) found that young women often reported having been initiated into drug use by their male partners and having subsequently begun committing offences to finance their (and often their partner's) use of illicit drugs. This is consistent with Australian research, which suggests that drug use may play a different role in the development of male and female offending (Makkai and Payne 2003; Johnson 2004), with men more likely than women to report involvement in offending *prior to* their first use of drugs. Loxley and Adams (2009) report that women's involvement in drug use and crime and their experiences of arrest typically occur when they are older than men. Although men are often involved in regular alcohol and cannabis use when first arrested, they are less likely than women to be using other illicit drugs (Loxley and Adams 2009). This leads Loxley and Adams (2009) to conclude that drug use among women leads to crime whereas among men crime leads to drug use or the two occur at the same time (see also Jamieson *et al*. 1999).

Other Australian analyses tend to confirm that there is a distinctive relationship between women's drug use and their involvement in crime. Willis and Rushforth (2003) concluded that women's drug use appeared to be a defining feature in their participation in crime with a stronger link between drug use and crime among women than among men. In particular, there was a strong relationship between women's drug use and their involvement in the distribution of illicit drugs, prostitution and various types of property crime. As Simpson and McNulty (2008: 170) note: 'women's initiation to drug use intersects with wider social factors, including the development of intimate relationships with men.' Dannerbeck *et al*. (2002) have suggested that women are more likely to start using drugs to cope with a traumatic event or to maintain a relationship with a drug user. There is further evidence that women tend to begin using methamphetamine to assist in weight loss or as a coping mechanism[1] whereas men's initial use tends to be experimental (Hartman *et al*. 2007). Among women, drug use may also be linked to negative experiences associated with living on the streets while co-morbidity may result in women using illicit substances to self-medicate (Shaffer *et al*. 2009). The criminalising and victimising potential of female drug use has been commented upon by Schwartz and Steffensmeier (2007: 50) who suggest that: 'Drug use is also more likely to initiate females into the underworld and criminal subcultures, expose them to potentially violent situations, and connect them to drug-dependent males who use them as crime accomplices or exploit them as "old ladies" to support their addiction.'

According to Bloom *et al*. (2004) the key factors that represent female pathways to criminal behaviour include histories of personal abuse, mental illness associated with early life experiences, substance misuse, economic and social marginality, homelessness and destructive relationships (also Dannerbeck *et al*. 2002). Because women's most common pathways to crime are based on survival of abuse, poverty and problematic substance use, Bloom *et al* (2004) argue that improving policy responses to women in conflict with the law needs to begin by addressing these factors through a focus on treatment for substance abuse and trauma recovery, the provision of education and training in employment and parenting skills and access to affordable and safe accommodation. Moreover, in view of women's different pathways to crime and addiction, their differing social circumstances and the complexity of their needs, drug treatment services for women should recognise both their differences from men and the differences *among* women (Shaffer *et al.* 2009).

Working with women in an attempt to support them to overcome problematic drug use therefore requires an acknowledgement of the fundamental differences relating to women as drug users, and as women within the criminal justice system. The gendered effects of policies and practice initiatives need to be considered in relation to both the use of drugs and the needs of drug users. As Bloom *et al.* (2003: 42) comment: 'Research indicates that gender differences play a role from an individual's earliest opportunity to use drugs; that the effects of drugs are different for women and men; and that some approaches to treatment are more successful for women than for men.'

Women, drugs and sentencing

Criminal justice drug policy affects women differently from men. In the USA, rather than addressing the needs of women with drug problems, recent policies have had a disproportionately punitive impact on women (Boyd 2004; Shaffer *et al.* 2009). For example, the introduction of mandatory minimum sentencing statutes for drug offences resulted in a significant increase in the number of women in prison. As Bush-Baskette (1998) argues, through ostensibly 'gender-neutral' sentencing laws (but see Wald 2001), the 'war on drugs' instigated in the USA in the 1980s became, in effect, a war against black women. 'Gender-neutral' sentencing laws failed to recognise and take account of the distinctions between major and minor players in drug organisations, with female couriers facing federal mandatory sentences of 15 years to life for a first felony conviction regardless of how 'culpable' they were or whether their involvement was coerced through threats of violence against themselves and/or their families. Women's punishment has been disproportionate to the harm they cause society and has included the penalising – through imprisonment, removal of their children and/or termination of parental rights – of drug-using women who are pregnant or who have children on the grounds that they have exposed their children to alleged risks.

Between 1986 and 1995 the number of women imprisoned for drug offences in the USA rose by 888 per cent, with the increase being more marked among states that had introduced severe penalties for drug offences; and among black women (Mauer *et al.* 1999). The proportion of women given probation for felonies, on the other hand, has decreased (Bloom *et al.* 2004). Danner (1998) predicted that not only would 'three strikes' and other harsh sentencing policies result in increased prisoner numbers, but resources would be taken from other social services – particularly those for women and children – to meet the costs of increased prison populations, with financial and social implications for both individuals and communities.

It has been argued that it is not only criminal justice policies associated with the 'war on drugs' that have had a disproportionately punitive impact on women. As Bloom *et al.* (2004) have commented, (drug-using) women in the USA have also borne the brunt of policies aimed at restricting access to welfare benefits, subsidised housing and educational opportunities (see also Campbell 2000). This includes lifetime prohibitions on the receipt of financial assistance and food stamps for people convicted of felonies involving the use or sale of drugs and denial of access to social housing for those convicted of drug offences or suspected of being involved in the use or sale of drugs. In the event that women with children are imprisoned – and typically serve an average of 18 months – less financial aid is provided to relative caregivers than to foster caregivers, yet the Adoption and Safe Families Act of 1997 made it mandatory for parental rights to be terminated in the event of a child being in foster care for 15 out of the preceding 22 months (Bloom *et al.* 2004). The loss of their children and restricted access to work, benefits, suitable accommodation and educational provision make it more difficult for women to recover from drug use and rebuild their lives.

In the UK, data from the Ministry of Justice indicate that just under 20 per cent of women in prison in England and Wales in June 2009 were foreign nationals (Ministry of Justice 2009), most of whom were in prison for a drug offence. Most foreign national prisoners are poor women who have been offered money to bring drugs into the UK and, as in the USA, are almost invariably a minor link in the international drug trade, having been recruited by organised criminal groups and having limited prior criminal involvement.[2]

Allen *et al.* (2003: 2) observe that there is 'evidence to suggest that coercion, against a background of violent, abusive and exploitative relationships, plays a part in the decision of some people to become drug couriers'. As in the USA, however, long sentences are imposed upon drug couriers as a deterrent – almost three-quarters of those in the period covered by Allen *et al.*'s (2003) analysis were serving sentences of four or more years – and little consideration is given to mitigating circumstances (such as extreme poverty or coercion) or to the impact of a lengthy custodial sentence on the woman's dependent children, even though most imprisoned drug couriers are single parents aged in their mid-thirties (Allen *et al*. 2003). In addition to having to cope with a long prison sentence, foreign national prisoners have to deal with a foreign culture, language and different food and they are less likely than other prisoners to receive support by way of visits, letters and telephone calls (Caddle and Crisp 1997).

Traditional responses to drug-related offending

The increase in problematic drug use by women impacted on the number of women arrested and sentenced for criminal offences from the late 1980s onwards, but there is little evidence that responses to this situation were either appropriate or effective. On the one hand, drug services often failed to take gender differences into account while, on the other, criminal justice interventions (in both prison and the community) failed to adequately address the needs of problem drug users – both men and women.

Drug services that have been traditionally designed to meet the needs of male heroin injectors may have difficulty moulding women into the resources they have created (Audit Commission 2002; Becker and Duffy 2002). Additionally, a woman's role as a mother can impact on the likelihood that she will use services, while the lack of childcare provisions can hinder access (Loucks *et al*. 2006). Similarly, fear of children being taken into care or of encountering judgemental attitudes (especially if they are pregnant) can prevent women from seeking or responding to support. These issues are exacerbated when women are drawn into the criminal justice system where the representations of drug using women that predominate are based on social constructions of 'appropriate femininities' (Malloch 1999) alongside an ideological expectation of the role of women in the family. In the UK, recent anxieties surrounding the competence of drug using 'parents' (Advisory Council on the Misuse of Drugs 2003; Scottish Executive 2003) have often targeted drug using 'mothers' who, in practice, are most likely to have responsibility for dependent children. This may have the potential to reduce the number of women approaching services for help which in turn is reflected in the provision of services that often assume that women drug users will not have any responsibility for children and therefore do not make the necessary arrangements for childcare facilities (Malloch and Loucks 2007). While this is clearly an important area for intervention, the presentation of the issues (and thereby responses) is not unproblematic.

Acknowledging the relatively small numbers of problem drug users who approach drug services for help, there appeared to be an optimism during the 1990s that the prison system could respond to problem drug use by making resources available for drug users in prison; or that measures could be put in place within prison to enable problem users to access resources following sentence. The high levels of reported drug use among prisoners has been noted above, many of whom may not have had any prior contact with treatment services before receiving a custodial sentence. The overall objective of introducing resources in prison was aimed at enabling individuals who may be unwilling or unable to access treatment in any other way to come into contact with services to address their drug use directly; providing a 'fast-track' entry to treatment services.

Growing concern about the number of women in prison and the extent of substance use problems among women prisoners was also contextualised by an increased awareness that many of these women also had experiences characterised by abuse, loss and mental health problems (Willis and Rushforth 2003; Loucks 2004; Butler and Kousoulou 2006). Indeed it was suggested that these experiences underpinned women's use of drugs (as self-medication) and that punishment (by imprisonment) was wholly inadequate in addressing these needs. As Bloom et al. (2004: 42) have observed: 'standard policies and procedures in correctional settings (e.g. searches, restraints, and isolation) can have profound effects on women with histories of trauma and abuse, and often trigger retraumatisation in women who have post-traumatic stress disorders.'

While the prison has been acknowledged as an appropriate point for intervening to reduce problem substance use, especially given the high prevalence of drug use among prisoners, there have been various criticisms about how prison-based 'treatment' actually operates in practice (Malloch 2001; Duke 2003) and how the 'unnatural' prison environment undermines treatment effectiveness once women return to the community (Richie 2008). For example, the emphasis on security and control within prisons raised serious questions about the viability of the prison system to facilitate drug treatment (Duke 2003) while the potential for offering therapeutic 'support' or 'treatment' for women drug users seemed particularly limited (Malloch 2000 and 2001). The many problems that women face as drug users in custody have been identified, presenting a challenge to the rhetoric that services are consistently operational and effective in all penal establishments

(Malloch 2001 and 2008; Borrill *et al.* 2003). Where services for women are available they often mirror those developed for men or, by reinforcing gender stereotypes, are sexist in nature (Shaffer *et al.* 2009). Drug treatment in prison, as in the community, tends to be oriented to white, opiate-using males (Simpson and McNulty 2008) and also tends to be focused on long-term prisoners instead of short-term prisoners, who are responsible for the majority of drug-related offending.

Despite prison service policies aimed at reducing levels of drug use in custody (education, support services, drug-free units, increased security) there is no evidence that the availability of drugs in prisons has reduced or that drug services in prison are adequate. Borrill *et al.* (2003: 2) noted that 'over a quarter of the women interviewed said they were still using heroin while in prison, albeit mainly on an occasional basis.' Their study highlighted that many women in prison have access to drugs most of the time, but only limited access to resources and counselling, a situation that is compounded by the complexity of women's needs and the relative scarcity of resources for female prisoners (Shaffer *et al.* 2009). As Richie (2008: 382) notes: 'women describe the conditions in correctional facilities as harsher; their sentences are longer and served in more isolated rural areas where there are fewer rehabilitation programmes available to them.'

Research conducted in the UK and elsewhere (e.g. Richie 2008; McIvor *et al.* 2009) suggests that women released from prison also face significant difficulties reintegrating into society and that imprisonment may serve to further marginalise already socially excluded women. The existing literature on women in prison indicates that female prisoners have a complex range of problems and needs (e.g. Loucks 2004) that are not usually addressed while they are in prison (Morris *et al.* 1995) and there is evidence that women's already fragile material circumstances can deteriorate further while they are in prison (Eaton 1993; Morris *et al.* 1995). Given that a high proportion of female prisoners report prior substance misuse (e.g. Singleton *et al.* 2005), successful resettlement (and desistance) will require that they avoid further drug use when they return to the community. However, throughcare is patchy and fragmented and compounded by the high turnover of female prisoners serving short sentences (Simpson and McNulty 2008) and there are a number of barriers – apart from its availability – to women accessing appropriate drug treatment and support when they leave prison. For example, the high turnover of female prisoners makes prison-based drug assessments particularly challenging and prevents the establishment of pre-release relationships with community-based workers that female prisoners appear to value (Fox *et al.* 2005; MacRae *et al.* 2006). Women are generally considered by drug agencies to be a hard-to-reach group who are reluctant to engage with drug services (MacRae *et al.* 2006), fearing removal of their children (Fox *et al.* 2005). However, while proactive approaches such as prison visits and gate pick-ups may encourage higher levels of service engagement (Fox *et al.* 2005; MacRae *et al.* 2006), drug misuse services need to be made more accessible to women, including mothers with children (Malloch 2004; Malloch and Loucks 2007).

While there have been improvements in the provision of drug services in prison, overcrowding throughout much of the female prison estate has impacted on the services and resources that are available and, more profoundly, on women's safety (Shaw 2005; Corston 2007). The recognition that prison is often inappropriate, and frequently dangerous for women drug users, has resulted in calls to expand and develop services in the community, increasing support options and expanding services that could operate as alternatives to custody (Home Office 2001; Scottish Executive 2002; Corston 2007). In particular, calls have been made for alternative ways to be considered of dealing with women who commit the frequent but relatively minor offences that are often associated with illegal drug use (Corston 2007).

More recent approaches to drug-related offending

While the criminal justice system has continued to be a gateway to drug treatment as a key component of more recent international drug strategies, addressing the needs of women involved in drug-related crime in the community rather than in prison has a number of advantages, including access to a wider range of more effective services, avoiding the damaging effects of separating mothers from their children and avoiding the negative impact of imprisonment on women. There is evidence that community-based interventions – which in the UK include arrest referral programmes, drug treatment and testing orders, drug rehabilitation requirements and drug courts – are better equipped to respond to the realities of women's lives and better meet their needs (Bloom *et al.* 2004; Hubbard and Matthews 2008).

Arrest referral

Women are often reluctant to seek treatment in relation to drug problems because of fears of reprisals for themselves or for their children and the considerable social stigma attached to female drug use (Malloch 1999; Simpson and McNulty 2008). Often, women's first contact with treatment and other services will be as a result of their offending and subsequent involvement with the criminal justice system. International evidence suggests that by the time they first come to the attention of the police, women are often already involved in regular illicit drug use. This, Schwartz and Steffensmeier (2007: 50) suggest, is because women have to overcome greater social and personal constraints against crime and 'need a greater motivational push to deviate'. As a result, women coming into contact with the criminal justice system are particularly vulnerable.

Although female detainees in Australia were found to be more likely than male detainees to report current or prior involvement in a drug or alcohol treatment programme, women were also more likely than men to report having been unable to access a treatment programme because of a lack of available places and were more likely to demonstrate high levels of personal distress at the point of arrest (Loxley and Adams 2009). Loxley and Adams (2009: xii) concluded that: 'Some drug-using women would profit from services to help them to deal with their drug use before they become deeply enmeshed in the criminal justice system.'

In the UK, arrest referral schemes were introduced as a means of 'fast-tracking' arrestees with drug and alcohol problems into appropriate treatment services, with schemes being established across England and Wales in the 1990s and slightly later in Scotland (Birch *et al.* 2006). Similar to initiatives in other jurisdictions across Europe and elsewhere, they aim to identify arrestees whose offending may be related to substance misuse and to refer them to appropriate treatment services and supports. The majority of arrestees interviewed by schemes are typically male. Analysis of national monitoring data for England and Wales indicated that women were more likely than men to report recent heroin, methadone, crack and benzodiazepine use, were more likely to have previously received treatment or currently be receiving treatment and were more likely to remain in their existing treatment or be referred to a specialist drug treatment service (Sondhi *et al.* 2001).

However, the proportion of women offered arrest referral appears to be variable, despite evidence that women assessed for arrest referral are 'riskier' than men and less likely to engage with treatment (Best *et al.* 2008). In Scotland, for example, the proportion of women among those who accepted the offer of referral varied across schemes, from 16 to 40 per cent (Birch *et al.* 2006) while some groups who might benefit from arrest referral – such as crack-using sex workers – have been identified as rarely being referred (Sondhi *et al.* 2002). Engagement with a scheme targeted upon street sex workers in a Midlands city was described as 'cautious', with the low take-up being attributed to factors such as the types of drugs used (which impaired women's ability to keep appointments with agencies), threats of violence from pimps and unstable living circumstances. It was also noted that women feared losing their children if their involvement in drug use and prostitution was known and that in previous contact with social services or other agencies women had met with 'stigmatisation and judgemental attitudes' (Pitcher and Aris 2003: 1).

Drug treatment and testing orders and drug rehabilitation requirements

Drug treatment and testing orders (DTTOs), which were introduced in the UK in the late 1990s, combined access to drug treatment, regular drug testing, case management and judicial review of progress and were aimed at offenders with an established pattern of drug-related crime who were at risk of imprisonment. National evaluations of DTTOs have shown that they are associated with reductions in drug use and drug-related offending (Eley *et al.* 2002; Turnbull *et al.* 2000; Hough *et al.* 2003; McIvor 2004). Given the frequent link between their offending and drug use, DTTOs were thought by policy-makers to hold particular promise for female offenders. Women made up 18 per cent of those given DTTOs in Scotland in 2006–07 and tended to be slightly younger than men (with half being under 26 years of age compared with around one-third of men) (Scottish Government 2007). However, women have also been found to breach DTTOs at a higher rate than men, with 41 per cent of women and 33 per cent of men given DTTOs in Scotland having their orders revoked as a result of breach in 2008–09 (Scottish Government 2010). The reasons for the higher breach rate among women are unclear but may include responsibilities for dependent children and the influence of drug-using partners. The absence of specific treatment services for women may also have resulted in lower levels of retention. In the longer term, sustained success is likely to require attention to women's social inclusion and the availability of appropriate resources and supports. Additionally, male drug users often have non-drug-using partners while the partners of female drug users are often drug users themselves (Simpson and McNulty 2008). This means that women are less likely than men to have a partner who actively supports them in their recovery from drugs (see also McIvor *et al.* 2006).

In England and Wales, the DTTO was replaced in 2005 by the community order with a drug rehabilitation requirement (DRR). Between August 2005 and July 2006, 25,495 women received a community order, representing 13.6 per cent of all offenders given this disposal. Nine per cent of requirements imposed on women given community orders during that period involved drug rehabilitation, with women being more likely than men to receive both supervision and drug rehabilitation requirements (Mair *et al.* 2007). However, breach rates for community orders and suspended sentence orders tend to be high (around a quarter of orders made) and it appears that these orders are replacing other non-custodial options rather than sentences of imprisonment. This, combined with the high breach rate, suggests that the net effect of orders might be an overall increase in the numbers of women going to prison (Patel and Stanley 2008).

Drug courts

Originating in the USA in the late 1990s, drug courts are a more recent approach to addressing drug-related crime in a number of jurisdictions (including the UK where they have been piloted in Scotland and, more recently, in England). Although 'by the time they reach drug court, most women are in a state of dire emergency with multiple problems – and multiple barriers to successful recovery' (D'Angelo and Wolf 2002: 386) drug court programmes have typically been designed for men and usually lack the necessary support for women with children. However, in the USA the first female drug court was established in 1992 in Kalamazoo, Michigan (Huddleston *et al.* 2008). Drug court programmes for women have subsequently been introduced in other states; for example, the Brooklyn Treatment Court, whose resources for women include an on-site health clinic, vocational counselling, support to help women re-establish links with their children and help finding affordable, good-quality childcare (D'Angelo and Wolf 2002).

In other jurisdictions the ability of drug courts – unless they have provision that is explicitly tailored to women – to engage effectively with female offenders has been questioned. For example, professionals in Scotland expressed concern at the absence of treatment and other services that were suited to women, and sentencers identified compliance as a particular problem for this group (McIvor *et al.* 2006). In New South Wales, Australia, the perceived lack of suitable treatment options for female drug court participants was considered to be a barrier to participation and the percentage of women entering the drug court would have been higher if it reflected the real level of need. Few residential rehabilitation facilities were said to be willing to accept women with their children at short notice and the high level of commitment required by the drug court regime may have disadvantaged those with parenting commitments, who found it more difficult to comply (Taplin 2002).

Internationally, evidence regarding completion rates and outcomes for women is somewhat mixed, with some studies suggesting lower retention rates for women than men (for example, McIvor *et al.* 2006) and others indicating higher rates of drug court programme completion (for example, Dannerbeck *et al.* 2002; Gray and Saum 2005). A qualitative study of female drug court participants in Northern California suggested that women welcomed the support, concern and understanding offered by sentencers and drug court staff and valued individualised treatment, services that accepted children, female counsellors (given their previous experiences of trauma and abuse) and the opportunity to participate in work or education (Fischer *et al.* 2007). Women participating in a drug court programme in Florida, who received enhanced services, had better retention rates and fewer positive drug tests (Beckerman and Fontana 2001) while women who participated in the Brooklyn Treatment Court for women had lower levels of self-reported drug use and recidivism than a comparison group but no improvements in self-reported economic well-being or health (Harrell *et al.* 2001).

A comparison of women sentenced to drug court with women given standard probation found lower rates of subsequent prosecutions among the drug court participants, though the difference was partly accounted for by probation violations (Shaffer *et al.* 2009). There is some evidence, however, that despite having more problems, women who use methamphetamine may have better recidivism outcomes than men (Hartman *et al.* 2007) and women may be particularly responsive to judicial interaction in a problem-solving court setting. For example, Johnson *et al.* (2000) found that women were more likely than men to state that regular court hearings helped them to remain drug-free while Saum and Gray (2008) found that women were more likely than men to be satisfied with their interactions with the judge. In comparison with men, women were more likely to value praise from judges and to believe that judges had given them an opportunity to relate their side of the story, had been fair to them, had treated them fairly and had treated them with respect. Saum and Gray (2008) suggest that women may have been better able than men to utilise judicial interaction to their advantage because they were able to develop meaningful connections with judges, to communicate their needs and to respond to the judges' requests. Being better able to express themselves in court may be both personally fulfilling for women and may facilitate aspects of the drug court process. Saum and Gray (2008: 115) argue that a 'care perspective' was operating in the drug court and that 'this more feminine model of justice appears particularly beneficial to the women who encompass it.'

Although they may represent a more appropriate response to women involved in drug-related crime through their relational focus, emphasis upon the development of a therapeutic alliance (Hubbard and Matthews 2008) and ability to offer more intensive levels of treatment and support (Hartman *et al.* 2007), drug court programmes are, in the main, based on services that have been developed for men and, as such, they are likely to fail adequately to respond to drug-using women's circumstances and needs. The emphasis, in the UK at least, on methadone and urine testing and the absence of provision that offers women necessary psychological and social support has been singled out for comment (Simpson and McNulty 2008). In the USA, even though women make up 24 per cent of drug court participants, the small scale of drug courts means that they often deal with relatively few women and, especially in rural areas, have difficulty offering specialised provision such as women-only groups (Dannerbeck *et al.* 2002).

General issues

Women who come into contact with the criminal justice system as a consequence of drug-related offending are often viewed as being non-cooperative and are subsequently up-tariffed (Malloch 2004). The chaotic circumstances of the lives of women drug users may indeed make it more difficult for women to comply with the requirements of community-based orders, but it is evident that there are long-standing challenges with the way that disposals are applied to women. Even the more specialist services aimed at addressing drug-related crime have been criticised for failing to respond to female clients. Women may require different forms of intervention or resources that take into account the context of their daily lives in order to enable them to meet the (often) stringent criteria of criminal justice disposals.

The important element in effective treatment in a criminal justice context is not the emphasis on coercion, but on engagement with services (Hough *et al.* 2003; Holloway *et al.* 2005). Identifying 'effective' resources can in itself be problematic. While initiatives such as drug treatment and testing orders and drug courts are intended to lessen the number of drug users sentenced to custody, the success of such initiatives is obviously dependent on available community resources. Regional variations in resources can result in a geographical lottery in accessing services, which is clearly of particular importance where criminal justice agencies refer clients to external service providers (Scottish Drugs Forum 2003). Follow-up support and aftercare is crucial for those nearing the end of court-ordered services, but is often extremely limited in practice, with support often weighted towards the initial stages of intervention.

Given the importance of engagement, it is crucial that resources across the criminal justice spectrum provide available, accessible and effective interventions. In particular, it is necessary that interventions link together to ensure that once engagement takes place, service users do not fall through gaps in services when they move between different criminal justice institutions (i.e. from prison to the community) (MacRae *et al.* 2006). Interventions must be strategic and accessible at the point of need, though recent analyses suggest that this is still not usually the case in the UK (Simpson and McNulty 2008). However, pockets of good practice are emerging that adopt a 'gender-sensitive' approach and that have the potential to provide a more relevant and effective service to women involved in drug use and offending.

A gender-sensitive approach

Given the acknowledged inadequacies of traditional and more innovative (penal) responses to women who encounter the criminal justice system, and women drug users in particular, the ongoing quest for appropriate models of intervention has continued. The needs and experiences of women (as both offenders and problem drug users) have often been subsumed under the needs and experiences of men in terms of criminal justice responses and support/treatment for drug problems. In particular, the disproportionately punitive impact on women of policies aimed at tackling drug-related crime has been criticised as a 'war on women' (Campbell 2000; Boyd 2004). Policies and practices that attempt to 'fit' women into systems dominated by, and designed for, men have been shown to be ineffective in responding to women and have led to increasing attempts to devise models for working specifically (and effectively) with women.

In 2003, Bloom *et al.* set out a comprehensive gender-responsive strategy for the US National Institute of Corrections, which drew on a number of theoretical distinctions that they used to set out a blueprint for responding to women involved with the justice system. These theoretical bases included: 'pathways' theory (women and men follow different pathways into crime); relational theory (acknowledging the importance of relationships for women); theories of trauma;[3] and addiction. They acknowledged that women differed from men in their experience across these areas and noted that a 'gender-sensitive' response required an acknowledgement of these distinctions (Bloom *et al.* 2003). Models of intervention based on this gender-responsive approach aim (within the constraints of criminal justice systems) to help women to address the emotional damage caused by the trauma of physical and sexual abuse, and to work towards repairing or recreating healthy relationships with self and others (Covington and Surrey 1997; Covington 2000).

This has enabled the identification of some key characteristics, considered crucial to effective programme development (Bloom *et al.* 2003; Holloway *et al.* 2005; Loucks *et al.* 2006), namely: that workers can be more effective when gender-responsive and gender-sensitive; they should be caring and available to clients; as far as possible have some shared experiences with the women they are working with; and be able to take a holistic approach in order to understand the experiences and to support the women with whom they are working. Furthermore, training should continue on an ongoing basis. Importantly, the environment where support and intervention takes place should be 'safe' and aftercare should form a key element in service provision (Covington 2000). This model has been used with some success (for example in Scotland, see Loucks *et al.* 2006).

Projects such as the 218 Centre in Glasgow (Loucks *et al.* 2006; Malloch and Loucks 2007; Malloch *et al.* 2008) demonstrate the value of a gender-responsive approach to the women who use the resources, even where its impact is difficult to measure in quantifiable terms. The centrality of relationships in engaging women with addictions, in conjunction with a flexible and comprehensive service, was considered to be crucial by workers, women using the service and other agencies.

Conclusions

For female drug users, a gender-specific application of rehabilitation (changing life circumstances) and recovery (from problematic substance use) is necessary, but not unproblematic (Thom 2010). Employing a gender-sensitive model for women with addiction issues, in practice, requires the presence of a number of factors. Research clearly shows that substance misuse is often central to women's offending, but also illustrates that this cannot be addressed in isolation from the contextual factors that both initiate and perpetuate it. Addressing women's addictions is critical, both to reduce their involvement in offending and to begin to address the resulting overarching chaos in their lives (Covington 2000).

Criminal justice responses have been shown to be limited in effect; indeed current criminal justice and wider social policies can actually make it more difficult for women to get out of these systems – a fundamental prerequisite of both rehabilitation and recovery. Responses can be improved pragmatically, but doing so requires that account is taken of women's pathways into crime and problematic drug use. The international evidence highlights that the problems experienced by women drug users in the criminal justice system are shared across international borders; presumably the solutions can also be shared. What is also evident is that the underlying factors for women's drug use may not be conducive to conventional 'treatment' but require addressing at the root. Rather than increasing criminal justice responses, which will invariably have an element of punishment by their very ethos, there is a need to identify and address the broader social contexts within which women's (problematic) drug use is initiated and propagated.

Notes

1 This also applies to other substances such as opiates and benzodiazepines.

2 For example, Allen *et al.* (2003) report that 90 per cent of Jamaican women in prison in England and Wales for drug offences were first offenders.
3 The recognition that many women who are in contact with the system have experienced various forms of trauma has increasingly come to inform the development of resources (Herman 1992).

References

Advisory Council on the Misuse of Drugs (2003) *Hidden Harm: Responding to the Needs of Children of Problem Drug Users*. London: ACMD.

Allen, R., Levenson, J. and Garside, R. (2003) *A Bitter Pill to Swallow: The Sentencing of Foreign National Drug Couriers*, http://www.rethinking.org.uk/informed/pdf/briefing5.pdf.pdf (last accessed 2 February 2010)

Anderson, T. (ed.) (2008) *Neither Villain nor Victim*. New Brunswick, NJ: Rutgers University Press.

Audit Commission (2002) *Changing Habits: The Commissioning and Management of Community Drug Treatment Services for Adults*. London: Audit Commission.

Becker, J. and Duffy, C. (2002) *Women Drug Users and Drugs Service Provision*. London: Home Office.

Beckerman, A. and Fontana, L. (2001) 'Issues of race and gender in court-ordered substance abuse treatment', *Journal of Offender Rehabilitation*, 33 (4): 45–61.

Bennet, T. and Holloway, K. (2004) *Drug use and Offending: Summary Results of the First Two Years of the NEW-ADAM Programme*. London: Home Office.

Best, D., Walker, D., Foster, A., Ellis-Gray, S. and Day, E. (2008) 'Gender differences in risk and treatment uptake in drug using offenders assessed in custody suite settings', *Policing and Society*, 18 (4): 474–85.

Birch, A., Dobbie, F., Chalmers, T., Barnsdale, L. McIvor, G. and Yates, R. (2006) *Evaluation of the Arrest Referral Pilot Scheme*. Edinburgh: Scottish Executive Social Research.

Bloom, B., Owen, B. and Covington, S. (2003) *Gender Responsive Strategies*. Washington, DC: US Department of Justice.

Bloom, B., Owen, B. and Covington, S. (2004) 'Women offenders and the gendered effects of public policy', *Review of Policy Research*, 21 (1): 31–48.

Borrill, J., Maden, A., Martin, A., Weaver, T., Stimson, G., Farrell, M. and Barnes, T. (2003) *Differential Substance Misuse Treatment Needs of Women, Ethnic Minorities and Young Offenders in Prison: Prevalence of Substance Misuse and Treatment Needs*. London: Home Office.

Boyd, S. (2004) *From Witches to Crack Moms*. Durham, North Carolina: Carolina Academic Press.

Bush-Baskette, S.R. (1998) 'The war on drugs as a war against black women', in S.L. Miller (ed.) *Crime Control and Women: Feminist Implications of Criminal Justice Policy*. Thousand Oaks, CA: SAGE.

Butler, P. and Kousoulou, D. (2006) *Women at Risk: The Mental Health of Women in Contact with the Judicial System*. London: Care Services Improvement Partnership.

Caddle, D. and Crisp, D. (1997) *Imprisoned Women and Mothers*. Home Office Research Study 162. London: Home Office.

Campbell, N. (2000) *Using Women: Gender, Drug Policy and Social Justice*. New York, NY: Routledge.

Corston, Baroness (2007) *The Corston Report: A Review of Women with Particular Vulnerabilities in the Criminal Justice System*. London: Home Office.

Councell, R. (2003) *The Prison Population in 2002: A Statistical Review*. London: Home Office.

Covington, S. (2000) 'Helping women recover', *Alcohol Treatment Quarterly*, 18 (3): 99–111.

Covington, S. and Surrey, J. (1997) 'The relational model of women's psychological development', in S. Wilsnack and R. Wilsnack (eds) *Gender and Alcohol: Individual and Social Perspectives*. New Brunswick, NJ: Rutgers Center of Alcohol Studies.

D'Angelo, L. and Wolf, R.V. (2002) 'Women and addiction: Challenges for drug court practitioners', *Justice System Journal*, 23 (3): 385–400.

Danner, M.J.E. (1998) 'Three strikes and it's women who are out: The hidden consequences for women of criminal justice policy reforms', in S.L. Miller (ed.) *Crime Control and Women: Feminist Implications of Criminal Justice Policy*. Thousand Oaks, CA: SAGE.

Dannerbeck, A., Sundet, P. and Lloyd, K. (2002) 'Drug courts: Gender differences and their implications for treatment strategies', *Corrections Compendium*, 27 (12): 1–5 and 24–26.

Duke, K. (2003) *Drugs, Prisons and Policy-Making*. Basingstoke: Palgrave MacMillan.

Eaton, M. (1993) *Women After Prison*. Buckingham: Open University Press.

Eley, S., Gallop, K., McIvor, G., Morgan, K. and Yates, R. (2002) *Evaluation of Pilot Drug Treatment and Testing Orders*. Edinburgh: Scottish Executive Central Research Unit.

Ettorre, E. (2007) *Revisioning Women and Drug Use*. London: Palgrave Macmillan.

Fischer, M., Geiger, B. and Hughes, M.E. (2007) 'Female recidivists speak about their experience in drug court while engaging in appreciative inquiry', *International Journal of Offender Therapy and Comparative Criminology*, 51 (6): 703–22.

Fox, A., Khan, L., Briggs, D., Rees-Jones, N., Thompson, Z. and Owens, J. (2005) *Throughcare and Aftercare: Approaches and Promising Practice in Service Delivery for Clients Released from Prison or Leaving Residential Rehabilitation*. Home Office Online Report 01/05.

Gray, A.R. and Saum, C.A. (2005) 'Mental health, gender and drug court completion', *American Journal of Criminal Justice*, 30: 55–69.

Harrell, A., Roman, J. and Sack, E. (2001) *Drug Court Services for Female Offenders, 1996–1999: Evaluation of the Brooklyn Treatment Court*. Washington, DC: Urban Institute.

Hartman, J.L., Listwan, S.J. and Shaffer, D.K. (2007) 'Methamphetamine users in a community-based drug court: Does gender matter?', *Journal of Offender Rehabilitation*, 45 (3/4): 109–30.

Herman, J.L. (1992) *Trauma and Recovery*. New York, NY: Basic Books.

Hoare, J. and Flatley, J. (2008) *Drug Misuse Declared: Findings from the 2007/08 British Crime Survey*. London: Home Office.

Holloway, K., Bennet, T. and Farrington, D. (2005) *The Effectiveness of Criminal Justice and Treatment Programmes in Reducing Drug-Related Crime: A Systematic Review*. London: Home Office Online Report 26/05.

Home Office (2001) *The Government's Strategy for Women Offenders*. London: Home Office.

Hough, M., Clancy, A., McSweeney, T. and Turnbull, P. (2003) *The Impact of Drug Treatment and Testing Orders on Offending: Two Year Reconviction Results*. London: Home Office Findings 184.

Hubbard, D.J. and Matthews, B. (2008) 'Reconciling the differences between the "gender-responsive" and the "what works" literatures to improve services for girls', *Crime and Delinquency*, 54 (2): 225–58.

Huddleston, C.W., Marlowe, D.B. and Casebolt, R. (2008) *Painting the Current Picture: A National Report Card on Drug Courts and Other Problem-Solving Court Programs in the United States*. Alexandria, VA: National Drug Court Institute.

Information Services Division (2008) *Drug Misuse Statistics Scotland 2008*. Edinburgh: Information Services Division.

Jamieson, J., McIvor, G. and Murray, C. (1999) *Understanding Offending Among Young People*. Edinburgh: The Stationery Office.

Johnson, H. (2004) *Key Findings from the Drug Use Careers of Female Offenders Study*. Canberra, ACT: Australian Institute of Criminology.

Johnson, S., Shaffer, D.K. and Latessa, E.J. (2000) 'A comparison of male and female drug court participants', *Corrections Compendium*, 25 (6): 1–9.

Loucks, N. (2004) 'Women in prison', in G. McIvor (ed.) *Women Who Offend*. London: Jessica Kingsley.

Loucks, N., Malloch, M., McIvor, G. and Gelsthorpe, L. (2006) *Evaluation of the 218 Centre*. Edinburgh: Scottish Executive Social Research.

Loxley, W. and Adams, K. (2009) *Women, Drug Use and Crime: Findings from the Drug Use Monitoring in Australia Program*. Canberra, ACT: Australian Institute of Criminology.

MacLeod, P., Page, L., Kinver, A., Iliasov, A. and Williams, R. (2009) *2008–09 British Crime and Justice Survey: Drug Use*. Edinburgh: Scottish Government.

MacRae, R., McIvor, G., Malloch, M., Barry, M. and Murray, L. (2006) *Evaluation of the Scottish Prison Service Transitional Care Initiative*.

Edinburgh: Scottish Executive Social Research, http://www.scotland.gov.uk/Publications/2006/02/08110928/0

Mair, G., Cross, N. and Taylor, S. (2007) *The Use and Impact of the Community Order and the Suspended Sentence Order*. London: Centre for Crime and Justice Studies.

Makkai, T. and Payne, J. (2003) *Key findings from the drug use careers of offenders (DUCO) study*, Trends and Issues in Crime and Criminal Justice No. 237. Canberra, ACT: Australian Institute of Criminology.

Malloch, M. (1999) 'Drug use, prison, and the social construction of femininity', *Women's Studies International Forum*, 22 (3): 349–58.

Malloch, M. (2000) 'Caring for drug users? The experiences of women prisoners', *The Howard Journal*, 39 (4): 354–68.

Malloch, M. (2001) *Women, Drugs and Custody*. Winchester: Waterside Press

Malloch, M. (2004) 'Women, drug use and the criminal justice system', in G. McIvor (ed.) *Women Who Offend*. London: Jessica Kingsley.

Malloch, M. (2008) 'A spoonful of sugar? Treating women in prison', in T. Anderson (ed.) *Neither Victims nor Villains*. New Brunswick, NJ: Rutger University Press.

Malloch, M. and Loucks, N. (2007) 'Responding to drug and alcohol problems: Innovations and effectiveness in treatment programmes for women', in R. Sheehan, G. McIvor and C. Trotter (eds) *What Works with Women Offenders*. Cullompton: Willan Publishing.

Malloch, M., McIvor, G. and Loucks, N. (2008) Time out for women: Innovation in Scotland in a context of change, *The Howard Journal*, 47 (4): 383–99.

Mauer, M., Potler, C. and Wolf. R (1999) *Gender and Justice: Women, Drugs and Sentencing Policy*. Washington, DC: The Sentencing Project.

McIvor, G. (2004) *Reconviction Following Drug Treatment and Testing Orders*. Edinburgh: Scottish Executive Social Research.

McIvor, G., Barnsdale, L., Eley, S., Malloch, M., Yates, R. and Brown, A. (2006) *The Operation and Effectiveness of the Scottish Drug Court Pilots*. Edinburgh, Scottish Executive, http://www.scotland.gov.uk/Publications/2006/03/28112035/0

McIvor, G., Trotter, C. and Sheehan, R. (2009) 'Women, resettlement and desistance', *Probation Journal*, 56 (4): 347–61.

McKeganey, N., Barnard, M. and McIntosh, J. (2002) 'Paying the price for their parents' addiction: Meeting the needs of the children of drug using parents', *Drugs: Education, Prevention and Policy*, 9 (3): 232–46.

McKeganey, N., Connelly, C., Knepll, J., Norrie, J. and Reid, L. (2000) *Interviewing and Drug Testing of Arrestees in Scotland: A Pilot of the Arrestee Drug Abuse Monitoring (ADAM) Methodology*. Edinburgh: Scottish Executive Central Research Unit.

Ministry of Justice (2009) *Population in Custody Monthly Tables June 2009 England and Wales*. London: Ministry of Justice.

Morris, A., Wilkinson, C., Tisi, A., Woodrow, J. and Rockley, A. (1995) *Managing the Needs of Female Prisoners*. London: Home Office.

Mumola, C.J. and Karberg, J.C. (2006) *Drug Use and Dependence, State and Federal Prisoners, 2004*. Washington, DC: Bureau of Justice Statistics.

Mwenda, L. (2005) *Home Office Statistical Bulletin: Drug Offenders in England and Wales 2004*. London: Home Office.

Patel, S. and Stanley, S. (2008) *The Use of the Community Order and the Suspended Sentence Order for Women*. London: Centre for Crime and Justice Studies.

Peters, R., Strozier, A., Murrin, M. and Kearns, W. (1997) 'Treatment of substance-abusing jail inmates: Examination of gender differences', *Journal of Substance Abuse Treatment*, 14 (4): 339–49.

Pitcher, J. and Aris, R. (2003) *Women and Street Sex Work: Issues Arising from an Evaluation of an Arrest Referral Scheme*. London: NACRO.

Richie, B.E. (2008) 'Challenges incarcerated women face as they return to their communities: Findings from life history interviews', *Crime and Delinquency*, 47 (3): 368–89.

Saum, C.A. and Gray, A.R. (2008) 'Facilitating change for women? Exploring the role of therapeutic jurisprudence in drug court', in T. Anderson (ed.) *Neither Villain Nor Victim: Empowerment and Agency Among Women Substance Abusers*. New Brunswick, NJ: Rutgers University Press.

Schwartz, J. and Steffensmeier, D. (2007) 'The nature of female offending: Patterns and explanation', in R.T. Zaplin (ed.) *Female Offenders: Critical Perspectives and Effective Interventions* (2nd edn). Boston, MA: Jones and Bartlett.

Scottish Drugs Forum (2003) *Response to the Scottish Executive National Review of Treatment and Rehabilitation Services*. Glasgow: Scottish Drugs Forum.

Scottish Executive (2002) *A Better Way*. Edinburgh: Scottish Executive.

Scottish Executive (2003) *Getting Our Priorities Right: Good Practice Guidance for Working with Children and Families Affected by Substance Misuse*. Edinburgh: Scottish Executive.

Scottish Government (2007) *Criminal Justice Social Work Statistics 2006–7*. Edinburgh: Scottish Government.

Scottish Government (2010) *Criminal Justice Social Work Statistics 2008–9*. Edinburgh: Scottish Government.

Shaffer, D.K., Hartman, J.L. and Listwan, S.J. (2009) 'Drug abusing women in the community: The impact of drug court involvement on recidivism', *Journal of Drug Issues*, Fall: 803–28.

Shaw, S. (2005) *The Death in Custody of a Woman and the Series of Deaths in HMP/YOI Styal August 2002–2003*. London: Prisons and Probation Ombudsman for England and Wales.

Simpson, M. and McNulty, J. (2008) 'Different needs: Women's drug use and treatment in the UK', *International Journal of Drug Policy*, 19 (2): 169–75.

Singleton, N., Pendry, E., Simpson, T., Goddard, E., Farrell, M., Marsden, J. and Taylor, C. (2005) *The Impact of Mandatory Drug Testing in Prisons*. Home Office Online Report 03/05, http://www.homeoffice.gov.uk/rds/pdfs05/rdsolr0305.pdf

Social Exclusion Unit (2002) *Reducing Re-offending by Ex-prisoners*. London: Social Exclusion Unit.

Sondhi, A., O'Shea, J. and Williams, T. (2001) *Statistics from the Arrest Referral Monitoring Programme for October 2000 to March 2001*. London: Home Office.

Sondhi, A., O'Shea, J. and Williams, T. (2002) *Arrest Referral: Emerging Findings from the National Monitoring and Evaluation Programme*. London: Home Office.

Staton-Tindall, M., Duvall, J.L., Oser, C.B., Leukefeld, C.G. and Webster, J.M. (2008) 'Gender differences in employment among drug court participants: The influence of peer relations and friendship network, *Journal of Social Work Practice in the Addictions*, 8 (4): 530–47.

Taplin, S. (2002) *The New South Wales Drug Court Evaluation: A Process Evaluation*. Sydney, NSW: New South Wales Bureau of Crime Statistics and Research.

Thom, B. (2010) 'Women and recovery', in R. Yates and M. Malloch (eds) *Tackling Addiction: Pathways to Recovery*. London: Jessica Kingsley.

Turnbull, P.J., McSweeney, T., Webster, R., Edmunds, M. and Hough, M. (2000) *Drug Treatment and Testing Orders: Final Evaluation Report. Home Office Research Study 212*. London: Home Office.

Wald, P.M. (2001) 'Why focus on women offenders?', *Criminal Justice*, Spring: 10–16.

Webster, J.M., Rosen, P.J., Krietemeyer, J., Mateyoke-Scrivner, A., Staton-Tindall, M. and Leukefeld, C. (2006) 'Gender, mental health, and treatment motivation in a drug court setting, *Journal of Psychoactive Drugs*, 38 (4): 441–8.

West, H.C. and Sabol, W.J. (2008) *Prisoners in 2007*. Washington, DC: Bureau of Justice Statistics.

Willis, K. and Rushforth, C. (2003) *The Female Criminal: An Overview of Women's Drug Use and Offending Behaviour*, Trends and Issues in Crime and Criminal Justice No. 264. Canberra, ACT: Australian Institute of Criminology.

Chapter 11

Managing risk in the community: How gender matters[1]

Janet T. Davidson

Introduction

Both institutional and community correctional populations have grown steadily over the past three decades. This growth has certainly captured the attention of scholars and some policy-makers, and more recently politicians concerned about the budgetary impact of such growth. Indeed, near the end of 2008 the Pew Centers released a report detailing that one in every 100 adults in the United States was incarcerated, a truly astounding number (Pew Center 2008). When the number of offenders serving community-based orders is included, the number of adults in the United States who are under correctional supervision is one in 31 (Pew Center 2009). Although less visible, correctional supervision in the community clearly remains the chief punishment strategy in the United States.

What has been less obvious and received far less attention, though, is the growth in the rate of female involvement in the criminal justice system – both in institutional and community correctional settings. Female offenders mark the fastest growing segment of the criminal justice system in the US (Bloom *et al.* 2003; Hannah-Moffat 2009; Holtfreter and Cupp 2007; Holsinger and Van Voorhis 2005; Glaze and Bonczar 2007; Sabol and Couture 2008). Female offenders have largely been rendered invisible due to their smaller numbers, relative to men (Belknap 2007; Bloom *et al.* 2003; Flavin and Desautels 2006; Holtfreter *et al.* 2004; McIvor *et al.* 2004; Owen 2003; Sommers *et al.* 2006). Indeed, female offenders represent, approximately: 24 per cent of all arrests (Federal Bureau of Investigation 2008); 13 per cent of

216

the total US jail population (Sabol and Minton 2008); 24 per cent of the total US probation population (Glaze and Bonczar 2007); 12 per cent of the total US parole population (Glaze and Bonczar 2007); 7 per cent of the US prison population (Sabol and Couture 2008); and 2 per cent of those on death row (Snell 2006).

Regardless, growing numbers of offenders, both male and female, have necessitated new ways of dealing with offenders. Increasing calls have been made to use evidence to manage our offenders in ways that are smarter and will both save money *and* increase public safety. Actuarial-based risk/need instruments have become, at least theoretically, the backbone of offender management in the community. These instruments are designed to manage both risk and programmatic needs of offenders. The application of these seemingly gender-neutral instruments to female offenders, though, does give cause for concern – mainly because gendered factors are still largely neglected at best or ignored at worst (Belknap and Holsinger 2006). This neglect may indeed have very tangible, negative consequences for female offenders.

The rise of the risk and need assessment model

Risk/need instruments remain a largely hidden method of controlling offenders, yet their use nonetheless impacts a significant number of offenders who serve time in the community in terms of case management (Holtfreter and Cupp 2007; Jones 1999; Vose *et al.* 2008) and recidivism prediction (Champion 1994; Hudson 2003). Actuarial risk assessment instruments generally involve (Harcourt 2007: 1):

> the use of statistical rather than clinical methods on large datasets to determine different levels of criminal offending associated with one or more group traits, in order (1) to predict past, present, or future criminal behavior and (2) to administer criminal justice outcome.

Risk assessment has historically involved the use of static, or unchangeable, factors that were utilised to 'score' offenders in terms of their likelihood to reoffend while serving time in the community. The more recent inclusion of dynamic factors, or factors that are changeable, allows for the crafting of case management, or treatment plans, and marks currently used third-generation risk/need assessment instruments as a significant improvement in offender management

(Hannah-Moffat and Shaw 2003; Van Voorhis 2005). While static factors still represent risks, criminogenic needs (the dynamic factors) are those linked to, and predictive of, criminal behaviour – yet they are also amenable to change (Bonta 1996).

Criminogenic needs can be reduced and, thus, so can the overall risk for recidivism via the correct interventions. Hannah-Moffat and Shaw (2003: 60) note that this represents a 'mixed model of government, wherein traditional rehabilitative strategies are reaffirmed and deployed to minimise and reduce risk'. This newer generation of instruments provides the simultaneous ability to predict (Petersilia 2003; Van Voorhis et al. 2008) as well as to reduce the likelihood of recidivism (Andrews and Bonta 2000; Jones 1999).

Risk, need and female offenders: One size does not fit all

The majority of instruments in use today, though, virtually ignore gender-specific variables otherwise informed via the pathways perspective or other gendered theoretical literature (Deschenes et al. 2006; Hannah-Moffat 2009; Maurutto and Hannah-Moffat 2007; Reisig et al. 2006; Van Voorhis et al. 2008). There exists evidence that certain demographic characteristics, such as gender, do and should matter in the creation and application of risk/need assessments (Deschenes et al. 2006; Maurutto and Hannah-Moffat 2007).

Abuse in the home, at the hands of family members and intimates, is undeniably linked to, and key to, understanding female offending (Belknap and Holsinger 2006; Bloom et al. 2003; Chesney-Lind 1997; Parsons and Warner-Robbins 2002; Reisig et al. 2006; Van Voorhis et al. 2008). Female offenders are more likely than their male counterparts to have sustained past and/or present victimisation. In turn, female offenders often turn to substance use as a means of dealing with this untreated trauma (Bloom et al. 2003; Comack 2006; Hollin and Palmer 2006).

These considerations, along with the myriad ways that patriarchy shapes female offenders' lives, are largely void in discussions regarding their management. Data indicate that 46.5 per cent of state prison female inmates had ever been physically abused and 39 per cent had ever been sexually abused, compared to male figures of 13.4 per cent and 5.8 per cent, respectively (Harlow 1999). Similar gender disparities exist for federal prison inmates, jail inmates and probationers. Other commonly cited factors related to offending for females (gender-specific needs) include the following:

- abuse (sexual and physical)-related trauma (Van Voorhis *et al.* 2008; Hubbard and Matthews 2008; Holtfreter and Cupp 2007; Bloom *et al.* 2003; Reisig *et al.* 2006; Widom 1995; Chesney-Lind and Pasko 2004; Hollin and Palmer 2006);

- childcare needs (Van Voorhis *et al.* 2008; Holtfreter and Cupp 2007; Hollin and Palmer 2006; Bloom *et al.* 2003);

- mental health problems (Van Voorhis *et al.* 2008; Hubbard and Matthews 2008; Holtfreter and Cupp 2007; Hollin and Palmer 2006);

- low social capital, including lack of education and employment skills (Holtfreter and Cupp 2007; Reisig *et al.* 2006);

- drug abuse (Holtfreter and Cupp 2007; Hollin and Palmer 2006; Reisig *et al.* 2006);

- problems with intimate relationships (Van Voorhis *et al.* 2008); and

- self-esteem and self-efficacy (Van Voorhis *et al.* 2008; Hubbard and Matthews 2008).

Few studies have specifically examined women's criminogenic risks and needs, separate from those of men (Hollin and Palmer 2006; Reisig *et al.* 2006; Holtfreter *et al.* 2004; Olson *et al.* 2003; Bloom and Owen 2002; Funk 1999; Richie 2001). Thus, it is not empirically known whether women's more prevalent histories of physical and/or sexual abuse, mental and physical health problems, and relationship and parental difficulties (as well as other gendered factors) are in fact relevant to current risk/need instruments (Reisig *et al.* 2006).

The Level of Service Inventory-Revised (LSI-R)

The Level of Service Inventory-Revised (LSI-R) is the most widely utilised third-generation risk/need instrument (Holtfreter and Cupp 2007; Vose *et al.* 2008) and is the instrument of focus for this research. It is specifically designed to measure criminogenic risks and needs (Bonta 1996). The instrument contains 54 items and is calculated, mainly, via the Burgess method of scoring. For example, the presence of a factor is scored as a one and the absence of the risk factor is a zero. The sum of all the scores provides the total, overall risk score. Further, the 54 items contained in the instrument are clustered into ten different domain areas.[2] In addition to the classification of risk level, the instrument is also designed to identify the domain area(s) that is most criminogenic for individual offenders and, hence, in need of treatment intervention.

An increasing number of studies have attempted to empirically address whether there are significant differences in predictors of recidivism for men and women (Bloom *et al.* 2003; Farr 2000; Olson *et al.* 2003, Bloom 2000; Funk 1999; Manchak *et al.* 2009; Smith *et al.* 2009; Van Voorhis *et al.* 2008; Veysey and Hamilton 2007; Fagan *et al.* 2007) yet these studies are still relatively few compared with male-based research. Especially poignant is the work highlighted by Holtfreter and Cupp (2007), which highlights that the majority of the research used to support the validity of the LSI-R for females has been based on males. Only 11 of the 41 empirical studies published from 1986 to 2006 actually reported statistics for female offenders. Twenty-six of these studies, over half, were based on male-only samples, only five included female-only samples. When studies have produced claims of gender neutrality, they are usually faulted on two fronts. First, they do not disaggregate gender. Secondly, they do not utilise representative samples of female offenders (Holtfreter and Cupp 2007).

Regardless, findings have certainly been mixed. Funk (1999) discovered that a female-only model with the inclusion of gendered factors demonstrated a higher adjusted R^2 than the male-only model. Child abuse, neglect and running away emerged as significant predictors of recidivism. Olson *et al.* (2003) found gendered differences in predictors of rearrest. Holsinger and Latessa (2003) found significant correlations between gender and overall LSI-R scores. Holtfreter *et al.* (2004) revealed that the LSI-R risk level dropped out as a significant predictor of recidivism once poverty status was controlled. Hubbard and Pratt (2004) found some gender differences in predictors of recidivism. Reisig *et al.* (2006) discovered that the LSI-R was only predictive for women whose offending context paralleled that of male offenders and did not work well for women who followed gendered pathways to offending. Heilbrun *et al.* (2008) noted significant gender differences on the financial and companion domains but these were not linked with outcome. Finally, Van Voorhis *et al.* (2008) demonstrated that the inclusion of gender-relevant factors created better predictors of outcomes than did gender-neutral factors.

On the other hand, Harer and Langan (2001) discovered that the same classification instrument was able to predict violence equally well for males and females. Lowenkamp *et al.* (2001) exhibited that the LSI-R was predictive of recidivism for males and females and that past victimisation did not enhance its predictive ability. Vose et al. (2008), in a meta-analysis, found the LSI-R to be predictive of recidivism for females and males, noting the instrument worked best for mixed samples, followed by male- and finally female-only samples. Manchak et al. (2009) discovered that the LSI-R worked well for women and that gender did not moderate the prediction of recidivism. Finally, Smith et al. (2009), in a meta-analysis of 25 published studies, demonstrated predictive validity for both males and females.

At face value, tools such as the LSI-R appear to be gender neutral because *some* studies demonstrate predictive validity for both males and females (Raynor 2007). Yet important gender patterns do emerge when gender is analysed separately, such as the importance of controlling for economic marginalisation (Reisig et al. 2006) or other gender-specific factors (Van Voorhis et al. 2008). Thus, the results so far indicate that gender matters in some respect (Manchak et al. 2009). And, since case management concerns will follow and not precede assessment, the *context* of women's offending should be included in any attempt at an actuarial classification instrument[3] designed to assess risk and triage offenders into treatment.

Current research

Data collected as part of an ongoing study of recidivism in the State of Hawaii, USA, were utilised to discern whether the LSI-R demonstrated gender-specific differences in overall scores, domain scores, and recidivism. Participants for this portion of the study included all parolees and felony probationers who were released to community supervision via parole or sentenced to felony probation between 23 January 1998 and 1 February 2005. All offenders who had an LSI-R assessment *and* who had at least a year of exposure in the community (at the time of data analysis) were included in this study. It is noteworthy that this sample included 462 women and 2,046 men, a relatively large female offender sample size for this type of research (Holtfreter and Cupp 2007).

The State of Hawaii uses a pre-screening instrument prior to the application of the LSI-R to ensure that the LSI-R is applied to the riskiest offender population. The proxy is a screening instrument comprised of three items, including age at first arrest, number of prior arrests, and current age. Thus the overall representativeness of *all* male and female offenders is not maintained in this sample.

Assessing whether risk *means* (content validity) the same thing for men and women requires a qualitative methodology. Specifically, 18 male and 13 female offenders who were under community correctional supervision (felony probation or parole) were interviewed to assess these risks – from their perspective. Sprague (2005) reminds us that by listening to groups who have been traditionally neglected in research (e.g. female offenders) we create enormous opportunities to uncover what quantitative analyses might have otherwise been obscured.

Findings

While recidivism rates were significantly lower for the female offenders in this sample, their overall level of assessed risk/need according to the total LSI-R scores was not significantly different from the males (Table 11.1). Male offenders in this study did score significantly higher than females on the criminal history (t=–7.686, p<.001) and leisure-recreation (t=–2.781, p<.001) domains.

Table 11.1 Overall LSI-R score by gender

Sample	Female	Male
Total sample	21.63	21.91
Probation only	21.67	21.96
Parole only	21.29	21.53

Note: Differences are not significant based on t-test for difference of means.

Female offenders in this sample scored significantly higher on the following domains: financial (t=5.704, p<.001), family and marital (t=3.598, p<.01), and emotional and personal (t=4.716, p<.001). Females were significantly more likely to report having a reliance on social assistance (t=8.313, p<.001), having a criminal spouse or family member (t=5.939, p<.001), having past (t=5.761, p<.001) and current (t=4.524, p<.001) mental health treatment, to having been assessed with a mental disorder that moderately interferes with daily living (t=2.087, p<.05), to have been frequently unemployed (t=2.148, p<.05) and to have never been employed for a full year (t=3.808, p<.001). There were no overall scoring differences between male and female offenders in terms of the following domains: education and employment, accommodation, and companions.

Correlation with outcome

The correlation between the LSI-R total score and recidivism was slightly stronger for men (r=.27, p<.001) than for women (r=.26, p<.001, see Table 11.2).[4] The strongest domain correlation with recidivism for women was the alcohol and drug domain (r=.27, p<.001), even though this is an area in which men actually scored slightly higher than women (though not significantly so). It is also worth noting that the correlation with recidivism for this domain is slightly higher than the total LSI-R score.

The education and employment domain remains a strong correlate of recidivism for women (r=.23, p<.001), but it does for men as well (it demonstrates the strongest correlation for the males in this sample). The family and marital domain on the LSI-R is also a significant predictor of recidivism for the women (r=.21, p<.001).

The companion domain is among the strongest correlates of recidivism (r=.19, p<.001) for females. Interestingly, the companion domain, for women, is correlated with other subscales in a manner not evident with the males. For example, the companion domain is correlated strongly with the following domains: alcohol and drug (r=.45, p<.001), accommodation (r=.41, p<.001), family and marital (r=.39, p<.001), education and employment (r=.32, p<.001) and attitudes and orientations (r=.32, p<.001) for females. The significant correlation with recidivism, and even stronger correlation with some

Table 11.2 Bivariate correlations with recidivism for LSI-R total score and domains for the entire sample and male- and female-only samples

Total LSI-R score and domains	Entire sample	Male only	Female only
Total LSI-R score	.27***	.27***	.26***
Criminal history score	.10***	.09***	.11*
Education and employment	.27***	.28***	.23***
Financial	.10***	.10***	.13***
Family and marital	.12***	.10***	.21***
Accommodation	.14***	.15***	.10**
Leisure and recreation	.14***	.13***	.19***
Companions	.21***	.21***	.19***
Alcohol and drug	.21***	.20***	.27***
Emotional and personal	.07**	.07**	.08
Attitudes and orientation	.13***	.12***	.17***

Note: * p<.05, ** p<.01, ***p<.001

223

of the other domains, may indicate that the choice of companions for many of these women is, in fact, a criminogenic one that exacerbates other areas of risk.

In sum, predictive validity was essentially identical for the males and females in this sample (yet these findings are likely affected by the exclusion of the less serious offenders). We may not be fully operationalising risks and needs of the female offenders, though, as evidenced by the stronger correlates of recidivism for women on domains with higher scores by the males.

Offender views on categories related to LSI-R domains – assessing content validity

Following is the analysis of the content validity of the LSI-R using qualitative data from this sample of interviewees. Some domains are left out in this work for two reasons. First, the domain did not exhibit substantial gendered differences. Second, the content validity was not challenged by the interview data for either males or females. The excluded domains include leisure and recreation; companions; and attitudes and orientation.

Criminal history

This portion of the LSI-R is largely concerned with past criminal history. The majority of the men committed either a crime against another person (56 per cent) or a property crime (35 per cent) as their instant offence. The men committed their crimes to obtain money or goods (71 per cent), because of personal problems (19 per cent), or because they were drug-affected or were fulfilling some other personal gratification (2 per cent). Most of the men committed their crimes alone (76 per cent) and most began their criminal careers as juveniles (88 per cent). It is not surprising that the majority of these male offenders were on parole (65 per cent). The men also tended to have more arrests than did the women.

Over half (53.8 per cent) of the women in this sample committed a drug offence, while the remaining committed an approximately equal number of violent and property crimes. Women tended to have less serious criminal histories than did the males. These data reveal that women's criminality was often situated within the context of an intimate relationship or in her substance use. Criminal acts often involved attempts to obtain drugs, use drugs, or get money to buy drugs. These data demonstrate that the pathway to drugs and crime is quite different for females when compared with males.

Education and employment

The education and employment domain within the LSI-R is described as 'straightforward' in terms of assessing risk for a community correctional population (Andrews and Bonta 2000). Yet the interviews demonstrate that this is not necessarily the case.

A significant number of men and women in this sample were either required or strongly encouraged to remain unemployed while they were in substance abuse treatment and/or living in a clean and sober living treatment environment. They instead relied on social assistance (44.4 per cent of the males and 61.5 per cent of the females), which is yet another risk factor per the LSI-R. Finally, an additional component for many was mental health treatment. While being unemployed, in mental health treatment and receiving social assistance may be criminogenic risk/need factors, being in treatment and/or in a clean and sober house is nonetheless protective.

Many of the women in this sample were abused as girls, which led them to become truant and/or to run away from home. They often gave up on or were unable to continue their education and worked in either illegal or other historically female positions that placed them subservient to men (e.g. the sex industry). Rose, for example, lost both of her parents when she was young – they both passed away from liver disease due to alcoholism. She lived in an abusive home and began to run away at an early age, dropped out of school and entered prostitution to earn money. Her first arrest for prostitution was at the age of 14. Although Rose did work, she had few legitimate jobs and a lack of education. She later earned her GED[5] in prison. Her work trajectory was guided by the context of her life circumstances rather than by a lack of work ethic.

Educational levels were low for many in this sample. Many of those who had obtained a GED did so in prison. Females were slightly more educated, though. Roughly one-third (30.8 per cent) of the females had a high school education or *less* (including GED), compared with 72.2 per cent of the males.

Financial

The LSI-R uses two questions to measure an offender's financial status: whether they have any financial problems (trouble meeting their basic needs, not just merely having debt) and whether they currently rely on social assistance. A greater percentage of the females (76.9 per cent) who were interviewed exhibited financial problems than did the males (61.1 per cent). Approximately three-fifths (61.5 per cent) of the females were currently dependent on social assistance compared with less than half of the men (44.4 per cent).

As discussed in the previous section, the interviews revealed contextual problems with the employment domain. To reiterate, drawing social assistance often requires the recipient to obtain mental health treatment – a risk factor per the LSI-R. This domain simply did not match the *context* of social assistance for many in this sample.

The males in this sample were typically on social assistance due to an addiction to drugs that preceded incarceration or probation. Some were living in clean and sober homes where they were required to go to treatment and remained unemployed until they completed treatment. They were typically either on welfare or on Supplemental Security Income (SSI).[6]

Many of the females in this study were in similar situations. Olivia is a 35-year-old French/Indian woman currently on probation for a drug offence. She had a GED along with a sporadic employment history. She was in a clean and sober home that contained a substance abuse treatment component. She receives $418 per month from welfare, of which $360 went to rent in the home, along with all of her food stamp money. Olivia noted that while this is not enough to live on, 'the rules of this house is that program first. Get your program done, next step is a job.' At the time of these interviews, most of the interviewees who received social assistance did so because they were in a recovery programme.

The LSI-R does not capture the connections between social assistance (counted as a criminogenic risk factor) and treatment that occurs in the context of clean and sober homes, treatment, and/or mental health treatment. Holtfreter *et al.* (2004) found, for example, that economically disadvantaged female offenders who did not have their immediate needs satisfied with social assistance were more, rather than less, likely to reoffend. The content validity of this domain seems to be challenged by these and other data.

Family and marital

The LSI-R scoring manual (Andrews and Bonta 2000: 8) states that: 'In general, this area is dynamic and is assessed on current marital/family interactions. There may well be historical issues from family/marital relationships that are present needs. Such needs may be noted in the Emotional/Personal area.' Slightly more females (46.2 per cent) than males (33.3 per cent) were classified as being dissatisfied with their marital or equivalent situation. An even greater disparity existed in terms of non-rewarding relationships with parents: 92.3 per cent for the females as compared to 72.2 per cent for the males. Females (46.2 per cent) also were more likely to have a non-rewarding relationship with other relatives than males (5.6 per cent). Finally, 46.2 per cent of the females interviewed, but none of the males, had a criminal spouse or significant other.

The females' histories of abuse, as children and adults, allow some of the dysfunction and abuse of a bad relationship to become normalised. This potentially clouds this section on LSI-R assessments. Women may *appear* satisfied because they have normalised bad or abusive relationships – there is a tendency for abused women to minimise their victimisation (Belknap 2007).

The female offenders interviewed for this study demonstrated that their current relationships were very much intertwined with their past histories of childhood abuse as well as those within their adult relationships. The LSI-R will document whether the female is currently dissatisfied with her relationship. The true dynamic nature of women's current relationships, though, is shaped by what they have learned from their abusive pasts. These effects are not likely to be captured from questions contained in this section of the LSI-R.

These gendered issues are further connected to other areas in the LSI-R. For example, Randi's unstable employment was an unwanted consequence of victimisation at the hands of her intimate partner. Vicki, on the other hand, turned to drugs as a way of dealing with relationship-related trauma. Randi's unemployment and Vicki's substance abuse would simply count as criminogenic needs (and place them at assessed higher risk) without regard to what those factors really mean for them. The context of relationships for women is simply qualitatively more complex and thus more likely to interact with other measures. Content validity is challenged on this domain.

Accommodation

The accommodation portion of the LSI-R measures the level of satisfaction with current accommodation, whether or not the offender has had three or more address changes in the prior year, and whether or not they live in a high crime area. Women were less likely (23.1 per cent) than men (44.4 per cent) to indicate that they had unsatisfactory accommodation. The women (46.2 per cent) and men (44.4 per cent) were equally likely to live in high-crime neighbourhoods. Women were more likely (53.8 per cent), however, to have had three or more address changes during the past year or in the year prior to incarceration compared with men (11.1 per cent).

Frequent address changes for female offenders often reflected relationship difficulties. Some women noted that they moved frequently in order to get away from abusive partners. Many women in this sample not only moved frequently, they were often homeless within high-crime neighbourhoods as well.

Maile, a 50-year-old local woman convicted of theft was living in a clean and sober house, and homeless at the time of her arrest. Following is what Maile had to say about her situation:

> Before I came here [current clean and sober home] I was living on Maui. I was homeless also on Maui, I was homeless for maybe … seven – eight years. Then because of the living situation, and the drugs, and, uhm, and I was doing prostitution just to get money and the drugs and stuff like that. And within those years by passing I was doing drugs I was getting into when I was doing, uhm, forging checks an[d] stuff like that to get money and stuff.

Homelessness and frequent address changes are indeed signs of trouble in terms of risk for future offending for both males and females. For women, this pattern is compounded by the nature of their relationships with men and their substance abuse. As such, unsatisfactory accommodation may be measuring something different for men as compared with women.

Alcohol and drug problems

The questions in this section centre on whether the individual has now or has ever had an alcohol or a drug problem, and the extent to which either alcohol or drugs have interfered with or affected their law violations, marital/family relationships, school/work, medical health, or other negative indicators. While most in this sample reported that they did not currently have an alcohol problem, over half of the women (53.8 per cent) reported having had a problem with alcohol at some point in their lives, versus 38.9 per cent of the males. However, a full 100 per cent of the women and 83.3 per cent of the men reported a drug problem at some period in their lives.

All of the women in this sample said that drugs or alcohol had affected their law violations, 84.6 per cent noted that it had affected their family or marital situations; *all* noted impacts on their school or work; 53.8 per cent noted problems with medical histories; and 69.2 per cent had other indicators of interference (mainly homelessness). For men, the numbers are slightly different: 83.3 per cent noted that their alcohol or drug problems had impacted their law violations; 72.2 per cent demonstrated that their family or marital relationships were affected; 61.1 per cent had their school or work affected; 22.2 per cent had a medical problem directly related to their substance use; and 11.1 per cent had other indicators of serious interference.

In general, women mainly talked about self-medication and escape as their entrée into substance use while the men discussed their use in terms of partying and 'hanging out' with friends. Female offender substance use was often intertwined with issues of abuse (physical, sexual and/or emotional) and isolation. Rose, for example, discussed the difficulties that drugs had caused her, including stealing from friends and family to support her habit. Rose began using heroin at the age of 14. She had been placed into foster care at the age of five and ultimately ended up living with an aunt and uncle. The aunt physically abused her while the uncle repeatedly sexually abused her. The untreated trauma surrounding the sexual abuse is what ultimately led to her drug use, running away, and later entrée into the world of prostitution, pimps, and other crimes all designed to support her habit. Although she had thoughts of suicide, she ultimately opted to use drugs to ease her pain. This is what Rose, whose first drugs at the age of 14 were barbiturates and heroin, had to say about what drugs did for her:

> The first time I stuck it in my arm, I fell in love ... I was pretty miserable, I was being molested, and my aunt was very abusive, I wanted to be with my dad. I loved my dad, regardless of how bad he was, you know. I just remember these young days driving around the country and with him while all his friends drinking, partying, and having fun, and that was the only images I had of him ... happy guy ... so I wanted that and, I was suffering where I was, you know, and uhm, when I shot up I didn't feel the pain that I was going through, you know, because there was times at a young age that I wanted to commit suicide.

While the LSI-R might do a good job in terms of identifying criminogenic risks for females in terms of their alcohol and drug abuse, the lack of *contextual* understanding renders this problematic for treatment purposes.

Emotional and personal

This section of the LSI-R measures the following: moderate interference or emotional distress (signs of anxiety or depression), severe interference or active psychosis, past or present mental health treatment, and whether a psychological assessment is indicated in the past 12 months (or whether characteristics are present, such as excessive fears, hostility, impulse control problems, etc.). While only one of the males and none of the females in this sample exhibited either moderate or severe interference due to emotional and personal problems, there were other differences between males and females. All the females reported past mental health treatment compared with roughly half of the men (55.6 per cent). At the time of the interviews 61.5 per cent of the women were in receipt of mental health treatment compared with only 22.2 per cent of the males.

Given the more prevalent histories of abuse in the lives of women, it is not surprising that they are more likely to have had or currently be in mental health treatment. It appears that mental health treatment, past or present, would be a protective factor and should not count against the women as a risk factor. Yet, the LSI-R does just that. It is the *lack* of treatment that seems to be a criminogenic risk factor.

Zoe, a 38-year-old on parole for auto theft, exemplified the need for mental health treatment. Zoe lived with her mum and dad until she was eight years old, at which time her mother committed suicide in front of her. Her dad remarried and she lived with him and her new stepmother until the age of 12, at which time she permanently ran away from home. She dropped out of school in the seventh grade.[7] She continued into a life of drugs, prostitution, abusive men and crime. She had in the past and at the time of the interviews engaged in much-needed mental health treatment.

The men in this sample were less likely to have been in mental health treatment. Additionally, the context of their treatment was typically different from that of females. Hector, for example, said that he never really sought mental health treatment, but did see a psychiatrist once as a requirement of disability payment qualification. He did not see this as helpful in any way.

In sum, the content validity of this section for women is challenged on two fronts. First, most of the females in this sample *need* mental health treatment. The lack of, rather than the presence of, mental health treatment is a real risk factor for these women. Secondly, for both men and women, the LSI-R does not take into account how some of the characteristics that are considered risk factors are connected. For many of these women (and men), the ability to seek treatment – both mental and substance – along with the financial ability to do so (albeit limited) appears quite protective and promising in the reduction of recidivism.

What's left out of the LSI-R: Histories of victimisation, health problems and childcare

Histories of abuse

The histories of abuse for these women were striking. Men and women were asked about three forms of abuse in the interviews: emotional, physical and sexual. Almost three-quarters of the female offenders reported emotional abuse as a child compared with about a third of the males. A full 100 per cent of the females reported having been emotionally abused as an adult compared with none of the men.

Many of the women in this sample experienced sexual abuse as both children and adults. Over two-thirds, 69.2 per cent, of the females compared with 11.1 per cent of the males, experienced childhood sexual abuse. The abuse continued into adulthood for about a third of the females (38.5 per cent) but for none of the males. Finally, 61.5 per cent of the females experienced childhood physical abuse compared with 22.2 per cent of the males. The physical abuse continued into adulthood for many of the women – 61.5 per cent of the women were abused as adults compared with none of the men.

Jackie was a 35-year-old Filipina woman on probation for a drug offence. Jackie had four children and said that all of her children were 'ice babies'.[8] Jackie's long history of serious drug addiction was originally connected to her unhappy, and often abusive, family life. Jackie experienced emotional, sexual and physical abuse as a child as well as an adult. Jackie's history is key to understanding how a woman like this could have, for example, four babies born addicted to ice – and all by different fathers. Jackie experienced significant emotional abuse early on, from both her real mother and her hanai[9] mother:

> I remember in the third grade, we had a contest and the contest was called build your future, and it was out of whatever you could possibly think of, you know, some people used the ice cream, popsicle sticks. Well, for me I used Legos, and, uhm, I built the future. I built a huge thing, I had to put it in a huge paper box. So, I came in second place and the first three places their awards got to be displayed in the library for a month. So I remember coming home a month later with my prize, he [Dad] was very proud, my hanai mom wasn't. I had placed the project on to the kitchen table. She saw that red ribbon, she, without a second of a doubt she grabbed the broom and she smashed it. And she just yelled at me and told me second place was not allowed in this house.

She also experienced regular physical abuse as a child at the hands of her hanai mother. This abuse continued for Jackie into adulthood. She entered several physically abusive relationships with men. One of these men stabbed her eight times on Christmas Day. Here is what Jackie had to say about that relationship and the impact of the abuse:

> If you notice this scar on the right side of my face, Christmas night … I was stabbed eight times by my ex-boyfriend, the father of my second child. Uhm, we were well in our disease [drug addiction], uhm, but see I stayed in these relationships cause like I mentioned earlier I was stuck. Was afraid of being alone. I had the low self-esteem. No confidence. No self-worth.

Jackie was largely estranged from her family due to years of emotional, physical and sexual abuse. As such, she did not want to go to her family of origin to escape these abusive relationships. Indeed, her hanai mother did not allow her to stay at home on the rare occasions that Jackie did try to go back – even with noticeable signs of physical abuse present.

Finally, Jackie discussed the issue of sexual abuse in her childhood, noting that she grew up in a family where a lot of sexual molestation occurred. She was the victim of sexual abuse at least twice as a child. She was first sexually molested at the age of eight. Here was the reaction from her hanai mother upon reporting the sexual abuse:

> I got slapped right across the face. They told me I deserved it, because I was wearing shorts. They called me puka, which is

slut. I was eight years old. So by the time that I was raped in the seventh grade, I never told anybody cause I thought it was my fault [she was raped by strangers on the way home from a school event].

It is not surprising, then, that Jackie began using drugs at the age of 13 and continued using into adulthood. Her drug use was initially connected to her family life and the issues of abuse therein. Like many female offenders, the substance abuse continued due to lasting and untreated trauma.

This research demonstrates the difficulty that prevalent histories of abuse, coupled with the lack of trauma-related treatment, pose for female offenders. While the LSI-R does capture some measure of mental illness and certainly substance use, the context of both, particularly trauma and depression, will simply remain hidden behind the drug use.

Health and children

The females in this sample were about twice as likely to have current health problems as were men (61.5 per cent and 38.9 per cent, respectively) and almost two-thirds (61.5 per cent) of the women were taking medications compared with 27.8 per cent of the men. These health problems, which are quite serious for some of the women (e.g. breast cancer, hepatitis C) are likely to impact on their ability to address other issues, namely trauma and substance abuse. The LSI-R may over-classify these women due to contextually hidden circumstances that include the receipt of social assistance, mental health and substance use treatment, and a lack of employment. At the very least, the added contribution of health problems compounds the demands already placed on these women.

Childcare and related responsibilities affect females differently from males. According to the latest national results, roughly one half of all inmates have at least one child under the age of 18. For women, the number is higher, almost two-thirds (65.3 per cent) have at least one child under the age of 18 compared with 54.7 per cent of the male inmates (Mumola 2000). For this sample of offenders, 69.2 per cent of the females had children compared with 44.4 per cent of the men. A third of these women had their first child under the age of 18, compared with none of the men. Finally, Child and Protective Services (CPS) were more likely to have been involved in separating the mother from her children (66.7 per cent) than for the males (37.5 per cent).

Discussion and conclusion

Agencies have readily incorporated the evidence-based strategy of actuarial-based risk/need assessments, in the main, because they aid in dealing with capacity problems – too many offenders to supervise in the community and not enough resources (officers, programmes or otherwise) to adequately do so. The good news about these instruments, from an ideological standpoint, is that they bring rehabilitation back into the correctional realm. However, if not utilised and managed properly, these instruments could end up unintentionally punishing more, not less. This is the main concern with their use for the management of female offenders in the community.

The quantitative data here and elsewhere indicate that the LSI-R does exhibit predictive validity for both males and females. The qualitative data nonetheless reveal that factors relevant to female offenders, especially those centred on past and present victimisation, are left out of risk and need assessment instruments. Thus, the appearance of gender neutrality, from a quantitative perspective, may be a spurious one. Female offenders' risk often masks the actual underlying root causes of their criminal offending and thus may not be useful for case management and treatment intervention.

Trauma, abuse, drugs and treatment, for many women, cannot be considered separate from one another. It is therefore suggested that female offenders' victimisation histories are an important part of a holistic approach to case-based classification for effective correctional intervention. The predominance of victimisation within female offender populations often connects with multiple psychological/ psychiatric problems compounded by ineffectual coping. This alone underscores the importance of offering intervention in this area. The LSI-R simply does not capture this victimisation piece, though.

It is thus certainly a fair criticism to state that the instrument tends to penalise women's attempts to heal from quite serious and extensive histories of abusive and related trauma via higher overall scores, thus higher risk classification, for behaviour such as seeking help with drug abuse and trauma issues. For example, many women seek mental health treatment for substance abuse and trauma-related issues, while also receiving social assistance. They are scored higher in these areas even though treatment and financial assistance seem to be protective.

If risk/need instruments do not consider gender, the misidentification and/or misunderstanding of criminogenic needs for female offenders means that women will not get the sort of supervision and help that will *best* benefit them and public safety. In essence, the true validity for current risk/need factors, and the absence of gender-specific ones, may affect the overall interpretation of the instrument in ways that ultimately deny needed services to female offenders (Blanchette and Brown 2006).

In light of evidence presented here and elsewhere, it seems that the most promising approach is to move towards a decidedly gender-centred method to risk/need assessment instruments. We need to craft instruments from the ground up, beginning with a gendered lens from creation through validation and ultimate use (Van Voorhis *et al.* 2008; Taylor and Blanchette 2009; Hannah-Moffat 2009; Blanchette and Brown 2006). If we did this we would likely end up with instruments that look different from the current gender-neutral ones (Van Voorhis *et al.* 2008; Holtfreter and Cupp 2007). The emergence of so-called fourth-generation instruments, which incorporate strengths and protective factors, seem more appropriate for female offenders, especially given their lower risk relative to men (Blanchette and Brown 2006).

Jurisdictions should also seriously consider whether current cut-off scores, in terms of classification levels, should be different for males and females. Given the current lack of context and attention to potentially spurious relationships, there is the danger of females being both over- and under-classified (Hollin and Palmer 2006; Reisig *et al.* 2006). Research has demonstrated that, specifically, women who are socially and economically marginalised tend to be over-classified with these instruments (Reisig *et al.* 2006). Over-classified women may be subject to too much surveillance or be subject to services that do not meet their needs. This, in turn, may set female offenders up for failure in terms of higher revocation rates via increased surveillance and failure due to inappropriate treatment. Under-classified women, on the other hand, may not be supervised enough and may not receive the services that meet their needs (Reisig *et al.* 2006).

In the end, there needs to be a system that recognises the disproportionate histories of abuse faced by female offenders, while not overly controlling them for factors that are, or were, beyond their control (Tonry 1987). Otherwise these instruments may become the veil behind which we continue to disadvantage female offenders, namely by treating them as 'objectively' similar to males. It seems appropriate to end this chapter with a quote from Zoe, one of the women interviewed for this study. The following passage is part of her comments regarding assessment, content and drugs:

The women's problems isn't the fucking addiction, it's what's behind the addiction. And if you're using one tool for screening people, in a cookie mould, and that screening is set for men [it's a problem]. Most of the women that are doing time right now are repeat offenders, most of the women are stuck in the revolving doors of recidivism. They are not targeting what they need. If you had a screening tool that targeted exactly what it was ... and the target is trauma. If you're not addressing their trauma then you expect them to be back.

Notes

1 Source: Davidson, Janet T. (2009) *Female Offenders and Risk Assessment: Hidden in Plain Sight*. El Paso, TX: LFB Scholarly Publishing.
2 The LSI-R contains ten domains, including: criminal history, education and employment, financial, family and marital, accommodations, leisure and recreation, companions, alcohol and drug, emotional and personal, and attitudes and orientations.
3 Hannah-Moffat and Shaw (2001: 15–16) present a detailed list of studies that have documented the context within which women often commit offences.
4 It is important to keep in mind that r values of .30 or greater are deemed ideal values for this type of prediction research (Van Voorhis *et al*. 2008). None of the reported bivariate correlations reached that value, but several were close.
5 GED refers to General Educational Development. The GED is a high school equivalency test. Individuals who pass the test are determined to have a knowledge base equivalent to those who earn a high school diploma. In the US, a GED often serves as a substitute for a high school diploma in work or higher educational settings.
6 Being addicted to drugs can be considered a disability and therefore allows one to draw SSI.
7 In the US, the seventh and eighth grades are considered middle or intermediate school levels, between elementary school (first to sixth grades) and high school (ninth to twelfth grades). Students in the seventh grade are generally between the ages of 12 and 13.
8 'Ice' is slang for methamphetamine in Hawaii.
9 Hanai refers to a practice of informal adoption in Hawaii.

References

Andrews, D.A. and Bonta, J. (2000) *The Level of Service Inventory-Revised: User's Manual*. Canada: Multi-Health Systems.

Belknap, J. (2007) *The Invisible Woman: Gender, Crime, and Justice* (3rd edn). Belmont, CA: Thomson.

Belknap, J. and Holsinger, K. (2006) 'The gendered nature of risk factors for delinquency', *Feminist Criminology*, 1: 48–71.

Blanchette, K. and Brown, S.L. (2006) *The Assessment and Treatment of Women Offenders: An Integrative Perspective*. Hoboken, NJ: John Wiley and Sons Ltd.

Bloom, B. (2000) 'Gender-responsive supervision and programming for women offenders in the community', *Responding to Women Offenders in the Community*. Washington, DC: US Department of Justice National Institute of Corrections.

Bloom, B. and Owen, B. (2002) *Gender-Responsive Strategies: Research, Practice, and Guiding Principles for Women Offenders*. Washington, DC: US Department of Justice National Institute of Corrections.

Bloom, B., Owen, B. and Covington, S. (2003) *Gender-Responsive Strategies: Research, Practice, and Guiding Principles for Women Offenders*. Washington, DC: US Department of Justice National Institute of Corrections.

Bonta, J. (1996) 'Risk-needs assessment and treatment', in A.T. Harland (ed.) *Choosing Correctional Options that Work: Defining the Demand and Evaluating the Supply*. Thousand Oaks: SAGE Publications, pp. 18–32.

Champion, D.J. (1994) *Measuring Offender Risk: A Criminal Justice Sourcebook*. Santa Barbara, CA: Greenwood Press.

Chesney-Lind, M. (1997) *The Female Offender: Girls, Women and Crime*. Thousand Oaks: SAGE Publications.

Chesney-Lind, M. and Pasko, L. (2004) *The Female Offender: Girls, Women, and Crime* (2nd edn). Thousand Oaks, CA: SAGE.

Comack, E. (2006) 'Coping, resisting, and surviving: Connecting women's law violations to their histories of abuse', in L. Alarid and P. Cromwell (eds) *In Her Own Words: Women Offenders' Views on Crime and Victimization*. Los Angeles: Roxbury Publishing Company, pp. 33–44.

Deschenes, E.P., Owen, B. and Crow, J. (2006) *Recidivism among Female Prisoners: Secondary Analysis of the 1994 BJS Recidivism Data Set*. Washington, DC: US Department of Justice, Bureau of Justice Statistics.

Fagan, A., Van Horn, M.L., Hawkins, D.J. and Arthur, M.W. (2007) 'Gender similarities and differences in the association between risk and protective factors and self-reported serious delinquency', *Prevention Science*, 8: 115–24.

Farr, K.A. (2000) 'Classification for female inmates: Moving forward', *Crime and Delinquency*, 46: 3–17.

Federal Bureau of Investigation (2008) *Crime in the United States, 2007.* Washington, DC: US Department of Justice, Federal Bureau of Investigation.

Flavin, J. and Desautels, A. (2006) 'Feminism and crime', in C.M. Renzetti, L. Goodstein, and S.L. Miller (eds) *Rethinking Gender, Crime and Justice: Feminist Readings.* Los Angeles, CA: Roxbury Publishing Company, pp. 11–28.

Funk, S.J. (1999) 'Risk assessment for juveniles on probation: A focus on gender', *Criminal Justice and Behavior*, 26: 44–68.

Glaze, L.E. and Bonczar, T.P. (2007) *Probation and Parole in the United States 2006.* Washington, DC: US Department of Justice, Bureau of Justice Statistics.

Hannah-Moffat, K. (2009) 'Gridlock or mutability: Reconsidering "gender" and risk assessment', *Criminology and Public Policy*, 8: 209–19.

Hannah-Moffat, K. and Shaw, M. (2001) *Taking Risks: Incorporating Gender and Culture into the Classification and Assessment of Federally Sentenced Women in Canada.* Canada: Status of Women Canada.

Hannah-Moffat, K. and Shaw, M. (2003) 'The meaning of "risk" in women's prisons: A critique', in B. Bloom (ed.) *Gendered Justice: Addressing Female Offenders.* Durham, NC: Carolina Academic Press, pp. 45–68.

Harcourt, B.E. (2007) *Against Prediction: Profiling, Policing, and Punishing in an Actuarial Age.* Chicago: University of Chicago Press.

Harer, M.D. and Langan, N.P. (2001) 'Gender differences in predictors of prison violence: Assessing the predictive validity of a risk classification system', *Crime and Delinquency*, 47: 513–36.

Harlow, C.W. (1999) *Prior Abuse Reported by Inmates and Probationers.* Washington, DC: US Department of Justice, Bureau of Justice Statistics.

Heilbrun, K., DeMatteo, D., Fretz, J., Yashure, K. and Anumba, N. (2008) 'How "specific" are gender-specific rehabilitation needs? An empirical analysis', *Criminal Justice and Behavior*, 35: 1382–97.

Hollin, C.R. and Palmer, E.J. (2006) 'Criminogenic need and women offenders: A critique of the literature', *Legal and Criminological Psychology*, 11: 179–95.

Holsinger, A.M. and Latessa, E.J. (2003) 'Ethnicity, gender, and the Level of Service Inventory-Revised', *Journal of Criminal Justice*, 31: 309–20.

Holsinger, K. and Van Voorhis, P. (2005) 'Examining gender inequities in classification systems: Missouri's development of a gender-responsive assessment instrument', *Women, Girls, and Criminal Justice*, 6: 33–48.

Holtfreter, K. and Cupp, R. (2007) 'Gender and risk asssessment: The empirical status of the LSI-R for women', *Journal of Contemporary Criminal Justice*, 23: 363–82.

Holtfreter, K., Reisig, M.D. and Morash, M. (2004) 'Poverty, state capital, and recidivism among women offenders', *Criminology and Public Policy*, 3: 185–208.

Hubbard, D.J. and Matthews, B. (2008) 'Reconciling the differences between the "gender-responsive" and the "what works" literature to improve services for girls', *Crime and Delinquency*, 54: 225–58.

Hubbard, D.J. and Pratt, T.C. (2004) 'The criminogenic needs of girls: What are the most important risk factors for delinquency and are they different from the risk factors for boys?', *Women, Girls, and Criminal Justice*, August/September: 57–63.

Hudson, B. (2003) *Justice in the Risk Society: Challenging and Re-Affirming Justice in Late Modernity*. Thousand Oaks, CA: SAGE Publications.

Jones, D.A. (1999) 'Case classification in community corrections: Preliminary findings from a national survey', *Topics in Community Corrections*. Washington, DC: US Department of Justice, National Institute of Corrections.

Lowenkamp, C.L., Holsinger, A.M. and Latessa, E.J. (2001) 'Risk/need assessment, offender classification, and the role of childhood abuse', *Criminal Justice and Behavior*, 28: 543–63.

Manchak, S.M., Skeem, J.L., Douglas, K.S. and Siranosian, M. (2009) 'Does gender moderate the predictive utility of the Level of Service Inventory Revised (LSI-R) for Serious Violent Offenders?', *Criminal Justice and Behavior*, 36: 425–42.

Maurutto, P. and Hannah-Moffat, K. (2007) 'Response to commentary: Cross-examining risk "knowledge"', *Canadian Journal of Criminology and Criminal Justice*, 49: 543–50.

McIvor, G., Murray, C. and Jamieson, J. (2004) 'Desistance from crime: Is it different for women and girls?', in S. Maruna and R. Immarigeon (eds) *After Crime and Punishment: Pathways to Offender Reintegration*. Portland, OR: William Publishing.

Mumola, C.J. (2000) *Incarcerated Parents and Their Children*. Washington, DC: US Department of Justice, Bureau of Justice Statistics.

Olson, D.E., Alderden, M. and Lurigio, A.J (2003) 'Men are from Mars, women are from Venus, but what role does gender play in probation recidivism?', *Journal of the Justice Research and Statistics Association*, 5: 33–54.

Owen, B. (2003) 'Differences with a distinction: Women offenders and criminal justice practice', in Barbara E. Bloom (ed.) *Gendered Justice: Addressing Female Offenders*. Durham, NC: Carolina Academic Press.

Parsons, M.L. and Warner-Robbins, C. (2002) 'Factors that support women's successful transition to the community following jail/prison', *Health Care for Women International*, 23: 6–18.

Petersilia, J. (2003) *When Prisoners Come Home: Parole and Prisoner Reentry*. Oxford: Oxford University Press.

Pew Center on the States (2008) *One in 100: Behind Bars in America*. Washington, DC: The Pew Charitable Trusts.

Pew Center on the States (2009) *One in 31: The Long Reach of American Corrections*. Washington, DC: The Pew Charitable Trusts.

Raynor, P. (2007) 'Risk and need assessment in British probation: The contribution of LSI-R', *Psychology, Crime and Law*, 13: 125–38.

Reisig, M.D., Holtfreter, K. and Morash, M. (2006) 'Assessing recidivism across female pathways to crime', *Justice Quarterly*, 23: 384–405.

Richie, B.E. (2001) 'Challenges incarcerated women face as they return to their communities: Findings from life history interviews', *Crime and Delinquency*, 47: 368–89.

Sabol, W.J. and Couture, H. (2008) *Prison Inmates at Midyear 2007*. Washington, DC: US Department of Justice, Bureau of Justice Statistics.

Sabol, W.J. and Minton, T.D. (2008) *Jail Inmates at Midyear 2007*. Washington, DC: US Department of Justice, Bureau of Justice Statistics.

Smith, P., Cullen, F.T and Latessa, E.J. (2009) 'Can 14,737 women be wrong? A meta-analysis of the LSI-R and recidivism for female offenders', *Criminology and Public Policy*, 8: 183–208.

Snell, T.L. (2006) *Capital Punishment, 2005*. Washington, DC: US Department of Justice, Bureau of Justice Statistics.

Sommers, I., Baskin, D.R. and Fagan, J. (2006) 'Pathways out of crime: Crime desistance by female street offenders', in L. Fiftal Alarid and P. Cromwell (eds) *In Her Own Words: Women Offenders' Views on Crime and Victimization*. Los Angeles, CA: Roxbury Publishing Company, pp. 237–45.

Sprague, J. (2005) *Feminist Methodologies for Critical Researchers: Bridging Differences*. Walnut Creek, CA: AltaMira Press.

Taylor, K.N. and Blanchette, K. (2009) 'The women are not wrong: It is the approach that is debatable', *Criminology and Public Policy*, 8: 221–29.

Tonry, M. (1987) 'Prediction and classification: Legal and ethical issues', in D.M. Gottfredson and M. Tonry (eds) *Prediction and Classification in Criminal Justice Decision Making*. Chicago: University of Chicago Press, pp. 367–413.

Van Voorhis, P. (2005) *Gender Responsive Assessments*. Presentation Given in Honolulu, Hawaii at the Department of Public Safety on 11 July 2005.

Van Voorhis, P., Salisbury, E., Wright, E. and Bauman, A. (2008) *Achieving Accurate Pictures of Risk and Identifying Gender Responsive Needs: Two New Assessments for Women Offenders*. Washington, DC: US Department of Justice, National Institute of Corrections.

Veysey, B.M. and Hamilton, Z. (2007) 'Girls will be girls: Gender differences in predictors of success for diverted youth with mental health and substance abuse disorders', *Journal of Contemporary Criminal Justice*, 23: 341–62.

Vose, B., Cullen, F.T and Smith, P. (2008) 'The empirical status of the Level of Service Inventory', *Federal Probation*, 72: 22–9.

Widom, C.S. (1995) *Victims of Childhood Sexual Abuse – Later Criminal Consequences*. Washington, DC: US Department of Justice, National Institute of Justice.

Chapter 12

Who cares? Fostering networks and relationships in prison and beyond

Jo Deakin and Jon Spencer

In this chapter we explore the changing role and significance of relationships between women who have served prison sentences, and the people that surround them. Using data from our recent study of ethnic minority (ex)-offenders[1] we consider how family and community connections are sustained during and after incarceration. Our findings illustrate the significance of supportive informal relationships with friends and family in the reintegration process, with positive relationships providing a form of social capital and acting as a significant form of social control. Additionally, we consider the impact of problematic relationships in the reintegration process.

Introduction

The rise in the female prison population across Western jurisdictions has been well documented (Barry and McIvor 2009; McIvor *et al.* 2009; Gelsthorpe *et al.* 2007; Deakin and Spencer 2003). A palpable consequence of this rise is an increase in the number of women returning to the community after serving their prison term. Contractually, the role of providing these women with suitable provision and support to help them desist from crime falls to the statutory and voluntary agencies. However, the reality of support for women leaving prison may come from a variety of other sources. Based on our case study analysis of seven ethnic minority women, this chapter addresses changes in notions of support prior to, during and after a prison sentence. Our findings indicate the significance of supportive informal relationships with friends and family in the reintegration process, where positive relationships provide a form of social capital and act as a significant form of social control.

Additionally, previous research, undertaken to consider the daily experiences of ethnic minority prisoners, suggests that race is an important daily issue for prisoners and staff (Spencer *et al.* 2009; Cheliotis and Leibling 2006; Leibling and Arnold 2002), provoking differential treatment, verbal abuse and other forms of 'institutional' discrimination in prisons (Haslewood-Poćik *et al.* 2006). Whilst tension is an everyday feature in the experience of *all* female prisoners, for ethnic minority prisoners there is an added layer of tension, some of which is embedded at the institutional level.

Reintegration

Drawing on the work of Maruna and Immarigeon (2004) and Visher and Travis (2003) we recognise 'reintegration' as a process that starts at the point of confinement, preparing the prisoner for success after release, and continuing for some time afterwards. In essence, then, reintegration encompasses 'the totality of work with prisoners, their families and significant others in partnership with statutory and voluntary organisations' (Association of Chief Officers of Probation, cited in Morgan and Owers 2001: 12).

However, with reoffending rates documented to be particularly high following imprisonment (Social Exclusion Unit 2009) the 'success' of reintegration strategies with women offenders is far from clear. Evidently, the transition from prison to the community is fraught with difficulties influenced by demographic characteristics, contextual factors and cultural experience. The links between these factors and women's recidivism have been explored in a large body of sometimes contradictory research from the US (see Kruttschnitt and Gartner 2003). In the UK most researchers agree that central to the success of this transition from prison to the community is an understanding of women's needs in relation to desistance (Gelsthorpe *et al.* 2007; Martin *et al.* 2009; Spencer and Deakin 2004) and, consequently, the reflection of those needs in the nature and quality of the support offered in the community (McIvor *et al.* 2009). For women leaving prison, community reintegration is not a straightforward unidimentional process; rather it must account for histories of economic and social marginalisation, and the distinct context of female offending.

Research focusing on the reintegration of female ex-offenders has considered their experiences of the services and support provided and, with the exception of more recent pockets of good practice,[2] has expressed concern that some programmes fail to account for women's needs (Hollin and Palmer 2006; Blanchette and Brown 2006; McIvor *et al.* 2009). Further, Huebner and colleagues discuss in their US study the additional problems faced by minority ethnic women, on re-entry to marginalised, disenfranchised communities and economically distressed neighbourhoods (Huebner *et al.* 2009). Gelsthorpe's work on the experiences and needs of ethnic minority women offenders finds them to be doubly neglected as 'the "other" other' (Gelsthorpe 2006).

The role of formal and informal support

There is a wealth of research evidence suggesting that close ties with friends and family members can play a significant role in improving post-release outcomes and easing an ex-prisoner's reintegration into their family and the community (Ohlin 1954; Glaser 1964; Holt and Miller 1972; Visher and Travis 2003). POPS (Partners of Prisoners and Families Support Group), a key voluntary sector agency working with prisoners and their families, highlights families as being 'a critical factor for change' (POPS 2007). The informal support from family, friends and significant others forms a key element of the reintegration process, coupled with formal interventions from statutory and voluntary organisations, and by a sense of self-determination (Maruna and Immarigeon 2004). As Farrell (2000) argues, most desistance occurs away from the formal provision of the criminal justice system through this process of self-determination and informal support. Further research has concluded that it is the processes of individual decision-making, lifestyle changes (including new or renewed social networks and social roles) and support for this new lifestyle that leads to desistance from crime (Laub and Sampson 2001). Most notably, for women leaving prison, it is close relationships (with children, parents or partners) that have been highlighted as a fundamental element of desistance (McIvor *et al.* 2009; Barry 2007). Additionally, research with women serving community sentences has highlighted the importance of social relationships and networks in fostering a sense of support and the increased confidence that can bring (Deakin and Spencer 2001). The research evidence presents a clear picture of close links between successful reintegration and positive lifestyle choices supported by prosocial networks.

Social networks and desistance

Previous research on social networks has looked at issues of isolation, lack of interaction (Lowenthal 1968) and role differentiation between formal and informal networks (Litwak 1965). Our research incorporates both these elements to provide a holistic, systematic analysis of the function of these networks in the daily tasks of reintegration and desistance for the women taking part in the study.

The social network that is the subject of this research is defined broadly as groups or individuals including the criminal justice system (CJS) and voluntary or statutory organisations, friends, family and significant others.

These groups are:

• An intimate group. These are usually close friends and some family members or significant others. This is the group that has been seen as the most influential in relation to desistance from crime (Laub and Sampson 2001). In most cases it is the group that provides the greatest amount of personal and emotional support and includes those with which the ex-offender has the most contact and interaction in the community;

• Semi-formal voluntary groups and organisations. These include religious organisations or charities such as NACRO, the crime reduction charity that may provide a helping function. These groups appear to gain in importance during custody and continue to be of relevance post release;

• Formal support such as that provided by the criminal justice system via prison and probation officers, social services and other governmental agencies. This group consists principally of political and economic entities that govern the nature and availability of basic entitlements such as health, housing, employment, education, behaviour and desistance. They aim to offer a range of services, entitlements and support based on principles of equality and rationality;

• Acquaintances, who may form additional links within the social network. These are often not seen as 'positive' relationships and were frequently linked to drug or alcohol use and offending.

These elements of the social network may interact and overlap, or may take a specific role in the overall support. As such this research is concerned with unravelling the role and value of personal relationships in offering support, how this role engages with and differs from that of the statutory and voluntary agencies, and the separate and interactive effects of elements of support as defined by the individual. Our analysis evaluates changes in the individual social networks and support structures at three points of the prisoner's journey: prior to custody (while offending behaviour is current); during custody and in preparation for release; and up to three months post release.

Methodology

Lengthy, in-depth interviews were conducted with seven female respondents at two stages of their reintegration: shortly before and shortly after release from a closed female prison in England. The interviews provided narrative case studies enabling us to explore experiences of 'reintegration', how positive kinship and community ties are maintained/re-established, and the effect of problematic relationships on the reintegrative process.

The sample of women varied in terms of age, ethnicity, social background and offending history. Their crimes included acquisitive offences such as theft and fraud, drug offences, aggravated acquisitive crimes such as robbery, and violent offences including grievous bodily harm and violence against the person.

The first interview conducted in the prison focused on the respondent's emotional, practical and social support networks at two different times: retrospectively, before coming into prison and during the sentence. The follow-up, community-based interview took place up to three months after release (about six months after the first interview) and focused on changes in the social network of respondents since leaving prison. The respondents were contacted via their probation officer, or using the contact details (sometimes of relatives) they had provided during the first interview. Research involving follow-up interviews has a notoriously high attrition rate (Farrington 1979), particularly after a change in location and circumstances of the respondents. However, five of our original seven respondents took part in the second interview, giving a high second-response rate for this type of study.

Criminal justice and voluntary sector professionals were also interviewed to provide different perspectives on the support networks of (ex)-offenders at various points in the reintegration process. These included probation officers, prison race relations officers and members of staff from charities working with ex-offenders. The purpose of these interviews was to gather information on the formal support available to people leaving prison and to explore alternative perspectives on the key themes of the research.

Findings

The journey of support

From the case studies we were able to build up a picture of supportive networks and how they had changed for the women over the period of imprisonment and after release. Before prison, informal support from family and friends featured heavily in terms of practical, social and emotional companionship and advice. During the sentence, the extent to which women prisoners rely on support from family and friends falls slightly, and this loss in 'outside' support is replaced by a rise in support from inside the prison coming from two main sources. Firstly, formal and semi-formal agencies, especially religious organisations and prison staff, take on a greater role in the respondents' social, practical and emotional needs. All the women discussed a close relationship with either a prison officer, one of the nurses or other medical staff in prison, or with a prison chaplain or visiting religious teacher. The frequent contact with prison staff and chaplains provides opportunities for those serving sentences to seek help, thereby replacing the support from family and friends that has become less easily accessible. Furthermore, the type of support required (including advice on internal prison issues) may be more suited to formal agencies within the prison than to outside help. Additionally some of the women were mindful not to cause concern to loved ones outside the prison and so directed their problems and needs towards others inside the prison.

Secondly, the women spoke of replacing the lost contact from those outside with informal support gained from new relationships developed with other prisoners. Friendships between female prisoners were a main source of emotional support providing 'a shoulder to cry on'. One respondent commented of her friend, 'She knows what it's like in here and she's always there for me, no matter what.' These friendships were also a vital social and practical resource, providing essential internal information about prison procedures, coping with daily life and 'working the system'. The friendships formed in prison reflect the exclusion felt by the women in our study from an outside world and the 'normal' relationships that were temporarily inaccessible. Other prisoners become substitutes for the closeness of family and friends and in one interview were described as 'a new family'.

The unique character of prison life creates a shared experience between prisoners (and to some extent with prison officers) that provides the opportunities for new, close relationships to form. However, while these relationships were important during the respondents' time in prison, few relationships were maintained after release. O'Brien (2001) describes the multi-level relationships that women in her study built while in prison as an essential part of successful reintegration. While she found that many of the relationships were maintained post prison, our own study saw only limited evidence of these relationships continuing after release. On release, the close relationships that were forged in custody were often severed as ex-offenders began their new lives. The families and friends of some of the women were unsupportive of continued relationships with other prisoners and ex-prisoners, preferring to sever all ties with the past. The intensity and brevity of many of the relationships the women formed in prison is typical of relationships that are formed in situations of crisis.

The informal support from friends and family members once again became the most important form of support as the women re-entered the community. They discussed practical assistance in finding accommodation and employment as being of particular importance on their release from custody. However, the strength of close relationships was expressed most commonly in the area of emotional support, with respondents relying on certain pivotal family members and close friends for advice and help. The key to valuable emotional support for respondents seemed to be an acceptance by the family or close friends of their offence and their sentence, and a positive and encouraging outlook towards a successful future with whatever support that entailed.

Whilst we found that respondents begin to rely more heavily on friends and family again after prison, the number of people they rely on seems to decrease. Certain key members of the family and significant friends become more important while other relationships, particularly with less significant friends, are diminished. Several women expressed their realisation of the importance of their family in their lives and actively sought to reduce their contact with friends.

Others realised the negative impact some friends could have on their lifestyle and behaviour and chose to avoid associating with them after release, deliberately severing ties with the original network. Some semi-formal agencies that had become more important to respondents while in prison continued to be important sources of support after release. Religious organisations continued to provide relevant, useful emotional and social support for several of the women. However, the formal agencies were not regarded so highly. Although respondents were more likely than they had been before prison to seek practical help from some formal agencies, such as support in finding a job or resolving debts, they still viewed the statutory support on offer as insubstantial.

Positive and negative relationships

The social networks of the women in the study in all cases included both positive and negative relationships. Positive, functional relationships are defined here as those that encourage independence, prosocial behaviour and desistance, and offer meaningful support to the ex-offender. This can include emotional, practical or social support such as general companionship and socialising, help with tasks of daily management, providing guidance in emotional matters, or help in times of illness or crisis. These positive, functional relationships were seen by the women as helping to reduce tension in their lives.

Negative relationships were defined as those that, in the women's view, encourage negative risk-based behaviours or criminogenic behaviour. Negative relationships may also include those that have a negative impact on the women's perceptions of self, linking closely with depression and low self-worth and having a negative impact on the desire to change. In general these relationships were defined by the women as those that add to tensions and problems in their lives. Other relationships may reflect a combination of positive and negative aspects at different times or in response to different situations.

For example, when discussing her pre-custody relationships, one respondent, Laya, provided examples of what, with hindsight, she saw to be destructive and inappropriate relationships she had developed with a number of men. She identified her lack of significant close relationships with family or friends as a catalyst to her compulsion to seek love and approval from other sources. She described these relationships as ones that she later found to be 'temporary and shallow', affirming her compulsive sexual behaviour and fuelling her drug taking:

I went into really inappropriate relationships so I got a lot of care and affirmation and all sorts of stuff from that. Married men or men that were unavailable or men that drank too much or any kind of inappropriateness, that was there a lot.

Several other women discussed how their primary relationships prior to going to prison were linked with crime. Sandie described how she lived in a house with a number of others with whom she would commit crimes on a daily basis. She explained how they would go out 'grafting' each day on different jobs including shoplifting, dealing drugs, prostitution and other 'activities'. The relationships within the house were her main sources of personal contact, but they offered little emotional or positive practical support. The crime- and drug-related nature of the relationships within the house provided a criminogenic, antisocial network of acquaintances and a ready source of criminal capital that, in retrospect, she felt were problematic despite seeing these relationships as normal at the time.

Negative relationships, isolation and drug use
Negative relationships were also described in women's experiences on leaving prison. Two of the women had returned to drug taking on leaving prison after previous sentences and had attributed this to negative relationships with family and friends. One of the more common stories we heard during the course of the fieldwork was of friends, partners and family members introducing respondents to drug use, or engaging in drug use with respondents as a social activity or a support mechanism. Michelle described the problematic relationship she had with her sister and how closely the relationship was bound up in drug addiction. After a previous prison sentence she returned to the community 'clean' only to restore links with her sister and quickly return to drugs and her previous criminal behaviour:

I was doing street robberies and that and I'd just turned 18 and I got two and a half years and when I come out, I was clean, I was off the drugs and my mum wanted to help again 'cause I was clean and that, and I ended up straight back on the drugs. And that's when I started living with my sister. We were like feeding each other's habits, if you know what I mean? And then I started street working; prostitution. She was like working already, and through me meeting a man, me and my sister, our relationship ... because I thought something was going on [with him] ... we just split up, we separated, me and my sister and that's when I ended up living in crack houses.

Michelle described her mother as a positive influence who wanted to help with her addictions. She had offered accommodation, financial support and emotional support when Michelle was released from prison. However, her return to drug use, facilitated by her sister, had resulted in Michelle no longer seeking her mother's help and engaging in prostitution and street robbery to pay for her addiction. It was during her second period of imprisonment for street robbery that we met Michelle. Unfortunately, Michelle did not turn up to her second interview in the community and after several more failed attempts at contacting her we received a message via her probation officer that she no longer wished to be a part of the research.

In the cases where very little or no support was available from family and friends, respondents expressed acute feelings of loneliness and isolation. Much of the isolation that was experienced before prison was linked with chaotic and problematic drug use, in particular, taking heroin and crack cocaine in 'crack houses'. Family and friends appear to drift or be driven away and these women were unlikely to make any efforts to maintain contact. Their sense of separation from reality and from 'normal' daily life is compounded by their feelings of isolation. Katie described her experiences of problem drug use and the link with depression and isolation:

With me being depressed, they're there. They are always there. These people are always there. These are the people I always used to see growing up. I never used to talk to them before. You know, I would walk past these people because me and them don't have the same thing in common. The minute you have this drug crack in common there isn't no barriers with who you talk to. It doesn't matter if you are a lawyer, a doctor, if you are smoking this drug, you will speak to any type of person because you want it and the worst thing is when you've got it you need somewhere to smoke it. And that's where it falls in, houses that are there for you to go to. And when you go into these houses it's dark. There ain't no daylight. And everybody, all types of people, from all walks of life and you are alone, it's the only place you can run to, to go to and smoke.

Claire also talked of her isolation from close friends and family:

> That's when my life sort of went, I went harder on the drugs, working a lot more, living in crack houses ... Yeah and if I wanted to talk, which I wouldn't you'd buy your friends ... cause I never had contact with my family, did I, 'cos of the drugs.

These respondents, who did not have significant relationships with family and friends, were also unlikely to access formal services for any form of support. The separation they experienced from relationships with family and friends was also reflected in their separation from society and any other forms of support available.

Relationships with intimate partners and children

Most of the women in this study were not in steady partnerships, although previous research has highlighted the importance of intimate partner relationships in the reintegration process. Research conducted in the US found that women who were living with a partner were less likely to be involved in non-drug crimes but were more likely to engage in drug taking, reflecting the complexity of the relationship between intimate relationships and criminality (Griffin and Armstrong 2003). One woman in our study, Debbie, discussed her relationship during the first prison interview: a six-year relationship characterised by alcoholism in both partners and punctuated with domestic violence. She described her hopes for her relationship when she returned home and felt that things would improve. During the second interview, ten weeks after her release, Debbie had separated from her partner but remained in a positive frame of mind.

There is evidence that the return to a role within the family of mother, wife or partner is, for many women, a key factor in their motivation to desist from crime (Huebner *et al.* 2009). In particular, attachment to children may have particularly positive effects on desistance (Steffensmeier and Allen 1996). Two women in our study had children who had been taken into care prior to their sentence. Towards the end of their sentences, both were focused on proving their worth as a citizen and mother in order to regain custody and return to family life. Both were determined to treat their substance and alcohol addictions and create a home for their children to return to. Neither had regained custody of her children by the time of the second interview.

Comparing two life stories

Most of the women in our study described life experiences that were punctuated by forms of physical, sexual and emotional abuse, problematic family relationships and addictions that had been ongoing and persistent. In the following section we draw themes from the stories of two of the women.

Sarah described a traumatic background and a deeply problematic relationship with her family. Initially living with her alcoholic father and stepmother, she was forced to leave, aged 14, after an altercation, and from this point on she stayed with a variety of friends. The breakdown in her relationship with her family coincided with her leaving school and experimenting with drugs (cannabis, poppers and magic mushrooms). For Sarah, life became more difficult and her level of vulnerability increased once she had left the family home. One of the consequences of this was that by the age of 16, she had begun taking amphetamines intravenously and by the age of 17 she had started to use heroin.

Laya suffers from clinical depression and had been diagnosed with a borderline personality disorder. She experienced a traumatic childhood caused by sexual abuse. Laya recounts that her parents have been supportive but that their relationship is problematic. Laya has a history of chaotic drug and heavy alcohol use. Both women have experienced abusive relationships, a chaotic lifestyle and drug and alcohol addictions. However, the critical difference is that Laya's parents remain supportive and connected whereas Sarah has no connection to family and relies on 'friends and acquaintances'.

On release from prison, Sarah was subject to a period of hospitalisation in a psychiatric unit and after a successful four weeks of treatment she was relocated to a hostel that is specifically designed to offer support to residents with mental health problems. However, once the institutional controls were relaxed and Sarah had more self-determination, her vulnerabilities resulted in a further drug-related offence and a recall to prison. Sarah, since her release, has had to rely on 'official' networks, mental health services, probation and other voluntary agencies to help her manage herself in the community. Sarah told us that during her prison sentence she had no contact with her family, and that her 'friendships' prior to prison were casual, drug-related acquaintances:

> Sometimes there was about ten or more in the house. I didn't know half of them; I couldn't say who they were. And 'cos

see when you're drugged up, off your face, you wake up and there's like loads of people there and you don't know none of them. Half me mates were just associates anyway, and I don't trust them as far as I can throw them.

This lack of robust and supportive social and friendship networks and Sarah's own vulnerabilities rendered desistance from drugs and offending highly problematic once Sarah was back in the community. Prison had achieved nothing in terms of provision of services that would allow Sarah to take charge of her own life on release and only further deepened the patterns of her pre-prison lifestyle.

For Laya the situation was different. On release from prison she had initially lived at a hostel but after a short period her probation officer allowed her to return to live at her own address. Laya made decisions to remove herself from networks that she considered to be a negative influence on her lifestyle:

it is mostly x ... y used to do a lot of cocaine and a couple of the other kind of people that I used to know who'd, I mean they could tolerate it they could do it but I just can't.

Consequently her social networks reduced in size but she was able to remove the more criminogenic influences and exert control over her networks:

it is people that I have chosen to be there rather than people that sort of just fall into your life.

Laya relied on her probation officer for practical support and was able to gain some distance from her parents, who continued to look after her children. It is apparent that Laya blurs the boundaries between formal and informal support; it is also apparent that some of the official agencies also blur boundaries between the legal requirements of their job and the need to provide practical and appropriate help.

These two narratives indicate the centrality of networks for women to be able to reconnect with positive relationships and the role that official and voluntary agencies play in this process. For Sarah the task of establishing positive networks was very difficult. The reconnection with her drug using acquaintances left her isolated from official sources of support. Sarah's period of imprisonment probably exacerbated that sense of distance from 'official' agencies and a consequent lack of trust in what they had to offer. Prison did little, or nothing, to counter the vulnerabilities and problems that Sarah had to deal with once she was released. The same could be said of Laya. Although she had accessed services when in prison, using the chaplaincy and probation officers as a form of support, Laya also needed to make significant readjustments on her release.

It was her conscious decision to avoid some previous acquaintances and narrowing of her social networks to exclude negative influences that probably led to Laya's more successful reconnection with her social networks. However, there is little in Laya's response to indicate that prison was a helpful or therapeutic element in her life. What is clear from comparing the two women's experiences is that whilst both had traumatic earlier lives, one of the women had managed to construct positive and self-validating social networks, which included family, friends and criminal justice professionals. For the other woman there is evidence that it was not possible to construct such positive social networks and the known, and to some extent, trusted prior-to-prison friendships were re-established. For Sarah there was no family or friendship support to enhance her own efforts and those of criminal justice agencies to assist her to live a life that desisted from crime. In our view the lack of family and close friendship networks places very severe burdens on women returning to the community after prison. The disruption to a woman's family and friendship ties that a prison sentence causes and the difficulty of re-establishing positive networks is a very real cost to women who serve custodial sentences.

Figure 12.1 illustrates the key relationships at three different phases of Laya's life. Each point of the triangle represents a specific type of support – social, practical or emotional – and the position of individuals within the triangle represents their role in Laya's life in relation to each type of support. Changes in the providers and quantity of support over the offending–prison–reintegration journey are clearly visible.

Conclusion

For many women, incarceration is damaging to their familial, social and support networks. Studies from the US, the UK and Canada suggest that incarceration can have a profoundly negative impact on women's lives, reducing ties to family and friends (Visher and Travis 2003; Lynch and Sabol 2001) and impacting on recidivism of both high- and low-risk offenders (Gendreau and Goggin 1994). Additionally

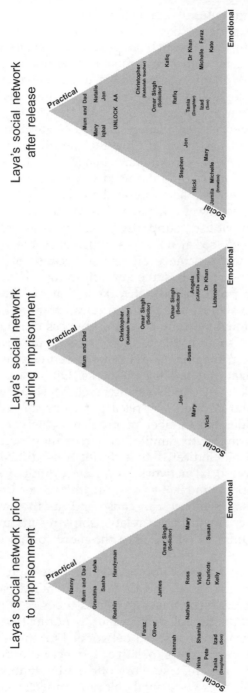

Figure 12.1 Laya's social networks – three key phases

women's racial and cultural ethnicities are seen to impact upon the reintegration experience both in prisons and in the community (Huebner *et al*. 2009). Our research suggests that a custodial sentence almost certainly affects women and their reintegration in a range of ways. We found that many women distance themselves from family and friendship networks and replace these by forging new supportive networks with other female prisoners and by relying on formal and semi-formal agencies (chaplaincy and other support groups) to provide support and assistance during the period of incarceration. There was a number of reasons for changes in the structure of women's networks, for example the need to protect family from the realities of their experience and the need to access knowledge from other prisoners about how to manage incarceration. This process of distancing from previously supportive relationships is potentially damaging to women's social networks and makes the reintegration process more difficult to achieve on release because of the need to rebuild and repair previous positive and affirming relationships. The main problem with prison-based networks is that the lifespan of the relationship is equivalent to the period of incarceration. Prison-based networks are functional but only have a usefulness during the period of incarceration and so add little to the process of reintegration.

Prison is highly damaging to a woman's self-esteem, her sense of self and her social and familial networks. Our research revealed experiences of breakdown and distancing in relationships with parents, siblings, children and partners. On release from prison, women have to manage a considerable number of problems (McIvor *et al*. 2009) including reconnecting with families and regaining access to their children. Our research indicated that during this difficult time the women's supportive social networks were more limited than before their period of imprisonment. Once again, this is testimony to the damage that a prison sentence can cause and, as the case of Sarah indicates, the further fracturing of relationships results in increasing the risk of reoffending on release once the more formal controls are reduced.

Our analysis, in this chapter, has focused on three types of support: social, practical and emotional, and provides a detailed picture of the movement and interaction of the sources and types of support at the three critical stages. Successful reintegration is not just dependent, in most cases, on the existence of social networks, but, more specifically, it depends on the existence of positive and active aspects of that social network. The informal support offered by family and close friends of ex-offenders plays a vital role in women's rehabilitation, and is likely to have a significant impact on their desistance from crime after release from custody. The nature of the support offered by friends and family is complex. For example, in Laya's case, where the relationship between Laya and her parents was problematic there still existed a positive provision of support by the continuing commitment of her parents to care for their grandchildren. The absence of family support and relationships can be seen as a critical issue in the case of Sarah and her relapse into drug misuse. However, families and friends can also provide mixed forms of support, some of which might be negative in terms of encouraging the very behaviours that lead some women to offend. Not all the relationships that women are engaged in after leaving prison have a positive effect on their desistance. The impact of 'negative relationships' is varied: such relationships may be crime generative, in that they actively encourage the woman to become involved in criminal activity; crime tolerant; reproduce a negative self-image or depression; enable or encourage drug and alcohol addictions; be centred on violence between intimate partners; or simply add to the tensions felt by the women.

In practice, we need to recognise the importance of close relationships, the strength of bonds and ties and also the potential problems that can emanate from family and friendship networks. It is our contention that close, functional family and friendship networks are, in many cases, intrinsically linked with the support necessary to promote behavioural and lifestyle changes in ex-offenders. For women, the involvement in positive social relationships provides valuable social resources for them on leaving prison. As Goldthorpe (1980) suggests, social networks can serve as 'channels of information and influence' in finding employment or accommodation, avoiding substance misuse, or tackling any of the other specific factors associated with offending.

Finally, a sense of belonging to a community has been seen, in some instances, to reduce crime (Wedlock 2006; Petersilia 2003). Our research highlighted the importance of community in the reintegration process: for example, having contacts in the local area, or being part of a religious community. Clearly, there are methods of support and current practices that focus on the importance of relationships as women return to the community. The focus for future policy and practice must be to address, through responsive intervention, the relationship between women who offend, their families, friends and the wider community, and to take into account the diverse needs of women from a variety of ethnic and cultural backgrounds. Central to any strategy for women offenders must be a recognition that in many instances women do not commit serious crimes; that prison sentences are highly damaging to family and friendship networks; and that it is necessary to radically change our practices in sentencing women who offend.

Notes

1 The study was funded under the EQUAL stream of the European Social Fund and commissioned by IMPACT (Innovation means prisons and communities together). The objective of this element of the funding stream was to improve the resettlement prospects of ethnic minority ex-offenders and as such the fieldwork was carried out with a sample of ethnic minority ex-offenders selected from custodial institutions. This paper focuses on the experiences of the women in the sample.

   For the purposes of the study a broad definition of the term minority ethnic was used, in line with Prison Service definition of black and minority ethnic prisoners. This includes white minorities, such as 'white other'.

2 See for example the 218 Centre in Scotland (Loucks *et al.* 2006) and the Asha Centre in England (Roberts 2002).

References

Association of Chief Officers of Probation, in R. Morgan and A. Owers (2001) *Through the Prison Gate, A Joint Thematic Review*, by HM Inspectorates of Prisons and Probation, London: Her Majesty's Inspectorate of Prisons.

Barry, M. (2007) 'The transitional pathways of young female offenders: Towards a non-offending lifestyle', in R. Sheehan, G. McIvor and C. Trotter (eds) *What Works with Women Offenders*. Cullompton: Willan Publishing.

Barry, M. and McIvor, G. (2009) 'Professional decision making and women offenders: Containing the chaos?', *Probation Journal*, 56 (4): 1–15.

Blanchette, K. and Brown, S.L. (2006) *The Assessment and Treatment of Women Offenders: An Integrated Perspective*. Chichester: John Wiley and Sons.

Cheliotis, L. and Liebling, A. (2006) 'Race matters in British prisons', *British Journal of Criminology*, 46: 286–317.

Deakin, J. and Spencer, J. (2001) *Evaluation of a probation groupwork programme for female offenders*. Unpublished final report.

Deakin, J. and Spencer, J. (2003) 'Women behind bars: explanations and implications', *Howard Journal for Penal Reform*, 42: 123–36.

Farrell, S. (ed.) (2000) *The Termination of Criminal Careers*. Burlington, VT: Ashgate/Dartmouth.

Farrington, D.P. (1979) 'Longitudinal research on crime and delinquency', *Crime and Justice*, 1: 289–348.

Gelsthorpe, L. (2006) 'The experiences of female minority ethnic offenders: The "other other"', in S. Lewis, P. Raynor, D. Smith and A. Wardak (eds) *Race and Probation*. Cullompton: Willan Publishing, pp. 100–20.

Gelsthorpe, L., Sharpe G. and Roberts, J. (2007) *Provision for Women Offenders in the Community*. London: Fawcett Society.

Gendreau, P. and Goggin, C. (1994) *The Effect of Prison Sentences on Recidivism*. Ottawa, Canada: Department of the Solicitor General, Public Works and Government Services.

Glaser, D. (1964) *The Effectiveness of a Prison and Parole System*. Indianapolis: Bobbs-Merrill.

Goldthorpe, J.H. (in collaboration with Llewellyn, C. and Payne, C.) (1980) *Social Mobility and Class Structure in Modern Britain*. Oxford: Clarendon Press.

Griffin, M. and Armstrong, G. (2003) 'The effect of local life circumstances on female probationers' offending', *Justice Quarterly*, 20(2): 213–40.

Haslewood-Poćik, I., Smith, E. and Spencer, J. (2006) 'The application of national legislation in relation to race and its application to prison service policy and practice (IMPACT: unpublished research report 2006).

Hollin, C. and Palmer , E.J. (2006) 'Criminogenic need and women offenders: A critique of the literature', *Legal and Criminological Psychology*, 11: 179–95.

Holt, N. and Miller, D. (1972) *Explorations in Inmate–Family Relationships*. Research Report (46). Sacramento, CA: California Department of Corrections.

Huebner, B., DeJong, C. and Cobbina, J. (2009) 'Women coming home: Long-term patterns of recidivism', *Justice Quarterly*, 27 (2): 225–54.

Kruttschnitt, C. and Gartner, R. (2003) 'Women's imprisonment', in M. Tonry (ed.) *Crime and Justice: A Review of Research* (Vol. 30, pp. 1–82). Chicago: University of Chicago Press

Laub, J.H. and Sampson, R.J. (2001) 'Understanding desistance from crime', in *Crime and Justice: An Annual Review of Research*, 28: 1–69. Chicago: Chicago University Press.

Liebling, A. and Arnold, H. (2002) *Measuring the quality of prison life*, Home Office Research Findings, No. 174. London: Home Office.

Litwak, E. (1965) 'Extended kin relations in an industrial democratic society', in E. Shanas and G. Streib (eds) *Social Structure and Family*. Englewood Cliff, New Jersey: Prentice Hall.

Loucks, N., Malloch, M., McIvor, G. and Gelsthorpe, L. (2006) *Evaluation of the 218 Centre*. Edinburgh: Scottish Executive Social Research.

Lowenthal, M.F. (1968) 'Social isolation and mental illness in old age', in B.L. Neugarten (ed.) *Middle Age and Aging*. Chicago: University Chicago Press.

Lynch, J.P. and Sabol, W.J. (2001) 'Prisoner reentry in perspective', *Urban Institute, Crime Policy Report*. Washington, DC: Urban Institute.

McIvor, G. (1998) 'Pro-social modelling and legitimacy: Lessons from a study of community service', in S. Rex and A. Matravers (eds) *Pro-social modelling and legitimacy: The Clarke Hall Day Conference*. Cambridge: University of Cambridge, pp. 53–62.

McIvor, G., Trotter, C. and Sheehan. R. (2009) 'Women, resettlement and desistance', *Probation Journal*, 56 (4): 347–61.

Martin, J., Kautt, P. and Gelsthorpe, L. (2009) 'What works for women? A comparison of community-based general offending programme completion', *British Journal of Criminology*, 49: 879–99.

Maruna, S. and Immarigeon, R. (2004) *After Crime and Punishment: Pathways to Offender Reintegration*. Cullompton: Willan Publishing.

O'Brien, P. (2001) *Making it in the free world: Women in transition from prison*. Albany, NY: Suny Press.

Ohlin, L. (1954) 'The stability and validity of parole experience tables', PhD thesis, University of Chicago, in C.A. Visher and J. Travis (2003) 'Transitions from prison to community: Understanding individual pathways', *Annual Review of Sociology*, 29: 89–113.

Partners of Prisoners and Families Support Group (POPS) (2007) 'Families … A Critical Time for Change', unpublished report for the Social Exclusion Unit. London: Cabinet Office. www.partnersofprisoners.org.uk/…/ Families_A_Crucial_Time_For_Change_April_2007.pdf.

Petersilia, J. (2003) *When Prisoners Come Home: Parole and Prisoner Re-entry*. New York, NY: Oxford University Press.

Roberts, J. (2002) 'Women-centred: The West Mercia community-based programme for women offenders', in P. Carlen (ed.) *Women and Punishment. The Struggle for Justice*. Cullompton: Willan Publishing, pp. 110–24.

Social Exclusion Unit (2009) *Short study on women offenders*. London: Social Exclusion Task Force, Cabinet Office, Ministry of Justice.

Spencer, J. and Deakin, J. (2004) 'Community reintegration for whom?', in G. Mair (ed.) *What Matters in Probation*. Cullompton: Willan Publishing.

Spencer, J., Haslewood-Poćik, I. and Smith, E. (2009) 'Trying to get it right. What prison staff say about trying to implement prison race relations policy', *Criminology and Criminal Justice*, 9: 187–206.

Steffensmeier, D. and Allen, E. (1996) 'Gender and crime: Toward a gendered theory of female offending', *Annual Review of Sociology*, 22: 459–87.

Visher, C.A. and Travis, J. (2003) 'Transitions from prison to community: Understanding individual pathways', *Annual Review of Sociology*, 29: 89–113.

Wedlock, E. (2006) *Crime and Cohesive Communities*. Online Report 19/06. London: Home Office.

Chapter 13

Mentoring

Chris Trotter

This chapter is about mentoring in criminal justice settings. It discusses definitions of mentoring, the literature on the effectiveness of mentoring and the general literature on effective work with offenders. It then reports on a small study undertaken in four Australian non-government organisations, each of which provides a different style of mentoring to offenders. It discusses the programmes, how clients respond to the programmes, and highlights some aspects of the programmes including some differences between the responses of female and male clients.

Mentoring in criminal justice

The nature and purpose of mentoring in criminal justice is described in different ways by different authors. Bouffard and Bergseth (2008), for example, suggest that while aftercare programmes focus on surveillance and services with a goal of reducing recidivism, mentoring programmes focus more on role modelling, support and the general well-being of offenders. Tolan *et al.* (2008: 3) refer to mentoring having certain common elements, which include interaction between two individuals over an extended period of time, an inequality of experience, knowledge, or power between the mentor and mentee, modelling and an 'absence of the role inequality that typifies other helping relationships'. Jolliffe and Farrington (2007: 2) refer to some of the practical aspects of mentoring and suggest that mentoring may 'provide both direct assistance (e.g. helping to fill in job applications or locate appropriate housing) and indirect support (e.g. encouragement or acting as a positive role model). This assistance would otherwise be unavailable to most offenders or 'at-risk' youths because of their family and social background.

There seems to be general agreement in the literature that mentoring involves a relationship between a professional or volunteer worker with high levels of contact on an informal basis, which involves modelling by the mentor and some practical assistance to the person being mentored. While the aim of mentoring is not necessarily to reduce offending this is often the aim, along with the aim of improving the client's well-being. Most of the literature on mentoring focuses on its impact on reoffending. For the most part the studies suggest that mentoring has a moderate impact on reoffending but this impact is greater if the mentoring is based on 'best practice' principles.

Jolliffe and Farrington (2007: 1) undertook 'a rapid evidence assessment of mentoring on reoffending'. They examined 18 studies, which included both mentoring and control or comparison groups. The review found that the research on impact on reoffending was limited but that overall mentoring reduced reoffending by four to 11 per cent (although they point out that the more rigorous studies found no significant impact). They found that while longer programmes were not more successful, mentoring was more successful if the mentor and mentee met at least once per week and for considerable periods. The more successful programmes involved four to eight hours per week contact between mentor and mentee. The programmes were also more successful if they were one of a number of interventions such as behaviour modification, employment or education programmes, a finding consistent with other studies, which suggest that multi-modal correctional interventions are generally more effective (Andrews and Bonta 2006). Jolliffe and Farrington (2007) conclude by saying that while mentoring shows some promise there is a need for more thorough research to determine its effectiveness.

A meta-analysis by DuBois *et al.* (2002), consisted of 55 evaluations of mostly American mentoring programmes. The study found a modest benefit for the average youth (mean age in each study under 19 years). The effects were enhanced when the mentoring was based on theoretical and empirical principles – for example the focus was on at-risk and disadvantaged youth; the programme included training, programme support and structured activities, parents were involved, there were clear expectations of frequency of contact and strong relationships were formed between mentors and young people.

Wilczynski *et al.* (2003: 1) undertook an Australian study of mentoring programmes with young offenders and they also suggested that more evaluation is needed. They argue that mentoring programmes should have 'tightly defined target groups, sufficiently trained staff to run the programme and provide support to participants, clear guidelines relating to the recruitment and screening of mentors, and well-developed links with a range of local agencies which can support the work of the programme'.

An American study by Spencer (2007) approached an evaluation from a different perspective by examining the reasons youth mentoring relationships fail. Based on interviews with mentors and clients they argue that they fail due to lack of motivation; unfulfilled expectations; deficiencies in mentor relational skills, including the inability to bridge cultural divides; family interference; and inadequate agency support. The support for mentoring programme is therefore somewhat mixed although mentoring appears to be more effective when consistent with 'best practice' principles. This reflects the general literature on supervision and support programmes for offenders. The research suggests generally that transitional support programmes for offenders lead to reduced recidivism. A review by Seiter and Kadela (2003), for example, found that transition programmes in the area of employment drug treatment, halfway houses, and working with sex and violent offenders were generally successful in reducing recidivism.

There is also support for transitional support programmes in the findings from the *Women After Prison* study (Trotter *et al.* 2007; McIvor *et al.* 2009). This study involved interviews undertaken in the two women's prisons in Victoria, Australia with 140 women and two follow-up interviews in the community, one within three months of release and one within 12 months of release. It was also found that women who made use of community-based services after their release had low reoffending rates. The women also did better if they were offered services that were holistic and intensive and were offered soon after they left prison.

There is also a voluminous and growing literature on what works in offender rehabilitation. A number of principles of effective practice have been developed in the literature and it is argued that these are general principles of good practice that apply to mentoring as much as to any other correctional intervention. These principles can be summarised as:

- Assist clients to address a wide range of issues that are related to their offending behaviour (criminogenic needs) such as drug

263

use, employment, criminal associates, criminal attitudes, family relationships, finances and housing;

- Address these issues through problem-solving approaches that involve reaching agreement between workers and clients on goals and on strategies to achieve them;

- Provide services in a collaborative or partnership manner. The worker–client relationship is an important factor in achieving positive outcomes;

- Provide prosocial models for clients, encourage and reinforce clients' prosocial comments and actions and appropriately challenge pro-criminal comments and behaviour;

- Help clients to understand the role of the professionals working with them, particularly their dual helper/social control role;

- Provide services to medium- to high-risk clients.

This is not an exhaustive list and more detail is available in Trotter (2006) or in many other publications (Andrews and Bonta 2006, for example). Other successful intervention methods – cognitive behavioural techniques, for example – have less relevance to mentoring and are not included here.

Evaluation of four Australian mentoring programmes

Outlined below is a description of an evaluation of four mentoring programmes offered to women and men following their release from prison in Victoria, Australia, and the responses of the offenders to the programmes. The aim of the evaluation was to consider the extent to which the clients found the mentoring helpful and which aspects of the mentoring they found most helpful.

The organisations

Two of the organisations offering the mentoring were low-budget organisations relying largely on volunteers and two were larger non-government organisations. Two of the organisations offer services exclusively to female offenders, the third to young women and men and the fourth offers mentoring to men. In all, 48 clients involved in the programmes were interviewed – 29 women and 19 men.

The first organisation is an interdenominational Christian organisation that operates on a small budget. It runs a number of programmes in the two Victorian women's prisons. These include arts and crafts programmes, a fitness programme and a Christian-based discussion group. Prison network staff and volunteers also meet individually with prisoners. Unlike professional visitors, they are able to meet prisoners on an informal basis in their open living areas. They also provide transport for children to see their mothers in the prison.

In addition to their role in the prison, the organisation has a role in supporting the women after they leave prison. In nearly all instances the first contact made with the women is within the prison even though on some occasions the contact in prison may be minimal. The staff often meet women at the door of the prison when they are released and they maintain contact with the women for as long as they need to after release. Once the women are released from prison the role of the mentors is one of support for the women. The role of the mentors fits clearly within definitions of mentoring referred to earlier. They are on call at any time and much of their work is done outside normal office hours. Much of the support provided to the women is provided over the phone, particularly if the women are not living in metropolitan Melbourne, but rather in regional or rural areas of Victoria.

The aim is to provide flexible, informal and voluntary support services to the women as they are needed – in many cases meeting needs that are not met by other services. The services offered by the programme were described by the staff as including counselling, mentoring, family work, financial assistance and emotional and practical support. The volunteers and staff also work with other agencies – housing, for example, when the need arises.

The second programme focuses on male prisoners, and was operating from the Barwon maximum-security prison in Victoria when the evaluation began in 2006 but moved to another maximum-security Victorian prison, Port Phillip Prison, in 2007. The programme, 'Lives in Transition', has both in-prison and after-prison components, and includes a series of personal development group sessions in prison followed up by mentoring after release. Volunteers are matched with, and meet, the prisoners prior to their release and soon afterwards. Prisoners volunteer for the LIT programme. The programme provides a series of group educational/counselling sessions for prisoners focusing on topics such as budgeting, decision making, reflection, relationships, character building and goal setting. It also offers

265

practical employment-related programmes such as a barista coffee making course and fork lift driving; it also maintains links with an industry-based employment programme, which provides employment opportunities for offenders after release. LIT also offers sessions in ceramics and education as well as opportunities for prisoners to study English and mathematics.

The LIT course in the prison is coordinated by a staff member and sessions are presented predominantly by volunteers. The volunteers are often also mentors and the prisoners have opportunities to choose mentors with whom they feel comfortable. A number of ex-prisoners are involved in the programme, both in the administration of the programme and as mentors. During the course the aim is to match each participant with a mentor. The mentor will then support the offenders after they leave prison and have a role in supporting offenders in relation to any issues around, for example, family, drugs or employment. They try to provide emotional support in terms of having someone to talk to about issues the men face following their imprisonment. In some instances the mentors are also able to offer practical support in terms of employment or housing. Contact with mentors may be in person. However, in some instances the mentors and the men may live some distance from each other and contact is by telephone. In addition to contact with the mentors the men may also maintain contact with staff and volunteers either personally or by telephone.

The third organisation offers a range of programmes for women offenders including a homelessness programme, youth and family programmes, and 'Women in Transition'. In addition, they provide support to offenders to address issues of personal well-being and social isolation. This involves the biweekly 'Women About' pro-gramme, which offers opportunities for women to go to the cinema, to attend a coffee shop group at the centre and to bring along family and friends. Other recreational activities include going to restaurants, and activities such as swimming with the dolphins. The women are subsidised in the activities but generally pay half the actual cost of them. One of the aims of this programme is to reduce isolation and help women to develop friendships. The staff in the programme (two workers) are often involved in assisting the women with issues or helping to mediate disputes with their family or others. In addition to the recreational and social activities, women may also be offered case management support. In terms of the definition referred to above, this programme has similarities to mentoring; the women are exposed to role models and have the opportunity to receive individual support through the recreational programmes or through case management support.

The fourth organisation deals with young offenders, most of whom have been involved in the juvenile justice system either through placement in youth training centres or on supervision or probation orders. Staff support young offenders in the community in relation to the issues they may face, with a particular focus on gaining employment. If possible, the aim is to gain employment for the young people before they are released from youth training centres.

The mentoring programme is also offered in groups and individually. The aim is to match young people with mentors before release and continue with the mentoring after release. Sports stars are often used as role models. Footballers and other sports stars may go into youth training centres and talk to young people, with many becoming mentors after the young people are released. In many cases the first person whom the young people meet after release from youth training centres will be the role model.

Each of these four programmes therefore has its own individual features. They are however characterised by the key element of mentoring – long-term, one-to-one supportive contact and role modelling with offenders; contact which for the most part is commenced in prison.

The clients

Forty-five clients from the programmes were interviewed in the community. It was anticipated that more interviews would be completed; however, the reliance on voluntary responses to posters displayed in offices limited the numbers and delayed the data collection. As a result the sample was not random. It constituted a proportion of the clients involved in the programmes.

As shown in Table 13.1 the majority of the clients were women: two of the organisations only accepted women.

Thirty-seven of the clients provided signed consent to access their police records. It was clear from the police records that the clients were serious offenders. The average age of first offence was 18 years, they had large numbers of prior offences and prior court appearances and an average of nearly five periods of imprisonment. The clients from the fourth agency were of course younger and had fewer prior offences recorded; nevertheless the police records suggest that these were also clients with an entrenched criminal history.

Table 13.1 Gender of clients in four mentoring programmes

Agency	Gender		
	Male	Female	Total
1	0	14	14
2	12	0	12
3	0	10	10
4	3	5	8
Total	15	29	44

More than 90 per cent of the clients had committed serious violent offences, from murder and grievous bodily harm to burglary and robbery. More than half had committed a drug-related offence (e.g. trafficking) and most admitted problems with drug use. In only one instance was the client a first offender (murder) and one individual client had 766 offences recorded against his name. As can be seen in Table 13.2 the women had slightly more prior offences than the men.

Level of contact

The contact between mentors and clients from each of the agencies was frequent and over a long period of time. The contact varied from five or six times a week to around once a month depending on the particular circumstances of the client.

Satisfaction with mentoring

The clients were very satisfied with the mentoring process with the average rating of nine as shown on their rating on a ten-point scale in Figure 13.1.

Women were slightly more satisfied than men with the mentoring process as shown in Table 13.4, although it is clear that both men and women experienced a high level of satisfaction.

Clients were asked to rate on a scale of 1–10 the extent to which the service helped them: where 1 = has not helped at all; 10 = excellent.

Table 13.2 Prior history of clients in mentoring programmes

Gender of client		Age of first offence	Number of prior offences	Number of court appearances with convictions	Number of sentences in prison	Age of client
Male	Mean	16.40	116.40	19.70	4.50	34.20
	N	10	10	10	10	15
	Std deviation	2.547	99.803	12.446	3.100	11.712
Female	Mean	19.17	183.04	23.43	5.09	33.59
	N	23	23	23	23	29
	Std deviation	5.416	198.934	21.708	3.976	8.244
Total	Mean	18.33	162.85	22.30	4.91	33.80
	N	33	33	33	33	44
	Std deviation	4.865	176.001	19.251	3.694	9.434

Table 13.3 Contact with the mentoring agency

Agency		Contact with the agency (in months, including prison if relevant)	Frequency of contact with workers from the agency
1	Mean	11.583	4.29
	N	12	14
	Std deviation	15.2537	1.267
2	Mean	18.846	3.64
	N	13	11
	Std deviation	38.0742	1.629
3	Mean	30.650	3.50
	N	10	10
	Std deviation	26.4911	1.354
4	Mean	52.500	4.00
	N	8	7
	Std deviation	37.2060	1.633
Total	Mean	25.826	3.88
	N	43	42
	Std deviation	32.7157	1.435

Rate on a scale of 1–10 the extent to which this service helped you, where 1 = has not helped at all; 10 = excellent

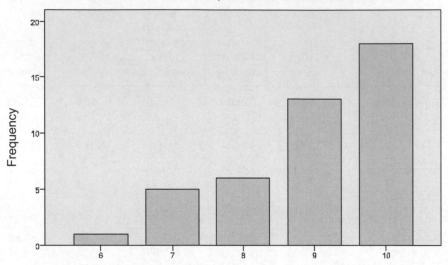

Figure 13.1 Helpfulness of the mentoring service

Table 13.4 Helpfulness of mentoring service for women and men

Gender of client	Mean	N	Std deviation
Male	8.67	15	1.113
Female	9.14	28	1.113
Total	8.98	43	1.123

Reoffending

In addition to being satisfied with the mentoring they were given, the clients also felt that the services helped them to stop reoffending as shown in Figure 13.2. Most clients felt that the service helped them to stop offending at least to some extent, with more than one in three clients reporting the mentoring helped significantly.

The clients involved in mentoring also had low rates of reoffending compared with offenders with similar risk levels. The police records were followed up an average of 30 months after the clients were released from prison. Ten clients (27 per cent) had received a period of imprisonment (or youth detention) during this period. The average

Did this service help you to stop offending again?

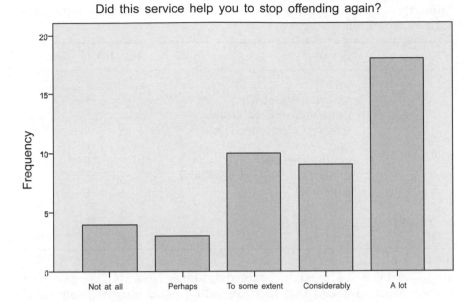

Figure 13.2   Helpfulness of the service in preventing offending

period of imprisonment was however only five months. Another ten clients had an action recorded against their names during this period. However, only three actually received a penalty (fine, Community Based Order or Intensive Corrections Order). The others received suspended sentences or adjournments as shown in Table 13.5.

A Victorian Department of Justice publication provides patterns of recidivism among prisoners released from custody in Victoria in 2002–03. Overall, 34.7 per cent of the cohort in that study was returned to prison within two years of release. The proportion returned to prison was however 52.6 per cent for prisoners who had four to five prior terms of imprisonment. The figure of 27 per cent returned to prison from those involved in the transition programmes compares favourably with these figures.

Progress and employment

We asked the clients a number of other questions relating to how they were progressing since their release. The clients were asked if they had been involved in offending since their release and 32 per cent of those who responded to this question (n=14; total n=43) said

Table 13.5 Penalties received by clients an average of 30 months after release from prison

Penalty	Number of clients
prison	9
suspended sentence	4
Community Based Order	1
Intensive Corrections Order	1
fine	1
youth detention	1
undertaking – good behaviour	2
adjourned	1
Total	20
No penalty	24
Total	44

they had been involved in some offending. However, 97 per cent (n=36; total n=37) said that their offending behaviour had improved since their contact with the agency.

Fifty-six per cent of study participants said they had been employed since their release whereas most (72 per cent) said that they had not been employed prior to their release. Clients reported that their family relationships were better with partners, parents and children in comparison to before they went to prison. Seventy-two per cent reported that they mixed less with criminal peers than before they went to prison with only twelve per cent saying they now mixed more with criminal peers. Ninety-three per cent of the clients (n=39; total n=42) indicated that they had used illicit drugs in the past. Only 29 per cent (n=12; total n=42) said that they were currently using illicit drugs.

It seems clear that the clients in these programmes had good outcomes and felt positively about the programme. They were also consistent with the best practice principles referred to earlier in this chapter.

Consistency with best practice principles

Strengths focus

The clients felt that their workers focused on the things they did well. We asked the clients if their worker spoke about what they did well and if the worker spoke about what they did not do well. This was rated on a five-point scale with the most common and mean response being 'often' in relation to things done well and 'occasionally' in relation to things done badly. There was a strong association between the clients' view that the worker helped them and the view that the worker often commented on the things the client did well.

The clients also commented that their workers were almost always punctual, reliable, honest and fair, key practices involved in prosocial modelling (Trotter 2006). A sense that their worker was fair was particularly important to clients, correlating strongly with the clients' views about the helpfulness of workers. The theme of clients valuing the workers' focus on the things they do well was also evident from the clients' comments in the interviews as illustrated below.

> You mean does she praise me? Yes, she does. She says I'm a good mother and I'm doing well.

> Often – to get self-esteem and motivation up. When I was incarcerated I got punished hard [length of sentence], it was my first offence. My self-esteem dropped to the point where I didn't want to live anymore.

> She's always positive and tells me that I cook well and I will make her fat.

> An appropriate amount of times, not so that it's fake. They actually celebrate when something goes well.

The workers were less inclined to challenge clients. The clients were asked what their workers did if 'you say something that is antisocial or pro-criminal or make excuses for your behaviour or behave in an inappropriate way'. The clients felt that their workers were clear about what they disapproved of but rarely criticised them.

Clear about role

The clients indicated that they were clear about what they and their worker were trying to achieve together (84 per cent; n=36; total n=43 indicated that they were clear or very clear about this). One female client expressed one of the key dilemmas in this work:

> Initially I found it hard to work out the differences between a worker and friend. I looked at her and thought are you my

friend, or my worker. Yeah, I struggled initially. Then I came to realise that the line between workers and friends is not clear. You meet people in different ways at different times in your life.

Clients' expectations

Fifty-four per cent of the clients said that their worker talked 'about what you want or expect from the service'. The clients indicated that their workers were less likely to talk about 'whether s/he has an authority role', for example whether they would 'have to report offences if you tell them' with only 21 per cent saying that they talked about this with their worker. However, the comments from the clients help to explain this. One woman commented:

> I guess it was an unspoken boundary, they're Christian and you know where they stand. I felt it was clear but it wasn't spoken about.

Addressing criminogenic needs

We asked the clients to identify the number of issues they were working on at the present time with the programme and the average was almost five issues. We then asked the clients to identify the specific issues on which they were working. As shown in Table 13.6 the men were particularly focused on finances and women were more concerned with support and family issues than the men.

How workers helped

We then asked the clients how the workers helped them with their problems. These data were analysed and coded manually and a number of consistent themes emerged. Many of the clients commented on the practical help they received from mentors and programme staff. For example, the clients referred to assistance with signing documents, taking children to appointments, helping sort out bills, and taking them to parole appointments. This is illustrated in the comments from clients set out below:

> For five years in prison I had no bank account. I had help with this, however, a fee made the account overdrawn and I needed more help to sort it out.

Table 13.6 Issues and problems which the clients were working on at the time of interview

Problems	Gender of client		
	Male	Female	Total
Financial	9	6	15
	60.0%	22.2%	35.7%
Employment	4	6	10
	26.7%	22.2%	23.8%
Drugs and alcohol	1	2	3
	6.7%	7.4%	7.1%
Family issues	0	4	4
	.0%	14.8%	9.5%
Mental health	0	1	1
	.0%	3.7%	2.4%
Lack of support	1	5	6
	6.7%	18.5%	14.3%
Housing	0	2	2
	.0%	7.4%	4.8%
Confidence	0	1	1
	.0%	3.7%	2.4%
Total	15	27	42
	100%	100%	100%

My worker helped me with housing maintenance issues, arranged hospital appointments, transported me to appointments for major things.

If something goes wrong she is there. It is hard to find someone when you need them.

I'm a talker and I can talk to my worker. I cry, get angry, I get frustrated.

I haven't been great at working on issues. I hide from them and slip into denial. Now I am trying to face up to issues.

Goal setting

We asked the clients if they set goals with their worker and 90 per cent (n=37; total n=41) of those who answered this question indicated that they did. Forty-nine per cent (n=19; total n=39) said that they (the client) set the goals, 49 per cent said that they set the goals together with the worker and only one client indicated that the worker set the goals. The clients were then asked to comment on the things they did to achieve their goals. They referred to a range of strategies including:

- enrolling in courses;
- turning up to appointments;
- modifying their expectations;
- evaluating thoughts; reading material provided by their workers;
- seeking housing;
- using a goal sheet to identify goals and strategies;
- contacting family members;
- learning to deal with frustrations; going to a retreat;
- mixing more with a sister who is a good influence;
- reviewing a list of goals and strategies;
- talking to workers about problems and not bottling things up;
- helping children with homework;
- cutting back drug use.

In all but three instances the clients interviewed were able to identify things that they had done or were doing to address their problems. In only three instances did the clients feel they were in a period of stalemate or not tackling their problems.

Help to stop offending

We then asked the clients to comment on how the service helped them stop offending and why. The following are examples of the clients' responses to this question:

> They taught me the difference from right and wrong, taught me to take account and be responsible for decisions and choices – someone 24/7 to turn to.

> I can talk about anything and I don't have to hide anything.

> They are more on-hand with their support and they had a wide range of workers in the group.

> Maintain contact, they keep checking, and they are not doing because they have to, they are volunteers.

Just being there for me. Having someone there, showing me I can do things.

They helped me get work and the same reasons I said earlier. Because maybe they gave me a different outlook on life and getting back into a routine, normal day to day things you know.

Differences in responses of men and women

It has already been noted that the female clients tended to be more satisfied with their mentoring and that women tended to focus on different issues from men in their interactions with mentors. They also reported that they worked on more issues than the men, that their workers were more likely to understand them and to be fair. They also had more frequent contact with the mentors over a longer period of time than the men.

Conclusion

In this chapter a definition of mentoring has been discussed and the literature on mentoring programmes has been briefly reviewed. The literature points to the value of intensive programmes that are consistent with the general principles of effective work with offenders. An evaluation of four mentoring programmes in Australia was then discussed. The programmes have been described, along with the clients' responses to the programmes. The clients' responses to the programmes were particularly positive and some comments have been made about aspects of the programmes that they found most helpful, in particular support for the things the clients do well and a sense that the worker is fair.

The mentoring programmes were generally consistent with the research about effective mentoring programmes. They offered intensive contact to high-risk offenders, focused on strengths, were clear about roles, addressed a wide range of needs and developed goals and strategies to address them.

The clients in this evaluation were not randomly selected. They are clients who volunteered to be interviewed in response to notices in waiting rooms and the provision of information from staff (in some cases perhaps influenced by the $AUS50 compensation provided to participants). The numbers were also too small to effectively undertake statistical analysis. Nevertheless the evaluation provides general support for mentoring based on best practice principles. It also provides some client views about the way these principles have been applied. Some differences between men's and women's responses have also been highlighted.

References

Andrews, D.A. and Bonta, J. (2006) *The Psychology of Criminal Conduct.* Newark, NJ: Anderson Publishers.

Bouffard, J.A. and Bergseth, K.J. (2008) 'The impact of re-entry services on juvenile offenders' recidivism', *Youth Violence and Juvenile Justice*, 6: 295–318.

DuBois, D.L., Holloway, B.E., Valentine, J.C. and Cooper, H. (2002) 'Effectiveness of mentoring programs for youth: A meta-analytic review', *American Journal of Community Psychology*, 30 (2): 157–97.

Jolliffe, D. and Farrington, D. (2007) *A rapid evidence assessment of the impact of mentoring on re-offending: a summary.* Cambridge University Online Report 11/07 http://www.homeoffice.gov.uk/rds/pdfs07/rdsolr1107.pdf

McIvor, G., Trotter, C. and Sheehan, R. (2009) 'Women re-settlement and desistance', *Probation Journal*, 56 (4): 347–61.

Seiter, R.P. and Kadela, K.R. (2003) 'Prisoner reentry: What works, what does not, and what is promising', *Crime and Delinquency*, July, 49 (3): 360–88.

Spencer, R. (2007) ' "It's not what I expected": A qualitative study of youth mentoring relationship failures', *Journal of Adolescent Research*, 22 (4): 331–54.

Tolan, P., Henry, D., Schoeny, M. and Bass, A. (2008) 'Summary of the systematic review effects on mentoring interventions in reducing crime: Mentoring interventions to affect juvenile delinquency and associated problems', *Campbell Systematic Reviews*, 2008: 16, http://www.campbellcollaboration.org/

Trotter, C. (2006) *Working with Involuntary Clients.* Sydney, NSW: Allen and Unwin.

Trotter, C., Sheehan, R. and McIvor, G. (2007) *Women After Prison.* Victoria, Australia: Department of Social Work, Monash University.

Wilczynski, A., Culvenor, C. and Cunneen, C. (2003) *Early intervention: Youth Mentoring Programs.* Canberra, ACT: Crime Prevention Branch, Australian Government Attorney General's Department.

Chapter 14

Community mentoring in the United States: An evaluation of the Rhode Island Women's Mentoring Program

Dawn M. Salgado, Judith B. Fox and Kristen J. Quinlan

The Rhode Island Women's Mentoring Program provided community support and guidance to women making the transition from prison for 17 years. This chapter examines the positive outcomes of this programme within the broader context of canvassing what factors promote long-term reintegration and reduce reoffending.

Women offenders in the US

In the United States, incarcerated women make up approximately 16 per cent of the prison population. Data over the past three decades indicate the number of women in prison has grown by over 800 per cent, or twice the growth rate for men (US Department of Justice 1999; West and Sabol 2008). In a large-scale study of over 270,000 male and female prisoners, 58 per cent of female prisoners were rearrested after release, 40 per cent were reconvicted, and 39 per cent were reincarcerated with or without a new sentence in a three-year period (US Department of Justice 2002). Other statistics from state prisons report that as many as 65 per cent of women in state prisons had been previously convicted (US Department of Justice 1999). Despite these alarming patterns, research in correctional settings tends to focus on male populations. Researchers have suggested that this is primarily due to women's minority status within the prison setting as well as the types of crimes they commit, which are typically non-violent and more likely to involve alcohol or drugs than their male counterparts (Bonta *et al.* 1995; Bradley and Davino 2002; Farr

2000; Richie 2001; Singer *et al.* 1995; US Department of Justice 1999; West and Sabol 2008). However, given the high numbers of female inmates who have recurrent involvement with the criminal justice system, some researchers and policy-makers have highlighted issues of reincarceration by identifying the need for, and availability of, services for incarcerated women.

Women in prison report a number of risk factors related to increased rates of incarceration and recidivism. They report having few educational and economic opportunities when in the community, as well as high rates of victimisation, substance use and other mental and physical health issues. Between 44–65 per cent of women in state prisons report not having completed high school, only 40 per cent were employed full-time, and most report being on public assistance at the time of their incarceration (American Correctional Association 1991; Singer *et al.* 1995; US Department of Justice 1999). Over half the women in state prisons report being under the influence of alcohol or drugs when committing the offence for which they were currently incarcerated (US Department of Justice 1999). Assessments of women while they are in prison indicate the vast majority not only have high rates of substance abuse/dependence (83 per cent according to Singer *et al.* 1995) but also meet the clinical range for depression and/or anxiety (64 per cent according to US Department of Justice 1999). Research on victimisation among women in prison also points to high rates of physical, psychological and sexual trauma (American Correctional Association 1991; Bradley and Davino 2002; Browne *et al.* 1999; Maeve 2000; Parsons and Warner-Robbins 2002; US Department of Justice 1999). In addition to mental health concerns, women in US prisons report higher rates of HIV infection than men in prison (4 per cent versus 2 per cent) and 5 per cent of women are pregnant at the time of incarceration (US Department of Justice 1999).

Despite the clear and well-documented needs of women in prison, research indicates that most women do not actually receive adequate services (Cotten-Oldenburg *et al.* 1997; Freudenberg 2002; Morris and Wilkinson 1995; Prendergast *et al.* 2002). Farr (2000) suggests that women's programmes and services suffer from a lack of funding and, when in place, are typically found to be inferior to men's programming. Further, women's programming often appears to be simply an offshoot of men's programming, and not designed to match women's specific needs (Farr 2000). Ineffective implementation of programmes for women can actually promote recidivism by reducing available funding for programmes that do work and decreasing the likelihood of successful reintegration after release (Travis and

Petersilia 2001). When considering the issues facing women involved in the correctional system, evidence points to an urgent need for gender-specific programming with accompanying empirical research to improve the provision of services.

Mentoring women in prison

Mentoring-based programmes offer one example and have been used in a number of contexts (e.g. educational, vocational, recreational) to provide access to positive role models, encourage the development of healthy interpersonal relationships with peers/elders, and promote individual change by impacting on social norms and positive self-perceptions (Hamilton et al. 2006; He 2009; Roberts 2000). Mentoring ex-offenders has quickly become a national priority, with federal legislation passed in April 2008, entitled the *Second Chance Act of 2007: Community Safety Through Recidivism Prevention* (US Public Law 110-1990: Bill HR 1593), that allocates funds specifically for non-profit organisations providing mentoring services to adults and juvenile offenders during their incarceration and/or post release. In May 2009, the US Office of Justice Programs (OJP) also released a call for grant proposals offering mentoring services for adult ex-offenders.

What little evidence exists suggests mentoring-based programmes may be particularly effective in reducing recidivism and encouraging successful reintegration among women in prison for a variety of reasons. First, meta-analytic results of women's prison-based programmes report behavioural-social learning intervention strategies (e.g. role-playing, modelling, and reinforcement) have larger treatment effects than traditional programming (Dowden and Andrews 1999). Second, many components found in mentoring programmes, including the existence of a strong female role model and an opportunity for women to develop supportive networks with peers, have been highlighted as promising approaches to working with incarcerated women (Morash et al. 1998). A report funded by the National Institute of Corrections on gender-responsive programmes also emphasised the role and importance of Relational Theory when considering effective intervention strategies among women in prison (Bloom et al. 2003). Relational Theory (Miller 1976, 1988) emphasises women's need for connection, mutuality and empathy to create growth-fostering relationships that can serve to increase knowledge of self and others, encourage personal empowerment, promote individual change, and foster the development of additional healthy relationships in the future. Thirdly, mentoring programmes tend to incorporate the principles of restorative justice into their programmatic structure and theory, which also emphasises personal accountability and empowerment (Van Wormer 2001). Finally, mentoring programmes for women can provide a 'seamless set of systems' (Travis and Petersilia 2001: 308) beginning in prison and continuing post release, which has been associated with successful reintegration into the community.

In summary, the structure of mentoring programmes may be especially beneficial for women since it encourages the development of relationships with individuals outside the prison environment, offers a means for social comparison, and grants women a much-needed source of non-judgmental support and guidance. While many aspects found in mentoring-based programmes would be considered useful in meeting the needs of women in prison (Dowden and Andrews 1999; Harrison 2001; Morash *et al.* 1998; Bloom *et al.* 2003; Travis and Petersilia 2001), mentoring programmes are rarely nor adequately evaluated for their effectiveness at reducing reincarceration, supporting successful reintegration into the community, or meeting the needs of women currently in prison and after release (Bauldry *et al.* 2009). For this reason, the remainder of this chapter discusses an evaluation of the Rhode Island Women Prison Mentoring Program.

Rhode Island Women's Prison Mentoring Program

The Rhode Island Women's Prison Mentoring Program began in 1991 with grant funds and volunteers from a local community leadership group. In the mid-1990s, funding for the programme was taken over by the Rhode Island Department of Corrections, making it among the few programmes in the country to be directly supported by a State Department of Corrections. Since its inception, approximately 400 women making the transition from prison (called mentees in the remainder of the chapter) were matched with community women mentors. The primary feature of the programme was to match women about to be released from prison with women in the community based on age, background characteristics, interests and geography in order to provide individual support to women moving from prison into the community. In order to qualify for the programme, women in prison who were recruited had to demonstrate motivation and commitment for continued involvement in weekly meetings and other programme-related events. Community women mentors agreed to volunteer for a minimum of one year, were screened by the Program Director, and then completed a training course covering a variety of topics (e.g. working within the prison walls, needs of women in prison, what to expect, what a mentor is). One evaluation of the programme has reported that mentees participating in the programme returned to prison at a lesser rate at one year post release than those women without mentors – 25 per cent versus 40 per cent, respectively (Roberti *et al.* 1996). Although these data provide supportive evidence of reducing recidivism, they did not intend to capture the programmatic experience of women in prison (and community women mentors), specific aspects of the mentoring relationship that might be most effective and important, and the overall programme's ability to create a more successful and positive reintegration experience for women leaving prison. As a result, the authors developed and implemented a mixed-method evaluation of the programme in order to further examine programmatic features while highlighting the voices of women who were previously incarcerated and women community mentors who volunteered.

Evaluation study participants and methods

All participants completed a brief survey containing items assessing demographic factors (e.g. age, educational attainment, housing status), mentee's prison background (e.g. time since last incarceration, number of sentences), and programmatic experiences (e.g. length of involvement, level of satisfaction, activities) followed by a confidentiality agreement. Quantitative data from survey items were analysed using the Statistical Package for the Social Sciences (SPSS 10.0 1999). The majority of previously incarcerated women were white, non-hispanic (87 per cent), between 31 and 50 years of age (M = 41.8 years, SD = 7.4), and had received at least a high school degree or its equivalent (93 per cent) at the time of the study. Mentees reported being currently employed on a full-time basis (33 per cent), on disability or sick leave (27 per cent) or unemployed (33 per cent). Mentees reported renting housing either alone or with others (53 per cent), living with family or friends (33 per cent), or owning their own homes (13 per cent). Past sentencing and incarceration items indicated mentees had served an average of 2.3 sentences (SD = 1.2, range from 1 to 4 sentences). Their first sentencing occurred at an average age of 30.6 years old (SD = 10.3, range from 15 to 55). Mentees reported having been out of prison for an average of approximately five years

(SD = 4.1, range from three months to approximately 15 years) with approximately a third (33 per cent) having been out for two years or longer. Most community women mentors were white, non-hispanic (82 per cent), between the ages of 45 and 65 years of age (M = 55.2 years, SD = 9.42), and college educated (55 per cent). Most mentors worked at least part-time (73 per cent) with the remainder retired or unemployed (27 per cent).

Focus groups were held separately for mentors and mentees, using a similar semi-structured focus group interview guide. Two focus groups were held with previously incarcerated women (N = 18) and an additional two focus groups were held with community women mentors (N = 11). Qualitative data were transcribed verbatim from the audiotaped focus groups. Following transcription, the data were cleaned to eliminate repetition (e.g. 'and then, and then I went'), unrelated sounds (e.g. 'um', 'uh', 'like', 'you know'), and possible identifiers. Qualitative data were analysed using a modified grounded theory method (Charmaz 2000; Glaser and Strauss 1967; Henwood and Pidgeon 2003), which consists of an interactive process of data collection and analysis that relies on building a theory rather than testing it. Questions in the focus groups explored: (a) programme participants' initial decision to become involved; (b) aspects of the mentoring relationship deemed important by mentees and mentors; and (c) an evaluation of the programme overall. Data were analysed using NVivo (version 1.3.146) with the overall coding structure focusing heavily on elucidating group consensus and general themes within the aforementioned topics.

Programme involvement and initial meetings

While in prison, women describe their motivation to become involved in the programme in a variety of ways. Mentees said they initially became involved to have some semblance of normalcy within the correctional system, to escape the boredom of prison life, and to have access to the privileges associated with the programme (meals, videos, etc.). One woman describes: '... honestly, it was something to do to stop sitting around just looking out the windows and things. And then when I did it [got involved] ... I wanted to better myself, to get myself back on track.' While the previous quote represents changes in motivations based on involvement, most of the mentees explicitly stated their programme involvement was an important decision aimed at improving their lives. One woman said:

The first time I was in prison I was still fighting it ... I wasn't ready. The second time when I came back that's when I was ready to take a look at what was really going on in my life ... I was starting to reach out and look for things within the system that would help me figure out why I kept going the way I was going ...

The central feature of the mentoring programme is meetings with community mentors within the prison facility every week. While some visits by mentors consist of structured components or topics, most meetings between mentors and mentees are open time whereby mentees and mentors have conversations, share information with each other, and connect with someone outside their regular social networks and other women in prison. Women in prison typically describe their relationships with family members and friends outside the prison walls as being strained. One woman described her experience as:

When I was in prison I pretty much burned all the bridges or blown up the bridges with everybody in my family. I really had nobody and upon leaving ... I knew I had to rid myself of all the past people in my life and start over.

Another woman who recognised the need for alternative sources of social support stated:

The reason I was interested was because I really needed a friend. Everyone that I associated with was either on drugs or on alcohol. And I knew that when I left the prison if I didn't ... talk to someone and get connected with someone that was on a sober [path] ... then I was going to end up going right back [to prison].

Even when family was present and supportive in the incarcerated woman's life, these individuals sought out community mentors as a source of non-judgemental support, as well as a sounding board in which to discuss their struggles and concerns while in prison. One mentee shares: 'I had plenty of family but they didn't understand ... So, to be able to talk to somebody that you don't know or you're not close to, it was easier for me to just let my feelings out ...'

Initial meetings between incarcerated women and community mentors began with a discussion with the Program Director, who provided

285

both parties with basic information about the other. When one previously incarcerated woman thought back on her initial meeting with the woman who would become her mentor, she described:

> [The Director] informed me, pretty much everything about her [the mentor] before I met her so I knew what she did for work and stuff like that and she knew because I told [the Director] to tell her about me, why I was in [prison] and stuff like that. So, I really didn't have to fill her in, she already knew …

Mentees found this sharing of information to be particularly beneficial, commenting that it took pressure off talking immediately about shaming experiences or details of their incarceration. However, nearly all the women mentees in prison reported feeling very apprehensive during the initial meetings with mentors, specifically pointing out that they were concerned about being judged or belittled by mentors based on stigma associated with their crimes or related to their being incarcerated. While some mentees spoke about forming a quick connection with their mentors, others reported having to get over their initial judgements about the mentors in order to give the mentoring relationship a chance to take root. Another common response among incarcerated women mentees was scepticism towards others in general:

> I didn't trust my family because they downed me left and right because of what I did when I was in my addiction. I didn't trust the system because the system is corrupt period … I didn't trust the streets any more because they whipped my permission, robbed things out of me. I didn't trust nobody …

Feelings of scepticism by women in prison also focused on the mentor's motivations for volunteering in a prison programme without compensation and expectation or the Program Director's ability to match them adequately. One mentee who had been matched with two mentors over a period of years admitted: 'I have trust issues … My first thought was, well what do they want in return? Everybody has a price and neither one of them [mentors] did, neither one of them.' Another mentee who has been matched with the same person now for over eight years said: 'when I first met her [mentor] she was an old white lady and I was like, you've got to be kidding … what is she going to do with me.'

Mentors reported that during the first meetings with mentees in prison, they sought to develop a secure foundation of trust and bridge experiential gaps while also acknowledging differences. One mentor described the struggle she experienced in those initial meetings, which continue even after several years:

> She [the mentee] was always testing me in the beginning, a lot of testing. She thought I was a society woman with nothing to do in my life and I was just out there to try to be a goody two shoes ... Every now and then it still comes up. I keep showing up and I'm not going to let her get the best of me.

For those mentors and mentees who were able to make a connection during those initial meetings, women in prison reported looking forward to meeting with mentors on a regular basis. One woman said: '... I was naïve ... and not trusting anybody ... but after the first couple of meetings I liked her. I can just say I liked her a lot. I looked forward to the meetings with her because I felt like I was getting something out of every one.' Another woman, who met her mentee regularly while incarcerated, confided that visits from her mentor were like '... a breath of fresh air because it was somebody different to talk to, who had a ... good outlook on life and it was just so comfortable to sit down and talk to somebody that wasn't negative.' These two mentees reported seeing their mentors as a welcome experience and something from which they regularly benefited. While these two instances reflect the importance of the mentoring relationship in terms of offering continued meetings and accessibility, it is also important to understand those aspects that mentees considered to be the most valuable in community women mentors.

Mentors in the programme also reported the experience of being in the prison and meeting with incarcerated women regularly as an eye-opening experience where similarities rather than differences seemed to foster connection. One mentor describes:

> I had never even thought about prison and didn't know anybody who had been in prison ... these women aren't any different from me. I've made mistakes, they've made mistakes. Unfortunately, their mistakes have had legal consequences, mine had other consequences.

Mentoring immediately before and after release

The time immediately before release from prison was described by many of the women in the programme as a time of not only hope but also fear and anxiety in dealing with pressures involved in attempting to re-establish their lives while meeting many of the same challenges they faced when initially imprisoned. When asked about the importance of having a mentor after release, one woman described it as:

> An excellent idea, the whole idea of the mentor is very necessary to anybody … especially on the verge of getting out because you're like, oh my God, this is a scary thought. You don't want to go back to where you came from and you don't want to make mistakes so you don't want to go back to the old friends and the old places. So it's a fresh start to meet somebody new and have a new friend. Somebody that you can call on and somebody that will understand and be there for you when you need them.

As seen in the quote above, mentees reported feeling especially vulnerable during the time immediately before and after release. Many reported they lacked social support from family and friends while moving from prison back into the community. One woman described: '… I didn't even believe in myself at the time. And to have somebody like that that would help you believe in yourself it was very important. It was beneficial, very beneficial coming out of prison.' Within this context, mentors were an important resource for previously incarcerated women, as demonstrated in the words of one woman: 'When everybody else has turned their back on you … you had burned all your bridges and you have nobody left, that person makes a big difference on whether you could keep going. It gives you an incentive.' Another woman who reported having the same lack of support immediately after release confided: 'I felt nobody's going to have nothing to do with me … and this person wanted to just pick me up and take me out for coffee and talk with me and it's like wow that was different. I didn't have anybody like that that was a positive role model in my life.' This opportunity for offering a seamless set of services, beginning in prison and continuing on after release was one of the most important features of the programme, mentioned by both mentees and mentors who were involved.

After release, many mentees continued to meet their mentors regularly, with activities being based on the combined interests of both parties, including socialising over coffee, sharing meals, going shopping, attending social events or movies, talking on the phone, and connecting with other community resources. One mentee, who described herself as an old-timer in the programme, described how her mentor would '... come and get me during the week and she's taken me into her world. She let me see what I was missing and kind of brought me back to reality. That was my favourite thing.' As mentors and mentees continued to meet after release, mentees reported their relationships being similar to family relationships (e.g. that of a sister, mother) or relationships with trusted others (e.g. sponsor, best friend, buddy). In fact, a full 85 per cent of mentees believed that their relationship with their mentor had made a critical difference in their staying on 'the right path' during and after their release.

Having previously met at scheduled times and events within the prison walls, the now-released mentees had to schedule time in the midst of other commitments and challenges while trying to re-establish their lives. According to mentors, the time after mentees were released was also a time in which they themselves often had to reconsider and re-evaluate their role and boundaries within the mentoring relationship. One mentor reflected on this struggle, stating: '... I'm not her probation officer. I'm not her shrink. I'm not her counsellor. I'm not a drug therapist and so I had to sort of rein myself in ...' Mentors also reported that they needed to continue bridging gaps between themselves and their relationships with mentees while also acknowledging that some limitations to the relationship may also exist. In the words of one mentor: 'You got to that point in the relationship with them that they knew where you lived ... it was just sad to me because I have to put up that wall ... in one aspect you want them to trust you and then in another aspect you're saying we are not on the same level here.' Finally, mentors reported the importance of showing continued commitment in the relationship even when disappointments surfaced (e.g. mentee relapsed, was rearrested, or even reincarcerated). One mentor, who described her continued commitment despite some major setbacks in her mentoring relationship, stated: '... to me, the bigger the challenges the more meaningful; when you get through it, the relationship is stronger.'

The mentoring relationship proved to be an important resource for mentees. According to mentees in the programme, community mentors offered not only an opportunity to provide a different perspective but also much-needed support while they were imprisoned, which continued on after release. Mentors reported participating in the programme an average of five years (SD = 5.0, ranging from 0.5 months to 14 years), spending an average of four days a month with mentees (SD = 3.6, ranging from 0.5 months to 12 days) and an average of two hours per meeting (SD = 0.8, ranging from 1.0 to 3.5 hours). This said, mentees pointed to a number of characteristics among mentors with whom they were matched that were instrumental in establishing and maintaining the relationship between themselves and the community women with whom they regularly met.

Characteristics of good mentors

Mentees reported that one of the most important characteristics of good mentors was their ability to be non-judgemental, trusting and honest. One mentee confided: 'I needed someone like a preacher that wasn't going to be judgemental to me and remind me of everything I did bad in the past. Someone that could make me look forward and towards the positive side of my life that I was hoping to find.' One community mentor echoed this notion, stating: '... we have a tendency in our culture to be very judgemental and we can't be because unless you walk in that person's shoes you have no idea.' Consistency on the part of mentors (e.g. coming to events, turning up at meetings, scheduling times to interact), was essential to mentees in demonstrating their commitment to the relationship. Mentees also reported that it was especially helpful if mentors were easy to bond with, actively listened and participated in conversations, and had a good sense of humour. These mentor characteristics seemed to ease the apprehension described by mentees during those initial meetings with mentors and also helped to establish the relationship early on.

As the mentoring relationship progressed, essential features of maintaining the relationship, according to mentees, were mentors' empathy and acceptance of their struggles and frustrations while in prison and after release. This said, mentees did not expect unconditional acceptance and also expected mentors to be strong, demanding, and direct when interacting with them. One mentee admitted:

> Mine [mentor] tells me where it's at ... being an addict and being an ex-inmate, we tend to manipulate the situation the

way we want them to be and she'll call me on it. She'll tell me just where I'm going with it and try to get me right back to step one again … she'll let me know if she can do something or if she can't. She'll put it right out there for me.

This mix of support and challenge was essential in not only creating and maintaining the mentoring relationship itself but also influencing the lives of mentees overall.

Programme impact

Mentees reported the programme, and the mentoring relationship specifically, fostered more positive self-perceptions, encouraged the development of healthy relationships with others, and helped them to make a successful transition back into the community. When thinking back on their time immediately after their incarceration, most of the mentees reported feeling powerless, unworthy, and unable to see beyond life in prison. As their involvement in the programme progressed, mentees reported changes in their view of themselves and their abilities. One mentee confided: 'My self-esteem ten years ago was so low it was pathetic. I had no confidence. I didn't think I could do anything right. Everything I did I felt like a failure. This programme allowed me to not think like that any more because no matter what, I'm not a failure.' Mentors act as the foundation for change to occur, encouraging accountability for past transgressions while also providing support and empowering mentees to be successful in the future. As one mentee said:

… I had really beat myself up over what I had done you know to myself, to my family, over my addiction … she [the mentor] helped teach me how to forgive myself basically. That it's okay and God forgives you. You've got to learn how to forgive yourself because if you can't do that you're going to stay stuck. You can't move forward. And that really helped me because I didn't know how to do that at the time. And it helped me move forward in my recovery and in my life.

Mentees in the programme reported that their relationships before, during and after imprisonment were typically characterised by strain and a lack of trust. This mentoring relationship provided an alternative source of support to any that mentees had previously experienced, encouraging the development of other healthier relationships in the future. As one mentee explained:

> I learned from the mentoring programme how to just bond with another woman ... You may have a roommate for two years it doesn't mean you trust them. It really doesn't. There's family members – they've been your siblings, Mom, Dad all your life and there's no trust. But there was a bonding that was a big part for me in the programme.

When mentees were asked about the reasons why they believed this programme was different from others, they highlighted the programme's structure and organisation. The Rhode Island's Women Prison Mentoring Program pairs one woman inmate with one woman community mentor, which was viewed by mentees as being integral in the development of long-lasting relationships. In the words of one mentee: 'It's all done by women and that's what I always liked ... I'm not discriminating against men but usually programmes are just different, most programmes have men and women in it. It's all about women ...' This one-to-one pairing also became a main strength of the programme. Another mentee stated:

> Most [programmes] are a group thing where the mentoring is a one on one ... somebody that you can trust and put your faith into and say anything to where in groups you might be hesitant or leery of what somebody's going to think of you or how they're going to react towards what you have to say, but when it's the one on one you feel free to come out with whatever needs to be said.

While many mentees had expressed scepticism early on regarding mentor motives for participating in the programme without compensation, this fact became a key strength of the programme when mentees were asked to compare this programme with others they had been involved in. One woman commented: '... this mentor programme has a personal touch ... and I think that's a big part ... If you're going into another programme, like one of the rehabs, it's not personal, it's a job you know.' For those women with substance use issues, mentees also distinguished between their relationship with their sponsors and their mentors. One woman explained: 'My sponsor is there to help me with just the recovery but a mentor is there to help you with anything ... you could talk to her about other things ...' In summary, mentors were viewed by mentees, not as paid employees doing a job, but individuals who were committed to them, their future and success. Most mentees reported that their involvement with the programme had been truly valuable and meaningful (86 per cent) with another 77 per cent of mentees reporting that their relationship with their mentor had had an important impact on their lives. In the words of one mentee: 'The mentoring program is about building friendships and building trust and going out into the community and hopefully connecting with a different type of people.' Almost all the mentees (93 per cent) reported that their mentoring relationships had developed into a friendship and 73 per cent reported that it had encouraged them to seek out other healthy relationships with other women.

For women who had been involved in the programme, many expressed wanting to become mentors to other women in prison. While 80 per cent of mentees reported that their involvement in the mentoring programme influenced their interest in volunteering in general, 100 per cent reported wanting to help other women coming out of prison as a result of this experience. One woman said:

I would like to be a mentor myself. I feel like I could help somebody get to where I am today. I had struggled many years to get where I am today and as you said, they are [mentors] all professional out there. Yes, you're right; you too can be there too. Believe it or not, I have a name on a card today. It took me a long, many years to get there but you know what, this programme allowed me to do that. The support system is just tremendous, it really is.

Conclusion

This chapter explains how mentoring programmes can be useful in reducing recidivism and influencing successful reintegration for women in prison. With research to date indicating that few women receive adequate services while in prison, the Rhode Island Women's Prison Mentoring Program integrates several theoretical frameworks considered to be effective in creating a more gender-responsive and strength-based approach to working with incarcerated women (Van Wormer 2001). Mentoring programmes such as the one described in this chapter can be instrumental in providing support to women in prison, promoting individual change, developing healthy relationships, and also encouraging successful reintegration after release.

Considering Miller's (1976, 1988) Relational Theory as it applies to working with women in prison, the mentoring relationship itself becomes a growth-fostering relationship, promoting individual change and personal empowerment by increasing self-knowledge. Women in prison saw their involvement with the mentoring programme as a positive step towards change and an opportunity to not only break the monotony of prison life but more importantly connect with another person outside of prison. Mentoring programmes such as the one described in this chapter are able to incorporate many types of behavioural-social learning interventions such as role-playing, modelling, and reinforcement within the mentoring relationship, which generally shows larger treatment effects (Dowden and Andrews 1999).

Through weekly meetings with community women mentors, incarcerated women reported that mentors became an important source of social support, especially among those inmates who had strained relationships with family and friends outside prison. While scepticism and apprehension were commonly experienced during the initial meetings with mentors, most of the female inmates developed a valued relationship with their mentor and saw these meetings as a highlight of their week. The mentoring relationship provided multiple opportunities for women in prison to develop supportive networks with strong female role models. Community women mentors became essential in offering alternative perspectives, sources of support, and guidance while mentees were in prison and after release. A previous study has shown that individuals having strong social ties to non-incarcerated individuals can be instrumental in reducing recidivism later on (Bales and Mears 2008). Mentees reported that they most valued mentors who could be described as warm, non-judgemental, and caring. However, they also wanted mentors who were direct, honest, and challenged them to become better people and make better choices in their lives.

Mentoring also provides a 'seamless set of systems' beginning in prison and continuing on post release, which is essential to encouraging successful reintegration and reducing recidivism rates among women in prison (Travis and Petersilia 2001). When mentees were released from prison back into the community, they reported feeling scared and anxious. Within this context, mentors remained an important resource for previously incarcerated women, acting as a new friend and person with whom to spend time. While mentees and mentors reported this time as a period in which their roles and boundaries were challenged, they maintained contact outside prison walls, meeting for coffee, talking on the phone, going shopping, or seeing movies.

In conclusion, research shows that when programmes and services are implemented effectively and based on inmate needs, they are an important intervention tool (American Correctional Association 1991; Brennan and Austin 1997; O'Brien 2001). Future programming and services for women in prison should consider the integration of mentoring-based strategies, which offer an economical way to provide continuous support to women while they are incarcerated and after release. In the current programme, mentoring relationships lasted well beyond the one-year commitment, with many lasting upwards of eight to ten years. It is the hope of the authors that the current chapter and discussion provides supportive evidence for the role of mentoring in prison to better meet the needs of incarcerated women.

References

American Correctional Association, (1991) *The Female Offender: What Will the Future Hold?* Arlington, VA: Kirby Lithographic Company.

Bales, W.D. and Mears, D.P. (2008) 'Inmate social ties and transition to society: Does visitation reduce recidivism?', *Journal of Research in Crime and Delinquency*, 45 (3): 287–321.

Bauldry, S., Korom-Djakovic, D., McClanahan, W.S., McMaken, J. and Kotloff, L. (2009, January) 'Mentoring formerly incarcerated adults: Insights from the Ready4Work Reentry Initiative'. Retrieved from http://www.ppv.org/ppv/publications/assets/265_publication.pdf

Bloom, B., Owen, B. and Covington, S. (2003) *Research, practice, and guiding principles for women offenders: Gender responsive strategies.* Washington, DC: US Department of Justice, National Institute of Corrections.

Bonta, J., Pang, B. and Wallace-Capretta, S. (1995) 'Predictors of recidivism among incarcerated female offenders', *The Prison Journal*, 75: 277–94.

Bradley, R.G. and Davino, K.M. (2002) 'Women's perceptions of the prison environment: When prison is "the safest place I've ever been"', *Psychology of Women Quarterly*, 26 (4): 351–9.

Brennan, T. and Austin, J. (1997) *Women in Jail: Classification Issues.* Washington, DC: US Department of Justice, National Institute of Corrections.

Browne, A., Miller, B. and Maguin, E. (1999) 'Prevalence and severity of lifetime physical and sexual victimization among incarcerated women', *International Journal of Law and Psychiatry*, 22 (3–4): 301–22.

Charmaz, C. (2000) 'Grounded Theory: Objectivist and constructivist methods', in N. Denzin and Y. Lincoln (eds) *Handbook of Qualitative Research.* London: SAGE.

Cotten-Oldenburg, N.U., Martin, S.L., Jordan, B.K., Sadowski, L.S. and Kupper, L. (1997) 'Pre-incarceration risky behaviors among women inmates: Opportunities for prevention', *Prison Journal*, 77 (3): 281–94.

Dowden, C. and Andrews, D.A. (1999) 'What works for female offenders: A meta-analytic review', *Crime and Delinquency*, 45: 438–52.

Farr, K.A. (2000) 'Classification for female inmates: Moving forward', *Crime and Delinquency*, 46: 3–17.

Freudenberg, N. (2002) 'Adverse effects of US jail and prison policies on the health and well-being of women of color', *American Journal of Public Health*, 92 (12): 1895–9.

Glaser, B.G. and Strauss, A.L. (1967) *The discovery of Grounded Theory: Strategies for qualitative research*. Chicago: Aldine.

Hamilton, S.R., Hamilton, M.A., Hirsch, B.J., Hughes, J., King, J. and Maton, K. (2006) 'Community contexts for mentoring', *Journal of Community Psychology*, 34 (6): 727–46.

Harrison, L.D (2001) 'The revolving prison door for drug-involved offenders: Challenges and opportunities', *Crime and Delinquency*, 4: 462–84.

He, Y. (2009) 'Strength-based mentoring in pre-service teacher education: A literature review', *Mentoring and Tutoring: Partnership in Learning*, 17 (3): 263–75.

Henwood, K.L. and Pidgeon, N.F. (2003) 'Grounded theory in psychology', in P.M. Camic, J.E. Rhodes and L. Yardley (eds) *Qualitative Research in Psychology: Expanding Perspectives in Methodology and Design*. Washington, DC: APA, pp. 131–55.

Maeve, M.K. (2000) 'Speaking unavoidable truths: Understanding early childhood sexual and physical violence among women in prison', *Issues in Mental Health Nursing*, 21: 473–98.

Miller, J.B. (1976) *Toward a New Psychology of Women*. Boston: Beacon Press.

Miller, J.B. (1988) *Connections, disconnections, and violations*. Retrieved from http://www.wcwonline.org/pdf/previews/preview_33sc.pdf

Morash, M., Bynum, T.S. and Koons, B.A. (1998) *Women offenders: Programming needs and promising approaches*. Washington, DC: US Department of Justice.

Morris, A., and Wilkinson, C. (1995) 'Responding to female prisoners' needs', *Prison Journal*, 75 (3): 295–305.

O'Brien, P. (2001) '"Just like baking a cake": Women describe the necessary ingredients for successful reentry after incarceration', *Families in Society*, 82 (3): 287–95.

Parsons, M.L. and Warner-Robbins, C. (2002) 'Factors that support women's successful transition to the community following jail/prison', *Health Care for Women International*, 23 (1): 6–18.

Prendergast, M.L., Farabee, D., Cartier, J. and Henkin, S. (2002) ' Involuntary treatment within a prison setting: Impact on psychosocial change during treatment', *Criminal Justice and Behavior*, 29 (1): 5–26.

Richie, B.E. (2001) 'Challenges incarcerated women face as they return to their communities: Findings from life history interviews', *Crime and Delinquency*, 47 (3): 368–89.

Roberti, M., Silvia, A.M. and Walsh, L. (1996) *Effects of mentoring on recidivism among women prisoners.* Unpublished report to the Rhode Island Department of Corrections.

Roberts, A. (2000) 'Mentoring revisited: A phenomenological reading of the literature', *Mentoring and Tutoring*, 8 (2): 145–67.

Second Chance Act of 2007, HR 1593, 110th Cong. (2007).

Singer, M.I., Bussey, J., Song, L.Y. and Lunghofer, L. (1995) 'The psychosocial issues of women serving time in jail', *Social Work*, 40 (1): 103–13.

SPSS Inc. (1999) *SPSS Base 10.0 for Windows User's Guide.* Chicago IL: SPSS Inc.

Travis, J. and Petersilia, J. (2001) 'Reentry reconsidered: A new look at an old question', *Crime and Delinquency*, 47 (3): 291–313.

US Department of Justice (1999) *Women offenders* (Special Report, NCJ 175688). Washington, DC: Bureau of Justice Statistics.

US Department of Justice (2002) *Recidivism of prisoners released in 1994* (Special Report, NCJ 193427). Washington, DC: Bureau of Justice Statistics.

Van Wormer, K. (2001) *Counseling female offenders and victims: A strengths-restorative approach.* New York, NY: Springer Publishing Company, Inc.

West, H.C. and Sabol, W.J. (2008) *Prisoners in 2007.* Bureau of Justice Statistics: December 2008. National Prisoner Statistical Data Series conducted by the US Bureau of Justice Statistics, Washington, DC: Bureau of Justice Statistics.

Chapter 15

Maintaining and restoring family for women prisoners and their children

Rosemary C. Sarri

Introduction

Recent estimates from the US Department of Justice indicate that 2.3 per cent of all children below 18 years in the United States have an incarcerated parent. Of the 114,852 women in prison, 61.7 per cent are parents of minor children (Glaze and Maruschak 2009). The number of incarcerated mothers more than doubled between 1991 and 2007, far faster than the increase for incarcerated fathers. There is relatively little public awareness of the extent and seriousness of this problem, as societal attention has been limited. Although the effects for children may be profoundly negative, without public acknowledgement of the situation, it is unlikely they will receive needed intervention. It is estimated that 10 million children in the US have had a parent or sibling who has been incarcerated (The Sentencing Project 2007). There is no requirement that frontline organisations serving vulnerable children – public schools, child welfare, and health care – inquire about or account for parental incarceration and its effects on children. The Child Welfare League of America (2004) surveyed the 50 states in the US and learned that most could not even provide basic demographic information about the children of incarcerated parents. In a famous class action case on behalf of women offenders (*Glover v. Johnson* 75 F 3d, 264), the state welfare department denied its responsibility for children of incarcerated mothers unless the court ordered them to do so, and failed to acknowledge that the parent had any right to participate in decision-making, even though custody may have been only temporarily transferred. Beckerman

(1994) found that welfare workers did not maintain contact with incarcerated mothers of children in foster care even when decisions had to be made about custody and related matters. Unfortunately, this had not changed a decade later (Moses 2006). Thus, when a woman returns home from prison, family reunification is often fraught with so much difficulty that family break-up occurs and recidivism results.

This chapter addresses the characteristics and needs of incarcerated mothers and their children with particular reference to the interventions required for successful family reunification. The chapter focuses primarily on the situation in the United States, but the problems of incarcerated mothers and their children is acknowledged in most countries so the discussion has general application.

Women in prison

While the number of incarcerated women is rising in many countries, the negative consequences for women who have been convicted of a criminal offence vary considerably because welfare systems in many countries are directly involved in diversion, community alternatives to incarceration, and decriminalisation of many crimes, so they do not rely as heavily on incarceration intervention as does the US (Walmsley 2005). In contrast, the US female prison and jail population has nearly doubled since 1990 to 203,100, the highest numbers since records were nationally available (Sabol *et al.* 2007). During this same period, the US eliminated many community-based programmes that had previously reduced the numbers incarcerated and thereby allowed mothers to maintain custody of their children in most instances. Table 15.1 provides a demographic overview of women admitted to state and federal prisons. Who are the mothers in prison today?

The crime rate of females has not risen, especially for serious violent crime, yet the rate of female incarceration in the US has grown far more rapidly than that of men. Women are now more often incarcerated for crimes that had previously allowed them sentences in the community: substance abuse, prostitution, welfare violations, credit card abuse, minor assaultive crime, property and public order violations. As of 2008, 32.3 per cent of women in prison were committed there for a crime of violence (Sabol *et al.* 2009). Thus, it seems likely that public safety would not have been jeopardised had more been treated in the community.

Table 15.1 Characteristics of women in prison (women in state and federal prisons at admission)

Race: percentage who are persons of colour	61.7%
Median age	33.4 years
Marital status: single parent	61%
Education:	
average no. of years completed	10.76
general education degree	65.57%
Employed at time of arrest	66.4%
Living with children when incarcerated	72.8%
Prior incarceration	71%
Previous receipt of public assistance	41.3%
Mental health problem	73.6%
Prior physical or sexual abuse	64.4%
Current offence for drugs	39%
Median sentence length	5 years
Committed for a violent offence	32.3%

Sources: Glaze and Maruschak 2009; Dallaire 2007; Mumola and Karberg 2006.

Gender is an important aspect of women's crime because many crimes involve relationships with family, friends and significant others (Glaze and Maruschak 2009; Covington 2003). Also, their greater exposure to abuse and addictions is related to pathways to crime that differ from those of men. Sentences are longer now than in the past, with little or no allowance for good behaviour. Recidivism has increased because of restrictive parole criteria, lack of access to community treatment programmes, and lack of community support after release, especially for women with children. Incarcerated women in the US are disproportionately poor, of colour, school dropouts, single mothers, unemployed when they are arrested, and have a high probability of substance abuse and/or mental health problems. Over-representation of women of colour is particularly serious. A woman of colour is six times as likely as a white woman to be incarcerated. Black children are seven and a half times more likely to have an incarcerated mother than are white children (Glaze and Maruschak 2009).

Discrimination on the basis of race, ethnicity, sexual orientation, class, county of residence and even commitment offences influence prison life and are the source of conflict among prisoners as well as between staff and prisoners. Few prisons or jails attempt to resolve problems associated with discrimination; therefore, it festers into an ongoing problem. In many ways, prisons are dumping grounds for people that society casts aside and prefers not to provide with treatment, education and other opportunities so that they can become law-abiding, effective members of society. From very young ages these individuals experience discrimination in education, access to health care, housing and neighbourhood segregation, and employment, which culminates in their vulnerability to crime arrests and incarceration.

Although 78 per cent of women in prison have a history of substance abuse, fewer than 20 per cent receive treatment while incarcerated. Similarly, among those who are seriously mentally ill, fewer than 25 per cent receive any services (Mumola and Karberg 2006). Three out of four have been sexually abused as children or adolescents, but few receive treatment so that additional serious problems result. Research now indicates sexual abuse has serious consequences for women throughout their lives with respect to their health, sexual behaviour and criminal activity (Goodkind *et al.* 2006).

The cycle of incarceration and its impact on mothers and children

Several phases occur in the cycle of a mother's incarceration and these often have continuing effects when a mother returns home from prison or jail. Prior to her incarceration it is probable that instability characterised family life and will continue to have lasting effects throughout her incarceration and beyond (Bernstein 2005; Wakefield 2007). Events surrounding the mother's leaving are usually traumatic for the children, especially those who are very young, and older children may be angry and resentful. Typically, the children will move to live with grandparents (44.9 per cent), other relatives (22.8 per cent), or friends (7.8 per cent) (Glaze and Maruschak 2009). Initially, a small percentage (10.9 per cent), are processed into foster care, but mothers often avoid formal foster care because they fear they may lose permanent custody of their children.[1] As a result, children lack access to mental health and social services and many also experience further instability in their housing, financial resources, health and socio-emotional well-being (Johnson and Waldfogel 2004).

Crises inevitably arise when a family member is incarcerated. Frequent family crises occur because of caregiver illness, problematic behaviour by children, discrimination by community residents, and disruption of the family's financial security. Adjustment to the rigidity of the prison environment is difficult for the female offender, and she may have little ability to maintain contact with her family. Women may be transferred to a facility that is several hundred miles from the family.

Several factors affect the impact of a mother's incarceration on her children:

- the child's age;
- location of the child in the family structure and relationships;
- the child's developmental needs;
- the status of the mother as primary caregiver;
- the kin network;
- distance between the prison and the child's residence;
- the organisation and availability of institutional support for the family.

Parke and Clarke-Stewart (2003) highlighted specific problems and issues that arise at different stages of development. Nationally, the mean age of children of incarcerated parents is eight years, ranging from birth to adolescence. Those separated at infancy cannot 'bond' with the mother, which can result in lifelong harm to their maternal attachment. The pain of separation is likely to delay their sense of autonomy and initiative (Parke and Clarke-Stewart 2003; Johnston 1995). They may develop sleep and eating disorders, and manifest anxiety in various ways. Although some may identify with the incarcerated parent, having a loving caregiver may alleviate the pain.

Older children (seven to 12 years) are also traumatised and experience school phobias, poor academic records, aggression and other inappropriate behaviour. Many experience discrimination because their mothers are in prison. In some countries and states, children may reside in prison with the mother for a specified period of time. Under some circumstances that may be appropriate, but it requires special facilities and assessment if it is to be more beneficial than harmful for the child.

Adolescents typically develop maladaptive coping patterns and conduct problems as a response to a parent's incarceration: delinquency, poor school performance, truancy, substance abuse, sexual acting out, pregnancy, and mental health problems (Eddy and Reid 2002; Phillips et al. 2002). The risk of violent antisocial behaviour is three to six times higher than for an adolescent with a non-incarcerated parent (Mumola 2000). Meyers et al. (1999) suggest that these children are five to six times more likely to enter the criminal justice system than those without an incarcerated parent.[2]

Incarcerated mothers reported higher rates of intergenerational incarceration than do male parents (Dallaire 2007). Evidence from several studies indicates that children of imprisoned parents are at risk through adolescence and even adulthood of criminal behaviour, as well as a variety of other serious problems in school, work and family (Murray and Farrington 2008; Kinnear *et al.* 2007). In a study of at-risk adolescent females, most of whom were not in the justice system at the time of the survey, we learned that 28 per cent had an incarcerated mother, 52 per cent had fathers who had been incarcerated and 34 per cent had incarcerated siblings (Goodkind *et al.* 2006). Their mothers' incarceration produced more negative effects on these adolescents as manifested in depression, suicide attempts, sexual acting out and delinquent behaviour. The risk of intergenerational incarceration is increasingly recognised as a serious problem because children of incarcerated parents are more likely to experience homelessness, lack health care and are often abused or neglected (Huebner 2007).

The stresses of incarceration

The prison experience is filled with many stressors for the mother, her children and their caregivers: the initial trauma of separation and adjustment to new environments, ongoing crises in the family, infrequent contact, uneven caregiving, the lack of legal services in the prison, and discrimination towards both the children in the community and their mothers in prison. There are numerous indicators of children's experience of stress varying by age. Children can internalise depression and feelings of abandonment, and may be unwilling to relate to others, and aggressive when blamed for family problems.

Imprisonment results in many stresses for incarcerated mothers. Maintaining contact with their children becomes difficult or impossible; they feel guilty about the reasons for their incarceration; they lack legal services to help them meet their parental responsibilities; and the dearth of opportunities in prison for self-improvement hinders them from becoming better parents. The mere removal of children from women offenders has been shown to increase a woman's criminal behaviour (Ross *et al.* 2004).[3]

Caregivers also experience stress as they care for children of incarcerated mothers. Most caregivers are grandparents (44.9 per cent) or other relatives who receive little or no compensation for their additional responsibilities. Because child welfare agencies are seldom involved, relative caregivers often fail to receive financial benefits for the children, even though they themselves may be living in poverty (Engstrom 2008; Dressel and Barnhill 1994; Ruiz 2002). For example, helping children maintain contact with parents by telephone and visits may require a great deal of effort and money because of restrictive correctional policies. Children living in poverty and unstable situations are likely to experience the same or greater economic insecurity than before the mother's incarceration (Seymour and Wright 2002). These numerous stresses strain the relationship between the grandmother and her daughter and may hamper the grandmother's caregiving.

Children manifest the stress of their mother's incarceration in many different ways: in acting-out behaviour at home, in denial of the reality of separation, in running away, in feelings of guilt because they think that they may have caused their mother's incarceration, and in depression and withdrawal. These children urgently need professional help, but unfortunately that is seldom available to them.

Contact during incarceration

What happens during incarceration to both the parent and the child, and the amount of contact during incarceration can significantly affect successful reintegration (Glaze and Maruschak 2009). The majority of mothers have very limited contact with children during their incarceration, either by mail, telephone or visits. Visits are particularly crucial for growing children, yet 58 per cent of this national sample never had a visit from their children, and 33 per cent had never spoken with them on the telephone (Glaze and Maruschak 2009). The latter situation results from the very high fees that are charged to the person calling an offender in prison. Since prison mail is routinely censored, contact through written correspondence also can be problematic. The difficulty in maintaining contact through various means hinders many children from having any contact with their incarcerated mothers, women whose average sentence is five years. The lack of understanding of the importance of visitation was raised in the *Overton v. Bazetta* (148 F Supp. 2d 813) case, but the US Supreme Court unanimously decided in 2003 that corrections departments were not obligated to allow relatives to visit offenders.

Even if children are able to visit, several factors diminish the ease of the visit. Because prisons are typically located a far distance from the children's home, transportation to the prison can be difficult to arrange and expensive. Entry into the prison requires invasive searches of the children. The configuration of prison visiting rooms discourages openness and intimacy between a mother and her children, and prison officials often allow only a very brief visit with no physical contact between mother and child. Prison policy may also prohibit family visits for those women who have a drug charge. Clearly these barriers limit the benefits of the visit for both mothers and children.

A small number of states have established visitation programmes for mothers and children that have had positive consequences for both (Fehr 2004; Minnesota Department of Corrections 2002; New York Women's Prison Association 2004). These include overnight visitation, as well as counselling of mothers as to appropriate behaviour with children during visits, on the telephone and in letters. Some local welfare and correctional agencies have established programmes to enhance visitation such as allowing imprisoned mothers to lead Girl Scout troops, and provide life skills training for both mothers and children (Moe and Ferraro 2007). Minnesota has an extensive array of alternatives to prison that involve mothers and children. Project SEEK in Michigan provides tutoring and support groups, family outings, emergency assistance and transportation for visits. At the Children's Centre in Bedford Hills Correctional Facility in New York, women offenders assist in furnishing a comprehensive range of services to children and parents. The New York Women's Prison Association (2004) provides community services with an emphasis on aiding women at re-entry and for the first year after their return to the community so that mothers can re-establish and strengthen family life. Parenting education is increasingly provided to women offenders, and evaluations show that positive results can be achieved (Kennon *et al.* 2009).

Legal services

In 1932, the US Supreme Court recognised access to counsel for indigents charged with a crime, but not until 1956 was this right extended to all criminal defendants (LaBelle 2002). Because the majority of women offenders cannot afford private counsel, they are most often represented by assigned attorneys who have very large caseloads or limited hours per case during trials. When the women enter prison, these attorneys are almost never available for further assistance, unless there is a provision for such service through public defenders. Thus, it is not surprising that those with private counsel are far less likely to be convicted or to receive prison sentences (LaBelle 2002).

In cases such as *Griswold v. Connecticut*, 381 US 479 (1965), the US Constitution recognised the right of a person to establish and maintain a family. Since incarcerated women cannot go to court when they receive orders pertaining to their custodial responsibilities, they urgently need legal services concerning child custody issues. The *Glover v. Johnson* case (75 F. Supp. 3d 364, 1994) shows that legal services in prison are essential if women are to address their custodial responsibilities successfully (LaBelle 2002). Incarcerated mothers may also need the assistance of legal services to retain or regain custody of children upon release from prison. Child support debt should not be a barrier to family reunification, and incarceration alone should not be a basis for termination of parental rights (Hirsch *et al.* 2005).

Women in prison as a result of assault in cases of domestic violence or abuse need access to legal services in order to appeal convictions, to secure divorce or other related matters. Human rights attorneys such as Deborah LaBelle (2002) have used the class action strategy successfully in many cases to extend legal services to women in prison. Some prisons provide paralegal training for inmates to assist other inmates in preparing legal briefs or grievances to address a variety of legal issues in prison. In addition, the availability of law books in prison libraries can provide necessary resources for women pursuing appeals or other legal actions.

Sexual assaults of women offenders by prison guards are finally being acknowledged as serious problems with long-term negative effects which affect their ability to function as parents. In several cases, LaBelle (2002) has obtained restraining orders as well as a variety of penalties against correctional departments. Following a series of successful court decisions for women offenders who had been assaulted by prison guards, the Governor of Michigan ruled that there would be no male guards in the housing units of women's prisons. Sexual assaults affect women's mental health and their ability to interact appropriately with their children in visits or in telephone calls.

As women prepare for release, legal services can assist them with the many barriers they might confront in the community:

1 With a felony drug conviction, they may be denied educational programmes and loans;

2 Unless effectively challenged, restrictions prevent access to educational programmes thereby closing many occupations to ex-felons;

3 Legal systems may declare women with a drug conviction ineligible for public assistance, food stamps or Medicaid when they return home (Allard 2002). Such decisions are particularly problematic if women have children for whom they assume full custodial responsibilities as soon as they are released. Women may also need legal services when they return home to obtain child support orders for children for whom they have custody;

4 Housing restrictions may apply to individuals with felony convictions;

5 Employers will often not consider hiring qualified applicants because of their criminal record. Providing incentives such as tax benefits or bonding insurance to potential employers may facilitate the hiring of ex-offenders (Holzer et al. 2004);

6 Women with ongoing problems within the criminal justice system, such as detainers, outstanding felony bench warrants or violations of probation need legal services (Hirsch et al. 2005);

7 In many states, ex-felons may not vote or participate freely as a citizen in their communities.

Many of these restrictive policies require legal challenges if ex-felons are to successfully reintegrate into society and be effective parents.

Human rights

During the past few decades, greater attention has been directed to the extension of the United Nations Human Rights Conventions to the criminal justice system for the protection of offenders and their families. These several conventions have been ratified by most countries, but it requires activists to call attention to them. Angela Davis (2005: 164), a noted activist, called for a 'new civil rights movement that critically examines the situation of the growing numbers of persons who cannot exercise their human rights because they are in prison'. She reminds us that a fundamental sense of personhood and human dignity lies in the right to exercise the rights that are denied to incarcerated persons. For her the prisoners' rights movement is located in race and class and in prison privatisation when she speaks of the 'prison industrial complex' in the United States.

Several international covenants can be considered with respect to the rights of women offenders, including:

• Convention on Elimination of All Forms of Discrimination Against Women;
• Convention on Elimination of All Forms of Racial Discrimination;
• Covenant on Civil and Political Rights;
• Convention Against Torture and Other Cruel, Inhuman or Degrading Treatment or Punishment;
• Convention on the Rights of the Child.

One of the areas for which international law and legal services may be particularly important today pertains to the detention, incarceration and subsequent deportation of immigrant and refugee women and its effect on their children (Zehr 2008). Their treatment in detention facilities and prisons is often very punitive and degrading as Human Rights Watch (2006) has documented. Moreover, women may experience severe trauma when they are forcibly removed from their children without being able to make arrangements for their care. In addition, the children may suffer grievously because they may not be notified when their parents are apprehended and taken into custody while at work. The children may be citizens of the county or city where they are residing, which will complicate the situation further if their mother is not a citizen.

Policy-makers in many countries utilise these covenants as guidelines in reviewing their own policies and actions and in suggesting new policies for implementation. Deborah LaBelle (2002) suggests that in her defence of women she often uses international laws and standards for extending rights to women offenders. She refers particularly to the UN Standard Minimum Rules for the Treatment of Prisoners. For example:

• If a child is born in prison, that fact is not to be noted on the birth certificate;
• All persons shall be treated with respect due to their inherent dignity and value as human beings. (UN 1990)

What then does our knowledge about the impact of incarceration on mothers and their children mean for re-entry programmes and reintegration?

Re-entry and reintegration: mothers

Incarcerated women eagerly await reunification with their children and do not anticipate the anger, apprehension or confusion that the child often feels when a parent returns (Bernstein 2005). Children are often hurt or angry about having been left alone or 'abandoned' or may have faced stressful situations in placements. Children may have become attached to other persons, and the mother may not understand their unwillingness to be close to her. On the other hand, children may expect the impossible of their mother when she is unable or unprepared to deliver because she may not have housing, employment, or financial resources (Freudenberg *et al*. 2005). A relative caregiver (e.g. a grandmother) may wish to be relieved of responsibility immediately. Thus re-entry is a challenging and difficult process during which women need a great deal of support and concrete assistance if they are to reintegrate successfully into the community. Still, today most offenders are released with nothing except the clothing they are wearing and a bus ticket.

Because nearly all women offenders will be returned to their families, prisons today should focus on family obligations and reunification to help prevent recidivism. The women should be provided opportunities to improve their education, treat their mental illness and addiction, train them in life skills and in parenting, and help them gain a sense of self-efficacy and competence. All too often, such programmes are the exception rather than the rule with only about 13 per cent of the prison population participating in any such programmes (Travis and Waul 2003). In contrast to the past, few prisons have social workers or other professionals on their staff to plan and manage reintegration for female offenders. Prisons today are primarily custodial facilities with the majority of prisoners having hours of 'idle' time each day. This situation is destructive both physically and psychologically and has many negative consequences for successful re-entry. Women return without housing, employment and transportation and may be struggling to stay substance-free. However dire their need, they may have their children returned to them the very day they are released or soon thereafter.

The most important correlates of successful re-entry are: safe, affordable and sufficient housing, supportive relationships from relatives or friends, having their children with them, treatment for substance abuse and health problems, sustainable employment, support from a parole officer and community attitudes of acceptance (Brown and Bloom 2009; O'Brien and Harm 2002). Several comments from women in Women Arise, a re-entry programme, are informative:

> The support group was the only opportunity we have to speak with former inmates, to share experiences (both good and bad) and resources. (34-year-old drug offender with one child)

> Women experience almost identical discriminatory responses from landlords as employers. When I reveal that I have a felony record, the answer is no. (30-year-old woman with three children)

> Transportation is a major problem because we have to find housing, employment, attend school, try to attend meetings and help our children get where they needed to go. (27-year-old woman with two children)

> Financial assistance from relatives is really helpful. I have been out of prison five years and with my family's help I have saved $15,000 for a down payment on a home. Discrimination was so bad that I had no choice but to buy a home for my family. (39-year-old woman with one child)
>
> (Phillips and Sarri 2003)

Despite their difficulties, all women expressed optimism about the future, wanted to remain in the support group, and said that they developed the ability to 'dust themselves off' after being discouraged or discriminated against (Phillips and Sarri 2003). These women were unanimous in saying that preparation for release and reintegration should start in the prison so that offenders can be prepared to manage their lives when they are released. That assistance should include special visits to children in the home community if possible, and communication with parole officers about activities to be undertaken prior to release concerning housing, education, employment and substance abuse treatment if that is necessary.

In order to foster family reunification and to help women gain access to needed community resources, the New York Women's

Prison Association (2004) provides case management services during a woman's prison term until three months after re-entry. This programme also provides transitional housing for women with their children, parenting training and support along with childcare services. Because substance abuse is one of the most prevalent problems for women offenders and because almost none receives intensive treatment while incarcerated, Covington's work in designing gender-responsive treatment models is particularly important. Her 'Helping Women Recover' and 'Sanctuary Model' provide approaches that have been widely tested (Covington 2003). She also emphasises the need for general supportive services if substance abuse treatment is to succeed. 'ReConnections', a successful re-entry programme in Chicago, provides a broad range of services beginning with immediate assistance (bus passes, ID card, clothing, etc.) up to whatever women need to survive in the community, multidimensional assessment and guidance in progressive steps to meet their basic needs (O'Brien and Lee 2006). Because employment is essential if women offenders are to succeed with their families and communities, immediate attention is necessary. National agencies such as Goodwill Industries have developed a variety of transitional work programmes. Women are placed in temporary wage-paying jobs supplemented by treatment and support services. Transitional employment provides ex-offenders with needed income in the period after release. It also allows programme staff opportunities to identify and try to resolve any workplace behaviours that would cause participants problems in permanent employment. After a few months in transitional jobs, participants are helped to secure permanent employment.

Relationships are critical for women returning to the community, but not only family relationships. Women may have initially been involved in crime because of personal relationships, either because of their association with others or because of the abuse they may have experienced from them. O'Brien and Harm (2002) observed that success in developing appropriate personal relationships was crucial to released women's success in the community as was the development of a sense of self-efficacy and competence in handling challenges. Women often experience abuse and violence in their relationships so they could benefit from social work treatment as well as peer support in establishing healthy relationships.

Most women returning to the community will have limited knowledge of the available services and how they can be accessed (Bloom *et al.* 2003). Human services need to be organised into a collaborative partnership arrangement so that services can be provided using wraparound and case management strategies to include: mental and physical health, substance abuse, sexual and physical abuse, family and child welfare services, emergency shelter, food, financial assistance and transportation, academic and vocational education, advocacy, and leisure and recreation. Successful reintegration requires partnerships and collaboration among agencies. For example, women with histories of substance abuse, who comprise the majority of returning offenders, would benefit from a web of services. Unless immediate resources are available, a stressful situation will almost inevitably cause them to resume abusing substances and thereby impede their ability to perform adequately their roles of mother, employee, citizen and friend. Most offenders are not familiar with ways to access community services so outreach services are essential. Substance abuse treatment must be available to provide immediate help to returning offenders at risk of relapse and return to prison. Professionally trained social workers functioning as parole officers can anticipate these stresses and assist women in obtaining treatment immediately before incidents occur that result in their relapsing into crime. They need to help women obtain welfare benefits initially denied because of drug offences (Allard 2002). In addition, correctional staff should provide information to parolees before release to secure a State ID, driving licence, social security number and birth certificate. Without proper identification materials, they can do almost nothing in the community. All should be given a brochure with the names, addresses, telephone numbers and addresses of key human service agencies they can contact and from whom they can expect to receive a positive response to their requests for assistance.

Re-entry and reintegration: children

Children of returning mothers equally need services since they too face problems in the reunification of family relationships and location. Younger children may adapt more easily than adolescents, assuming that they have had loving and effective caregiving while their mother was incarcerated. Helping children avoid delinquent behaviour is very important both in the short term and throughout life because of their high risk for criminal careers (Murray and Farrington 2008; Wakefield 2007). Children who have been in non-relative foster care may experience difficulty in responding to contrasting parenting behaviour. For adolescents and young adults, the re-establishing of close relationships may be particularly difficult and not possible for some. The struggles of family reunification following a parent's incarceration could well exacerbate the already significant amount of turmoil most adolescents experience. Bernstein's poignant accounts of the stories of children of the incarcerated highlight the need for long-term counselling and support if children are to successfully recover from a parent's incarceration (Bernstein 2005). These children are at very high risk for mental health disorders, for substance abuse, for school problems and for arrests, which may lead to their commitment to a correctional facility. Murray (2007) highlights some of the types of social exclusion that children experience because of their parents' incarceration and how they could be counteracted.

Conclusions and recommendations

From this analysis it seems quite clear that the incarceration of mothers with children has innumerable negative consequences for all concerned. Furthermore, it is also clear that far more attention must be directed to how correctional policy can be changed to reduce incarceration and recidivism. For those who must be incarcerated, the need for intensive re-entry and reintegration programmes cannot be overemphasised. The feminist and child welfare movements have given women's imprisonment little attention despite the growth of incarceration and its long-term negative consequences. It is as if this is a population to be ignored unless a serious crisis occurs. The fact that most of the women and children are poor and persons of colour may well be a factor in the lack of attention. Women's pathways to crime differ significantly from those of men because their crime often involves relationship problems, a characteristic that may need special attention in treatment. Human service workers and educators were active in the justice system in the past, but their presence has declined sharply since the early 1990s. They are urgently needed to assist women offenders in community agencies but also to serve as probation and parole officers.

Proposals for future policies and practices need to focus on strategies for reducing incarceration, increasing crime prevention, decriminalisation of substance abuse crimes, diversion of minor offenders to community treatment programmes, revision of statutes in areas such as domestic violence, and increased alternative sentencing. Also overdue for change are policies that require commitment to prison of persons who are mentally ill or addicted when mental health or substance abuse treatment facilities could far better serve

313

their needs. The overwhelming majority of women offenders do not threaten public safety, so alternative non-institutional sentencing for those who have been convicted of crime deserves serious attention. These alternatives include diversion and community service, probation, civil penalties, fines, contract treatment, and suspended sentences. In addition, sentences for all penalties need to be shortened to the duration of those existing in several developed countries. There is no evidence that the length of sentence is correlated with recidivism. Rather, the quality and extent of reintegration programmes are critical factors in reducing recidivism. If community-based programmes are used extensively, family units need not be broken up because of a mother's crime. For women in correctional facilities, education, mental health, substance abuse, parenting, and relationship services are imperative. The maintenance of contact between parents and children is essential, along with active involvement of child welfare workers. Lastly, for those who are incarcerated, services to prepare for release and reintegration in the community should be available throughout the entire period of incarceration and for several months after release.

Notes

1 Women face many obstacles in trying to maintain parental rights. In 25 states there are laws terminating parental rights when a parent is incarcerated for a specific period of time (Genty 1995) The Safe Family and Adoption Act of 1997 created many obstacles for incarcerated parents because there are limits on the length of time that can elapse before a child is placed for adoption when a parent is separated from the child. The law shifted policy away from family preservation and reunification and towards adoption.
2 Intergenerational incarceration experience is a growing phenomenon in the US and it may be due to 'labeling' and social exclusion of children, which increases the likelihood of incarceration if one has a parent or other immediate relative who has been incarcerated.
3 Part of the explanation for the increase in the women's criminal behaviour may be a reaction to the removal of her children because of abuse and/or neglect.

References

Allard, P. (2002) *Denying Welfare Benefits to Women Convicted of Drug Offenses.* Washington, DC: The Sentencing Project.

Beckerman, A. (1994) 'Mothers in prison: Meeting the prerequisite conditions for permanency planning', *Social Work*, 39 (1): 9–14.

Bernstein, N. (2005) *All Alone in the World: Children of the Incarcerated*. New York: The New Press.

Bloom, B., Owen, B. and Covington, S. (2003) *Gender-Responsive Strategies: A Summary Research, Practice and Guiding Principles for Women Offenders*. Washington, DC: National Institute of Corrections. NIC Number 018017.

Brown, M. and Bloom, B. (2009) 'Reentry and renegotiating motherhood: Maternal identity and success on parole', *Crime and Delinquency*, 55: 313–36.

Child Welfare League of America (2004) *An Overview of Statistics on Children of Incarcerated Mothers*. http://www.cwla.org/programmes/incarcerated/cop_factsheet.htm

Covington, S. (2003) 'A woman's journey home: Challenges for female offenders and their children', in J. Travis and M. Waul (eds) *Prisoners Once Removed*. Washington, DC: The Urban Institute, pp. 67–104.

Dallaire, D., (2007) 'Incarcerated mothers and fathers: A comparison of risks for children and families', *Family Relations*, 56: 440–53.

Davis, A. (2005) *Abolition Democracy: Beyond Empire, Prisons and Torture*. New York: Seven Stories Press.

Dressel, P. and Barnhill, S. (1994) 'Reframing gerontological thought and practice: The case of grandmothers with daughters in prison', *The Gerontologist*, 34: 685–91.

Eddy, J.M. and Reid, J.B. (2002) 'The antisocial behavior of adolescent children of incarcerated parents: A developmental perspective', Presentation at the *Prison to Home* Conference, Washington, DC, 30–31 January 2002.

Engstrom, M. (2008) 'Involving caregiving grandmothers in family interventions when mothers with substance abuse problems are incarcerated', *Family Process*, 47 (3): 357–71.

Fehr, L. (2004) 'Female offender re-entry programmes combine transitional services with residential parenting', *Corrections Today*, October: 82–7.

Freudenberg, N., Daniels, J., Drum, M., Perkins, T. and Richie, B. (2005) 'Coming home from jail: The social and health consequences of community re-entry for women, male adolescents and their families and communities', *Public Health Matters*, 95: 1725–36.

Genty, P. (1995) 'Termination of parental rights among prisoners', in K. Gabel and D. Johnston (eds) *Children of Incarcerated Parents*. New York: Lexington Books, pp. 167–82.

Glaze, L. and Maruschak, L. (2009) *Parents in Prison and Their Minor Children*. Washington, DC: US Department of Justice Office of Justice Programmes, NCJ222984, August.

Goodkind, S., Ng, I. and Sarri, R. (2006) 'The impact of sexual abuse in the lives of young women involved or at risk of involvement with the juvenile justice system', *Violence Against Women*, 12 (5): 456–78.

Hirsch, A., Dietrich, S. Landau, R., Schneider, P. and Ackelsberg, I. (2005). *Every Door Closed: Barriers Facing Parents with Criminal Records*. Washington, DC: Centre for Law and Social Policy.

Holzer, H., Raphael, S. and Stott, M. (2004) 'Will employers hire former offenders? Employer preferences, background checks, and their determinants', in M. Patillo and B. Western (eds) *Imprisoning America*. New York: Russell Sage Foundation, pp. 205–46.

Huebner, B. (2007) 'Effects of maternal incarceration on adult offspring involvement in the criminal justice system', *Journal of Criminal Justice*, 35 (3): 283–96.

Human Rights Watch (2006) *A Threat to Society? Arbitrary Detention of Women and Girls for 'Social Rehabilitation'*. New York, NY, 18 (2): 1–39.

Johnson, E.I. and Waldfogel, J. (2004). 'Children of incarcerated parents: Multiple risks and children's living arrangements', in M. Patillo, D. Weiman and B. Western (eds) *Imprisoning America: The Social Effects of Mass Incarceration*. New York: Russell Sage Foundation, pp. 97–135.

Johnston, D. (1995) 'Incarcerated parents', in K. Gable and D. Johnston (eds) *Children of Incarcerated Parents*. New York: Lexington Books, pp. 3–20.

Kennon, S., Mackintosh, V. and Myers, B. (2009) 'Parenting education for incarcerated mothers', *Journal of Correctional Education*, 60 (1): 10–30.

Kinnear. S., Alati, R., Najman, J. and Williams, G.M. (2007) 'Do paternal arrest and imprisonment lead to child behavior problems and substance use?', *Journal of Child Psychology and Psychiatry*, 48 (11): 1148–56.

LaBelle, D. (2002) 'Women, the law and the justice system: Neglect, violence and resistance', in J. Figueira-McDonough and R. Sarri, *Women at the Margins: Neglect, Punishment and Resistance*. Binghamton, NY: Haworth, pp. 347–74.

Meyers, B., Smarsh, T., Amlund-Hagen, K. and Kennon, S. (1999) 'Children of incarcerated mothers', *Journal of Child and Family Studies*, 8 (1): 11–25.

Minnesota Department of Corrections (2002) *Report on the Women's Prison*. St. Paul: Minnesota Department of Corrections.

Moe, A. and Ferraro, K. (2007) 'Criminalized mothers: The value and devaluation of parenthood from behind bars', *Women and Therapy*, 29 (3): 135–64.

Moses, M. (2006) 'Does parental incarceration increase a child's risk for foster care placement?', *National Institute of Justice Journal*, 205: 1–3.

Mumola, C. (2000) *Incarcerated Parents and their Children*. Report No. NCJ-182335. Washington, DC: US Department of Justice, Bureau of Justice Statistics.

Mumola, C. and Karberg, J. (2006) *Mental Health Problems of Prison and Jail Inmates*. Washington, DC: US Department of Justice, Bureau of Justice Statistics, NCJ 213600.

Murray, J. (2007) 'The cycle of punishments and social exclusion of prisoners and their children', *Criminology and Criminal Justice*, 7: 55–81.

Murray, J. and Farrington, D. (2008) 'Parental imprisonment: Effects on boys' antisocial behaviour and delinquency through the life course', *Journal of Child Psychology and Psychiatry*, 46 (12): 1269–78.

New York Women's Prison Association (2004) *Breaking the Cycle of Despair: Children of Incarcerated Mothers*. New York, NY: Women's Prison Association and Home, www.wpaonline.org

O'Brien, P. and Harm, N. (2002) 'Women's recidivism and reintegration: two sides of a coin', in J. Figueira-Mcdonough and R. Sarri (eds) *Women at the Margins: Neglect, Punishment and Resistance*. Binghamton, NY: Haworth Press, pp. 296–320.

O'Brien, P. and Lee, N. (2006) 'Moving from needs to self-efficacy: A holistic system for women in transition from prison', *Women and Therapy*, 3: 106–19.

Parke, R. and Clarke-Stewart, K.A. (2003) 'Effects of parental incarceration on children', in J. Travis and M. Waul (eds) *Prisoners Once Removed*. Washington, DC: Urban Institute, pp. 189–233.

Phillips, A. and Sarri, R. (2003) *Evaluation of Prove, A Re-entry Program for Women Offenders*. Detroit, MI: Women Arise.

Phillips, D., Burns, B., Wagner, R., Kramer, T. and Robbins, J. (2002) 'Parental incarceration among adolescents receiving mental health services', *Journal of Child and Family Studies*, 11 (4): 385–99.

Ross, T., Khashu, A. and Warnsley, M. (2004) *Hard Data on Hard Times: An Empirical Analysis of Maternal Incarceration, Foster Care and Visitation*. New York City Administration on Children's Services and the Vera Institute.

Ruiz, D.S. (2002) 'The increase in incarcerations among women and its impact on grandmother caregivers: Some racial considerations statistical data included', *Journal of Sociology and Social Welfare*, 29 (3): 179–98.

Sabol, W., Minton, T. and Harrison, P. (2007) *Prison and Jail Inmates at Midyear 2006*. Washington, DC: US Department of Justice, Office of Justice Programs, NCJ 217675.

Sabol, W., West, H. and Cooper, M. (2009) *Prisoners in 2008*. Washington, DC: US Department of Justice, Office of Justice Programs, Bureau of Justice Statistics, NCJ 228417.

Seymour, C.B. and Wright, L.E. (2002) 'Working with children and families separated by incarceration', *Handbook for Child Welfare Agencies*. Washington, DC: CWLA Press.

The Sentencing Project (2007) *Women in the Criminal Justice System*. Washington, DC, www.sentencingproject.org

Travis, J. and Waul, M. (2003) *Prisoners Once Removed: The Impact of Incarceration and Reentry on Children, Families and Communities*. Washington, DC: The Urban Institute.

United Nations (1990) *Proceedings of the 45th Session of the General Assembly*. 'Model treaty on supervision of offenders conditionally sentenced or conditionally released'. New York, NY, pp. 222–4.

Wakefield, S. (2007) *The Consequences of Incarceration for Parents and Children*. PhD dissertation, UMI Number 3273803, Ann Arbor, MI: ProQuest Information and Learning CO.

Walmsley, R. (2005) *World's Prison Population* (6th edn). London: International Centre for Prison Studies, Kings College, London.

Zehr, M.A. (2008) 'Iowa's school districts left coping with immigration raid's impact', *Education Week*, 21 May: 4.

Court cases

Glover v. Johnson {75 F. 3d 364, 1994}
Griswold v. Connecticut (381 US 479, 1979)
Overton v. Bazzetta et al. [148 F. Supp. 2d 813] (ED Mich. 2001)

Chapter 16

Connecting to the community: A case study in women's resettlement needs and experiences

Becky Hayes Boober and Erica Hansen King

Introduction

The state of Maine, USA has introduced gender-responsive transitions into the community, recognising the different pathways for women and men into offending and their differing needs from programmes to give them better outcomes. This chapter discusses these initiatives and how they might be applied in other contexts. The authors would like to recognise and thank the Maine Department of Corrections (DOC) and Volunteers of America Northern New England for their leadership and exemplary work with women, as well as their support for accessing data and relevant information to inform this piece.

Trudi's experience

Trudi transferred to the Women's Re-entry Centre (WRC) when it opened in November 2007. The small, community-based centre houses 40 women for the last 6–18 months of their state prison sentences, using a model of evidence-based, gender-responsive programming and community involvement to improve re-entry experience for women in Maine, a rural state in the north-eastern Atlantic coast of the United States.

She was eased into community life, wearing street clothes on frequent community outings with staff to the library, church and the Department of Labour Career Centre. She helped in the kitchen; she took classes at a local college; she volunteered to be featured on a local television segment about the new centre.

Once she earned community status, she was hired by a local restaurant chain willing to transfer her to one of their sites near her home after her release. In addition to working, Trudi participated in many of the centre's programmes and treatment interventions. She learned about healthy relationships and redirected her thinking to a more prosocial focus. She and her case manager designed a post-release life. They identified friends, family and professional community providers to be her re-entry team. Before release, Trudi had a detailed re-entry plan that addressed her key recidivism risks, family and community reunification issues, mental health treatment, employment, health care, prosocial recreational opportunities and support networks. The plan heavily structured her first days post release, including appointments with community providers, her work schedule, recreational activities and family reunification activities. She received follow-up calls from the centre staff and had ongoing support from her re-entry team.

Trudi's experience at the WRC highlights its programmes and services. The WRC was developed in response to a rapidly growing female incarceration population, but focused on reducing recidivism through effective programming and relationship building. A broad network of systemic and local collaborative partnerships was created to support women as they made the transition into their community of choice. Maine's WRC model capitalises on those connections, to promote thriving re-entry outcomes for transitioning women while implementing principles of evidence-based practice and gender responsivity. It offers opportunities and lessons for replication in other jurisdictions.

National landscape: The United States and Maine context

In January 2008, the US imprisoned 2.94 million of its over 309 million citizens, more than the 26 European countries with the largest inmate populations combined (Warren 2008). This 'mass incarceration' occurred even though arrests and reported crimes decreased between 1973 and 2005 (Bureau of Justice Statistics 2007). Women are disproportionately affected by this increase in imprisonment. During the past 30 years, the number of women incarcerated in the US increased 757 per cent, while the incarceration of men rose 386 per cent (Frost *et al.* 2006).

Maine's incarceration rate is the nation's lowest, at 149 per 100,000 residents. However, Maine experienced an increase of 114 per cent in the number of women incarcerated between 1999 and 2004, the nation's largest increase for that period (Frost *et al.* 2006). Its incarceration rate for females increased 53 per cent in 2002 alone, rising to 12 per 100,000 (Commission to Improve the Sentencing, Supervision, Management and Incarceration of Prisoners 2004). Women comprise 9 per cent of the total adult prison population in Maine (Benson and Montana 2003) and 7 per cent nationally (Harrison and Beck 2005) and 12 per cent in US jails (Solomon *et al.* 2008). The decade saw a 61 per cent increase in female arrests to over 10,000. Maine's prison for women housed almost double its capacity within five years of opening (Boober and Fortuin 2006).

Maine's trends in female arrests and incarceration reflect US and other nations' statistics. Compared with male offenders, women commit fewer serious and violent crimes. They are more likely than men to be incarcerated for a drug offence (29 per cent versus 19 per cent) or property offence (30 per cent versus 20 per cent) and less likely than men to be incarcerated for a violent offence (35 per cent versus 53 per cent) (The Sentencing Project 2007). Only one in seven violent offenders is a woman. Twenty-eight per cent of women are imprisoned for violent crimes, but three-quarters of these committed simple assault. Over a third of women incarcerated in state prisons are convicted of drug offences, representing an increase for these crimes of 888 per cent between 1986 and 1996. Not surprisingly, since women and children are the fastest growing segment of those living in poverty, 27 per cent are imprisoned for property crimes (University of Cincinnati 2004).

Maine women's offence trends are consistent with the pathways research (Bloom *et al.* 2003; Chesney-Lind and Pasko 2004a, 2004b; Daly 1992; Gilfus 1992) that describes women's offences as more likely to be economically motivated (e.g. forgery, embezzlement, theft) or more trauma reactive (e.g. substance abuse) and relational (e.g. assault). Their criminal activity often occurs in response to fractured relationships, and women are often accomplices to crimes initiated by their male partners. In a study of Maine's women offenders (King 2009), five offence types (n=880) accounted for 79 per cent of misdemeanour offences committed by women: assault and threatening (n=362), operating under the influence (n=239), drugs (n=119), theft (n=108) and forgery (n=52). Similarly, five offence types accounted for 80 per cent of women's felony offences: drugs (n=295), theft (n=209), burglary (n=97), forgery (n=63) and assault and threatening (n=56).

As these statistics suggest, women's pathways to offending are different from and often more complex than men's. Their criminogenic needs are compounded by multiple, interconnected problems that reflect individual, family systems, and micro and macro environmental factors, including social stratification of privilege. Women's offending behaviours are often linked to factors such as the struggle to support themselves and their children in a society that gives fewer economic privileges to women; a history of trauma and victimisation; substance abuse issues; mental illness often tied to early abuse; economic and social marginality; homelessness; low self-efficacy; and relationship issues or pressures (Bloom *et al.* 2005). Because their pathways are different, women's recidivism risks and transition needs vary from those of their male counterparts and require a different approach and interventions (Boober and Fortuin 2006).

Maine's approach: Integrating knowledge

WRC was designed to better address women's pathways to offending and their unique transition needs while alleviating overcrowding. Rather than simply build another facility that would house women and then release them unprepared for community life, Maine examined women's pathways into the criminal justice system and designed a comprehensive programme merging best practices from both the evidence-based practice (EBP) and gender-responsive principles (GRP) research to increase women's successful re-entry.

Maine commits to full implementation and fidelity to two, sometimes viewed as dichotomous, bodies of literature defining work with criminal justice-involved women. The first, often referred to as 'what works', evidence-based practices and/or principles of effective correctional intervention (Andrews and Dowden 2006; Gendreau *et al.* 1996), has professionalised the field of corrections, impacting on prisoner re-entry by providing a prescription for intervening. Essentially, EBP guides practitioners to assess risks and target needs (mostly criminogenic) with appropriate services and dosage and with high adherence. As one of the two National Institute of Corrections' demonstration sites for implementation of EBP in community corrections, Maine is particularly invested in this model.

The movement towards EBP is criticised by some advocates, feminists and scholars. At the heart of the debate is whether the risks and needs underlying women's criminal behaviours are qualitatively different from men's and if different interventions are warranted. Some refute the utility of risk assessment (Hannah-Moffat 2009), cognitive behavioural therapy (Bloom 2000) and related approaches with women, who are marginalised in many respects. One criticism is that the research underlying the risk-need-responsivity model is limited by quantitative methods, ignoring compelling qualitative research that includes the voices of women offenders (Kendall 2004). Another critique is that EBP research is based on predominantly white, male samples and has been overgeneralised with all offenders, without regard to gender, ethnicity or race (Porporino 2005). Meanwhile, others (Dowden and Andrews 1999; Smith *et al.* 2009) assert that traditional risk domains apply equally to women, questioning the validity of women-only studies. Neither position in this debate, when viewed dichotomously, serves the work of re-entry with women optimally.

Recently, more integrative approaches to women offenders have emerged (Taylor and Blanchette 2009; Blanchette and Brown 2006a, 2006b; Van Dieten 2002, 2007), and women-only studies (Salisbury 2007; Van Voorhis *et al.* 2010) have shed new light on what risk assessment and interventions for women might be. As a current implementation site of the National Institute of Corrections' Women Offender Case Management Model (WOCMM) (Van Dieten 2007), Maine actively works to maintain mutual fidelity to these two bodies of knowledge. While some (Morash 2009) question whether this can be achieved realistically, Maine remains committed to using the best knowledge available to rehabilitate women offenders.

Maine integrates the six GRP into its programming along with EBP. Its programming involves both correctional facility staff and community supervision (probation) in initiatives such as the WOCMM (Van Dieten 2007) to ensure a more therapeutic and seamless transition for women. In addition to addressing traditional risk domains, such as substance abuse, education/employment and attitudes, Maine's model attends to gendered risk factors such as mental health and medical re-entry (Van Voorhis *et al.* 2010). This integration of EBP and GRP prompts Maine's best work with women involved with the criminal justice system.

To support effective programme operations at the line level, Maine recognises and employs a multilevel practice approach to facilitate integration at the macro (policy), mezzo (organisational) and micro (operational, programme staff, women) levels, helping women internalise strategies and develop stronger external supports. For example, as women faced limited access to health care and as women-only literature correlates medical stability with women's recidivism, Maine Department of Corrections (DOC) generated an interdepartmental memorandum of understanding (MOU) with the Maine Department of Health and Human Services (DHHS) to streamline the pre-release application process at the macro level. At the mezzo level, Maine DOC has protocols and staff education on the MOU. Then, staff (micro) schedules appointments and transfers medical records 30 days prior to release. As a result, women experience better continuity of care and access health insurance and needed physical and behavioural health services more efficiently post release (see Figure 16.1).

Maine's approach: Women's re-entry programming

Maine integrated EBP and GRP in its Women's Centre (WC) which opened in 2002 as a gender-responsive unit and Maine's only female state prison. However, the state recognised a need for a quality re-entry preparation opportunity for women (Van Voorhis 2005). Therefore, in 2006 it committed resources to open a Women's Re-entry Centre (WRC) incorporating both EBP and GRP and emerging re-entry best practices. Maine included elements the National Governors' Association recommended as evidence-based re-entry programming:

- Begin re-entry planning at intake and build on individual risks, needs and strengths;
- Use validated risks and needs assessment tools to determine appropriate programming to mediate risks/needs;
- Improve access to and engagement of local service providers;
- Improve how release decisions are made;
- Improve how and when release from the facility occurs;
- Develop a detailed, specific transition plan with structured time for the first hours and days after release;
- Assist with applications for supportive benefits prior to release;
- Prior to release, provide the individual with proper state identification, needed to access services and jobs;
- Use wraparound, integrated case management approaches to planning and supervision;
- Support residents to find social services and health supports, safe housing, jobs and related community supports;
- Build on natural supports;
- Develop programmes in communities where a large percentage of prisoners return; and
- Notify victims. (NGA 2005)

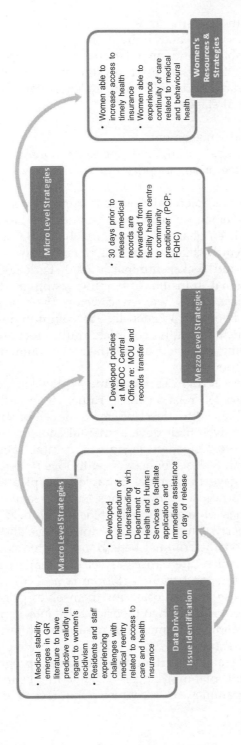

Figure 16.1 Integrated practice model – medical stability

WRC integrates these elements with a gender-responsive twist. The work incorporates GRP and builds on strengths-based principles of positive psychology and on relational theory. Strategies such as motivational interviewing are used throughout the process to enhance women's engagement and motivation. Release planning is organised in three operational stages:

1 Assessment and engagement;
2 Team building, goal setting and re-entry planning; and
3 Community integration, support and stability.

To examine Maine's implementation, it is important to understand its theoretical basis. Female re-entry programmes are based on positive psychology, which emphasises prevention by building on strengths that make life worthwhile at societal, community and individual levels (Seligman and Csikszentmihalyi 2000; Park 2003). Designing women's correctional transition planning using a strengths-based and relational focus helps women develop their strengths within the environmental context. Women live in communities that support and/or restrict them through a complex, multidirectional interaction. In addition to being impacted on by their environment, women can help shape their community.

Relational theory recognises that females develop psychologically within the context of relationships, rather than adhering to the separation model used to describe male development (Covington and Surrey 1997). Given their developmental and socialised emphasis on relationships, women often engage in criminal behaviour in an attempt to maintain a close connection with loved ones. For example, women might engage in criminal behaviour to please a partner or to provide for the needs of loved ones, such as children or elderly parents. Maine has women incarcerated for embezzling funds to pay for their elderly parents' prescription drugs and other health care costs. Additionally, criminal behaviour is often compounded by substance abuse, which often arises as self-medication due to painful personal relationships and trauma (Bloom *et al*. 2005). Women must learn skills to choose and advocate for themselves prior to release.

The WRC integrates these two theories fully into its programming, release planning and community follow-up by adhering to the six research-based GRP (Bloom *et al*. 2005). These principles are central to decisions made at the systemic, operational, programmatic and individual resident planning levels. Daily, the centre emphasises people, not programmes. It recognises the fact that humans are complex and encounter an elaborate web of influences; they are not just a manifestation of their recidivism risks. Therefore, the Women's Re-entry Centre is a strengths-based, therapeutic community environment emphasising skill building, treatment and self-efficacy. Transition planning is multidimensional, addressing social, cultural and therapeutic issues. Re-entry activities consider gender-responsive factors such as relational violence, family and natural support relationships, substance abuse, co-occurring disorders, poverty, cultural norms and non-privileged status (Bloom *et al.* 2005).

Stages of re-entry

To understand how this works, it is helpful to examine how the centre, operated under DOC contract by Volunteers of America Northern New England, incorporates GRP into three stages of re-entry planning and execution.

1 Assessment and engagement

Re-entry begins at the initial time of incarceration. The assessment and engagement stage includes both EBP and GRP assessment of a woman's risks, needs and strengths. Women receive a thorough physical examination, mental health screening, validated criminogenic risk assessment, strengths assessment, substance abuse evaluation, trauma screening, and level of custody/confinement evaluation. Data collected by trained staff using motivational interviewing techniques become the foundation for determining an individualised rehabilitation plan incorporating the appropriate, prioritised programming for each woman. Treatment dosage is linked to levels of risk.

Originally, Maine used the Level of Service Inventory-Revised (LSI-R) (Andrews and Bonta 1995). However, drawing on the state's experience with wraparound services and on research recommending that the LSI-R be supplemented with a more gender-sensitive assessment of needs, especially economic needs (Holtfreter *et al.* 2004), Maine later adopted the strengths-based Service Planning Instrument for Women (SPIn-W) assessment (Robinson *et al.* 2005) to measure both criminogenic risks and protective/strengths factors. It is used with the LSI-R, which is required by departmental policy, to inform risk classification and case management.

Assessing social capital assets and needs becomes critical for women's re-entry programming and planning. Female offenders living in poverty tend to have social networks that can offer only lower levels of emotional, social and instrumental (such as financial) support (Reisig *et al*. 2002). Assisting women with skills that enhance their social capital can reduce recidivism risks. Therefore, an Ecomap is used to assess formal and informal community support for the women. These data become important in identifying the composition of the re-entry team and planning for social capital support.

Data from all of these assessments drive the individualised plan of programming. Maine's diverse programming adheres to both EBP and the GRP. Educational interventions focus on skills women need to succeed after release. Tutors and adult education services both on site and in the community help women earn a General Equivalency Diploma. At the WRC, women can enrol in any of the area's five colleges and universities. The WRC partners with organisations that help women apply for financial assistance. Philanthropists also fund tuition and support for college/university costs. Study stations with computers in the centre's day room facilitate homework activities.

Other skills are developed at the WRC as well. 'Earning and Learning' enhances knowledge about personal budgeting and financial management. After completing this programme, women may open a matching savings account through Women, Work and Community to save for education, to buy a home, or to start a business. 'Boundaries', a favourite among the women, teaches skills to establish healthy personal boundaries in relationships. Skills are practised daily at WRC. Parenting classes and support groups teach skills that are integrated into family visitation.

The WRC also addresses trauma, mental health and substance abuse. In the US, over 50 per cent of women prisoners report experiencing childhood abuse and over 75 per cent report being abused as an adult. Sixty-one per cent report past physical abuse and 54 per cent past sexual abuse. In Canada 81 per cent of women in criminal justice report experiencing abuse in their current relationship (Bureau of Justice Statistics 2007). At the WRC, as many as 55–99 per cent of female residents at any given time are victims of trauma. Trauma is frequently linked to substance abuse, depression, anxiety disorders and PTSD. To address trauma issues, WRC adopted *Seeking Safety* (Najavits 2002) and *Moving On*, intervention programmes designed specifically for women involved with the criminal justice system (Van Dieten and MacKenna 2001; Van Dieten 2007). The local domestic violence project offers onsite awareness training. They also provide transitional housing for women who need to avoid returning to dangerous home situations. While participating in these trauma interventions, some women recognise for the first time that their relationships are unhealthy. In this emotionally vulnerable time, they require access to quality mental health services.

Contracted treatment providers and DOC professional staff provide mental health treatment at WRC. Women begin seeing community mental health providers prior to release to enhance continuity of care and compliance with post-release mental health treatment. Providers selected have expertise in women's mental health needs, trauma and family reunification.

The Differential Substance Abuse Treatment (DSAT) model addresses substance abuse (Jamieson *et al.* 1999). This cognitive behavioural programme with separate curricula for women offers 15 three-hour sessions in Level 3 and 26 sessions in Level 4 for women with severe substance abuse histories. The two levels cover motivation, triggers, problem solving, assertiveness, constructive thinking, support, self-care, stages of change, refusal skills, managing emotions, controlling self-defeating thoughts, the relationship between substance abuse and criminal behaviours, and effective communication. Next, women take a transitional DSAT programme to reinforce skills as they spend time in the community, with potential exposure to triggers. After completing these programmes, women make the transition into community DSAT groups, which support their sobriety post release. Participants most value insights on triggers and the community follow-up treatments (Van Voorhis 2005).

Women also engage in prosocial recreational activities and community involvement. They register to vote and participate in elections. They volunteer at the local thrift shops and food banks. They participate in community events and professional meetings. These activities often establish new, prosocial interests and hobbies.

Each woman uses a personal portfolio to document her programming accomplishments, growth and changes, employment-readiness efforts, job-seeking documents, goals and treatment engagement. This portfolio is used for applications for early release programmes, for job searching, and for initial meetings with probation. It also helps a woman's self-efficacy by serving as a visual documentation of her growth. The centre's culture also prepares women for release by modelling healthy environments. Correctional staff members are trained in gender-specific classes and motivational interviewing and are expected to model appropriate behaviours and relationship skills consistently. This is built into job performance evaluations. Whenever possible, correctional officers co-facilitate community building activities and cognitive behavioural groups.

Gender-responsive programming requires an environment with safety, respect and dignity. Because of high rates of trauma and abuse histories for female prison residents, the centre uses strategies to maintain security while avoiding procedures such as invasive searches that might retraumatise. Staff and 'veteran' residents model appropriate boundaries, respect, support and opportunities for personal empowerment and healthy relationship skills. Policies and procedures promote positive personal growth. Consensus management is used. Rules, expectations and sanctions are clear, consistent, reasonable and inclusionary. Women give input that helps shape these rules. This assists them in internalising appropriate boundaries. At weekly town meetings, residents share concerns, celebrations, input about policies and operations, and community opportunities. They address issues through community problem solving, resolve their own conflicts and develop prosocial decision-making skills. Deliberate attention is given to creating a more equal power distribution than traditionally is found in prison environments. It is within these healthy relationships and culture that women are motivated to change.

All this assessment and programming prepares each woman for her release. Intensive release planning begins six months prior to release. It builds on the skills the woman has developed, on her strengths, and on her prosocial community network. The next two stages further shape her re-entry experience.

2 Team building, goal setting and re-entry planning

Women need comprehensive, creative community placement and referrals to become self-sufficient after leaving the correctional system. Using strengths and risks assessment data, the woman establishes key post-release goals. She works with her case worker to identify natural supports and professional community providers who serve as an individualised re-entry team. Although the team includes her facility case manager and key treatment staff, most of the team members are community providers and natural supports such as family and friends. If the woman will have probation, her probation officer is automatically included on the team so s/he will participate in meetings where the woman's strengths are emphasised. This often creates a more positive relationship between the woman and the officer and enhances compliance.

The case worker contacts each team member and describes the process and expectations for team meetings and activities. Process guidelines establish how often the team will meet, ground rules for maintaining an emotionally safe meeting, and a shared vision of success. This pre-meeting process builds a cohesive team and lays the groundwork for the strengths-based focus of the meetings. Team members share their ideas to add to the woman's strengths list, which is then written on flip chart paper posted in the meeting room.

The re-entry team meets one to three times during the last four months prior to release, often using video-conferencing to overcome geographic and transportation barriers. The team first reviews the posted strengths and adds additional strengths. This process validates the woman and sets the tone for the meetings. When a team member prematurely brings up problems or needs, the meeting facilitator (usually the case manager or woman) gently redirects them to focus on strengths at this stage of the meeting. Next, the woman describes how she can use these strengths to reach her re-entry goal(s). Only then are her risks, needs and challenges to reaching her goal addressed. Team members brainstorm with her strategies and resources, emphasising the strengths and resources she has already identified.

Working with the resident, the team develops a comprehensive transition plan that builds on strengths, enhances outcomes and reduces risks. A detailed schedule of the first 24 hours and of the first weeks is designed. Recognising the complexity of services for multiple needs such as employment and treatment with family reunification demands, the plan accommodates scheduling complications. For example, transportation, childcare and treatment appointments are conducted so that they do not interfere with work opportunities. Referrals and appointments are made prior to release to support these goals. Whenever possible, community providers participate in re-entry team meetings to build rapport with the woman. The team identifies and prioritises community resources and social capital and develops specific steps to facilitate successful transition.

While the re-entry plans are individualised, the key areas emphasised on most women's plans include financial stability, safe housing, transportation, treatment (physical, mental, and behavioural health), family reunification, crisis/safety planning, and prosocial recreation/peers. Women need to be empowered to improve their individual and the social socio-economic conditions for women. Because women offenders are often heads of households, it is essential to create solid self-sufficiency plans. WRC mediates socio-economic barriers by engaging DHHS in the release planning to determine eligibility for temporary assistance for needy families

(TANF), food stamps, other emergency assistance and child welfare services. Eligibility is determined as far as 45 days prior to release and services are available on the day of release. When appropriate, applications for Social Security Supplemental Security Income/Social Security Disability Insurance (SSI/SSDI) governmental income for the disabled are completed online at the Social Security Administration (SSA) website and interviews to determine eligibility are conducted at the local SSA office or through a telephone interview. SSA trains medical records staff at DOC so all pertinent medical records are submitted with the application, greatly reducing the likelihood of eligibility denials. Other financial stability options are pursued, such as establishing child support payments.

Jobs provide financial stability for most women. The WRC works closely with the Department of Labour (DOL) Career Centre (an employment search and support office), Women Unlimited, area community colleges and universities, and Women, Work, and Community to assist women with employment opportunities. When women first arrive at the WRC, DOL staff assesses their work readiness and enrols them in appropriate DOL programmes. For many, an initial community activity is a DOL Job Readiness course at the Career Centre. Practice interviews, résumé writing, links to area employers, and other employment search supports improve women's job options, economic independence and stability. To prevent childcare from being an employment barrier, women with children apply for publicly assisted childcare months prior to release so that their name is on the waiting list, in the hope that their childcare slot will be available by the time of their release.

To assure that vocational training prepares women for careers in high demand/high growth industries, WRC consults with DOL to align vocational programming with labour market statistics and with DOL's insights into industries most receptive to hiring persons with criminal convictions. Green construction is a growing industry paying living wages and hiring women, often due to contractual incentives. In response, Women Unlimited (WU) partners with the WRC, teaching the women non-traditional trades onsite and in the community. Green construction trades, Occupational Safety and Health Administration (OSHA) safety courses, blueprint reading, construction mathematics and reading are among the popular classes. Upon successful completion, women receive certifications that enhance their employment opportunities in the non-traditional trades. WU staff assists graduates to find employment that often provides high wages with benefits such as health insurance. One resident who had always worked in office jobs discovered in a WU class that she loved welding. An area employer selected her to train in its new, specialised welding procedures and paid her a training wage. After training, she was hired full time by the company at a wage almost double what she had previously earned. She worked for them for six months prior to release and continues to work for them, earning wage increases and promotions.

In addition to planning for financial stability, adequate transition planning links women to resources in the community through comprehensive, collaborative partnerships (Bloom *et al.* 2003, 2005). WRC benefits from active state inter-agency collaboratives that facilitate needed systemic changes. DOC and Maine State Housing Authority (MSHA) jointly provide subsidised housing using federal Department of Housing and Urban Development funds through Rental Assistance Coupons Plus (RAC+), a two-year transitional housing voucher programme for full rental value. The transitioned woman pays $US50 or one-third of her income and participates in a Personal Responsibility Contract (her re-entry plan) to stay in the programme. Coupons are available state-wide.

Family reunification planning helps women integrate into households with children. Nationwide, about 1.5 million children have an incarcerated parent. Two-thirds of women in the US correctional facilities plan to reconnect with their children after release. Planning for reunification requires safety planning and supportive services, especially when children are in the foster care system (NGA 2005). Reunification motivates women to make difficult but needed changes. Ninety-two per cent of women with children in a Davidson County Sheriff's Office survey said their families were critical to their personal success (Solomon *et al.* 2008). An example of reunification planning was a situation where child welfare notified a WRC resident, informing her that her parental rights would be terminated unless she could prove within 30 days that she could care for her children. WRC assisted her to invite the child welfare worker to her re-entry team. He was impressed with her conduct in the meetings, her strengths as expressed by the team, her participation in WRC programmes, and her re-entry plan. He became her strong ally in convincing the court that she could successfully reunify with her children when released. This strongly motivated her to complete treatment and job readiness components of her re-entry plan.

Women may apply for short family reunification community passes when they are within two months of release to have private time with their children in the community. Passes are for up to four hours to enjoy a local children's museum or a meal at a nearby restaurant with their children. As women get close to their release date, they can also apply for a weekend pass for family reunification and to seek housing and other services in their home community.

3 Community integration, support and stability

Community integration begins in earnest a month prior to release. WRC works with Vital Statistics so each woman has a copy of her birth certificate. From the Division of Motor Vehicles, women get a state photo identification card or driving licence, a necessity for obtaining a job or applying for public assistance programmes. Applications for public assistance and MaineCare (Medicaid public health insurance) are completed. MaineCare is especially critical in the US since it pays for physical and mental/behavioural health services and substance abuse treatment.

As part of re-entry planning, victims are notified of pending releases by the state Victim Services Offices. They are offered a support team planning process, similar to the re-entry team process, to prepare them for the offender's release with needed services. They can give feedback to the re-entry team. Since victims are sometimes family members or friends, this process can create smoother reunification.

The re-entry day sets the tone for a woman's transition experience. The re-entry plan details activities for the first few days. Transportation with a natural support is arranged. The woman usually will need to stop by the local DHHS office to activate her public assistance. She might need to move into new lodgings. Specific, prosocial family reunification celebratory activities are planned. Helping a woman plan ahead for recreational celebrations of her release can help her avoid triggers or situations that might lead to recidivism.

As NGA (2005) notes, timing of release and planning for the moment of release can be critical to a woman's success (Solomon *et al*. 2008) Some jurisdictions drop people off in the middle of the night into risky communities. The centre no longer releases during the night except in unique situations. One such incident was when the media hounded a woman with a high-profile crime just prior to her release. They planned to aggressively pursue her. The resident worried for her physical and emotional safety. Therefore, the WRC arranged for her family to pick her up at 12:01 a.m. at a different entrance in the building, so her privacy and safety could be respected.

Following a woman's release, staff support her in the community for at least 90–180 days. The case worker calls several times during the first week after release, at least weekly for the first month, and frequently thereafter for the first six months. Soon after her release, the re-entry team meets again. The woman gives updates, and the team celebrates her successes. They also help her identify emerging needs and opportunities. Adjustments are made to the re-entry plan to reflect her current status. Additional community linkages are made if needed. The woman might get a job promotion that requires modifications in her childcare, for example. She might have accomplished her initial re-entry goals and be ready to establish new ones requiring different resources and social capital. The team asks what internal and external supports she needs and helps her modify her plan. It is essential during the first year post release to intervene early when problems arise. For example, if a woman with a substance abuse history relapses, the team can immediately help her get needed assistance and guide her in identifying unexpected triggers and in learning new strategies. Rather than being punitive, a strengths-based approach is used so the relapse becomes as a teachable moment.

Without rehabilitative preparation and re-entry support, women are at a distinct disadvantage when released. Not surprisingly, the traditional recidivism rate for women in the US is 60 per cent, including 40 per cent being arrested for a new conviction (Deschenes *et al.* 2006). During its first year of operation, WRC's recidivism rate was 10 per cent for probation violations, technical violations, and/ or new crimes. Recognising women's gendered needs, providing appropriate programming and planning for re-entry supports to mediate their needs and risks make the difference. The WRC's three stages of re-entry provide a model for quality transitions for women leaving prisons.

The model for the WRC has been described in this chapter. The authors openly disclose that implementation has not always been as clean as described here. To assist other sites considering development of their own re-entry programming for women, it is important to explore the potential barriers.

From ideal to real: Implementation challenges and strategies

Implementing evidence-based, gender-responsive interventions requires special efforts and dedication. Programme goals will be achieved over time as the result of intentional implementation strategies and ongoing quality improvement processes. Maine's model has, as have most sites, encountered its share of implementation challenges.

A recent meta-analytic study and resulting monograph on implementation (Fixsen *et al*. 2005) provides a helpful context for identifying, evaluating and overcoming such challenges. Implementation science provides a roadmap 'that can help ensure that what is known through science is implemented with integrity' (Fixsen *et al*. 2005: 77). Implementation happens in stages: exploration, installation, initial implementation, full implementation, innovation and sustainability. The first four stages take up to four years (Fixsen *et al*. 2005). As a three-year-old programme (in October 2010), which endured multiple contextual changes since the programme was conceptualised, Maine is moving from *initial* to *full* implementation.

Staff selection, client–programme matching and community engagement

Lessons learned in the first three years of implementation include three important areas of attention: staff selection and retention, client–programme matching, and community engagement. Staff recruitment and retention challenges, which the programme encountered in its first year, reflect the dynamic nature of implementation. 'Any human service organisations are thinly resourced and face high rates of turnover at practitioner and leadership levels that are disruptive to any attempts to systematically implement practices of any kind' (Fixsen *et al*. 2005: 72). Changes in administration, director transitions and line staff turnover all impacted on programme stability in its formative stages.

Another challenge is the fact that many women sent to the centre do not meet programme admission criteria. To keep the programme full, women sometimes are transferred to WRC before completing prerequisite mental health, substance abuse and medical treatment. Therefore, they have acute needs for which the centre was not designed originally. The focus on jobs, education and economic factors is compromised when women relapse or do not adjust because of unmet substance abuse and mental health needs. Programming was altered to intensify focus on emotional regulation, mental health and substance abuse services.

Thirdly, community engagement is critical to the mission of the WRC. Unless all stakeholders within and outside the system recognise 'that a change in corrections is needed, is affordable, and does not conflict with its sentiments regarding just punishment, an innovative project has little hope of surviving, much less succeeding' (Petersilia

1990: 144). To this end, Maine engaged community providers and other stakeholders. Contributing to the initial success of the centre is the culture of collaboration in Maine's interdepartmental efforts. A statewide Maine Re-entry Network Steering Committee uses an Integrated Practice Model to oversee infrastructure to identify and resolve systems issues and barriers to interdepartmental service integration. Infrastructure building and operations alignment begins with a data-driven process to identify challenges. For example, because Maine-specific data confirmed that employment was a protective factor against recidivism (King 2009), DOC used Labour Market Statistics to focus vocation training on careers in high-demand/high-growth industries.

Conclusion

Maine's response to dramatic increases in women's incarceration incorporates implementation of evidence-based, gender-responsive principles to help women return to their communities better equipped. While the programme is relatively new, the outcomes of initial implementation appear promising. Even though the WRC is one model of gender-responsive re-entry programming in a rural state of a developed country with no universal health care system, many of its concepts can be readily adopted by other jurisdictions and countries with appropriate adaptations. Of primary importance to sites interested in replication is: (1) the integration of GRP and EPB; and (2) the multilevel systemic approach to supporting women's re-entry. By adopting the six principles of GRP, the WRC model helps women enhance their personal development and strengths while reducing their risks of recidivism as they make the transition back into their families and communities. Gender responsivity is strategically addressed at the multiple levels of the individual (micro); facility programming/community, re-entry team, local community (mezzo); and system (macro). Using a wraparound, strengths-based approach with an emphasis on relational theory and practice, the WRC gives women such as Trudi the skills and practice they need to exercise positive relational skills, boundaries, self-efficacy and motivation to support their thriving in the community. Re-entry planning responds appropriately to the complexity women offenders face living within their families and communities. Their strengths and ongoing connections give women the hope, skills and courage they need for their challenging re-entry journey.

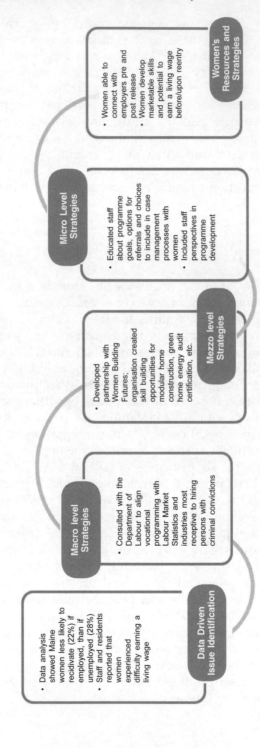

Figure 16.2 Integrated practice model – economic and employment opportunities

References

Andrews, D.A. and Bonta, J.L. (1995) *LSI-R: The Level of Service Inventory: Revised.* Toronto: Multi-Health Systems Inc.

Andrews, D. and Dowden, C. (2006) 'Risk principle of case classification in correctional treatment: A meta-analytic investigation', *International Journal of Offender Therapy and Comparative Criminology,* 50: 88–100.

Benson, J. and Montana, M. (2003) *Prison population trends: Preliminary report.* Augusta: Maine State Planning Office.

Blanchette, K. and Brown, S. (2006a) 'Gender-informed correctional practice: Integrating gender-neutral and gender-specific/responsive paradigm', *Women, Girls and Criminal Justice,* 7 (4): 49–64.

Blanchette, K. and Brown, S.L. (2006b) *The Assessment and Treatment of Women Offenders: An Integrative Perspective.* Somerset, NJ: John A. Wiley and Sons, Inc.

Bloom, B. (2000) 'Beyond recidivism: Perspectives on evaluation of programs for female offenders in community corrections', in M. McMahon (eds) *Assessment to Assistance: Programs for Women in Community Corrections.* Lanham, MD: American Correctional Association.

Bloom, B., Owen, B. and Covington, S. (2003) *Gender-responsive Strategies: Research, Practice, and Guiding Principles for Women Offenders.* Washington, DC: National Institute of Corrections. NIC accession no. 018017.

Bloom, B., Owen, B. and Covington, S. (2005) *Gender-responsive Strategies for Women Offenders: A Summary of Research, Practice, and Guiding Principles for Women Offenders.* Washington, DC: National Institute of Corrections. NIC accession no. 020418.

Boober, B.H. and Fortuin, B. (2006) 'Re-entry without walls or cash: Building relationships that work', *Journal of Community Corrections,* 15 (2): 6–13.

Bureau of Justice Statistics. (2007) *Four Measures of Serious Violent Crime, 1973–2005.* Washington, DC. Available at: http://www.ojp.usdoj.gov/bjs/glance/cv2.htm (accessed on 20 October 2009).

Chesney-Lind, M. and Pasko, L. (2004a) *Girls, Women, and Crime: Selected Readings.* Thousand Oaks, CA: SAGE Publications.

Chesney-Lind, M. and Pasko, L. (2004b) *The Female Offender: Girls, Women and Crime.* Thousand Oaks, CA: SAGE Publications.

Commission to Improve the Sentencing, Supervision, Management, and Incarceration of Prisoners (2004) *Report of the Commission to Improve the Sentencing, Supervision, Management, and Incarceration of Prisoners Part 1: Immediate Needs.* Augusta, ME:

Covington, S. and Surrey, J. (1997) 'The relational model of women's psychological development: Implications for substance abuse', in S. Wilsnack and R. Wilsnack (eds) *Gender and Alcohol: Individual and Social Perspectives.* New Brunswick, NJ: Rutgers University Press.

Daly, K. (1992) 'Women's pathways to felony court: Feminist theories of law-breaking and problems of representation', *Southern California Review of Law and Women's Studies,* 2: 11–52.

Deschenes, E.P., Owen, B. and Crow, J. (2006) *Recidivism among Female Prisoners: Secondary Analysis of the 1994 BJS Recidivism Data Set.* Unpublished Report for the US Department of Justice.

Dowden, C. and Andrews, D. (1999) 'What works for women offenders: A meta-analytic review', *Crime and Delinquency*, 2 (4): 438–52.

Fixsen, D.F., Naoom, S.F., Blasé, K.A., Friedman, R.M. and Wallace, F. (2005) *Implementation Research: A Synthesis of the Literature.* Tampa, FL: University of South Florida, Louis De La Parte Florida Mental Health Institute, The National Implementation Research Network (FMHI Publication #231).

Frost, N., Greene, J. and Pranis, K. (2006) *The Punitiveness Report. Hard Hit: The Growth in the Imprisonment of Women, 1977–2004.* Institute on Women and Criminal Justice. Women's Prison Association. Available at: http://www.wpaonline.org/institute/hardhit/ (accessed 30 October 2007).

Gendreau, P., Little, T. and Goggin, C. (1996) 'A meta-analysis of the predictors of adult offender recidivism: what works!', *Criminology*, 2: 575–607.

Gilfus, M. (1992) 'From victims to survivors to offenders: Women's routes of entry and immersion into street crime', *Women and Criminal Justice*, 4 (1): 63–89.

Hannah-Moffat, K. (2009) 'Gridlock or mutability: Reconsidering "gender" and risk assessment', *Criminology and Public Policy*, 8 (1): 209–19.

Harrison, P.M. and Beck, A.J. (2005) *Prisoners in 2004.* Bureau of Justice Statistics Bulletin. Washington, DC: US Department of Justice Office of Justice Programs. NCJ 210677.

Holtfreter, K., Reisig, M. and Morash, M. (2004) 'Poverty, state capital, and recidivism among women offenders', *Criminology and Public Policy*, 3 (2): 185–208.

Jamieson, W., Beals, E., Graves, G. and Associates (1999) *Differential Substance Abuse Treatment (DSAT) Model.* Augusta, ME: State of Maine Department of Behavioural and Developmental Services Office of Substance Abuse and Department of Corrections.

Kendall, K. (2004) 'Dangerous thinking: A critical history of correctional cognitive behaviouralism', in G. Mair (ed.) *What Matters in Probation.* Cullompton, Devon: Willan Publishing, pp. 55–89.

King, E. (2009) *Maine Women Offenders: What do We Know?* Portland, ME: University of Southern Maine Muskie School of Public Service.

Morash, M. (2009) 'A great debate over using the Level of Service Inventory-Revised (LSI-R) with women offenders', *Criminology and Public Policy*, 8 (1): 173–81.

Najavits, L. (2002) *Seeking Safety: A Treatment Manual for PTSD and Substance Abuse.* NY: Guilford Press.

National Governors' Association Centre for Best Practices (2005) *Issue Brief: Improving Prisoner Re-entry Through Strategic Policy Innovations.* Washington, DC.

Park, C.L. (2003) 'The psychology of religion and positive psychology: Presidential address APA division 36 presented at the 111th annual convention of the American Psychological Association', *Psychology of Religion Newsletter: American Psychological Association Division* 36, 28 (4): 1–8.

Petersilia, J. (1990) 'Conditions that permit intensive supervision', *Crime and Delinquency*, 36 (1): 126–45.

Porporino, F.J. (2005) 'Revisiting responsivity: Organizational change to embrace evidence-based principles and practices', in *American Correctional Association (2005) What Works and Why: Effective Approaches to Re-entry*. Lanham, MD: American Correctional Association.

Reisig, M.D., Holtfreter, K. and Morash, M. (2002) 'Social capital among women offenders', *Journal of Contemporary Criminal Justice*, 18 (2): 167–87.

Robinson, D., Van Dieten, M. and Millison, B. (2005) *SPIn-W: Service Planning Instrument for Women*. Ottawa, Ontario: Orbis Partners, Inc.

Salisbury, E. (2007) *Gendered Pathways: An Empirical Investigation of Women Offenders' Unique Paths to Crime*. Unpublished dissertation. University of Cincinnati.

Seligman, M.E.P. and Csikszentmihalyi, M. (2000) 'Positive psychology', *American Psychologist*, 55 (1): 5–14.

Sentencing Project (2007) *Women in the Criminal Justice System Briefing Sheets*. Washington, DC. Available at: www.sentencingproject.org (accessed 22 February 2010).

Smith, P., Cullen, F. and Latessa, E. (2009) 'Can 14,737 women be wrong? A meta-analysis of the LSI-R and recidivism for female offenders', *Criminology and Public Policy*, 8 (1): 183–208.

Solomon, A.L., Osborne, J.W.L., LoBuglio, S.F., Mellow, J. and Mukamal, D.A. (2008) *Life after Lockup: Improving Re-entry from Jail to the Community*. Washington, DC: Urban Institute.

Taylor, K. and Blanchette, K. (2009) 'The women are not wrong: it is the approach that is debatable', *Criminology and Public Policy*, 8 (1): 221–9.

University of Cincinnati (2004) *Commission Research Projects: Maine Presentation*. Cincinnati, OH: University of Cincinnati.

Van Dieten, M. (2002) *Moving On*. Ottawa, ON: Orbis Partners, Inc.

Van Dieten, M. (2007) *Women Offender Case Management Model*. Ottawa, Ontario: Orbis Partners, Inc.

Van Dieten, M. and MacKenna, P. (2001) *Moving On Facilitator's Guide*. Ottawa, ON: Orbis Partners, Inc.

Van Voorhis, P. (2005) *The Women's Centre: Maine Correctional Centre, Maine Department of Corrections*. Washington, DC: US Department of Justice National Institute of Corrections.

Van Voorhis, P., Wright, E., Salisbury, E. and Bauman, A. (2010) 'Women's risk factors and their contributions to existing risk/needs assessment', *Criminal Justice and Behavior*, 37: 261–88.

Warren, K. (2008) *One in 100: Behind Bars in America 2008. Public Safety Performance Project*, PEW Charitable Trust Report. Available at: http://www.pewceneronthestates.org/ (accessed on 22 February 2010).

Chapter 17

Working with women offenders in the community: What works?

Rosemary Sheehan, Gill McIvor and Chris Trotter

In recent years the main aim of correctional services has been to reduce reoffending. The extraordinary increase in women entering prison, for reasons explored in this book, has encouraged governments to concentrate on reducing the number of women in prison, increasing the use of community orders for women. We are seeing, in ways discussed in the book, significant investments in community provision, offering approaches that recognise the different underlying factors and circumstances that influence female offending. What is clear is that financial problems, high levels of sexual and physical victimisation in childhood and as an adult, relationship problems, mental health issues, childcare difficulties and problems related to substance misuse are related to women's offending in ways they are usually not to offending by men. The authors in this book demonstrate that interventions and supports must focus on these factors if they are to be relevant to women who offend. What is also apparent is that if women are to benefit from them, services and interventions need to be delivered in ways that are meaningful to them.

As we noted in the Introduction, this book concentrates on the needs of women who offend, the principles that inform the development of policies on which to build expertise in working with women in the community, and gender-responsive practices that have been implemented. In this concluding chapter we discuss the themes that have been developed and put forward some conclusions about key approaches that are likely to enhance the efficacy of community-based responses to women who offend. In doing so we hope to offer a template for effective community correctional interventions for women who offend aimed at promoting women's reintegration in the community and encouraging their desistance from crime. However, while there is growing consensus about the potential benefits of theoretically informed gender responsive services – agreement that the needs of criminalised women are best met within the community and a recognition that gender-responsive community-based sanctions may have the potential to reduce the high number of very short custodial sentences that are imposed upon women who offend – the contributors to this book also identify a number of significant and ongoing challenges.

Women in the criminal justice system

Whilst women's offending is generally less serious than men's, Hedderman (Chapter 2) highlights the escalating use of custody after arrest, despite evidence that women remanded in custody are much less likely than men to receive a custodial sentence subsequently. Hedderman suggests that media attention to women's offending has shaped statutory responses. It is her view that the reaction to increases in women dealt with for violence, currently close to that for men, has persuaded the media to press courts to use custody and not let offenders 'go free from court' by using community sentences. Yet the arrest rate for women remains significantly lower than that for men (53 per 1,000 population in England and Wales, while it is 10 per 1,000 for women) and women are more likely to be cautioned where violence is concerned. Hedderman reminds that women's involvement in crime has become only a little more prevalent and the seriousness of their offending has increased marginally. The perceived increase in serious offending by women is heightened by the overall smaller number of women offenders, so slight increases appear major by comparison. What has changed is a tougher community climate towards offending, in particular drug offending, and governments generally now have a preferred 'get tough' on drugs stance, which permeates legislation and sentencing practices. In England and Wales, not only were many new criminal offences created but also the sentencing powers of magistrates decreased in their discretion (for example, in relation to breaches of community orders) in ways that disproportionately affect women – whose breaches may relate to childcare, transport and money issues rather than to overt non-compliance. While previously this may have been understood as a need for practical supports, and magistrates dealt with breaches in this context, changes to breach provisions in legislation have meant that these less serious matters could easily end up in imprisonment. Hedderman underlines these impacts on women, noting that in England and Wales in 2008 there were over twice as many women as men with no previous convictions (23 per cent compared with 11 per cent) under community supervision.

Given that more than two-thirds of women receive sentences of less than one year, this approach – rather than that of community sentences – not only further marginalises already vulnerable women but increases the potential for reoffending. Such short disposals make it less likely for women to access the support services and programmes they need to address their health and relational difficulties, and improve their chances of desistance. Sharpe (Chapter 8) refers to a parallel criminalisation and punishment of young women in England and Wales. The same media attention referred to by Hedderman is given to the perceived growing 'problem' of girls' offending behaviour. It is these same media calls that have influenced changes in police and court processing approaches that have inflated girls' official crime rates and propelled them into the youth justice system. Sharpe outlines how these girls have become increasingly criminalised: girls who appear in court, for offences such as minor assaults, are receiving more intrusive and more often custodial responses than previously, and the rate at which they are punished for non-compliance has also increased. This community and statutory attention to girls and violence has, suggests Sharpe, overtaken sexuality as the central site of anxiety about young womanhood and girlhood delinquency. It has certainly expanded the female youth custodial population; even when community penalties are imposed, the conditions attached can be so onerous, or lacking 'fit' with the lives of the young women, that the rate at which there are breaches for non-compliance has increased significantly.

The Australian experience mirrors this. Sheehan (Chapter 4) found there was an increase in the number of women entering prison custody for serious violent offences (i.e. robbery offences and offences against the person) and drug-related offending. What was found was that women were being increasingly remanded into custody, which was less to do with their offences and more to do with inadequate accommodation and complex treatment and support needs. Despite general government recognition that women in prison were among the most socially disadvantaged, women's needs that lead to offending have received negligible real attention. Whilst in Engand and Wales the Women's Offending Reduction Programme (WORP) recognised women's welfare needs, it has not translated into approaches that lead to women avoiding custody. This is in part explained by singling out drug offences, and legal responses, which are required to impose a higher tariff on an offender, as part of the aforementioned 'get tough on drugs' approach now favoured by governments and communities. Malloch and McIvor (Chapter 10) report the extraordinary 414 per cent increase in the number of women imprisoned for drug offences in England and Wales (1992–2002); and the impact of drug offending is evidenced in almost two-thirds of women in prison in England and Wales having a drug problem. Whilst programmes have been introduced in prisons to tackle drug problems, Malloch and McIvor comment that they do not respond to the associated social and personal difficulties that affect women, and which are heightened by incarceration. Nor is drug offending effectively addressed by traditional community-based responses to women's offending, failing to focus on the practical (lack of housing and vocational skills to gain employment) and personal (social isolation, victimisation – either past or current – mental health concerns and family difficulties, which may include children in care). This lack of remediation can lead to statutory orders being breached and women reoffending. A singular focus on drug offending features also in the USA, noted by Buell, Modley and Van Voorhis (Chapter 3), with mandatory prison sentences for drug use and sales. They comment that it is this which has caused the growth of women in the criminal justice system rather than increases in serious crimes per se. The female prison population in the US has grown by 832 per cent from 1977 to 2007 compared to 416 per cent for males during the same time period (Bureau of Justice Statistics 2008). They note also that the wholesale closing of state mental health hospitals has contributed to this increase, given what is known about women's pathways into offending and the extent to which victimisation and health problems are factors in this.

Buell *et al.* (Chapter 3) outline US responses to the major explosion in female incarceration in the US, underpinned by an ethos that corrections emphasise incapacitation rather than rehabilitation. The National Institute of Corrections has recognised the need to offer distinct and distinctive interventions to women, and has supported the development of specific risk/needs assessments to do this. The NIC acknowledged that if they were to reduce the number of women going to prison then they had to understand the circumstances of female offenders. They put in place a range of approaches to tease out and describe the key aspects of gender-informed programme interventions, and these were to be spearheaded by practitioners who understood women's pathways to offending. The Women Offender Case Management Model (WOCMM) was designed in 2005 to offer a seamless case management model that would accompany a woman throughout her sentence – from prison to community release and supervision. What is significant about this approach is that it combines evidence-based and gender-responsive principles and research to identify risks and needs for women as they make the transition from prison to community. Strong emphasis on pre-release planning with a 'team' of correctional case manager, human and health service providers and other supports identifies how to support women after release and, by mobilising their strengths, reduce offending. In England and Wales, the Women's Offending Reduction Programme (WORP) was developed in 2002 primarily to address the social exclusion needs of women who had offended in the community. Hedderman suggests that whilst it is embedded in being 'tough on crime', its attention to tackling issues such as poverty and unemployment could, at least in the longer term, reduce offending. The caveat however is that no new or specific funding was allocated to secure delivery. Sharpe (Chapter 8), moreover, reminds us that girls and young women have been completely overlooked within this system; no formal attention has been given to proactive responses to girls in difficulty despite their entering the formal justice system in increasing numbers and receiving more restrictive penalties.

Limitation of risk assessment and cognitive behavioural interventions

The development of interventions for offenders has traditionally been driven by research on (young, white) men, despite the accumulating evidence of different pathways and explanations for female crime. It is often assumed that men and women have broadly similar needs and that 'generic' interventions need only be modified slightly to make them appropriate for women. However, there is evidence that women have different needs from men and that even apparently 'similar' needs may intersect with women's offending in different ways (Hedderman 2004; Hollin and Palmer 2006; McIvor 2007; Gelsthorpe, Chapter 7 this volume). Similar assumptions have been applied to the technology of risk assessment with the consequence that the effects of gender and diversity and the impact of social and economic constraints are absent from both an academic and practice perspective (Shaw and Hannah-Moffat 2004; Hannah-Moffat

2009). As Davidson (Chapter 11) illustrates, at a superficial level, risk assessment tools such as the LSI-R may *appear* equally adept at predicting male and female recidivism. However, additional qualitative data challenge such a conclusion by contextualising women's needs: for example, Davidson (Chapter 11) and Pollack (Chapter 6) argue that LSI-R tends to penalise women's attempts to seek help in relation to victimisation, trauma or substance misuse by associating these behaviours with higher risk scores while giving women lower ratings of risk if they are in a relationship, which is assumed to bring 'stability' into women's lives (Pollack, Chapter 6).

By redefining 'needs' as risk factors related to recidivism (rather than as a statement of entitlement to services and supports), structured risk assessments redirect and limit the scope of interventions to those 'risk' factors that can be directly linked empirically to the risk of recidivism (Shaw and Hannah-Moffat 2004) and divert attention away from the structural barriers that are important in understanding and explaining women's involvement in crime (Kendall 2002). Because risk assessment tools fail to consider a number of factors thought to be more relevant to women, resulting interventions tend to prioritise psychological factors rather than addressing gender-responsive needs (Buell *et al.*, Chapter 3). Furthermore, Pollack (Chapter 6) argues that risk narratives can transform women's abuse by men into risk factors for women by equating 'relationships' with criminal behaviour in such a way that 'risk' and relationships become intertwined. The redefining of 'welfare needs' as 'psychological needs' related to 'risk' (Hudson 2002) has, it has been argued, resulted in more women being imprisoned: this is because women have more 'needs' than men with the result that risk assessment practices construe them as 'riskier' than they actually are (Carlen 2003; Davidson, Chapter 11). Sharpe (Chapter 8) likewise suggests that practitioners need to be alert to the danger of redefining girls' complex needs as 'risks' and over-intervening through unnecessarily intrusive criminal justice interventions.

Structured actuarial risk assessment is closely linked to the emergence of cognitive behavioural programmes, which are derived from social learning theory, cognitive theory and behaviourism. The underlying assumption of programmes of this kind is that there is a relationship between thoughts, feelings and behaviour and that offending is a result of offenders having failed to acquire particular cognitive skills. Although cognitive behavioural interventions are now widespread in use with male offenders, there is little evidence that programmes of this type 'work' with women (Gelsthorpe, Chapter

7), with their appropriateness for women having been challenged on empirical, methodological and theoretical grounds (McIvor, forthcoming).

For example there have been few evaluations of cognitive behavioural interventions with female offenders and those that have been conducted provide little evidence of an effect upon recidivism (Lart *et al.* 2008). Cann (2006), for instance, found no evidence that female prisoners who had participated in accredited cognitive skills programmes had lower reconviction rates than matched prisoners who had not. Significantly, Cann suggests that because the programmes were designed to address male criminogenic needs using methods compatible with the learning styles of men, there was no evidence that they targeted appropriate 'criminogenic' needs among female prisoners. It has also been argued elsewhere that even when adapted for use with women (or developed specifically for women) the relevance of cognitive behavioural programmes tends to be constrained by a narrow focus on factors that are predicted to bring about reductions in crime, thereby drawing attention away from the structural inequalities of women's lives and, by teaching women that their problems are a result of their own deficient thinking, holding them responsible for their own oppression (Kendall 2002; Shaw and Hannah-Moffat 2004). Some women *may* benefit from a relatively structured exploration of how their attitudes and beliefs may have contributed to their offending but this should seek to build on women's existing strengths and competencies (Porporino and Fabiano 2005) in the context of severely constrained choices as a result of women's offending often being a response to deep-rooted and enduring socio-economic conditions that are difficult to change (Worrall 2002).

Effective approaches to working with women in the community

The National Institute of Corrections in the US established the need for gender-responsive treatment principles if intervention strategies for women offenders were to be effective (Buell *et al.*, Chapter 3). These general principles acknowledged, first and foremost, that gender makes a difference. Second, they address the intervention contexts for women, to create an environment based on safety, respect and dignity. Third, the focus is on relationships, on policies, practices and programmes that promote healthy connections to children, family, significant others and the community. Fourth, services and supervision must be appropriate to women's health and personal needs, comprehensively assessed and integrated as well as culturally relevant. Fifth, women are to be provided with opportunities to improve their socio-economic conditions. Sixth, a system of community supervision is to be established to include comprehensive, collaborative services to facilitate re-entry. Buell *et al.* present the growing empirical support for broader case management and counselling approaches, when working with women offenders, with a focus on self-efficacy, childcare, parenting, substance abuse and trauma (Bloom *et al.* 2003). Drawing more broadly across the contributions to this volume, it is possible to identify a number of themes that emerge as relevant to effective work in the community with women who offend.

Gender specific

Buell *et al.* (Chapter 3) describe how the NIC partnered with the University of Cincinnati in the USA in 2004 to construct a gender-responsive risk/needs assessment for women, which would inform assessment strategies for women offenders. They developed scales that could measure: self-esteem, self-efficacy, victimisation as an adult, child abuse, parental stress, and relationship dysfunction. What was different about this was that, in contrast to many gender-neutral assessments, items were added to identify strengths, or protective factors, such as support from others and educational assets, to inform more effective ways for working with women to divert them away from crime and reduce recidivism. The process also involves identifying and mobilising the woman's strengths. The WOCMM approach they describe focuses very much on identifying a woman's strengths and resilience, and on building partnerships with service providers to offer accessible and ongoing supports to women, in much the same way as the TWP in England and Wales.

Gelsthorpe (Chapter 7) confirms that the consistent messages from the research literature on women offenders include the fact that women offenders tend to have a history of unmet personal, health and structural needs, compounded very often by substance misuse and childcare responsibilities. If strategies to reduce offending are to be effective then they must respond to this complexity of factors that shape women's pathways into crime, and provide more broadly based responses that can be individually tailored. Gelsthorpe reminds us that Blanchette and Brown's (2006) 'responsivity' principle underlines the importance of strengths-based approaches and the 'good lives' model, as much as 'women-specific' factors such as health care, childcare and mental health in offering structured interventions. However, such interventions must be mindful to accommodate how women learn if they are to be truly 'responsive'.

Sharpe (Chapter 8), in reviewing the needs of girls who offend, confirms that, to be effective, programmes need to be gender-specific and acknowledge the victimisation and deprivation they experience, rather than simply delivering programmes designed for boys, or for adult women. Interventions must acknowledge how the lives of these young women have often been characterised by rejection and conflict, by homelessness or unstable living arrangements, and by high levels of psychiatric disturbance, self-harm and substance misuse making them more vulnerable than both young men and adult women when in detention. Malloch and McIvor (Chapter 10) also highlight the need for interventions and resources directed at women involved in substance misuse to take into account the contexts of their daily lives. Drawing on work from Bloom et al. (2004), they note that because women's most common pathways to crime are based on survival of abuse, poverty and problematic substance use, responses to women offenders must focus on treatment for substance abuse and trauma recovery, the provision of education and training in employment and parenting skills, and access to affordable and safe accommodation. There are fundamental differences relating to women as drug users, and also as women within the criminal justice system, which give the differing contexts that surround drug use by women and men.

Davidson (Chapter 11) proposes that gender-centred risk/need assessment can bring renewed focus on causes of criminal offending and facilitate case management and treatment intervention. However, they do need to be gender-responsive, as too often risk/need instruments have been used as a method of controlling offenders. She argues however that the good news about these instruments, from an ideological standpoint, is that they bring rehabilitation back into the correctional realm. The main concern is that they are not over- inclusive and end up unintentionally punishing more, not less. This is a particular concern for their use with female offenders in the community. Boober and King (Chapter 16) describe how the US state of Maine in 2007 designed a comprehensive programme entitled the Women's Re-entry Centre to assist women's transition needs into the community, recognising the different pathways for women and men into offending. They drew from research evidence and gender-responsive principles to translate women's risks and needs into preparing them for community life and delivering them better outcomes.

The importance of relationships

It is becoming increasingly clear that women tend to attach considerable importance to the relational aspects of supervision. This is consistent with Gilligan's (1982) feminist theory of psychological development and with research that suggests that women and men have different learning styles, and has implications for the types of interventions that are likely to engage women successfully in the process of change (Gelsthorpe and McIvor 2007). Deakin and Spencer (Chapter 12) found in their study of women shortly before, and shortly after, release from a closed female prison in England that supportive informal relationships with friends and family had a significant influence on their experience of the reintegration process, with positive relationships providing a form of social capital and acting as a significant form of social control. This has particular resonance for ethnic minority prisoners whose experience of prison is one of discrimination and difficulty, and whose re-entry to the community may return them to challenged and economically distressed communities, with few resources to support them. The women identified that in prison they relied on formal support from agencies, especially religious organisations and prison staff; their help replaced the support from family and friends that they relied on before prison, now less accessible to them in prison. They were relationships that were not generally sustained after prison; on release women's circumstances changed, the crisis of imprisonment had passed, and families and friends of some of the women were unsupportive of continued relationships with other prisoners and ex-prisoners, preferring women to have a fresh start. Where relationships were positive and 'prosocial' they helped reduce tension in women's lives. However, some relationships were negative and drew women back into previous problems; this was especially evident when women returned to drug use.

Nugent and Loucks (Chapter 1) profiled a range of initiatives for women in Scotland where caseworkers encouraged women to identify the relationships in their lives that are positive, and those that are not, in order to support them to move away from the latter relationships. To do this however it needs to be recognised that caseworkers must have the time and opportunity to give this discursive space to their work with women; the space needed to listen to women and work with their concerns. Sharpe (Chapter 8) identified this need for time and space when working with young women offenders; they told the researchers that they wanted practical support and someone who would listen to their experiences in a supportive and non-judgemental way. Girls' relationships with workers were particularly important; they looked for workers who could be trusted, who were there to talk to, and understand their life context. These attributes mattered more than the worker's professional background. These relationships played a central role in the girls' development; they could harness the positive aspects of girls' relationships and perhaps also work with their families, with whom girls' relationships are often troubled and a source of distress. The principles developed by the NIC give particular emphasis to young girls and relationships and also, if possible, to work with their families, with whom girls' relationships are often the underlying cause of their distress.

However, as already noted, Pollack (Chapter 6) cautions that this attention to relationships in gender-responsive interventions has been co-opted by correctional services to reconstruct women's relationships as criminogenic with the result that 'intimate relationships ... become a gendered site of surveillance and regulation of the criminal justice system' (p. 119). Through these risk discourses, Pollack argues, women are encouraged to see themselves as deficient with respect to their relationships and this, in turn, fosters self-regulation and compliance with the norms of correctional practice.

Women's roles as mothers

Central relationships for women are those with their children, yet these are fragmented when women go into prison, and made more difficult by distance between prison and children's residence. Nugent and Loucks (Chapter 1) confirmed that mothers report that being away from their children is the hardest part of being in prison and, for many, being back with their children is the main motivating factor for desistance. 'Social capital' for women can often mainly mean the role of being a mother. When women lose this role it becomes incredibly difficult for them to rebuild their lives. Losing this role may make desistance from further offending less likely. Malloch and McIvor (Chapter 10) reported that women's loss of their children and restricted access to work, benefits, suitable accommodation and educational provision make it more difficult for women to recover from drug use and rebuild their lives. They found women are often reluctant to seek treatment in relation to drug problems because of fears of reprisals for themselves or for their children; reprisals which very likely include losing their children.

Sarri (Chapter 15) finds significant fragmentation for women in the USA, in terms of their relationships with their children. There are no formal requirements for key organisations serving vulnerable children, such as schools, child welfare and health care, to inquire about or account for parental incarceration and its effects on children. Yet, because nearly all women offenders will return to their families, greater attention needs to be paid to family obligations and reunification – as well as to training in life skills and in parenting – to help women gain a sense of self-efficacy and competence and prevent recidivism.

Peer support

Peer relationships are recognised as a key support for women exiting prison, with greater benefits than the 'expert' model of service delivery which Nugent and Loucks (Chapter 1) find can be exclusionary and oppressive. Scotland's Routes out of Prison (RooP) Project is a peer support approach that works with women's strengths while providing support to offenders in the community. Nugent and Loucks argue that this approach could be used in future as part of an alternative to custody. The Routes out of Prison (RooP) Project is made up primarily of ex-offenders who act as peer support workers to help women and men who are not entitled to statutory support to access the support they need in the community. Women can relate better to workers who have 'been there' and understand the difficulties they face. Salgado *et al.* (Chapter 14) describe how US mentoring-based programmes with women offenders use peer relationships as positive role models, to encourage women to develop supportive networks with peers and enjoy healthy interpersonal relationships. Strong female role models offer important opportunities for individual change, and steer women into accommodating social norms that improve community membership and increase desistance. Sharpe (Chapter 8) found that the young women in her study were positive about relationships with befrienders and lay mentors. They believed they could trust them more than formal agencies such as social services, which had often let them down even when they asked for help.

Trotter (Chapter 13) reports on the evaluation of four mentoring programmes with individuals exiting prison. He found that women valued what mentoring offered them: intensive levels of informal contact; practical assistance; and, importantly, the mentor being a role model for how to manage relationships and daily life issues and resolve problems. What was key to these approaches was their holistic emphasis, that one person could provide a range of contacts to deal with the multilayered problems offenders face with reintegration. However, Trotter reminds us that it remains inconclusive as to the extent to which these mentoring approaches reduce recidivism.

Empowerment, agency and self-efficacy

A number of writers in this book demonstrate, through the programmes they describe, the importance of interventions that concentrate on the empowerment of women, reducing their powerlessness and promoting agency and self-efficacy. Nugent and Loucks (Chapter 1) outline the extensive research that indicates that women who are involved in offending often have a history of physical and sexual abuse in childhood and into adulthood. They argue that approaches which work on women's strengths and promote resilience, identifying what has helped them through their experiences of victimisation, can promote their desistance from offending. These approaches must include support networks that can build and maintain such resilience, as they cope with significant social and personal stresses associated with reintegration. Sharpe (Chapter 8) concurs, arguing that interventions with young women offenders must foster their strengths and aim to empower them to make positive decisions, if they are to be effective. Most particularly since young women and girls are faced with overwhelming structural obstacles, and have multifaceted needs, better met by holistic approaches and ongoing follow-up. Buell *et al.* (Chapter 3) outline how key to the effectiveness of WOCMM is identifying and mobilising a woman's strengths. It is an approach that has women contributing to their own case plans, outlining what changes they seek to make to manage reintegration and turn away from offending. The WOCMM team (and the administrators of its representative agencies) ensures essential partnerships with service providers and resources are available and readily accessible, and that these are continuous for women long after their contact with the justice system has finished.

Non-authoritarian, women-only environments

As Buell *et al.* (Chapter 3) indicate, women-only caseloads are increasingly being used by community-based agencies in the USA. Where they expressed a preference, girls in Sharpe's English research (Chapter 8) indicates that they preferred having a female worker on the basis that they found them easier to talk to and better able to empathise with them. Moreover, in view of their previous experiences, young women often had a generalised fear and distrust of men. Sharpe (Chapter 8) highlights the need for work to be undertaken with young women, as far as possible, in non-authoritarian settings and in women-only environments in which they feel 'safe'. As Gelsthorpe (Chapter 7) indicates, theoretical work on gender and learning points also to the need to work with women in non-authoritarian cooperative settings where women are empowered to engage in social and personal change. There is, for example, emerging evidence that group work in non-authoritarian settings is likely to be most suited to girls' collaborative learning styles (Sharpe, Chapter 8).

Gelsthorpe (Chapter 7) reminds us that, in addition to being generally more flexible (with respect to who they are able to work with and for how long), voluntary sector providers are non-coercive. Coercion, as Blackwell (Chapter 5) notes, can create a sense of powerlessness among women and undermine their compliance with community supervision. Blackwell identifies a number of different levels at which coercion may operate and impact upon female offenders and makes the important point that even if they are not subject to statutory measures of supervision, women may face a range of other sanctions for failing to cooperate with criminal justice and other public agencies. Although coercion is often used or justified as a means of engaging women with a view to improving – in the longer term – their quality of life, little is known empirically about the impact of coercive practices on offenders.

Holistic and flexible provision

The case management model developed as WOCMM is holistic in its approach and offers 'wraparound' services that focus as much on the health and well-being of women and their families as on aiming to reduce future criminal behaviour. This model was guided by an extensive review of the criminal justice, mental health and child welfare literature, and in consultation with both practitioners and researchers. A team approach is adopted which involves the woman, correctional case manager, human and health service providers and other supports. At its centre is the woman herself, working with practitioners and others on what she identifies as her needs and challenges (Buell *et al.*, Chapter 3). The fact that women have complex needs that require a holistic response – and one that includes a focus on victimisation histories, which cannot be considered separately from other issues such as trauma and substance misuse – is highlighted by a number of other contributors (e.g. Nugent and Loucks; Gelsthorpe; Sharpe; McIvor and Malloch; Davidson).

Gelsthorpe (Chapter 7) reports how voluntary sector providers offer a greater degree of flexibility and freedom to meet women's real needs by being able to provide personalised and tailored services; statutory agencies, by contrast, are more likely to have narrow eligibility criteria and narrow agency boundaries that do not fit well with the complexity of women offenders' lives. There are strong arguments to be made for provision that is sufficiently flexible and capable of engaging with women even after their statutory involvement with agencies has ended: thus the service developed as WOCMM is intended to be 'limitless' and available to women and their families long after their formal system supervision has ceased (Buell *et al.*, Chapter 3). Seeking to expand women's ongoing access to community services is a key component of recent programmes across jurisdictions (including, for example, WOCMM in the USA, the Asha Centre and Together Women Programme in England and the 218 Centre in Scotland). As some contributors (for example, Nugent and Loucks in Chapter 1 and Trotter in Chapter 13) argue, this should include access to affordable and accessible leisure facilities and other resources that are 'normalising' and non-stigmatising and may have the additional benefit of providing opportunities for women's achievements to be recognised (Sharpe, Chapter 8).

In the UK, 'contestability' – the procurement of services by the statutory sector through a competitive tendering process – has, Gelsthorpe (Chapter 7) suggests (and despite having other obvious disadvantages), facilitated greater links with third sector providers who have experience of working with women in the community. A major challenge for voluntary/third sector providers, however, is securing stable and sufficient funding for them to be innovative, flexible and effective. Many gender-responsive initiatives have not survived as a result of financial constraints or have found their focus driven in unhelpful ways by the need to 'chase' funding (Gelsthorpe, Chapter 7). Survival of innovative projects has also been jeopardised by a lack of evaluative research (Buell *et al.*, Chapter 3). A solution that is suggested by both Sharpe (Chapter 8) and Gelsthorpe (Chapter 7) is that resources to support gender-responsive services are transferred to the voluntary sector so that community provision to meet women's needs is funded by statutory bodies but is delivered by third sector providers.

Ongoing challenges

Acknowledging and accommodating diversity

As several of the contributors to this volume have commented, a major limitation of so-called 'gender-neutral' services and interventions in the criminal justice system is that they fail to take account of important gender differences in types of and reasons for offending, including pathways into crime. However, as Malloch and McIvor (Chapter 10) observe, it is important also not to lose sight of the important differences *among* women as well as their differences from men. This is necessary if services are to accommodate women's different pathways to crime and addiction, their differing social circumstances and the complexity of their needs. For example, while it would appear that the features of effective engagement with women are likely in many ways to be similar to those associated with successful interventions with girls, there are also likely to be important differences, such as the role of families and peers as a significant reference point for girls. Likewise, older women – who are forming an increasing proportion of criminal justice caseloads – will have different needs from younger women who continue to make up the majority of women in prison or subject to probation or parole (e.g. Wahidin 2005).

Provision for women in the community also needs to be culturally appropriate. As Worrall (2000) has indicated, 'what works' in one cultural context may bear little relation to what is effective in another. However, as Goulding (Chapter 9) observes, penal policy assumes that the needs of indigenous women in Australia can be met through mainstream services for women, with the result that levels of engagement with services in prison and beyond are typically low. She argues that services for indigenous women need to take into account their needs as women but also their social and economic marginalisation from mainstream Australian culture. She discusses a culturally appropriate arts-based programme that was developed and delivered by Aboriginal women to urban Aboriginal women prior to release from prison in Western Australia; it aimed to facilitate engagement with the training organisation on release. Attendance rates at the prison-based programme were high, with this being ascribed to the programme's cultural specificity and the use of Aboriginal trainers. However, engagement and retention rates were more difficult to quantify in the community-based training programme and appeared overall to be much lower, despite attempts to make the programme more relevant and appealing to indigenous

357

women. This might reflect the wider challenges that the women faced on leaving prison before being ready to engage with a programme of this kind.

Penal expansion and social welfare

Despite the growing policy interest in and attention to women in the criminal justice system across jurisdictions, courts continue to send increasing numbers of women to prison and, although there is evidence from some jurisdictions that the average prison sentence is getting longer, increasing proportions of women are serving short custodial sentences (Hedderman, Chapter 2; Sharpe, Chapter 8) that are personally and socially disruptive and unlikely to address the issues underlying their offending. Prisons are less likely to be effective in reducing women's risk of reoffending because of their damaging effects on women while they serve their sentences and the fact that women are likely to return to even worse circumstances when they are released (Gelsthorpe and Sharpe 2007; McIvor *et al.* 2009). Moreover, interventions in prison are less likely to be effective because they are offered in an environment that is far removed from the realities of women's lives on the outside.

Yet, worryingly, there is evidence that prison is often used as a means of accessing resources or as a respite from chaotic lives in the community. As Nugent and Loucks (Chapter 1) observe, the use of prison as a 'welfare panacea' results in women avoiding facing up to the issues that resulted in their imprisonment in the first place and that are likely to bring them back to prison again if they are not addressed. While Nugent and Loucks base their observations on practice in Scotland, there is wider evidence from the contributions in this book of the adverse impact on women of the increased penalisation of the welfare state (Wacquant 2009). Thus, as Malloch and McIvor (Chapter 10) note, the 'rolling back' of the welfare state to meet the costs of increasing prison populations in the United States has had a particularly severe impact on criminalised women with drug problems, while Sharpe (Chapter 8) argues that the retrenchment of the welfare state – and, in particular, a reduction in services for young people in difficulty – has been followed by a significant expansion of the youth justice system in England and Wales as a means of 'plugging the gap' that has been left by the absence of state welfare services. Girls interviewed by Sharpe reported that their experiences of welfare services were poor and that a neglect of their welfare and development needs resulted in their turning to alcohol, drugs and alternative means of relieving boredom and gaining recognition from their peers. Although the youth justice system was welcomed by some young women as a means of accessing welfare support, increasing numbers of young people – especially girls – are being brought unnecessarily into contact with a criminal justice system whose legitimacy is undermined by the absence of prior state support.

De-centering punishment: Legislating for change?

The need to move away from punishment to address the causes of women's offending has been highlighted in several contributions to this volume (for example, Hedderman, Chapter 2; Malloch and McIvor, Chapter 10). However, there is also evidence that making more and 'better' community disposals available to courts or providing sentencers with more information about available community options is insufficient to bring about significant changes in sentencing practice: the recent decrease in the average daily female prison population is, argues Hedderman (Chapter 2), a result of an increase in the number of women receiving short prison sentences, while less serious cases – that might previously have been dealt with by way of a fine or discharge – are increasingly likely to attract a community order (leaving women consequently at risk of imprisonment if they are breached). As Sharpe (Chapter 8) observes, the rate at which girls are given community supervision has also increased at the same time as the use of discharges and fines has decreased. Similarly, Gelsthorpe (Chapter 7) suggests that, despite their clear benefits to the women who make use of them, innovative gender-responsive projects in the UK – such as the 218 Centre and the Together Women Programme – appear as yet to have had a limited impact on the use of custody.

Gelsthorpe identifies other possible sites for positive and effective engagement with women caught up in the criminal justice system, including referral for assessment as an alternative to prosecution (that is, via conditional cautions) and problem-solving courts. Malloch and McIvor (Chapter 10) agree that the relational basis of problem-solving courts has the potential to offer a more gender-appropriate response to women in conflict with the law, though only if the services that they make available have been designed specifically to meet women's needs. Hedderman argues in Chapter 2, however, that *legislative reform* is required to prevent courts from sending women (and men) to prison for short periods of time. She suggests that curtailing magistrates' powers to imprison women would have an immediate and positive effect on imprisonment rates, as would taking away the courts' power to remand individuals in custody for offences that are insufficiently serious ultimately to result in a custodial sentence. Evidence that, with political will, legislative change of this type is possible can be seen in Scotland where, as Nugent and Loucks (Chapter 1) indicate, changes to legislation mandating the use of supervised attendance orders as an alternative to imprisonment for fine default has had a dramatic effect on the number of women imprisoned for short periods of time for non-payment of a fine: whereas there were 525 adult female receptions to prison in Scotland for fine default in 2003–04, five years later this figure had decreased to 89 (Scottish Government 2009). More ambitiously, in 2008 a commission set up to examine the use of prison and non-custodial sentences in Scotland advocated the abolition of prison sentences up to six months (Scottish Prisons Commission 2008), along the lines of the approach previously adopted in Western Australia in 2003 (Eley *et al.* 2005). While, in response, the Scottish Government agreed that many offenders given short prison sentences could be dealt with in the community instead (Scottish Government 2009), the legislation subsequently introduced[1] disappointingly stopped short of abolition and instead advocated a *presumption against* custodial sentences of only three months. This reluctance to 'grasp the nettle' and make a decisive commitment to decarceration undoubtedly reflects political concerns about public attitudes towards crime and punishment, which are perceived to be characterised by (increasing) intolerance for supposedly 'lenient' responses to crime.

In conclusion

As Gelsthorpe (Chapter 7) observes, our understanding of what is effective in reducing offending among women does not yet have a strong empirical basis, with interventions often under-theorised and how they relate to changes in women's behaviour not yet adequately assessed. There is even less evidence about what works with girls who offend because few gender-specific programmes have been developed and even fewer have been evaluated (Sharpe, Chapter 8). However, as the contributions to this volume have shown, it is possible on the basis of contemporary understanding of female offending to identify emerging lessons for effective work with women in the community (Gelsthorpe *et al.* 2007). An important starting point is an acknowledgement of women's distinctive pathways into crime and the implications this has for the types of services and interventions that may meet their needs. Women who offend are likely to have complex problems and needs and, compared with men, require more intensive support. In addition to addressing issues that are relevant to women's offending – such as poverty, victimisation, trauma and substance misuse – services and supports should be women-friendly (providing a safe environment in which their problems can be addressed), accessible and holistic, with appropriate provision to meet women's childcare needs. Flexibility with respect to patterns of contact and enforcement will also be necessary to ensure that services are appropriately responsive (particularly in times of crisis) and to avoid unnecessary breach.

As several contributors to this book have indicated, the 'one stop shop' model – exemplified in services such as the Asha Centre, 218 Centre and Together Women Programme – offers much promise. As Gelsthorpe (Chapter 7) observes, women appear to benefit from holistic 'wraparound' support, access to 'women-only space', empowering and enabling cultures, the use of mentors and volunteers to offer practical and emotional support – also to the women's children and families – and opportunity for training and education. Moreover, voluntary sector involvement means that women perceive their involvement in services as less stigmatising and the multitask approach means that their needs can be addressed in a more coherent way. This, however, is also dependent upon effective multi-agency cooperation at the local level supported by integrated social policies that enable women to access the services and support their need to achieve a sense of social justice and self-efficacy through an improved quality of life. Furthermore, as Malloch and McIvor (Chapter 10) remind us, the effectiveness of services for women will be severely hampered unless steps are taken to address wider social and penal policies that impact adversely on women and impair their ability to successfully address their problems and rebuild their lives.

Note

1 The Criminal Justice and Licensing (Scotland) Act received royal assent in August 2010.

References

Blanchette, K. and Brown, S. (2006) *The Assessment and Treatment of Women Offenders*. Chichester: John Wiley and Sons.

Bloom, B., Owen, B. and Covington, S. (2003) *Gender-Responsive Strategies: Research, Practice and Guiding Principles for Women Offenders*. Washington, DC: National Institute of Justice.

Bloom, B., Owen, B. and Covington, S. (2004) 'Women offenders and the gendered effects of public policy', *Review of Policy Research*, 21 (1): 31–48.

Bureau of Justice Statistics (2008) *Prisoners in 2007*. Washington, DC: US Department of Justice.

Cann, J. (2006) *Cognitive skills programmes: Impact on reducing reconviction among a sample of female prisoners*. Home Office Research Findings 276. London: Home Office.

Carlen, P. (2003) 'A strategy for women offenders? Lock them up, programme them ... and then send them out homeless', *Criminal Justice Matters*, 53: 36–7.

Corston, Baroness (2007) *The Corston Report: A Review of Women with Particular Vulnerabilities in the Criminal Justice System*. London: Home Office.

Eley, S., McIvor, G., Malloch, M. and Munro, B. (2005) *A Comparative Review of Alternatives To Custody: Lessons From Finland, Sweden And Western Australia*. Edinburgh: Scottish Parliament Justice 1 Committee.

Gelsthorpe, L. and McIvor, G. (2007) 'Difference and diversity in probation', in L. Gelsthorpe and R. Morgan (eds) *Handbook of Probation*. Cullompton: Willan Publishing, pp. 322–51.

Gelsthorpe, L. and Sharpe, G. (2007) 'Women and resettlement', in A. Hucklesby and L. Hagley-Dickinson (eds) *Prisoner Resettlement: Policy and Practice*. Cullompton: Willan Publishing, pp. 199–233.

Gelsthorpe, L., Sharpe, G. and Roberts, J. (2007) *Provision for Women Offenders in the Community*. London: The Fawcett Society.

Gilligan, C. (1982) *In a Different Voice*. Cambridge Mass.: Harvard University Press.

Hannah-Moffat, K. (2009) 'Gridlock or mutability: Reconsidering "gender" and risk assessment', *Criminology and Public Policy*, 8: 209–19.

Hedderman, C. (2004) 'The "criminogenic" needs of women offenders', in G. McIvor (ed.) *Women Who Offend*. London: Jessica Kingsley.

Hollin, C. and Palmer, E. (2006) 'Criminogenic need and women offenders: A critique of the literature', *Legal and Criminological Psychology*, 11 (2): 179–95.

Hudson, B. (2002) 'Gender issues in penal policy and penal theory', in P. Carlen (ed.) *Women and Punishment: The Struggle for Justice*. Cullompton: Willan Publishing, pp. 21–46.

Kendall, K. (2002) 'Time to think again about cognitive behavioural programmes', in P. Carlen (ed.) *Women and Punishment: The Struggle for Justice*. Cullompton: Willan Publishing, pp. 182–98.

Lart, R., Pantazis, C., Pemberton, S., Turner, W. and Almeida, C. (2008) *Interventions Aimed at Reducing Re-offending in Female Offenders: A Rapid Evidence Assessment*. London: Ministry of Justice, http://www.justice. gov.uk/publications/docs/intervention-reduce-female-reoffending.pdf (last accessed 16 October 2009).

McIvor, G. (2007) 'The nature of female offending', in R. Sheehan, G. McIvor and C. Trotter (eds) *What Works with Female Offenders*. Cullompton: Willan Publishing.

McIvor, G. (forthcoming) 'What works with women who offend?', in R. Taylor, M. Hill and F. McNeill (eds) *21st Century Social Workers: A Resource for Early Professional Development*. Venture Press.

McIvor, G., Trotter, C. and Sheehan. R. (2009) 'Women, resettlement and desistance', *Probation Journal*, 56 (4): 347–61.

Porporino, F. and Fabiano, E. (2005) 'Is there an evidence based supportive of women-centred programming in corrections?', *Corrections Today*, October: 26–8.

Scottish Government (2008) *Protecting Scotland's Communities: Fair, Fast and Flexible Justice*. Edinburgh: Scottish Government.

Scottish Government (2009) *Prison Statistics Scotland 2008–9*. Edinburgh: Scottish Government.

Scottish Prisons Commission (2008) *Scotland's Choice: Report of the Prisons Commission*. Edinburgh: Blackwell.

Shaw, M and Hannah-Moffat, K. (2004) 'How cognitive skills forgot about gender and diversity', in G. Mair (ed.) *What Matters in Probation*. Cullompton: Willan Publishing, pp. 90–121.

Wacquant, L. (2009) *Punishing the Poor: The Neoliberal Government of Social Insecurity*. Durham, NC: Duke University Press.

Wahidin, A. (2005) 'The needs of older men and women in the criminal justice system: An international perspective', *Prison Service Journal*, 160.

Worrall, A. (2000) 'What works at One Arm Point?', *Probation Journal*, 47 (3): 243–9.

Worrall, A. (2002) 'Missed opportunities? The probation service and women offenders', in D. Ward, J. Scott and M. Lacey (eds) *Probation: Working for Justice*. Oxford: Oxford University Press, pp. 134–48.

Index